MESSIANIC IDEAS AND MOVEMENTS IN SUNNĪ ISLAM

MESSIANIC IDEAS AND MOVEMENTS IN SUNNĪ ISLAM

Yohanan Friedmann

THE HEBREW UNIVERSITY OF JERUSALEM
AND SHALEM COLLEGE, JERUSALEM

ONEWORLD
ACADEMIC

Oneworld Academic
An imprint of Oneworld Publications

Published by Oneworld Academic in 2022

A CIP record for this title is available from the British Library

ISBN 978-0-86154-311-3
eISBN 978-0-86154-312-0

Typeset by Tetragon, London
Printed and bound in Great Britain by Clays Ltd, Elcograf S.p.A.

Oneworld Publications
10 Bloomsbury Street
London WC1B 3SR
England

For Zafrira, Yasmin, Tamar, Adi, Tom,
Stav, Yarden, Shiraz and Ethan

Contents

Preface

Expectation of a redeemer is a widespread phenomenon in many civilizations. The hidden, innermost thoughts and aspirations of a civilization can be gauged from its description of its forthcoming redeemer, of its messianic age. Like adherents of other civilizations, Muslims have also cultivated the hope that at some time in the future a redeemer will appear and transform the nature of human existence for the better. Classical Islamic traditions maintain that this redeemer will establish justice where injustice and oppression prevailed, will destroy Judaism and Christianity, transform Islam into the sole religion, bring about religious uniformity in the world and cause Islam to reign supreme. He will attain this goal in collaboration with Jesus who will return to this world as a Muslim and play a central role in this apocalyptic endeavour.

Contrary to current scholarly ethos which values comparative studies, this work will not attempt to compare the Muslim *mahdī* movements and their ideas with messianic movements in other faiths. The amount of material on Muslim movements which needs to be surveyed, analysed and interpreted is enormous and even this material could not be used in its entirety in the preparation of the present work. I have therefore preferred to concentrate on the main purpose of the book rather than engage in comparisons with other civilizations. There will of course be a comparison of the Sunnī Muslim *mahdī*s with each other. This is the focus of the last chapter of the book.

In choosing to include some of these Sunnī *mahdī* claimants in my analysis, I am not passing judgment on the sincerity or otherwise of that person's messianic claim. Anyone who advanced a claim to be a *mahdī*, convinced a substantial number of people to accept it and left behind documentation which enables us to study his thought may be a *mahdī* for the purposes of this study. One thinker whose thought I have analysed does not fit this definition: Abū al-Aʿlā Mawdūdī (d. 1979) developed a theory relevant to the *mahdī* phenomenon, but as far as I know was not a messianic claimant himself. I also need to say that as a matter of principle I do not speak of *mahdī*s and "pseudo-*mahdī*s".[1] No messianic claimant so far has been able to deliver on his promises and therefore all claimants are "pseudo-*mahdīs*" in a significant sense.

There have been numerous *mahdī* claimants in the Sunnī branch of Islam and it is not possible to discuss all of them within the framework of this work.[2] For the purpose of the present book, I have chosen to deal with four messianic claimants from different periods and different regions. The North African Ibn Tūmart (d. 1130) and the Indian Muslim Sayyid Muḥammad Jawnpūrī (d. 1505) operated in medieval times and under Muslim rule. In the endeavour of the Sudanese *mahdī* Muḥammad Aḥmad (d. 1885), anti-British struggle was paramount and intimately related to his religious thought. The messianic claim of Mīrzā Ghulām Aḥmad (d. 1907) and the controversy concerning the nature of the *mahdī* in modern Muslim India transpired under British rule and included extensive polemics against Christianity and the Christian missionaries in India, but in the main did not entail anti-British activity. The substantial differences between these *mahdī*s are a good example of the interpretative possibilities available to Muslim thinkers and religious leaders who want to use classical Muslim thought and tradition, and reinterpret them in a manner appropriate for their time and place.

Since the idea of the *mahdī* in the Shī'a branch of Islam has been subject of extensive research, the focus of this book is the messianic idea in the Sunnī branch, which has received much less attention. The various chapters will touch upon the political history of the Sunnī *mahdī* movements only to the extent that this is essential for the understanding of their religious thought. The *mahdī*s who had political significance, such as Ibn Tūmart and the Sudanese *mahdī* Muḥammad Aḥmad, have been frequently studied with their political and social perspectives in mind. Their religious thought, on the other hand, has received less attention. This will be the principal concern of this book. Wherever possible, there will be an attempt to relate

1 This is the term used by Yoginder Sikand in his work about messianic movements in modern Muslim India.

2 By way of example, I would like to mention the several North African and Andalusī *mahdī*s analysed in the seminal work of Mercedes García-Arenal, the modern Indian *mahdī* movements described by Yoginder Sikand and the group of Juhaymān al-'Utaybī which took over the mosque of Mecca in 1979.

the *mahdī*s' thought to classical Muslim ideas on the apocalypse. In order to make this feasible, the first chapter of the book will survey and analyse the main elements of classical Muslim thinking on the appearance of the *mahdī* and the related apocalyptic drama.

The *mahdī* idea is usually associated with Shīʿī Islam and there is an enormous amount of research on the Shīʿī view of apocalyptic redemption. The centrality of the *mahdī* idea in Shīʿī thought – both medieval and modern – is beyond question. Its contemporary centrality can be gauged from the fact that article 5 of the Iranian constitution of 1979 implies that the government of the "just and God-fearing jurisprudent" (*faqīh-i ʿādil o muttaqī*) – meaning the present government of Iran – will last only until the manifestation of the *mahdī*.[3] It is also reflected by the existence of dedicated institutions in Iran and Iraq which produce a constant stream of books on the *mahdī* and his importance. Some scholars dedicate their books to the *mahdī* and even ask him "to accept" their works. It is, however, noteworthy that according to many Shīʿī scholars, the *mahdī* idea is not specifically Shīʿī: it belongs to Islam in general. Numerous books by Shīʿī scholars have been written in recent years in order to advance the notion that the *mahdī* idea is common to both major branches of Islam. Some writers even consider it as a possible tool for rapprochement between the Sunna and the Shīʿa.

The perception of the *mahdī* idea as primarily a Shīʿī one is among the reasons that pertinent Sunnī ideas and the numerous Sunnī claimants have received much less attention. This imbalance needs to be redressed. Goldziher – and Friedländer before him – asserted that "in Sunnī Islam the pious awaiting of the *mahdī* never took the fixed form of dogma".[4] This view is correct in the sense that it does not appear in the classical compendia of articles of faith (*ʿaqāʾid*),[5] but this should not be understood to mean that the idea has little importance in Sunnī Islam. While some

3 "During the Occultation of the Walī al-ʿAṣr (may God hasten his release), the *wilāyah* and leadership of the Ummah devolve upon the just (*ʿādil*) and pious (*muttaqī*) *faqīh*, who is fully aware of the circumstances of his age; courageous, resourceful, and possessed of administrative ability, will assume the responsibilities of this office in accordance with Article 107." Article 107 describes the procedure for electing the leader of the Islamic Republic of Iran.

4 Friedländer, *Die Messiasidee im Islam*, p. 15; Goldziher, *Introduction*, p. 200. See a survey of the early research on the topic and a critique of it in D. Cook, *Studies in Muslim Apocalyptic*, p. 30.

5 See the discussion of this in Chapter 1, at notes 133–134.

Sunnī scholars took pains to undermine the *mahdī* traditions and even considered them unreliable, numerous Sunnīs made messianic claims throughout Islamic history. None of them commanded universal acceptance, but the *mahdī*s made considerable impact in the regions where they emerged. In two major cases – Ibn Tūmart and Muḥammad Aḥmad – they managed to establish political units. The Almohad empire lasted for about 140 years; the state established by the Sudanese *mahdī* lasted for eighteen years only, but during these periods both movements produced Muslim regimes which are highly significant for the evaluation of radical Muslim movements and their objectives in modern times.

The apocalyptic drama also has modern relevance. A large number of contemporary Muslim writers have interpreted various details of the apocalyptic drama as relating to modern personalities and situations. Both Sunnī and Shīʿī writers have interpreted events and personalities in the apocalyptic drama as relating to contemporary events. The evil participants in that drama – mainly the *dajjāl* – are identified with oppressive rulers in modern times, as well as with communism, capitalism, materialism, Zionism and the United States of America. Perhaps the most bizarre attempt at actualization of the apocalyptic drama was the Nazi idea to identify the coming of Hitler with the second coming of Jesus and to identify the false messiah (*dajjāl*) with a monstrous Jewish king, to be killed by the new incarnation of Jesus – Adolf Hitler.[6]

The belief systems analysed in this book (except the Aḥmadī one) provide us with historical depth for understanding radical movements in modern Islam. The excommunication (*takfīr*) of opponents, the uncompromising imposition of the *sharīʿa* in its literal interpretation (which was also the hallmark of the Khawārij), the demand of absolute obedience to the leader, the demand to leave one's place of residence and to perform *hijra* to the area under the jurisdiction of the radical groups – all these exist in one or more of the *mahdī* groups and prefigure what we see in some contemporary radical movements. The recurrent appearance of *mahdī* movements serves as a reminder that radical interpretations of Islam appeared time and again in Muslim history, but so far have not achieved enduring success.

The planning of this book went through several stages. Looking at the research works devoted to Ibn Tūmart – and especially at the seminal article

6 Motadel, *Islam and Nazi Germany's War*, pp. 89–90.

of Goldziher which was published in 1887 before any of the Almohad books were in print and which was therefore based solely on manuscripts – I was reminded of the pre-Islamic poet ʿAntara b. al-Shaddād who said in the first hemistich of his famous ode: "Have the poets left anything to be patched up ... (*hal ghādara ʾshshuʿarāʾu min mutaraddamī* ...)?" Consequently, I doubted whether I should include a chapter on Ibn Tūmart in this work. After consulting several colleagues, however, I came to the conclusion that a book on the *mahdī* idea in Sunnī Islam cannot stand without a chapter on Ibn Tūmart. I am apparently taking my lead from ʿAntara who wrote his extensive ode though he doubted whether his predecessors left him with anything new to say.

The decision on Muḥammad Aḥmad, the Sudanese *mahdī* was easier. Though there is plenty of research on his movement, most of it is devoted to its political and military aspects and not to the religious thought which is the focus of my work. The Mahdawī movement in medieval India and the controversy relating to the nature of the *mahdī* in modern Muslim India did not raise problems of this sort at all: research which has been devoted to these topics is much less extensive.

I used some of the material included in this book in the first Al-e Ahmad Suroor Memorial lecture ("Some aspects of the Messianic idea in Sunnī Islam") which I delivered at the Jamia Millia Islamia University in New Delhi on 16 October 2008. An edited version of the lecture was published in *The Third Frame: Literature, Culture and Society* 2 (2009), pp. 1–23. I wish to thank Professor Mushir al-Hasan of blessed memory for inviting me to deliver the lecture. On 9 May 2016, I delivered the 18th Zalman Chaim Bernstein memorial lecture (in Hebrew) at the Shalem College in Jerusalem on "The messianic idea in Islam". I wish to thank Vice President Dr Dan Polisar for inviting me to do so.

Most of the book was written in the National Library of Israel in Jerusalem and in the British Library in London. I thank the staff of both libraries for their efficient help over the years of writing it.

My thanks go to Ella Landau-Tasseron who read Chapter 1 and suggested significant improvements. Eyal Ginio provided me with information on attitudes to the Sudanese *mahdī* in the Ottoman empire. Muzaffar Alam, Albert Arazi, Meir Bar Asher, Yoram Bilu, Sujata Ashwarya Cheema, Marc Gaborieau, Isaac Hasson, Etan Kohlberg, Sivan Lerer, Aharon Maman, Maria Pakkala, Frank Stewart, Sara Sviri and Nurit Tsafrir helped me in various ways. I am indebted to the anonymous reviewer for his thoughtful comments, to Elizabeth Hinks for her attentive and professional copy-editing, and to Paul Nash for guiding the book through the production process. Jonathan Bentley-Smith deserves my gratitude for expeditiously seeing the book through the review process. It goes without saying that any errors of fact or infelicities of style are solely my responsibility.

YOHANAN FRIEDMANN
Jerusalem, May 2021

1

Mahdī, Jesus and *dajjāl*: The apocalyptic drama in Sunnī religious thought

1 "PORTENTS OF THE HOUR" (*ASHRĀṬ AL-SĀʿA*)

The Qurʾān contains numerous verses of eschatological content and the Day of Judgment plays a cardinal role in it,[1] but the messianic idea in Islam cannot be directly derived from the Qurʾān. The Hebrew word *mashiʾaḥ* (Aramaic: *meshiḥā*), from which the English "Messiah" and "Messianism" are derived, appears several times in the Muslim scripture in the form *al-masīḥ*, but it seems to have been used as a proper name of Jesus rather than as a title with eschatological content. In Hebrew, the term means a personality symbolically anointed with oil in preparation for a sacred duty or a dignified position of leadership. Classical commentators on the Qurʾān tend to seek an Arabic etymology for the word and maintain that it means someone whom Allah blessed or purified from sin. Even those who are aware of the word's Hebrew or Aramaic extraction maintain that it is a proper name which was arabicized like the names of other biblical prophets, such as Ismāʿīl (= Yishmaʿel) or Isḥāq (= Yizḥaq).[2]

1 For a survey of apocalyptic material in the Qurʾān, see Arjomand, "Islamic Apocalypticism in the Classic Period", pp. 238–248.

2 Donner, "La question du messianisme ...", pp. 220–221; Ṭabarī, *Jāmiʿ al-bayān*, vol. 3, p. 270 (on Qurʾān 3:45); vol. 6, p. 35 (on Qurʾān 4:171).

In the vast corpus of Muslim prophetic traditions, known as the *ḥadīth*, the situation is different. The *mahdī* is not mentioned in the celebrated collections of Muḥammad b. Ismāʿīl al-Bukhārī (d. 870) and Muslim b. Ḥajjāj (d. 875), but the Qaḥṭānī, another clearly messianic (South Arabian) figure, is mentioned by both.[3] Other canonical collections of *ḥadīth* do include chapters on the coming of a redeemer; however, the term describing him is in the great majority of cases not *al-masīḥ*, but rather the original Arabic term *mahdī*, "the rightly guided one". The idea of divine guidance (*hudan*) is central in the Qur'ān, but the passive participle *mahdī* is not Qur'ānic; nevertheless, it gained the upper hand in the Muslim descriptions of the messiah and served as the preferred title of messianic pretenders throughout Muslim history. The centrality of divine guidance (*hudan*) in Muslim religious thought, as well as the clearly Arabic provenance of the term, are the likely reasons for the prevalent acceptance of the term *mahdī* for the redeemer in the Muslim tradition.

According to the classical Muslim *ḥadīth*, the *mahdī* is part of an eschatological drama which will take place at some unspecified time before the Day of Judgment. His appearance is integrated into a series of wondrous, dramatic and terrifying events – "Portents of the Hour" – expected to precede and herald the Last Day (*ashrāṭ al-sāʿa, āyāt al-sāʿa, al-fitan wa al-malāḥim*):[4] the sun will rise from the West; a huge fire will erupt in the Yemen in order to drive all humanity to the place of the Last Judgment; a frightful beast carrying Solomon's ring and Moses' staff will appear; a one-eyed false messiah called *al-dajjāl* will come forth, having the word "infidel" (*kāfir*) inscribed on his forehead; the earth will collapse in the East, in the West and in the Arabian Peninsula; there will be a solar eclipse; the Euphrates will recede, revealing a mound of gold; Gog and Magog will be freed from their chains in the East and move West. Muslims will fight the

3 Madelung, "Apocalyptic Prophecies in Ḥimṣ", p. 149, quoting Bukhārī, *Ṣaḥīḥ*, *Kitāb al-fitan* 23 (vol. 4, p. 380) and Muslim b. Ḥajjāj, *Ṣaḥīḥ*, *Kitāb al-fitan* 60 (vol. 4, p. 2232).

4 There is no clear difference between these terms and they are used interchangeably. Nevertheless, we can discern some distinctions. *Ashrāṭ* is more commonly used for natural miracles, such as earthquakes or sunrise in the West, while *fitan* is more frequently used for events initiated by mythical beings such as the *dajjāl* or Gog and Magog. *Malāḥim* is used for the apocalyptic battles, crowned by the conquest of Constantinople, sometimes dubbed *al-malḥama al-kubrā*, "the big *malḥama*", cf. Livne-Kafri, "Some Notes on the Muslim Apocalyptic Tradition", pp. 72–74.

Indians,[5] the Turks[6] and the Jews.[7] Constantinople will be conquered. All these events will take place at a time characterized by senseless killings, religious instability, prevalence of infidelity over belief and a disproportionately high number of women in the population. People who were believers in the morning turn infidels by nightfall. All normalcy will come to an end. Facing these trials and tribulations (*fitan*), the few remaining believers will be helpless; at most, they will attempt to seclude themselves on uninhabited mountaintops to save their faith.[8] The nineteenth-century Egyptian scholar al-Ḥamzāwī (d. 1886)[9] adds some modern woes to these classical descriptions of the *ashrāṭ*:

> The Qur'ān is taken as something to be sung. It is sung in meetings, markets and coffee houses. Coffee houses are built in greater numbers than mosques which are places of worship, of remembering God and of useful knowledge – while [the coffee houses] are places of slander, defamation and vice. There is also smoking which came into vogue in these times. It is a blameworthy innovation in all religions because it distracts from remembering God, the Only One, the Judge. (*ittikhādh al-Qur'ān mughannan yughannā bihi fī ṣudūr al-majālis wa al-aswāq wa al-qahāwā wa minhā ʿimārat al-qahāwā akthar min al-masājid allatī hiya maḥall al-ʿibāda wa al-dhikr wa al-fawā'id wa al-qahāwā maḥall al-ghība wa al-namīma wa al-mafāsid wa minhā ma ḥadatha fī hādhā al-zamān min shurb al-dukhān fa-innahā bidʿa munkara fī sāʾir al-adyān li-annahu yulhī ʿan dhikr Allah al-qāhir al-dayyān.*)[10]

The classical *ashrāṭ* constitute a catastrophic, frightful and awesome series of events immediately preceding the apocalypse and leading to it. We may note here that since the very beginning of apocalyptic literature in Islam,

5 Nasā'ī, *Sunan*, vol. 6, pp. 42–43; Nuʿaym b. Ḥammād, *Kitāb al-Fitan*, pp. 252–253.
6 Bukhārī, *Ṣaḥīḥ*, *Kitāb al-jihād*, 95 (vol. 2, p. 230); Muslim, *Ṣaḥīḥ*, vol. 4, pp. 2233–2234 (nos. 62–66); Nuʿaym b. Ḥammād, *Kitāb al-fitan*, pp. 412–417.
7 Bukhārī, *Ṣaḥīḥ*, *Kitāb al-jihād*, 94 (vol. 2, pp. 229–230); Muslim, *Ṣaḥīḥ*, vol. 4, pp. 2238–2239 (nos. 79–82).
8 These traditions are ubiquitous in the Muslim tradition and have been exhaustively analysed in Cook, *Studies in Muslim Apocalyptic*. By way of example, see Ibn Māja, *Sunan*, vol. 2, pp. 1343–1366 (*Kitāb al-fitan*, nos. 4045–4081).
9 See for him, Brockelmann, *GAL*, vol. 2, p. 486.
10 Ḥamzāwī, *Mashāriq al-anwār*, p. 183. On the controversy concerning coffee consumption in the sixteenth to eighteenth centuries, see Maḥāmīd and Nissim, "Ṣūfīs and Coffee Consumption", *passim*.

the expectation of these events should be seen against the background of a general philosophical underpinning: an ingrained pessimism regarding the development of Muslim (or generally human) history. The *ḥadīth* compilers may not have shared this interpretation; after all, the seemingly irreversible decline will eventually result in the eschatological triumph of Islam.[11] For the time being, however, things are moving from bad to worse. Ibn Māja has included in his *Sunan* a chapter entitled "the adversity of time" (*shiddat al-zamān*) which includes the following prophetic tradition:

> This matter will increase only in adversity, this world will move only backward and the people will only become more parsimonious. The Hour will occur only when people are the worst and there is no *mahdī* except Jesus the son of Mary. (*lā yazdādu al-amr illā shiddatan wa lā al-dunyā illā idbāran wa lā al-nās illā shuḥḥan wa lā taqūmu al-sā ʿa illā ʿalā shirār al-nās wa lā al-mahdī illā ʿĪsā b. Maryam.*)[12]

Or, in another formulation:

> The best of my community is the generation in which I was sent, then those who follow them, then those who follow them. (*khayru ummatī al-qarn alladhī bu ʿithtu fīhi thumma 'lladhīna yalūnahum thumma 'lladhīna yalūnahum.*)[13]

The latter *ḥadīth* has no apocalyptic significance; its main intention is to extol the Muslims of the Prophet's generation, and to assert that Islam started its existence at the pinnacle of glory, to be followed by an irreversible decline. Nevertheless, it should be read in conjunction with traditions which give historical substance to the deterioration of Islam after the Prophet's death. The political instability of the caliphate, best exemplified by the murder of three of the "righteous caliphs" and the various struggles which plagued Muslim history in the first century AH and – significantly enough – are also called *fitan*, must have contributed to the idea according to which the deterioration of the Muslim community and the "countdown" to the eschaton started almost immediately after the emergence of Islam. In several of these traditions negative and positive apocalyptic events – such

11 I owe this insight to my friend and colleague Ella Landau-Tasseron.

12 Ibn Māja, *Sunan*, vol. 2, pp. 1340–1341 (no. 4039).

13 See Bukhārī, *Ṣaḥīḥ*, vol. 2, p. 416 (*Kitāb faḍa ʾil aṣḥāb al-nabī, bāb* 1).

as the conquest of Constantinople – are mixed with actual historical events from the earliest Muslim period. In one tradition, a mysterious person clad in white tells the Muslim participants in a raid on Ṭawāna:

> Be steadfast, because this is a community receiving [divine] mercy. God decreed for it five tribulations and five prayers. I said: "Name them for me." He said: "... One of them is the death of their Prophet ... then the murder of ʿUthmān ... then the rebellion of Ibn al-Zubayr ... then the rebellion of Ibn al-Ashʿath." Then he turned around saying: "[Only] misfortune (*al-ṣaylam*) remained, [only] misfortune remained ..."[14]

Other lists of "Portents of the Hour" also include both negative and positive events: the death of the Prophet, the conquest of Jerusalem, the settlement of the Muslim community in Syria, a dissension which will afflict every Arab house and a truce with the Byzantines.[15]

A general observation about the nature of the classical apocalyptic literature is in order here. As is well known, the decades of Islamic history which followed the death of the Prophet in 632 CE were characterized by unprecedented military triumphs. The resounding victories of the Muslims and the phenomenal expansion of Muslim rule over huge areas of the Middle East and North Africa could easily be seen as very positive developments and even signs of divine support for Islam. Nevertheless, the Muslim apocalypticists completely ignore these positive features of early Islamic history – except for the conquest of Jerusalem which is interpreted as a "portent" of the Hour – when they describe the first century of Islamic history as a period of deterioration of Islam and as a countdown to the imminent end of the world. It is as if the classical historians of early Islam and the apocalypticists operate in distinct, disconnected spheres which are unaware of each other. The conquests of the seventh century CE were accomplished simultaneously with the internecine struggles and the perceived moral deterioration which plagued the Muslim community, but only these negative aspects of early Muslim history are taken into account when the apocalypticist makes his gloomy predictions. The apocalypticist's disregard of the Muslim military successes seems to be a

14 Nuʿaym b. Ḥammād, *Kitāb al-fitan*, p. 26. David Cook identifies Ṭawāna with Adana in modern Turkey. See his *The Book of Tribulations*, p. 14.

15 Nuʿaym b. Ḥammād, *Kitāb al-fitan*, p. 26 (D. Cook, *The Book of Tribulations*, pp. 13–14).

result of ingrained asceticism, disregard for worldly achievements, disdain for this world, absolute concentration on promoting the religious standards and bemoaning their deterioration.

Both the Qur'ān and the classical collections of *ḥadīth* can easily be used to substantiate the belief in the proximity of the apocalypse. The expected Hour (*al-sā'a*) is mentioned in dozens of Qur'ānic verses. The very famous tradition according to which the Hour is as close to Muḥammad's mission as his two fingers are to each other[16] points in the same direction. This motif is further developed in the earliest collection of apocalyptic traditions, the *Kitāb al-fitan* by Nu'aym b. Ḥammād (d. 844). Nu'aym adduces several traditions listing the earliest *fitan* which will adversely affect the Muslim community. Some are phrased in general, vague terms and include unspecified tribulations, plagues and internecine struggles in the Muslim community. Others include clear political advocacy, such as the tradition according to which "people will live in prosperity as long as the kingdom of the 'Abbāsīs is not toppled; when it is toppled, they will experience tribulations (*fitan*) until the rising of the *mahdī*" (*lā yazālu al-nās bi-khayrin fī rakhā' mā lam yunqaḍ mulku banī al-'Abbās fa-idhā 'ntaqaḍa mulkuhum lam yazālū fī fitan ḥattā yaqūma al-mahdī*).[17]

In this way Nu'aym b. Ḥammād creates the impression that almost the whole Muslim history, beginning with the Prophet's death, is a prelude to the apocalypse.[18] Similar traditions appear in the *Ṣaḥīḥ* of al-Bukhārī, in the *Sunan* of Ibn Māja and in al-Naysābūrī's *al-Mustadrak*.[19] The idea is mentioned in numerous apocalyptic works and we shall see a much more developed version of it in our analysis of the thought of Ṣiddīq Ḥasan Khān in Chapter 5.[20]

---

16 Bukhārī, *Ṣaḥīḥ*, vol. 4, p. 231 (*Kitāb al-riqāq* 39) and elsewhere; see Wensinck, *Concordance*, s.v. *bu'ithtu*.

17 Nu'aym b. Ḥammād, *Kitāb al-fitan*, p. 123.

18 Nu'aym b. Ḥammād, *Kitāb al-fitan*, pp. 25–32. Translation by Cook, *Studies in Muslim Apocalyptic*, pp. 11–22.

19 Bukhārī, *Ṣaḥīḥ*, vol. 2, pp. 297–298 (*Kitāb al-jizya*, 15); Ibn Māja, *Sunan*, vol. 2, pp. 1341–1342 (no. 4047); Naysābūrī, *Mustadrak*, vol. 5, p. 600 (no. 3436). The commentators on al-Bukhārī's *Ṣaḥīḥ* have nothing to say about the significance of including the death of the Prophet among the *ashrāṭ*, seemingly agreeing to the idea that the countdown to the apocalypse began immediately after the Prophet's death, and consequently the days of human history on earth were numbered. See al-'Aynī, *'Umdat al-qāri'*, vol. 15, pp. 99–100; 'Asqalānī, *Fatḥ al-bārī*, vol. 6, pp. 277–279; al-Qasṭallānī, *Irshād al-sārī*, vol. 7, p. 95; al-Khaṭṭābī, *A'lām al-ḥadīth*, vol. 2, pp. 1468–1469.

20 See Chapter 5, at notes 5–7.

II JESUS AND THE *MAHDĪ* – A DISPUTED IDENTIFICATION

Three figures play major roles in Muslim eschatology: the *dajjāl*, Jesus and the *mahdī*. Muslim traditions vary concerning the identity of the latter and it stands to reason that his identity changed because of considerations of politics or religious polemics. Several early collections of *ḥadīth* – compiled between the ninth and the eleventh century CE but evidently including much earlier material – maintain that "the *mahdī* is none else than Jesus" (*lā al-mahdī illā ʿĪsā*);[21] or, in another formulation, "the *mahdī* is Jesus b. Maryam".[22] A tradition related on the authority of Ibn ʿAbbās maintains that "the *mahdī* is one of us and he will hand over [his office?] to Jesus the son of Mary" (*al-mahdī minnā yadfaʿuhā ilā ʿĪsā b. Maryam ...*).[23] However, the identification of Jesus with the *mahdī* eventually lost currency and was even declared spurious by several medieval scholars of *ḥadīth*.[24] Jesus' role as the *mahdī* must have been embarrassing to Muslims in their polemics with Christianity, though most traditionists held that Jesus would be a Muslim when he descends to earth for the second time.[25] David Cook has convincingly argued that the identification of Jesus with the *mahdī* was renounced because Muslims felt ill at ease having an eschatological hero who was also "the god of another faith".[26] It is certainly not possible

21 Ibn Māja, *Sunan, Kitāb al-fitan* 24 (vol. 2, pp. 1340–1341, no. 4039); Naysābūrī, *al-Mustadrak*, vol. 5, pp. 629 (no. 8412); Dānī, *al-Sunan al-wārida fī al-fitan*, pp. 80 (no. 217) and 200 (no. 590); Iṣfahānī, *Ḥilyat al-awliyāʾ*, vol. 9, p. 172.

22 Ibn Abī Shayba, *al-Muṣannaf*, vol. 8, p. 678 (no. 192); Nuʿaym b. Ḥammād, *Kitāb al-fitan*, p. 230.

23 Nuʿaym b. Ḥammād, pp. 228–229; cf. al-Sulamī, *ʿIqd al-durar*, p. 26.

24 See al-Bayhaqī, *Bayān khaṭaʾ man akhṭaʾa ʿalā al-Shāfiʿī*, pp. 296–305; Ibn al-Jawzī, *al-ʿIlal al-mutanāhiya*, vol. 2, pp. 862–863; al-Dhahabī, *Siyar aʿlām al-nubalāʾ*, vol. 10, p. 67; *idem*, *Talkhīṣ kitāb al-ʿIlal al-mutanāhiya li-Ibn al-Jawzī*, pp. 320–321 (no. 959); Ibn Qayyim al-Jawziyya, *al-Manār al-munīf*, pp. 89–90; al-Saffārīnī, *Ahwāl al-qiyāma*, pp. 29–30; al-Shawkānī, *al-Fawāʾid al-majmūʿa*, p. 439 (no. 1428). For a negative attitude of a modern scholar, who also uses this opportunity to attack the Aḥmadīs, see al-Albānī, *Silsilat al-aḥādīth al-ḍaʿīfa*, vol. 1, pp. 175–105 (no. 77). But see also Ibn Kathīr, *al-Fitan wa al-malāḥim*, p. 53, who does not see any contradiction between this tradition and traditions which identify the *mahdī* as a person different from Jesus: he thinks that there may be more than one *mahdī*. The tradition is mentioned in Baghdādī, *Taʾrīkh Baghdād*, vol. 4, p. 221 without comment. *Pace* E. Dickinson, *The Development of Early Sunnite ḥadīth Criticism*, Leiden: E. J. Brill, 2001, p. 27, note 63: it is not reasonable to say simply that "Sunnites hold that the *mahdī* will be ʿĪsā."

25 See my *Prophecy Continuous*, pp. 115–116.

26 See Cook, *Studies in Muslim Apocalyptic*, p. 323.

to agree with Zniber who argues that the prevalent view among Muslim scholars is that the *mahdī* is identical with Jesus.[27]

Nevertheless, some scholars attempted to maintain the authenticity of this *ḥadīth* by giving it a restrictive interpretation. Al-Qurṭubī (d.1273), for instance, devotes to this issue an extensive passage in which he asserts that *lā al-mahdī illā ʿĪsā* stands in contrast with numerous relevant traditions, has been transmitted by unreliable people and is therefore not authentic (*lā yaṣiḥḥu*). At the end of his discussion al-Qurṭubī tries to "save" the *ḥadīth* by providing it with a restrictive interpretation, saying that "there is no *perfect mahdī* except Jesus" (*lā mahdī illā ʿĪsā kāmilan*),[28] but the thrust of his discussion is against its acceptance.[29]

In *al-Manār al-munīf*, Ibn Qayyim al-Jawziyya (d. 1350) rejects the *lā mahdī illā ʿĪsā b. Maryam ḥadīth* because it is based on a weak *isnād* while the other traditions on the identity of the *mahdī* have a stronger one.[30] But later in the discussion he mentions a view – without identifying its supporters – according to which the authenticity of the *ḥadīth* can be accepted if interpreted as meaning that

> there is no *mahdī* in reality except Jesus, even if there are other *mahdī*s. [This usage is the same] as when you say that there is no knowledge except the useful and there is no property except what protects its owner's honour. In the same way, it is correct to say that "Jesus the son of Mary is indeed the *mahdī*, meaning the perfect, the infallible one." (*fa-yaṣiḥḥu an yuqāl: lā mahdī fī al-ḥaqīqa siwāhu wa in kāna ghayruhu mahdiyyan. kamā yuqāl: lā ʿilma illā mā nafaʿa wa lā māla illā mā waqā wajha ṣāḥibihi. wa kamā yaṣiḥḥu an yuqāl: innamā al-mahdī ʿĪsā b. Maryam yaʿnī al-mahdī al-kāmil al-maʿṣūm.*)[31]

This means that there is more than one *mahdī* and Jesus is the perfect one. Another view is expressed by Ibn ʿAbd al-Ḥalīm: the *mahdī* does not have to accomplish his tasks in the whole world. If he appears in a certain

27 Zniber, "L'iteneraire psycho-intellectuel d'Ibn Toumert", p. 15.
28 This means that there may emerge other, "non-perfect" *mahdī*s besides Jesus, cf. Ibn ʿAbd al-Ḥalīm, *Kitāb al-ansāb*, p. 264.
29 Qurṭubī, *al-Tadhkira*, pp. 1205–1206.
30 Ibn Qayyim al-Jawziyya, *al-Manār al-munīf*, pp. 89–90.
31 Ibn Qayyim al-Jawziyya, *al-Manār al-munīf*, p. 95.

place and accomplishes what the prophetic *ḥadīth* expects of him, he is to be accepted. This implies that each geographical region can have its own *mahdī*s.[32]

The view of al-Barzanjī (d. 1764) is ambivalent: on the one hand he suggests that the *ḥadīth* means that "if we say that Jesus is the *mahdī*'s *wazīr*, no word of his [can be accepted] unless he consulted Jesus". This means that Jesus and the *mahdī* are two different personalities. But immediately after saying that, and following the view of Ibn Qayyim al-Jawziyya, he gives an alternative interpretation according to which "there is no absolutely infallible *mahdī* except Jesus" (*lā qawla li-'l-mahdī illā bi-mashwarat ʿĪsā ... in qulnā annahu wazīruhu aw lā mahdī maʿṣūman kāmilan illā ʿĪsā ...*)[33] This means that Jesus is the "perfect, infallible" *mahdī*, but there may be other persons bearing the messianic title. In effect, both Ibn Qayyim al-Jawziyya and al-Barzanjī increase the importance of Jesus by implying that there may be numerous *mahdī*s, but Jesus will be superior to all.

At this point we need to address a further interpretation of the term *mahdī* which can be used to undermine the messianic role of Jesus and the *mahdī* idea in general. It is related to Qurʾān 3:46 and 5:110 according to which Jesus was miraculously given the ability to speak while he was still an infant in the cradle (*mahd*); this was the reason why he was called *mahdī* and not because of any messianic status.[34]

The Shīʿīs also objected to the fusion of the *mahdī* with Jesus: the undisputed identification of the *mahdī* in the Twelver Shīʿī tradition with the twelfth *imām* made this fusion impossible. At times we also hear other reasons for the rejection of this *ḥadīth*, such as the unreliability of transmitters and the traditions in which Jesus and the *mahdī* appear as two distinct personalities in the apocalyptic drama.[35] Modern Muslim scholars normally take a similar approach.[36] However, the widespread criticism of the *ḥadīth* under discussion does not mean that Jesus lost his eschatological role completely: even without holding the messianic title,

32 Ibn ʿAbd al-Ḥalīm, *Kitāb al-ansāb*, p. 265.
33 Al-Barzanjī, *al-Ishāʿa*, pp. 236, 251.
34 See Yāqūt, *Muʿjam al-buldān*, s.v. "Mahdiyya;" Ibn Khaldūn, *Muqaddima*, p. 301; translation by Rosenthal, vol. 2, pp. 185–186. For the polemical use of this interpretation against Ibn Tūmart, see Chapter 2 at notes 70–71.
35 Ganjī, *al-Bayān*, pp. 458–460.
36 See, for instance, the editor's note in Dānī, *al-Sunan al-wārida fī al-fitan*, p. 80, note on tradition no. 217. Cf. Albānī, *Silsilat al-aḥādīth al-ḍaʿīfa*, vol. 1, pp. 175–177. Albānī uses the presumed inauthenticity of this *ḥadīth* in order to attack the Aḥmadī beliefs.

he continued to play a major part in the extraordinary events preceding the Day of Judgment.

Before we describe the eschatological role of Jesus, we need to analyse the reasons for the controversy regarding his messianic status and for the urge felt by numerous traditionists to strip him of the title of *mahdī*. We have already mentioned David Cook's explanation of this[37] and it is now time to place the downgrading of Jesus in a wider context. At the present time I am not able to chart the timeline of this development, but it stands to reason that this downgrading is comparable to the process in which Muslim tradition gradually abandoned ritual details adapted from Judaism and Christianity and developed rituals that are distinctively Islamic. Changing the *qibla* from Jerusalem to Mecca, abandoning the Jewish fast on the tenth of the first month (*ʿāshūrāʾ*, *yom ha-kippurim*) in favour of Ramaḍān, and replacing the call to prayer with *shofar* or *nāqūs* by *adhān* with a human voice are cases in point. The belief in Jesus as *mahdī* is of course not a ritual, but it is part of a wider process in which Islam progressively dissociated itself from religious elements characteristic of Judaism and Christianity and developed a distinctive system of its own.[38]

III THE *DAJJĀL*, JESUS AND THE DESTRUCTION OF JUDAISM AND CHRISTIANITY

It is time now to describe the eschatological drama in greater detail. The amount of relevant material is enormous and it will not be possible to refer to all pertinent works. Because of the great variety and number of the relevant traditions, the chronology of the events is not lucid. The apocalyptic traditions are frequently phrased in an abstruse fashion and use outlandish vocabulary, probably intended to intensify the atmosphere of awe and mystery. In most cases, the story begins with the supernatural occurrences described earlier and the appearance of the false messiah (*al-dajjāl*), who will be

> short, walking with his thighs wide apart, having curly hair, having one eye while the other is obliterated, neither protruding nor

37 See earlier, at note 26 in this chapter.
38 For further details on this process, see Friedmann, *Tolerance and Coercion*, pp. 28–33.

> sunken. Should you become confused, know that your Lord is not one-eyed. (*rajul qaṣīr afḥaj ja ʿd a ʿwar maṭmūs al- ʿayn laysa bi-nāti ʾa wa lā jaḥrā ʾ fa-in ulbisa ʿalaykum fa-ʾ ʿlamū anna rabbakum laysa bi-a ʿwar.*)[39]

In other descriptions, the *dajjāl* was born during the time of the Prophet and was a Jew, accompanied by Jewish troops (*junūd min al-yahūd*); sometimes he hails from the Jewish quarter of Marw or Iṣfahān.[40] In a very rare tradition, he is accompanied by Turks.[41] In a fourteenth-century source, after the destruction of Baghdad by the Mongols, he is said to be accompanied by 70,000 "Tatars"[42] who replace the Jews of the classical traditions. It thus seems that the *dajjāl*'s entourage changes with the changing identity of the enemies of Islam. In some descriptions he claimed to be God while in others he asked the Prophet to testify that he (i.e., the *dajjāl*) was a messenger of God. He had a huge, frightful body that would fill his entire house. According to some traditions, God banished him to an island.[43] It is noteworthy that the classical traditions about the "Jewish connection" of the *dajjāl* inspired modern Muslim writers to identify him with contemporary Jews and with the modern State of Israel.[44]

The Prophet will protect the believers from the *dajjāl* if he appears during the Prophet's lifetime; if not, every believer will have to fend for himself by reciting the opening verses of *Sūrat al-Kahf* (Qur ʾān 18)

39 Abū Dāwūd, *Sunan*, vol. 4, p. 165. The last sentence is meant to deny the *dajjāl*'s claim to divinity; see Qurṭubī, *Tadhkira*, p. 1282. For an extensive collection of traditions about the *dajjāl*, see Nu ʿaym b. Ḥammād, *Kitāb al-fitan*, pp. 315–352. For an analysis of the traditions about *al-dajjāl*, see Halperin, "The Ibn Ṣayyād Traditions ..." and, more recently, Raven, "Ibn Ṣayyād as an Islamic 'Antichrist'".

40 Nu ʿaym b. Ḥammād, *Kitāb al-fitan*, pp. 323, 327; Muslim, *Ṣaḥīḥ*, vol. 4, p. 2266 (no. 163); Ibn Kathīr, *Kitāb al-fitan wa al-malāḥim*, p. 153; Saffārīnī, *Lawā ʾiḥ al-anwār*, vol. 2, p. 82 *infra*.

41 Nu ʿaym b. Ḥammād, *Kitāb al-fitan*, pp. 414. For the changing image of the Turks in Muslim apocalypse, see D. Cook, "The Image of the Turk ...", *passim*.

42 Ibn Kathīr, *Kitāb al-fitan wa al-malāḥim*, p. 153. Elsewhere, his hosts include "Zoroastrians, Jews, Christians and non-Arab polytheists". See ibid., p. 157.

43 Balkhī, *al-Bad ʾ wa al-ta ʾrīkh*, vol. 2, pp. 186–187.

44 For a convenient collection about the connection of the *dajjāl* with the Jews, see Ibn Kathīr, *Kitāb al-fitan wa al-malāḥim*, pp. 152–155. For a modern work on the *dajjāl*'s "Jewish connection", see Qasmi, *Emergence of dajjāl, the Jewish King*. See also D. Cook, *Contemporary Muslim Apocalyptic Literature*, pp. 184–200 and notes 186–189 to the present chapter. For the identification of the *dajjāl* with Christians, see Chapter 5, at notes 100–110.

in the *dajjāl*'s face. The *dajjāl* will remain on earth for forty days, but each of these may last for a year, a month or a week. When this period comes to an end, Jesus will descend – next to the white minaret located east of Damascus.[45]

The actions to be committed by Jesus after his descent will come as a surprise to those who know Jesus from the Qur'ān and from the Christian tradition. In the Qur'ān and parts of the *ḥadīth* literature, Jesus is described as one of God's prophets; there are references to his pious mother Mary, to his miraculous birth, to his miracles and to the denials of his being a son of God. In Ṣūfī literature he is also a model of humility and an ascetic way of life.[46] In eschatological literature, his image undergoes a substantial change. In this literary genre, during his second coming, Jesus is expected to be a rather pugnacious figure of a warrior who will perform a number of violent deeds designed to bring about the ultimate defeat of Christianity and the triumph of Islam:

> The Prophet said: "There was no prophet between me and him [i.e., Jesus][47] and he is about to descend. You will recognize him when you see him: a man of medium height and bright complexion, wearing two pieces of cloth. His head seems to be dripping, though not wet. He will fight the people for the sake of Islam, will crush the cross, kill the swine and abolish the poll-tax. In his time, God will annihilate all religions except Islam. He will kill the false messiah and remain on earth for forty years; then he will die and the Muslims will pray at his funeral." (*inna al-nabī ... qāla: laysa baynī wa baynahu – ya'nī 'Īsā - nabī wa innahu nāzil*

45 The famous fourteenth-century scholar Ibn Kathīr reports that during the year 741 AH/1340–1341 CE this white minaret was renovated at the expense of the Damascene Christians who were accused of burning it in the past: "God determined that this minaret will be built at the expense of the Christians so that Jesus the son of Mary can descend upon it to kill the swine, to break the cross, and not to accept from them *jizya*. Those of them who will embrace Islam – good and well; the others will be killed. This will also be the fate of all infidels of the earth on that day." See Ibn Kathīr, *al-Fitan wa al-malāḥim*, p. 173.

46 There is an enormous amount of research on the image of Jesus in the Qur'ān and the *ḥadīth*. A good bibliography can be found in Neal Robinson, "Jesus", *Encyclopaedia of the Qur'ān*, s.v.

47 This *ḥadīth* assumes that the pre-Islamic Arab prophets, such as Hūd, Ṣāliḥ and Shu'ayb, lived before the times of Jesus. Since the dates of these prophets are not clear in the relevant traditions, to make this assumption is not difficult for the traditionists.

fa-idhā ra'aytumūhu fa-''rifūhu: rajulun marbū' ilā al-ḥumra wa al-bayāḍ bayna mumaṣṣaratayn ka-'anna ra'sahu yaqṭur wa in lam yuṣibhu balal fa-yuqātil al-nās 'alā al-islām fa-yaduqqu al-ṣalīb wa yaqtul al-khinzīr wa yaḍa'u al-jizya wa yuhlik Allah fī zamānihi al-milal kullahā illā al-islām wa yuhlik al-masīḥ al-dajjāl fa-yamkuth fī al-arḍ arba'īna āman thumma yutawaffā fa-yuṣallī 'alayhi al- muslimūn.)[48]

Not all collections of *ḥadīth* are so explicit regarding the military exploits of Jesus: some have a shorter version which metaphorically mentions the breaking of the cross, the killing of the swine and the abolition of the *jizya*. The commentators, however, usually follow the more detailed version of the *ḥadīth* and interpret this tradition in terms of real warfare: Jesus is expected "to fight the people for the sake of Islam until Allah annihilates in his time all the religions except Islam".[49]

In one place, the text of the tradition is uncertain: some editions read *yaḍa' al-jizya* ("he will abolish the poll-tax") while others have *yaḍa' al-ḥarb* ("he will abolish war").[50] In Krehl's edition of Bukhārī's *Ṣaḥīḥ* we have *yaḍa'u al-ḥarb* in one place and *yaḍa'u al-jizya* in two places.[51] In one Egyptian edition, we have *yaḍa'u al-jizya* in the text and *yaḍa'u al-ḥarb* as a variant on the margin.[52] The bilingual Arabic-English edition by Muḥammad Muḥsin Khān has *yaḍa'u al-ḥarb* in the Arabic text, but translates "there will be no *jizya*".[53]

The expression *yaḍa'u al-jizya* is cryptic. Lexically it could mean that Jesus will impose the *jizya*[54] or abolish it. We need therefore to turn to the

48 Abū Dāwūd, *Sunan*, vol. 4, p. 167 (no. 43240); cf. Ibn Kathīr, *al-Fitan wa al-malāḥim*, p. 173.

49 Tirmidhī, *Ṣaḥīḥ*, vol. 9, p. 78 (Ibn al-'Arabī al-Mālikī's commentary); al-Qasṭallānī, *Irshād al-sārī*, vol. 5, p. 419; al-'Asqalānī, *Fatḥ al-bārī*, vol. 7, p. 304.

50 The consonantal skeletons of *jizya* and *ḥarb* are similar and this may be reason for the variation.

51 Bukhārī, *Ṣaḥīḥ*, ed. Krehl, vol. 2, p. 370 (*Kitāb al-anbiyā'* 49) – *yaḍa'u al-ḥarb*; vol. 2, p. 40 (*Kitāb al-buyū'* 102); vol. 2, p. 107 *Kitāb al-maẓālim wa al-ghaḍab* 31) – *yaḍa'u al-jizya*.

52 Bukhārī, *Ṣaḥīḥ*, Cairo: Dār Iḥyā' al-Turāth al-Arabī, n.d., vol. 4, p. 205.

53 Muḥammad Muḥsin Khān, ed., *Ṣaḥīḥ al-Bukhārī*, Beirut: Dār al-'arabiyya, 1985, vol. 4, p. 437.

54 For the possibility of such an understanding, see al-'Aynī, *'Umdat al-qāri'*, vol. 16, p. 39, lines 4–5: *wad'u al-jizya mashrū' fī hādhihi al-umma fa-lima lā yakūnu al-ma'nā taqarrur al-jizya 'alā al-kuffār min ghayr muḥābāt?*

commentators in order to learn how it was understood. The meaning of abolition is prevalent and the commentators concentrate on the question, what are the reasons for the abolition of the *jizya* at the end of days? Abū Sulaymān al-Khaṭṭābī (d. 988) says that it could be understood in two ways. According to the first interpretation, the *jizya* will lapse because Jesus will force all people to embrace Islam; as a consequence, there will not exist any scriptuary liable to pay the *jizya*. The alternative explanation for its abolition assumes that the *jizya* was originally imposed on the scriptuaries in the interest of Islam, for the empowerment of Muslims, for buying horses (to be used in *jihād*) and for supporting the Muslim poor. In apocalyptic times Islam will have no adversary, and there will be abundant money for everyone; the reasons for levying the *jizya* will therefore exist no longer.[55] It is noteworthy that al-Khaṭṭābī considers the payment of the *jizya* a tool for the strengthening of the Muslims and their state rather than a means to humiliate the scriptuaries intimated in Qur'ān 9:29.

The Shāfiʿī scholar al-Nawawī (d. 1277) concurs with the view according to which the apocalyptic policies of Jesus will be uncompromising. He maintains that the *sharʿī* right of infidels to pay the *jizya* and retain their religion will lapse at the end of days. Even if they do pay the *jizya*, they will not be left alone: in contradistinction to historical times, Jesus will give them only the options of conversion to Islam or death (*lā yaqbalu min al-kuffār illā al-islām wa man badhala minhum al-jizya lam yukaffa ʿanhu bihā bal lā yaqbalu illā al-islām aw al-qatl*).[56]

For al-ʿAsqalānī (d. 1449) and al-ʿAynī (d. 1453), the *yaḍaʿu al-jizya ḥadīth* entails additional problems. Al-ʿAynī deems it necessary to make it clear that this *ḥadīth* does not allow Muslims to break the crosses and kill the swines of the *dhimmī* Christians whose safety and religious freedom are guaranteed by the *dhimma* treaty; this is permitted only regarding the *ahl al-ḥarb* (non-Muslims who live outside *dār al-islām*) who have not received the protection of the Muslim community. Another question discussed by these two scholars is whether the abolition of the *jizya* by Jesus does not mean that he will be entitled to abrogate a law which was part of the Muslim *sharīʿa*. This is not so: when Jesus comes at the end of days, he will follow the law of the Prophet Muḥammad and will abolish

55 Khaṭṭābī, *Aʿlām al-ḥadīth*, vol. 2, pp. 1098–1099.
56 Nawawī, *Sharḥ Ṣaḥīḥ Muslim*, vol. 1–2, p. 549 (the pagination of the two volumes is continuous).

the *jizya* not on his own initiative, but rather on Muḥammad's orders as expressed in our *ḥadīth*.[57]

It is noteworthy that some modern commentators also stress this aspect of the policies of Jesus in apocalyptic times. Anwar Shāh Kashmīrī sees a precedent for these uncompromising policies of Jesus in the Prophet's refusal to accept *jizya* from Jews and Christians in the Arabian Peninsula, and in his decision to expel them rather than to grant them the *dhimma* status which entails the payment of *jizya*.[58]

A more "peaceful" version of the same tradition, which does not mention the abolition of the *jizya* is quoted in Ibn Ḥanbal's *Musnad*:

> ʿĪsā b. Maryam will descend as a just *imām* and a righteous judge, will break the cross, kill the swine, restore the peace (*yurjiʿ al-silm*) and transform the swords into sickles (*yattakhidhu al-suyūfa manājila*).[59] The venom of every scorpion will disappear (*tadhhabu ḥumatu kulli dhī ḥumatin*)[60] so that a boy will play with a snake without being harmed.[61]

Ibn Māja records a considerably expanded version of the tradition in which the peaceful conditions follow the total defeat of the Jews. In this version, Jesus descends while a few Arabs perform the morning prayer in Jerusalem, led by a righteous *imām*. When the *imām* recognizes Jesus, he expresses his desires to relinquish his place as the prayer leader in Jesus' favour. Jesus, however, declines to take over and instructs the *imām* to retain his place in the front. According to Muslim b. Ḥajjāj, Jesus refused to take over because the Muslims are "amīrs over each other, as a token

57 ʿAynī, *ʿUmdat al-qāriʾ*, vol. 13, pp. 27–28; cf. ibid., vol. 12, p. 34 and vol. 16, pp. 38–39; ʿAsqalānī, *Fatḥ al-bārī*, vol. 6, pp. 490–492. Cf. Qasṭallānī, *Irshād sl-sārī*, vol. 5, pp. 182, 488; vol. 7, p. 406.

58 See Kashmīrī, *Fayḍ al-bārī*, vol. 4, pp. 43–44 and the commentary of Muḥammad Shafīʿ (1897–1976). On Kashmīrī, see *al-Taṣrīḥ*, p. 92, notes 3–4. Muḥammad Shafīʿ served as the chief *muftī* of Pakistan. The Prophet's refusal to accept *jizya* in the peninsula has been traditionally explained by the idea that "no two religions will coexist in the Arabian Peninsula" (*lā yajtamiʿu fī jazīrat al-ʿarab dīnāni*). See Friedmann, *Tolerance and Coercion*, pp. 90–93.

59 Or: "use the swords as sickles". Cf. Isaiah 2:4.

60 For an explanation of this expression, see Ibn Māja, *Sunan*, vol. 2, p. 1362 (*Kitāb al-fitan, bāb 33*, no. 4077).

61 Ibn Ḥanbal, *Musnad*, vol. 2, pp. 482–483; Ibn Kathīr, *al-Fitan wa al-malāḥim*, p. 112. Cf. Isaiah 11:6–8.

of Allah's respect for this community" (*inna baʿḍakum ʿalā baʿḍin umarāʾ takrimata ʿllāhi hādhihi al-umma*).[62] When the prayer is over, Jesus tells the worshippers to open a certain door. The *dajjāl* appears behind that door, accompanied by seventy thousand Jews, each having an ornamented sword and a shawl (*sāj*).[63] When the *dajjāl* sees Jesus, he runs away. Jesus catches up with him near the eastern gate of the city of Lydda and kills him. At the same time, God defeats the Jews. They have no place to hide: wherever they try, be it under a tree, under a stone, or next to a wall – that object will say: "O Muslim servant of God, here is a Jew! Come and kill him!" Having also mentioned the breaking of the cross, the killing of the swine, the abolition of the *jizya* and the idyllic conditions prevailing in the animal realm, Ibn Māja continues:

> The earth will be filled with peace like a vessel with water. The declaration of faith (*kalima*) will be one. None except Allah will be worshipped, and war will come to an end (*wa taḍaʿ al-ḥarb awzārahā*).[64]

The peaceful conditions described here result from the religious uniformity which Jesus sets up by rather violent means.

In a similar vein, a tradition adduced by Ibn Ḥanbal and others reads:

> It will be one of the signs of the Hour that the swords will not be engaged in [waging] *jihād*, and that [the pleasures of] this world will be sought after by feigning piety. And another version reads: ... that the swords will be transformed into sickles. (*min ashrāṭ al-sāʿa an tuʿaṭṭala al-suyūfu min al-jihād wa an tukhtala al-dunyā bi-'l-dīn wa ruwiya: an tuttakhadha al-suyūfu manājila.*)[65]

This "eschatological disarmament" will be brought about by the destruction of Judaism and Christianity at the hands of Jesus. This idea has immense

62 Muslim b. Ḥajjāj, *Ṣaḥīḥ*, vol. 1, p. 137 (*Kitāb al-īmān bāb*, 247).

63 The *sāj* is traditionally defined as a shawl worn by Jews. See Suyūṭī, *al-Aḥādīth al-ḥisān fī faḍl al-ṭaylasān*, pp. 51–52, 58. Arazi, "Noms de vêtements", pp. 138, 146.

64 Ibn Māja, *Sunan*, vol. 2, pp. 1361–1362 (*Kitāb al-fitan, bāb* 33, no. 4077); cf. Qurṭubī, *Tadhkira*, p. 1295 and Ibn Kathīr, *al-Fitan wa al-malāḥim*, pp. 111–112, 122, 140.

65 Ibn Ḥanbal, *Musnad*, vol. 2, p. 482 *infra*; Zamakhsharī, *al-Fāʾiq fī gharīb al-ḥadīth* (Cairo 1945), vol. 1, p. 329 (s.v. *kh-t-l*); Ibn al-Athīr, *al-Nihāya fī gharīb al-ḥadīth wa al-athar* (Cairo 1311 AH), vol. 1, p. 281 (s.v. *kh-t-l*).

value for the medieval Muslim polemicists: what could be more humiliating for their Christian adversaries than having Jesus inflicting the ultimate defeat on their faith?[66]

IV THE DESCENT OF JESUS IN QUR'ĀNIC EXEGESIS

We have seen that the apocalyptic descent of Jesus is copiously discussed in *ḥadīth* literature. The Qur'ān has ample material on Jesus, but it does not include an explicit statement regarding his descent at the end of times. We may conclude from this that the apocalyptic role of Jesus was not central to the religious message of Muḥammad and is, in this regard, similar to the coming of the *mahdī* who has not been mentioned in the Qur'ān either. Yet the Sunnī commentators invested much ingenuity to find Qur'ānic substantiation for the role of Jesus in the apocalyptic drama. In the same way as their Shī'ī counterparts looked in the Qur'ān for veiled references to the *mahdī*,[67] the Sunnī exegetes worked hard to find in it references to the second coming of Jesus. We will see in Chapter 5 that these verses have been extensively discussed in modern polemical encounters between Muslim factions as well as between Muslims and Christians.

Qur'ān 3:55 is a case in point. It is relevant because it speaks of Jesus' ascension to heaven. If this verse hints at the death of Jesus, the idea of the second coming becomes problematic: it would require that God resurrects him ahead of the general resurrection and this possibility is not mentioned in the *ḥadīth*. The verse reads:

> When God said, "Jesus, I will take you to Me and will raise you to Me (*innī mutawaffīka wa rāfi'uka ilayya*) and I will purify you of those who believe not. I will set your followers above the unbelievers till the Resurrection Day. Then unto Me shall you return, and I will decide between you, as to what you were at variance on. As for

66 This is a short account of a huge literary corpus dealing with the events preceding the Last Day and the coming of the *mahdī*. This account is necessary in order to put the following chapters in perspective and connect them to the classical tradition about the *mahdī*. I have been able to be so brief because the subject has received exhaustive and excellent treatment in D. Cook, *Studies in Muslim Apocalyptic*.
67 See Section V of this chapter.

> the unbelievers, I will chastise them with a terrible chastisement in this world and the next; they shall have no helpers."[68]

The crucial words for our discussion are *mutawaffīka* and *rāfiʿuka*. The common Arabic expressions such as *tuwuffiya, tawaffāhu Allah bi-raḥmatihi* and *wafāt*, as well as the Persian *wafāt kard*, immediately conjure up the meaning of death. Gabriel S. Reynolds who recently subjected the Qurʾānic material on Jesus to intense analysis has no doubt that this was the originally intended meaning.[69] Yet classical commentators are far from agreeing on it and numerous translators have followed the views of the commentators rather than the plain meaning of the Qurʾānic text. Muqātil b. Sulaymān (d. 767) understands *mutawaffīka* in its plain meaning, but maintains that *mutawaffīka* and *rāfiʿuka* should be read in reverse order (*taqdīm*): "I am raising you to myself now and causing you to die after killing the *dajjāl*" (*innī rāfiʿuka ilayya al-ān wa mutawaffīka baʿda qatl al-dajjāl*).[70] In the commentary of al-Ṭabarī, who is also aware of the *ḥadīth* predictions of the second coming, most interpretations do not take *mutawaffīka* to indicate death. One of them glosses *mutawaffīka* as "I am causing you to sleep and raising you in your sleep" (*innī munīmuka wa rāfiʿuka fī nawmika*). Another explains: "I am taking you from earth alive into my presence" (*innī qābiḍuka min al-arḍ ḥayyan ilā jiwārī*).[71] There is also an interpretation which explicitly speaks of the apocalyptic task of Jesus:

> He whom I raised to myself is not dead; I shall send you against the one-eyed false messiah and you will kill him. Then you will live

---

68 Translation by Arberry, *The Koran Interpreted*, vol. 1, p. 81 (slightly modified).

69 See Reynolds, "The Muslim Jesus", *passim*. Cf. Zahnisser, "The Forms of *tawaffā* in the Qurʾān ...", *passim*, and Ayoub, "Towards an Islamic Christology ...", *passim*.

70 Muqātil b. Sulaymān, *Tafsīr*, on Qurʾān 3:55. This has already been noted by Reynolds, "The Muslim Jesus: Alive or Dead", p. 245.

71 It may not be superfluous to note that the Muslim tradition includes the idea that Muḥammad will not be left in his grave for more than three days (there are references to different lengths of time in other traditions) before ascending to heaven. See the important and lucid analysis of these traditions by Szylágyi, "A prophet like Jesus?", pp. 139–146. Traditions which include this idea did not gain entry into the canonical collections of *ḥadīth*, but the reasons for their emergence can be understood: they serve as a riposte to the Christian polemicists who used to compare Jesus who is alive, sitting at the right hand of God in heaven, with Muḥammad who is buried in Medina, with his bones decayed. See Friedmann, *Prophecy Continuous*, pp. 112–115.

> twenty-four years after which I shall cause you to die like [any] living being. (*laysa man rafaʿtuhu ʿindī mayyitan. wa innī sa-abʿathuka ʿalā al-aʿwar al-dajjāl fa-taqtuluhu thumma taʿīshu baʿda dhālika arbaʿan wa ʿishrīna sana thumma umītuka mītat al-ḥayy.*)[72]

In a similar vein, al-Bayḍāwī studiously avoids the sense of irreversible death for *innī mutawaffīka*:

> I will complete your lifetime and let you live until your appointed time, protecting you from their [i.e., the Jews'] killing; or taking you from the earth – as you say: – I took my money; or I am taking you sleeping, because it was said that he was raised sleeping; or I am killing you (to remove) your desires which impede the ascension to the world of the kingdom (of God). And it was said that God killed him for seven hours and then raised him to heaven. This is the belief of the Christians. (*ay mustawfī ajalika wa muʾakhkhiruka ilā ajalika al-musammā ʿāṣiman iyyāka min qatlihim aw qābiḍuka min al-arḍ min tawaffaytu mālī aw mutawaffīka nāʾiman idh ruwiya annahu rufiʿa nāʾiman aw mumītuka ʿan al-shahawāt al-ʿāʾiqa ʿan al-ʿurūj ilā ʿālam al-malakūt wa qīla amātahu Allah sabʿa sāʿāt thumma rafaʿahu ilā al-samāʾ wa ilayhi dhahaba al-naṣārā.*)[73]

It is, however, noteworthy that in his commentary on *lammā tawaffaytanī* in Qurʾān 5:122, al-Bayḍāwī is more receptive to the sense of death and says that *tawaffī* is "taking a thing when it is full and death is one type of such taking (*wa al-tawaffī akhdh al-shayʾ wāfiyan wa al-mawt nawʿun minhu*).[74] On the other hand, al-Ṭabarī also quotes the view of Ibn ʿAbbās who maintained that *mutawaffīka* means "I cause you to die" (*mumītuka*) without specifying the time for this.[75] Al-Zamakhsharī also includes this meaning in his commentary, though the thrust of his explanation is that Jesus will die only after completing his apocalyptic role.[76]

---

72 Ṭabarī, *Jāmiʿ al-bayān*, vol. 3, pp. 289–290; cf. Ibn Kathīr, *Tafsīr*, vol. 3, p. 70.
73 Al-Bayḍāwī, *Anwār al-tanzīl*, vol. 1, p. 158.
74 Al-Bayḍāwī, *Anwār al-tanzīl*, vol. 1, p. 281.
75 Ṭabarī, *Jāmiʿ al-bayān*, vol. 3, p. 290 *infra*. For the use of the view of Ibn ʿAbbās in nineteenth-century polemics, see Chapter 5, at note 122.
76 Zamakhsharī, *al-Kashshāf*, vol. 1, p. 566.

Qur'ān 43:61 is another verse in which the commentators have found an indication of Jesus' role at the end of times: "It is knowledge of the Hour, doubt not concerning it and follow me. This is the straight path" (*innahu la-ʿilmun*) (or *ʿalamun*) *li-'l-sāʿa fa-lā tamturunna bihā fa-'ttabiʿūnī hādhā ṣirāṭun mustaqīm*). The commentators needed much ingenuity to arrive at this interpretation. Jesus is mentioned in Qur'ān 43:57 and 43: 59 as "a sign for the Children of Israel" which has no apocalyptic significance. There are two readings of the letters ʿ *l m* in the verse, and the traditionists quoted by al-Ṭabarī are all in agreement that the verse means – in all its readings – that the descent of Jesus is the "knowledge" (*ʿilm*) or the "sign" (*ʿalam*) of the approaching Day of Judgment.[77] Al-Bayḍāwī quotes in his commentary the famous *ḥadīth* on the apocalyptic exploits of Jesus after his descent, adding that he will also "destroy the churches and the synagogues and kill the Christians except those who believe in him" (*yukharribu al-biyaʿ wa al-kanāʾis wa yaqtul al-naṣārā illā man āmana bihi*).[78]

Qur'ān 4:158 comes after the verse denying the crucifixion of Jesus and this context makes it clear that the verse speaks about Jesus: "There is not one of the People of the Book but will assuredly believe in him before his death and on the Day of Resurrection he will be a witness against them." The commentators are not of one opinion on this verse. Some say that "his death" refers to the death of Jesus and explain that all People of the Book will believe in Jesus before he dies. From this they draw the conclusion that Jesus is alive with God who raised him to Himself, will descend before the Day of Judgment and will die only after killing the *dajjāl*. Since Jesus is expected to be a Muslim at his second coming, this means that all Jews and Christians will embrace Islam at that time. Other commentators assert that "his death" refers to the death of a scriptuary; if this is the case, the verse does not support the idea that Jesus is alive and will descend before the Day of Judgment. And the reading "before their death" (*qabla mawtihim*) – which is attributed to Ubayy b. Kaʿb – completely precludes the interpretation according to which the scriptuaries will believe in Jesus before the death of Jesus; they will believe in him before *their own* death.[79]

77 Ṭabarī, *Jāmiʿ al-bayān*, vol. 25, pp. 90–91; Ibn Kathīr, *Tafsīr*, vol. 12, p. 323.
78 Bayḍāwī, *Anwār al-tanzīl*, vol. 2, p. 241 *infra*. Bayḍāwī also gives another explanation in which the verse speaks about the Qur'ān rather than about Jesus. Cf. Zamakhsharī, *Kashshāf*, vol. 5, pp. 453–454 and Muqātil, *Tafsīr*, vol. 3, p. 800.
79 Ṭabarī, *Jāmiʿ al-bayān*, vol. 6, pp. 18–23; see also Ibn Kathīr, *Tafsīr*, vol. 4, pp. 341–346. Al-Bayḍāwī (*Anwār al-tanzīl*, vol. 1, pp. 240–241 gives both views without expressing his own.

The Sunnī commentators make a valiant effort to find in the Qur'ān support for the *ḥadīth* material about the apocalyptic role of Jesus – *mutatis mutandis*, like the Shī'īs who look for verses which can be explained as predicting the coming of the *mahdī*. Yet the apocalyptic descent of Jesus raises also problems for Muslim traditionists. First of all, they had to affirm that he will not descend as a prophet and will not bring a new *sharī'a* – different from that of Muḥammad – because this would contradict the idea that Muḥammad was the last prophet. Al-Qurṭubī mentions even traditionists who maintain that the obligation to observe the religious law will lapse with the descent of Jesus (*bi-nuzūl 'Īsā yartafi' al-taklīf*), so that he cannot be a messenger who will issue commandments and prohibitions to the people of that time. Al-Qurṭubī rejects this idea, but he does maintain that when Jesus descends, he will be a Muslim and a follower of Muḥammad. He will be an ordinary Muslim rather than a prophet, and is therefore made to decline the offer to lead the Muslims in prayer after his descent and is made to pray behind the Muslim *imām*. Furthermore, some traditionists ask why it was necessary to include Jesus in the apocalyptic drama at all. They opine that this was necessary because the Jews always insisted that they had killed him – contrary to the Qur'ānic account.[80] God therefore afflicted them with humiliation,[81] deprived them of power (*quwwa*, *shawka*) and sovereignty (*sulṭān*) in any part of the world and will keep them in this humble condition until the Day of Judgment. Then He will send Jesus who will defeat them together with their leader the *dajjāl*, eliminate those of them who refuse to embrace Islam and cleanse the earth of all infidels.[82]

Jesus performs these tasks as a Muslim. Some traditions say so explicitly, stating that he will come "believing in Muḥammad, adhering to his religion" (*muṣaddiqan bi-Muḥammad ... wa 'alā millatihi*).[83] In other traditions, Jesus' affiliation with Islam can be inferred from the fact that immediately following his descent, he prays under the leadership of a Muslim *imām*; and when he dies, Muslims pray at his funeral. This may come as a surprise to some readers; however, describing Jesus in this manner is easily understandable within the Islamic world view according to which

80 Cf. Qur'ān 4:157.

81 Qur'ān 2:61.

82 Qurṭubī, *Tadhkira*, pp. 1301–1303.

83 Ibn Kathīr, *al-Fitan wa al-malāḥim*, pp. 123–124.

Islam (indicating the absolute and exclusive submission to Allah)[84] is not only the name of the religion and the civilization founded by the Prophet Muḥammad at the beginning of the seventh century CE, but also the name of the primordial monotheistic belief which existed since the creation of mankind. The most celebrated case in which a pre-Islamic personality is perceived as Muslim is that of Abraham about whom the Qur'ān says that he was "neither a Jew nor a Christian but a *ḥanīf* Muslim and was not one of the idolaters".[85] While the Qur'ān does not explicitly describe Jesus in the same manner, it is certainly not surprising to find Jesus and other prophets perceived as Muslim in the Islamic tradition. A very clear case of such an approach can be found in the works of Ibn Taymiyya who asserts that "the religion of all the prophets, from Noah to Jesus, was Islam" (... *anna al-anbiyā' kullahum kāna dīnuhum al-islām, min Nūḥ ilā al-Masīḥ*).[86] Jesus is a prophet like all the others and if he had been a Muslim during his initial mission, it would only be natural if he retained his erstwhile religious affiliation during the second coming.

V JESUS AND THE *MAHDĪ* IN HISTORICAL TIMES

We now need to discuss additional traditions about Jesus. These traditions are not included in all the canonical books of *ḥadīth* and some Muslim scholars have therefore declared them as spurious. We need to discuss these traditions because of two considerations. First, from our point of view, non-canonical traditions reflect trends which may have been important in medieval Muslim thought, but were excluded from the canon for some reason. This exclusion does not diminish their importance from a

84 Of the numerous studies devoted to the elucidation of the term Islam, the following may be mentioned: H. Ringrren, *Islam, aslama and Muslim*. Uppsala 1949; D. Z. Baneth, "What Did Muḥammad Mean When He Called His Religion Islam? The Original Meaning of *aslama* and its Derivatives", *Israel Oriental Studies* 1 (1971), 183–190; J. I. Smith, *An Historical and Semantic Study of the Term 'Islām' as Seen in a Sequence of Qur'ān Commentaries*, Missoula: Scholars Press, 1975.

85 Qur'ān 3:67.

86 Ibn Taymiyya, *Ghurbat al-islām*, p. 16. The idea that leaders of pre-Islamic religions were actually Muslims is not restricted to the classical tradition. Ṣiddīq Ḥusayn, the leader of the twentieth-century Dīndār Anjuman – who strove for the conversion of Hindūs to Islam – maintained that figures such as Rāmā and Krishna actually preached Islam and therefore Hindūs who embrace Islam should not be considered traitors to their religious heritage. See Sikand, *Pseudo-Messianic Movements*, pp. 31, 36 and elsewhere.

historian's point of view. Second, these traditions were widely used in modern polemics about the apocalyptic role of Jesus which will be discussed in Chapter 5.

The first tradition relates to the life of Jesus from his second coming to his death. It reads:

> The messenger of God ... said: "Jesus the son of Mary will descend to earth, will marry and beget children. He will live for forty-five years. Then he will die and will be buried with me in my grave. I and Jesus will rise [from the dead] from the same grave, between [the graves of] Abū Bakr and 'Umar." (*qāla rasūl Allah ... yanzilu 'Īsā b. Maryam ilā al-arḍ fa-yatazawwaju wa yūladu lahu wa yamkuthu khamsan wa arba'īna sana thumma yamūtu wa yudfanu ma'ī fī qabrī fa-aqūmu anā wa 'Īsā b. Maryam min qabrin wāḥid bayna Abī Bakr wa 'Umar.*)[87]

This tradition significantly differs from the "canonical" view of the activities of Jesus during his second coming. It completely disregards the classical descriptions in which Jesus actively participates in the apocalyptic wars and creates the impression that Jesus descended to earth only in order to lead a normal life of a married man, to die as any mortal, to be buried in the Prophet's grave and to rise from the dead in his company. It is another expression of the special, very intimate relationship between the Prophet Muḥammad and Jesus, based on the traditional statement of the Prophet that "there was no prophet between myself and Jesus".[88] No special apocalyptic role is assigned to Jesus in this *ḥadīth* and the second coming is not related to the end of days at all.[89] Some traditions combine this tradition with an apocalyptic one and maintain that after killing the *dajjāl* Jesus will perform the pilgrimage, will go to visit the Prophet's grave in Medina, will die there and will be buried in his grave.[90] Another

87 Ibn al-Jawzī, *al-Muntaẓam*, vol. 2, p. 39; *idem*, *al-'Ilal al-mutanāhiya*, vol. 2, p. 915; Qurṭubī, *Tadhkira*, pp. 1299, 1301. Cf. Ibn Kathīr, *al-Fitan wa al-malāḥim*, p. 174 who says that Jesus will die in Medina and will be buried in the "prophetic chamber" (*yudfanu bi-'l-ḥujra al-nabawiyya*). See also Tirmidhī, *Ṣaḥīḥ*, *Kitāb al-manāqib* 1 (vol. 13, p. 104); Nu'aym b. Ḥammād, *Kitāb al-fitan*, p. 354.

88 See earlier, at note 48 in this chapter.

89 See Chapter 5, at note 126, for the use of this *ḥadīth* in modern anti-Aḥmadī polemics.

90 Qurṭubī, *Tadhkira*, p. 1348.

tradition – also unrelated to the end of days – tells us that the Prophet saw both Jesus and the *dajjāl* performing *ṭawāf* around the Kaʿba. The compilers of this *ḥadīth* do not perceive any oddity in the scene in which the *dajjāl*, the arch-enemy of Jesus, and Jesus himself are seen performing a Muslim ritual together.[91]

An additional tradition seems to indicate that Jesus will indeed come at the end of days, but the *mahdī* will appear in the "middle" of history and the world will not come to an end after his appearance. The tradition reads:

> A community in which I am at the beginning, Jesus at the end and the *mahdī* in the middle will not perish. (*lan tahlika ummatun anā fī awwalihā wa ʿĪsā fī ākhirihā wa al-mahdī fī wasaṭihā.*)

Several late authors have attributed this tradition to works as early as the *Musnad* of Ibn Ḥanbal and the *Sunan* of al-Nasāʾī, but I have not been able to locate it in either of them.[92] Since mainstream Muslim eschatology considers Jesus and the *mahdī* as actors in the same apocalyptic drama, the tradition describing them as coming at different times did not gain entrance into the canonical literature; however, it has become

91 Mālik b. Anas, *al-Muwaṭṭaʾ*, vol. 2, p. 920; Muslim b. Al-Ḥajjāj, *Ṣaḥīḥ*, vol. 1, pp. 154–156 (*Kitāb al-īmān bāb 75*). In some versions the Prophet sees Jesus and the *dajjāl* in a dream.

92 Yūsuf b. Yaḥyā al-Maqdisī al-Sulamī (d. 1286; see Brockelmann, *GAL G* I, p. 431; *GAL S* I, p. 769) attributes it in his *ʿIqd al-durar* (pp. 146, 148) to the *Musnad* of Ibn Ḥanbal, to the *Sunan* of al-Nasāʾī and to the *ʿAwālī* of al-Iṣfahānī. The editor of *ʿIqd al-durar* has not found it in the first two works. The tradition does appear in several works by al-Suyūṭī, *al-Jāmiʿ al-ṣaghīr*, p. 453 (no. 7384), in *al-ʿArf al-wardī*, p. 222, *al-Iʿlām bi-ḥukm ʿĪsā*, p. 340 and in Munāwī, *Fayḍ al-qadīr*, vol. 5, p. 383 (no. 7384); Suyūṭī and Munāwī attribute it to Nuʿaym b. Ḥammād's *Akhbār al-mahdī*, but the version found in Nuʿaym's *Kitāb al-fitan* (p. 353) does not mention the *mahdī* and reads: "How can perish a community which begins with me and ends with the *masīḥ*? (*kayfa tahliku ummatun anā awwaluhā wa al-masīḥ ākhiruhā?*). Ibn ʿAsākir includes two versions of this *ḥadīth* in his *Taʾrīkh madīnat Dimashq* (vol. 47, pp. 521–522): one mentions both the *mahdī* and Jesus while the other mentions Jesus only. Ibn Ḥajar al-Haytamī (*al-Qawl al- mukhtaṣar*, p. 40) says that the *mahdī* will appear "close to the end" (*qarīb ākhirihā*), trying to explain away the appearance of the *mahdī* in the "middle" in order to save the idea that both the *mahdī* and Jesus will appear simultaneously at the end of days. This interpretation is accepted by al-Muttaqī al-Hindī (*al-Burhān*, vol. 2, p. 799) and by al-Barzanjī (*al-Ishāʿa*, p. 236).

The scholars who found this tradition in the canonical collection must have had at their disposal a version of the canonical works which was different from that available to us.

a godsend proof-text for messianic thinkers who desired to transform the *mahdī* into a historical leader, expected to change the world for the better without waiting for the eschaton.[93] The tradition can easily be interpreted as indicating that Muslim history will continue after the coming of the *mahdī* and facilitates conferral of the title of *mahdī* to historical leaders. Ella Landau-Tasseron has shown comparable ideas in Zaydī thought where she identified a tendency for the *mahdī* and the *imām* to be used for one and the same person, a historical leader and restorer of religion.[94]

VI THE *MAHDĪ*

Despite the central role which Jesus is expected to play in the drama to be enacted at the end of days, his identification with the *mahdī* lost its primacy. Instead, Jesus was "demoted" to a figure merely paving the way for the *mahdī*'s appearance.[95] As we have shown, this downgrading should be understood as a part of the process through which Islam has gradually dissociated itself from Judaism and Christianity and assumed a distinct character of its own.[96] As for the *mahdī* himself, he was now expected to be a descendant of the Prophet, bearing his name and genealogy. The *mahdī*'s genealogy is sometimes described in terms which could be used in support of various messianic claimants. The tradition according to which "the *mahdī* will be from my descendants, from the sons of Fāṭima" (*al-mahdī min ʿitratī, min wuld Fāṭima*)[97] could be used in support of Shīʿī messianism, while the ʿAbbāsī claim to legitimacy found endorsement in the identification of the *mahdī* as "a descendant of my uncle al-ʿAbbās".[98] Evidently enough, all these utterances bestow upon the *mahdī* an unquestionably Muslim character and mitigate the

93 See, for instance, Shāh Dilāwar, *Khaṣāʾiṣ*, p. 10 where this *ḥadīth* is used to substantiate the messianic claim of Sayyid Muḥammad Jawnpūrī. See also Gaborieau, *Le mahdī incompris*, pp. 222–226 for the use of this *ḥadīth* in support of the mahdist claims of Sayyid Aḥmad Shahīd.

94 Landau-Tasseron, "Zaydī *imāms* as Restorers of Religion", p. 255.

95 For a discussion of the possible background of this process, see earlier, at note 38 of this chapter.

96 For a discussion of this process, see Section II of this chapter.

97 Abū Dāwūd, *Sunan*, Cairo 1983, vol. 4, p. 151 (no. 4284). See the discussion of this tradition in Elad, "The Struggle for Legitimacy ...", pp. 46–49.

98 Ibn al-Jawzī, *al-ʿIlal al-mutanāhiya*, p. 316.

embarrassment of having Jesus performing such a decisive role during the eschatological cataclysm.

The *mahdī*'s actions are described in a less detailed fashion than those of Jesus. He is expected to reign five, seven, or nine years to establish justice and create unlimited wealth on the face of the earth. Sometimes he has only one day to accomplish this task before the Day of Judgment comes.[99] In view of the classical idea according to which agriculture and animal husbandry are likely to interfere with *jihād*, the *mahdī* will deprive Muslims of landed property so that the necessity to tend to their crops and flocks does not impede their participation in the eschatological wars.[100] The *mahdī* is also expected to usher in a period in which supply of money is unlimited: he will give away any amount for the asking.[101] His basic task is described as follows:

> ...The Prophet said: If only one day remained of this world, ... God would prolong that day ... until he sends a man related to me – [or: a man] from my household whose name will correspond to mine and whose father's name will correspond to that of my father ... He will fill the earth with equity and justice, even as it had been replete with wrong and iniquity. (*law lam yabqa min al-dunyā illā yawmun ... la-ṭawwala Allāh dhālika al-yawm ... ḥattā yab'atha fīhi rajulan minnī, - aw - min ahli baytī - yuwāṭi'u 'smuhu 'smī wa 'smu abīhi 'sma abī yamla'u al-arḍ qisṭan wa 'adlan kamā muli'at ẓulman wa jawran.*)[102]

In this and in similar traditions the *mahdī*'s appearance is part of the eschatological drama. If we merge the activities of the *mahdī* and of Jesus, we can understand the nature of the early Muslim community's messianic expectations. Jesus is portrayed as a pugnacious figure, engaged in the establishment of religious uniformity through the violent destruction of Judaism and Christianity and the consequent transformation of Islam into the sole religion. In contradistinction to Muslim history, Muslim tradition recognizes only wars caused by reasons of religion; it is therefore only

99 See D. Cook, *Studies in Muslim Apocalyptic*, p. 144.
100 Nu'aym b. Ḥammād, *Kitāb al-fitan*, p. 218. For the connection between landed property and *jihād*, see Kister, "Land Property and *jihād*", pp. 284–285.
101 Ibn Māja, *Sunan*, vol. 2, p. 1368 (no. 4083).
102 Abū Dāwūd, *Sunan*, vol. 4, p. 151.

natural that religious uniformity, though achieved by violent means, is expected to result in universal peace. Once peace is established by Jesus, the *mahdī* will transform the messianic period into one of unprecedented prosperity and justice.

VII THE *MAHDĪ* IN MUSLIM CREEDS

The fact that the *mahdī* is mentioned neither in the Qur'ān nor in the celebrated collections of prophetic traditions by al-Bukhārī (d. 870) and Muslim b. al-Ḥajjāj (d. 875) created different trends in the study of the messianic idea in Sunnī Islam. For the historian of religious ideas, the absence of the idea from the Qur'ān is important because it indicates that the Prophet Muḥammad did not consider it central to his religious message, though eschatology as such stood at its core. On the other hand, the absence of the idea from al-Bukhārī and Muslim is not very significant for the historian, because the idea appears in other collections of prophetic tradition from the late ninth century; this is a sufficient indication of the fact that at some point between the seventh and the ninth centuries the messianic idea acquired considerable importance in Sunnī Muslim religious thought. The reasons for this development need further investigation, but the inclusion of the *mahdī* theme in the *ḥadīth* is undeniable. Suffice it to say that the *Sunan* of Abū Dāwūd (d. 889), Ibn Māja (d. 886), al-Tirmidhī (d. 892), as well as the *Musnad* of Ibn Ḥanbal (d. 855), which are certainly part of the canonical tradition, include copious material about the *mahdī*. Furthermore, traditions about the *mahdī* do appear in *al-Mustadrak ʿalā al-Ṣaḥīḥayn* by al-Naysābūrī (d. 1014) – a collection of traditions which have a sound *isnād* in the view of al-Naysābūrī, but were nevertheless not included in the *Ṣaḥīḥ*s of al-Bukhārī and Muslim b. Ḥajjāj.[103] This indicates that the exclusion of the *mahdī* idea from the *Ṣaḥīḥ*s of al-Bukhārī and Muslim was not acceptable to all scholars of *ḥadīth*.

The absence of the idea from the Qur'ān and from the two "authentic" (*ṣaḥīḥ*) collections gave rise to the notion that the idea did not originate with the Prophet and therefore does not belong to the core of Muslim religious thought. David Cook correctly asserted that "there are virtually no Qur'ānic citations to be found in the [Sunnī] cycles about the

103 Naysābūrī, *al-Mustadrak*, vol. 5, pp. 770–773.

mahdī".[104] The situation in Shīʿī tradition is different. This work does not focus on Shīʿī scholarship, but the Shīʿī attempts to find in the Qurʾān hints at the *mahdī*'s appearance are significant for us because they are used to substantiate the argument that the *mahdī* idea is not a sectarian Shīʿī one, but belongs to the whole of Islam, including its Sunnī variety. For the Shīʿī scholars, the expectation of the *mahdī*, frequently referred to as *qāʾim al-zamān* or *ṣāḥib al-amr*, became a cardinal article of faith. The absence of an explicit reference to the *mahdī* in the Qurʾān brought about Shīʿī attempts to interpret certain Qurʾānic expressions as hinting at his future appearance. These attempts can be found in the earliest Shīʿī sources which perceive hints to the *mahdī* in numerous Qurʾānic verses. In many cases, these interpretations need much exegetical ingenuity and imagination. A few examples are in order. Qurʾān 2:3 speaks of "those who believe in the Unseen" (*alladhīna yuʾminūna bi-ʾl-ghayb*); this is taken to refer to the rising of the *mahdī*.[105] The "unseen" (*ghayb*) is understood as a hint at the *mahdī*'s occultation (*ghayba*). Another verse used in a similar way is Qurʾān 2:148 where the divine promise "to bring you all together" (*yaʾtī bikum Allah jamīʿan*) is understood to hint at the *mahdī* and his entourage.[106] In Qurʾān 3:200, the expression "endure, be steadfast and persevere" (*iṣbirū wa ṣābirū wa rābiṭū*), which is usually interpreted as enjoining perseverance in *jihād*, is understood by a Shīʿī author as meaning "tie yourselves to the Imām *mahdī* – peace be upon him – and tie your spirits to him" (*shuddū anfusakum bi-ʾl-imām al-mahdī ʿalayhi al-salām wa ʾrbuṭū arwāḥakum bihi* ...).[107] Al-Ṭūsī explains the downtrodden of earth whom God will make into "*imāms* and inheritors" (Qurʾān 28:5) by saying that they are "the family of Muḥammad whose *mahdī* Allah will send and will honour them after their tribulations and will humiliate their enemy" (*hum āl Muḥammad yabʿathu Allah mahdiyyahum baʿda juhdihim fa-yuʿizzuhum wa yudhillu*

104 D. Cook, *Studies in Muslim Apocalyptic*, p. 278.

105 Ṭabrisī, *Majmaʿ al-bayān*, vol. 1, p. 82; Majlisī, *Biḥār al-anwār*, vol. 51, p. 52; Baḥrānī, *al-Burhān*, vol. 1, p. 124; Riẓwī, *al-Mahdī al-mawʿūd*, pp. 65–66. See also Ibn Babūya, *Kamāl al-dīn*, p. 17.

106 Ṭabrisī, *Majmaʿ al-bayān*, vol. 1, p. 65; Majlisī, *Biḥār al-anwār*, vol. 51, p. 53; ʿAyyāshī, *Tafsīr*, vol. 1, p. 85; Ṭūsī, *Ghayba*, p. 176; Baḥrānī, *al-Burhān*, vol. 1, p. 347.

107 Shīrāzī, *al-Mahdī fī al-Qurʾān*, pp. 24–25. In Sayyārī's *Kitāb al-qirāʾāt*, the interpretation is less explicit: *rābiṭū ʿalā al-aʾimma* (see Kohlberg and Amir-Moezzi, *Revelation and Falsification*, p. 36 of the Arabic text, no. 127). In ʿAyyāshī, *Tafsīr*, vol. 1, p. 237: *rābiṭū yaʿnī al-aʾimma*; the same in Baḥrānī, *al-Burhān*, vol. 1, p. 733.

ʿaduwwahum.)[108] Al-Majlisī's *Biḥār al-anwār* includes a whole chapter dealing with Qurʾānic verses which are to be interpreted as hinting at the coming of the *mahdī.*[109] Al-Majlisī's compilation includes an interpretation of Qurʾān 9:34[110] – which is usually interpreted as relating to the mission of the Prophet Muḥammad – as if it related to the appearance of the *mahdī*. This is indicative of the length to which the Shīʿī tradition is willing to go in order to find a Qurʾānic basis for the eschatological return of the hidden *imām*, the *mahdī.*[111] This approach is alive also in modern times. As part of the attempts to narrow the gap between the Shīʿa and the Sunna, numerous books have been written in recent decades, in order to prove that the belief in the *mahdī* is Qurʾānic and therefore should be regarded as common to all Muslims rather than as a sectarian Shīʿī one. These books list dozens of Qurʾānic verses which were interpreted in classical Shīʿī commentaries as relating to the *mahdī* or predicting his reappearance.[112]

The Shīʿīs substantiate the idea that the *mahdī* idea is common to all Muslims also by the fact that many Sunnī *ḥadīth* collections include the *mahdī* idea. This method of proof is easier than the previous one, because the *mahdī* idea is common in Sunnī *ḥadīth* and has explicit support among Sunnī scholars. Those who support the idea of rapprochement between the Sunna and the Shīʿa also use the existence of the *mahdī* idea in both traditions in order to promote their goal. A good example of their approach can be seen in al-Nāṣirī's "The *imām mahdī* in traditions common to the Sunna and the Shīʿa" (*al-Imām al-mahdī fī al-aḥādīth al-mushtaraka bayna al-sunna wa al-shīʿa*). The suitability of the *mahdī* idea for promoting the Sunnī–Shīʿī rapprochement is explicitly stated in the preface and the book's structure is also relevant: Sunnī and Shīʿī traditions concerning the *mahdī* are quoted after each other.[113] A similar approach is taken by the editors of the "Mahdī Encyclopaedia" (*mawsūʿat al-mahdī*) who include

108 Ṭūsī, *Kitāb al-ghayba*, p. 184.

109 Majlisī, *Biḥār al-anwār*, vol. 51, pp. 44–64.

110 "It is He who has sent His messenger with the guidance and the religion of truth in order to make it prevail over all religions, though the polytheists be averse."

111 See Majlisī, *Biḥār al-anwār*, vol. 51, pp. 50, 60, 61.

112 Abū Maʿāsh, *al-Imām al-mahdī fī al-Qurʾān wa al-sunna*; Riẓwī, *al-Mahdī al-mawʿūd fī al-Qurʾān al-karīm*; Shīrāzī, *al-Mahdī fī al-Qurʾān*. A similar approach is visible in Qazwīnī, *Mawsūʿat al-mahdī*, vol. 1, pp. 36–48.

113 Nāṣirī, *al-Imām al-mahdī fī al-aḥādīth al-mushtaraka bayna al-Sunna wa al- Shīʿa*, pp. 7–8 and *passim*. See also Mīlānī, *al-Imām al-mahdī* (pp. 10–11) where a long list of Sunnī scholars who supported the *mahdī* idea is given.

in the introduction to this multi-volume work a list of fifty Sunnī writers who mentioned the *mahdī* idea in their works.[114] It is evident also in Fāźil Lakhnawī's "The last crown holder of the *imāma*" which mentions, among others, Ibn al-ʿArabī, Sibṭ b. al-Jawzī and ʿAbd al-Wahhāb al-Shaʿrānī as Sunnī scholars who adduced traditions about the expected coming of the *mahdī*.[115]

In Sunnī theological literature the situation is different. In the early Muslim creeds attributed to Abū Ḥanīfa, the *mahdī* is not mentioned even in places where other participants in the eschatological drama, such as the *dajjāl*, Jesus and Gog and Magog, do appear.[116] The same is true for a substantial number of other creeds, including that of Aḥmad b. Ḥanbal.[117] The Ḥanbalī theologians al-Barbahārī (d. 941) and Ibn Baṭṭa (d. 997) mention in the eschatological chapter of their creed the descent of Jesus and the appearance of the *dajjāl*, but do not mention the *mahdī*.[118] The Shāfiʿī scholar al-Lālakāʾī (d. 1027)[119] mentions, in a passage describing the beliefs of Aḥmad b. Ḥanbal, the *dajjāl* and his killing by Jesus, but leaves the *mahdī* unmentioned.[120] Al-Nasafī (d. 1142), his commentator al-Taftāzānī[121] and the Ḥanbalī jurist Ibn Qudāma al-Maqdisī (d. 1223)[122] follow suit.

Nevertheless, Ibn Ḥanbal's attitude to the *mahdī* idea is not necessarily negative. Al-Suyūṭī quotes Ibn Ḥanbal as saying that "three books are baseless: [those on] the military expeditions [of the Prophet], on eschatology and on exegesis" (*thalāth* [sic] *kutub lā aṣla lahā: al-maghāzī, al-malāḥim wa al-tafsīr*). The reason for this rather surprising judgment is said to be the weak chains of transmission characteristic of material on these topics.

---

114 Qazwīnī, *Mawsūʿat al-mahdī*, vol. 1, pp. 8–11. The inclusion of al-Bukhārī in this list (p. 10) is gratuitous.

115 Lakhnawī, *Ākhirī tāj-dār-i imāmat*, *passim*, especially pp. 52–63, 72.

116 Abū Ḥanīfa, *al-Fiqh al-akbar*, n.p. 1874(?), p. 9; *Kitāb al-fiqh al-akbar wa sharḥuhu li-ʿAlī al-Qāriʾ*, p. 92; al-Maghnīsāwī, *Sharḥ al-fiqh al-akbar*, pp. 49–50. Cf. Wensinck, *The Muslim creed*, p. 244.

117 Watt, *The Formative Period*, pp. 292–293; see also Ibn Ḥanbal, *al-ʿAqīda*, *passim*; Watt, *Islamic Creeds*, *passim*; Ṭaḥāwī, *ʿAqīda*, p. 16.

118 Ibn Abī Yaʿlā, *Ṭabaqāt al-Ḥanābila*, vol. 2, p. 20; Laoust, *La profession de foi d'Ibn Baṭṭa*, p. 58 (text), p. 106 (translation).

119 Brockelmann, *GAL G I*, p. 181; S I, 308.

120 Lālakāʾī, *Sharḥ uṣūl al-iʿtiqād*, pp. 159, 166.

121 Taftāzānī, *Sharḥ al-ʿaqāʾid al-nasafiyya*, pp. 201–202; Elder, *A Commentary on the Creed of Islam*, pp. 165–166.

122 Ibn Qudāma al-Maqdisī, *ʿAqīda*, p. 558.

Goldziher seems to have taken its attribution to Ibn Ḥanbal at face value,[123] but the sentence quoted is not found in Ibn Ḥanbal's *Musnad*. Conversely, the *Musnad* does include references both to the miraculous events preceding the Day of Judgment (*malāḥim*) and to the *mahdī* specifically.[124] It is therefore not possible to conclude that Ibn Ḥanbal viewed the idea of the *mahdī* with suspicion or deemed it unworthy of inclusion in his main compilation. It seems that in Ibn Ḥanbal's view the *mahdī* tradition was not worthy of inclusion in the formal creeds, but was acceptable in *ḥadīth* literature.

In later Sunnī creeds the situation changed and the *mahdī* idea has gradually found its way into some Sunnī credal statements. Al-Qāriʾ al-Harawī (d. 1607) included the *mahdī* idea in his commentary on *al-Fiqh al-akbar* (II), though the idea is absent from *al-Fiqh al-akbar* itself.[125] The Shāfiʿī scholar Ibn Ḥajar al-Haytamī (d. 1567) adduces at the beginning of his work on the *mahdī* the tradition according to which "whoever denies the *dajjāl* is an unbeliever and whoever denies the *mahdī* is an unbeliever" (*man kadhdhaba bi-'l-dajjāl fa-qad kafara wa man kadhdhaba bi-'l-mahdī fa-qad kafara*).[126] In another work of his, he also supports the *mahdī* idea and extensively quotes the pertinent classical traditions. At the same time, he scathingly denounces "a group who claims that a man who died forty years ago was the *mahdī* whose appearance was promised at the end of times and that whoever denies that he was the *mahdī* is an infidel".[127]

---

123 Suyūṭī, *Itqān*, vol. 4, pp. 472–473; Harawī, *al-Maṣnūʿ*, pp. 178–179 (no. 421). According to Harawī, this *ḥadīth* relates not only to some specific books of exegesis and *maghāzī*, but to all books of eschatological content (*malāḥim*) which include only a few authentic traditions. Cf. Goldziher, *Richtungen*, p. 57.

124 See Ibn Ḥanbal, *Musnad*, vol. 3, pp. 37, 52: "I am bringing you the good tidings about the *mahdī* who will be sent to my community when the people will be at variance with each other ..." (*ubashshirukum bi-'l-mahdī yubʿathu fī ummatī ʿalā 'khtilāfin min al-nās* ...). For different views on this tradition, see Albānī, *Silsilat al-aḥādīth al-ḍaʿīfa*, vol. 4, pp. 91–92. For other traditions, see Wensinck, *Concordance* ..., s.v. *mahdī*. These traditions are used by a Shīʿī scholar to support the view that the *mahdī* idea is not a specifically Shīʿī one, but rather belongs to all Muslims. See Jalālī, *Aḥādīth al-mahdī fī Musnad Aḥmad b. Ḥanbal*, *passim*.

125 ʿAlī al-Qārī *Sharḥ al-fiqh al-akbar*, p. 92. On the other hand, al-Maghnīsāwī (*Sharḥ al-fiqh al-akbar*, pp. 49–50) omits the reference to the *mahdī* in his commentary on the same work.

126 Haytamī, *al-Qawl al-mukhtaṣar*, p. 27. The modern editor of the work quotes several medieval scholars who thought that this tradition is forged (*mawḍūʿ*). Suhaylī (*al-Rawḍ al-unuf*, vol. 2, p. 431) adduces this *ḥadīth*, but says that it has an extremely strange (*gharīb*) *isnād*. Cf. Sulamī, *ʿIqd al-durar*, p. 157 and al-Muttaqī al-Hindī, *al-Burhān*, vol. 2, p. 844.

127 Haytamī, *al-Fatāwa al-ḥadīthiyya*, p. 26 *infra*. The *mahdī* traditions are adduced on pp. 27–31.

Al-Haytamī died in 1567 CE and it stands to reason that the *mahdī* who died "forty years ago" is Sayyid Muḥammad Jawnpūrī (d. 1505).[128]

The Ḥanbalī scholar al-Saffārīnī (*c.* 1702–1774)[129] devoted a substantial part of his theological treatises *Lawā'iḥ al-anwār*[130] and *al-Buḥūr al-zākhira* to eschatology and included in them many classical traditions on the *mahdī*, the *dajjāl* and the second coming of Jesus. He also included the *mahdī* concept in his versified *'aqīda* and commented on it extensively. The description of the deeds of the *mahdī* makes it clear that the *mahdī* is for al-Saffārīnī a central figure in the apocalyptic drama. He is expected to take hold of the whole world (like Alexander and Solomon), to fight on behalf of the *sunna*, remove blameworthy innovations (*bida'*) and restore cohesion to the Muslim community. The symbolic actions of breaking the cross and killing the swine, which were to be performed by Jesus according to the classical accounts, are now attributed to the *mahdī* though they are also retained in the list of deeds to be performed by Jesus.[131] It is also interesting to observe that al-Saffārīnī rejects the idea that the *mahdī* is identical with Jesus, asserting that he is a different figure who will appear before the descent of Jesus. He maintains that the traditions concerning the *mahdī* have such copious chains of transmission they must be considered substantively unassailable (*tawātur ma'nawī*), and they became an article of faith for Muslims. Like al-Haytamī before him, he quotes approvingly the *ḥadīth* according to which denial of the *dajjāl* or the *mahdī* amounts to infidelity. Summing up, he says that "the belief in the coming of the *mahdī* is obligatory, as has been decided by the scholars" (*fa-'l-īmān bi-khurūj al-mahdī wājib kamā huwa muqarrar 'inda ahl al-'ilm*).[132] The nineteenth-century scholar al-Qundūzī expresses similar opinions.[133]

---

128 On Jawnpūrī, see Chapter 3.

129 For his biography, see Brockelmann, *GAL S* II, p. 449.

130 Al-Saffārīnī's *Aḥwāl yawm al-qiyāma* seems to be a modern extract from the *Lawā'iḥ*.

131 Saffārīnī, *Lawā'iḥ al-anwār*, vol. 2, p. 72; on Jesus, see ibid., p. 90. See also *idem*, *al-Buḥūr al-zākhira*, vol. 1, p. 442.

132 Saffārīnī, *Lawā'iḥ al-anwār*, vol. 2, pp. 79–80. See also *idem.*, *al-Buḥūr al-zākhira*, vol. 1, pp. 469–470. Cf. D. Cook, *Studies in Muslim Apocalyptic*, p. 146.

133 See Qundūzī, *Yanābī' al-mawadda* p. 536: "Whoever denies the (future) coming of the *mahdī*, disbelieves in what was revealed to Muḥammad; whoever denies the (second) coming of Jesus, is an infidel; whoever denies the coming of the false messiah is an infidel (*man ankara khurūj al-mahdī fa-qad kafara bi-mā unzila 'alā Muḥammad wa man ankara nuzūl 'Īsā fa-qad kafara wa man ankara khurūj al-Dajjāl fa-qad kafara*). I am indebted to my friend and colleague Etan Kohlberg for this reference.

When Goldziher said that "in Sunnī Islam the pious awaiting of the *mahdī* never took the fixed form of dogma", he was right only in the sense that the *mahdī* idea was not included as an article of faith in the early Sunnī creeds. However, this does not diminish the importance of the idea in the rest of the Sunnī tradition. First, as we have seen, the *mahdī* idea did find its way into late medieval Sunnī creeds; second, a distinct Sunnī literary genre dealing with the idea of the *mahdī* came into being. Mention should be made of Nuʿaym b. Ḥammād (d. 844) whose *Kitāb al-fitan* includes abundant material on the *mahdī* and its importance was highlighted in the works of David Cook. This *Kitāb al-fitan* did not gain entrance into the canonical literature, but it does reflect the views of a significant segment of Muslim opinion in the first half of the ninth century. It was followed by a substantial number of works by scholars such as al-Qurṭubī (d. 1273), al-Sulamī (d. 1286), Ibn Kathīr (d. 1373), al-Suyūṭī (d. 1505), al-Haytamī (d. 1567), al-Barzanjī (d. 1764), al-Saffārīnī (d. 1774), Ḥusayn al-ʿAdawī al-Ḥamzāwī (d. 1886) and Ṣiddīq Ḥasan Khān (d.1890).[134] All of them make extensive use of Nuʿaym b. Ḥammād's work. The aforementioned books are of course in addition to numerous other works which include chapters relevant to our theme.

In contradistinction to the trend which reflects the increasing importance of the *mahdī* in late medieval Muslim thinking, we need to mention Ibn Khaldūn who entertained grave doubts about the *mahdī* idea. This is understandable. Ibn Khaldūn was not part of the theological tradition; on the contrary, he is going against its grain. Though he did not explicitly express his own view on the *mahdī* idea, the tone of his discourse and the material adduced by him leave little doubt that he did not support it. He adduced numerous pertinent traditions from the *ḥadīth* collections, analysed their chains of transmission and found that many of them included transmitters who are considered unreliable.[135] He rejected the centrality of the *mahdī* idea as expressed in a *ḥadīth* which says that "he who denies the *mahdī* is an infidel and he who denies the *dajjāl* is a liar" (*man kadhdhaba bi-'l-mahdī fa-qad kafara wa man kadhdhaba bi-'l-dajjāl fa-qad kadhaba*) by asserting that the *ḥadīth* includes a *ḥadīth*-forger in its chain of transmission and is "extremist" (*wa ḥasbuka hādhā*

134 A list of these works is given in D. Cook, *Studies in Muslim Apocalyptic*, pp. 24–26. Cf. Naysābūrī, *al-Mustadrak*, vol. 5, pp. 657, 771–773.

135 Ibn Khaldūn, *Muqaddima*, pp. 290–301; translation by F. Rosenthal, *The Muqaddimah*, vol. 2, pp. 156–184.

ghuluwwan) in content.[136] Later in the survey, Ibn Khaldūn says: "These are all the traditions concerning the *mahdī* and his coming at the end of days, included by the religious scholars [in their compilations]. As you have seen, only very few of them are above criticism" (*fa-hādhihi jumlat al-aḥādīth allatī kharrajahā al-a'imma fī sha'n al-mahdī wa khurūjihi ākhira'l-zamān wa hiya kamā ra'ayta lam yakhluṣ minhā min al-naqd illā al-qalīl wa al-aqall minhu*).[137] He also attributes the *mahdī* idea to "the common, stupid multitude, those who have no recourse in this to guiding intelligence" (*mā tadda'īhi al-'āmma wa al-aghmār min al-dahmā' mimman lā yarji'u fī dhālika ilā 'aqlin yahdīhi*).[138] Ibn Khaldūn uses traditional methods of *ḥadīth* criticism in order to debunk the idea of the *mahdī*,[139] but it is reasonably clear that he would have been critical of the *mahdī* idea even if the *isnād*s of the relevant traditions had been unassailable. As we shall see later in this chapter as well as in Chapter 5, Ibn Khaldūn's ideas were taken up by several modern Muslim critics of the *mahdī* idea.

VIII *MAHDĪ*S IN HISTORY

In parallel with the eschatological conception of the *mahdī*, a trend which conferred this title on historical personalities came into being. There were also very early traditions which harmonized the two and envisaged "historical" *mahdī*s in addition to eschatological ones:

136 Ibn Khaldūn, *Muqaddima*, p. 291; translation by F. Rosenthal, vol. 2, p. 159.
137 Ibn Khaldūn, *Muqaddima*, p. 301; translation by F. Rosenthal, *Muqaddimah*, vol. 2, p. 184.
138 Ibn Khaldūn, *Muqaddima*, p. 306; translation by F. Rosenthal, vol. 2, p. 196.
139 A modern scholar, Aḥmad b. Muḥammad al-Ṣiddīq (d. 1960), devoted a monograph to the refutation of Ibn Khaldūn's views. See his *Ibrāz al-wahm al-maknūn min kalām Ibn Khaldūn aw al-murshid al-mubdī li-fasād ṭa'n Ibn Khaldūn fī aḥādīth al-mahdī*. N. Matar ("The English Merchant ...", p. 50, at note 1), maintains that this book was written around 1590. This is not possible because al-Ṣiddīq mentions at the beginning of his work (pp. 4–5) scholars such as al-Zurqānī (d. 1710), al-Saffārīnī (d. 1774), al-Shawkānī (d. 1839) and Ṣiddīq Ḥasan Khān Qannawjī (d. 1890). See also Kaḥḥāla, *Mu'jam al-mu'allifīn*, vol. 1, p. 285 (s.v. *Aḥmad b. al-Ṣiddīq*). The Indian Muslim scholar Ashraf 'Alī Thānawī (d. 1943) also wrote a refutation of Ibn Khaldūn's views (*Mu'akhkhirat al-ẓunūn 'an Ibn Khaldūn*), but this work was not available to me. See al-Barzanjī, *al-Ishā'a*, p. 191 note 1.

> The *mahdī*s are three: the *mahdī* of goodness (*mahdī al-khayr*) who is ʿUmar b. ʿAbd al-ʿAzīz; the *mahdī* of blood (*mahdī al-dam*) in whose times blood will stop flowing, and the *mahdī* of religion (*mahdī al-dīn*), Jesus the son of Mary, during whose times his community will embrace Islam.[140]

By necessity, the trend which disconnected the *mahdī* from its eschatological content transformed the term into an honorific title used to extol rulers or enhance the legitimacy of political pretenders. This trend emerged very early in Muslim history, probably even before the development of the eschatological dogma. If the *mahdī* is a historical figure, a mortal who lives and dies, it is only natural that human history will continue after his death in the same way as before him. There will be nothing "messianic" in the period following the *mahdī*'s death, and the internecine struggles in the Muslim community will go on without much interruption.[141]

The separation of the *mahdī* idea from the eschaton has been extensively studied by several leading scholars. Madelung maintains that this use of the term started with the Prophet himself who was called *mahdī* by the poet Ḥassān b. Thābit,[142] but this may be an exaggerated conclusion from a single verse in Ḥassān b. Thābit's poetry. Furthermore, the verse can easily be interpreted as saying that Muḥammad was guided by Allah, without any eschatological connotation. More massive evidence for this trend is provided by Crone and Hinds who have shown that both Umayyad and ʿAbbāsī caliphs were honoured by this title, mainly in poetry.[143] Similar material was collected by ʿAbd al-ʿAzīz al-Dūrī, though in some of his examples the term *mahdī* could be interpreted in a non-technical sense.[144] Further evidence in the same direction can be found in the early *ḥadīth* collections. In a difficult passage included in Ibn Abī Shayba's *Muṣannaf*, Ibrāhīm b. Maysara is quoted as saying to Ṭāwūs:

> [Was] ʿUmar b. ʿAbd al-ʿAzīz the *mahdī*? He said: "He was rightly guided, but he was not the *mahdī*."[145] When the *mahdī* comes, the

140 Nuʿaym b. Ḥammād, *Kitāb al-fitan*, p. 222. The last part of this tradition speaks about the "second coming" of Jesus. Cf. Suyūṭī, *al-Arf al-wardī*, p. 238.

141 Nuʿaym b. Ḥammād, *Kitāb al-fitan*, p. 235.

142 Madelung, "Mahdī", in *EI*², s.v.; Ḥassān b. Thābit, *Dīwān*, vol. 1, p. 269 line 2.

143 Crone and Hinds, *God's Caliph*, index, s.v. *mahdī*.

144 Dūrī, "al-Fikra al-mahdiyya", *passim*.

145 This is the understanding of Madelung; see "Mahdī", *EI*², s.v.

> generous will increase in their generosity and the wrongdoers will be forgiven for their wrongdoing. He will spend money and be tough with the governors and merciful to the needy. (*ʿUmar b. ʿAbd al-ʿAzīz al-mahdī? qāla: kāna mahdiyyan wa laysa bihi inna al-mahdī idhā kāna zīda al-muḥsin fī iḥsānihi wa tība ʿan al-musīʾi min isāʾatihi wa yabdhulu al-māl wa yashtaddu ʿalā al-ʿummāl wa yarḥamu al-masākīn.*)[146]

This passage seems to be hesitant about the standing of ʿUmar b. ʿAbd al-ʿAzīz, but there are traditions in which he is designated as *mahdī* without any hesitation (*ʿUmar b. ʿAbd al-ʿAzīz huwa al-mahdī ḥaqqan*).[147] And when the Umayyad caliph Sulaymān [b. ʿAbd al-Malik] (r. 715–717) "manifested what he manifested", Abū Yaḥyā was asked: "Is this the *mahdī* who is mentioned [in the traditions]?" He responded: "No, he is not even similar [to him]" (*lammā qāma Sulaymān fa-aẓhara mā aẓhara, qultu li-Abī Yaḥyā: hādhā al-mahdī alladhī yudhkar? qāla: lā wa lā al-mutashabbih*).[148] David Cook and Amikam Elad have analysed the way in which claims of being a *mahdī* were made for Muḥammad b. ʿAbd Allah *al-nafs al-zakiyya*, and there is a tendency to surmise that the tradition, according to which the name of the *mahdī* will be identical with the name of the Prophet, was initially coined for Muḥammad b. ʿAbd Allah *al-nafs al-zakiyya*.[149] D. S. Attema and Wilferd Madelung analysed a tradition with messianic overtones which was circulated in support of the so-called "anti-caliph" ʿAbd Allāh b. al-Zubayr who rebelled against the Umayyad rule in the 680s.[150] Madelung also analysed several traditions in which the ʿAbbāsī revolution was promoted as having messianic characteristics. One of them reads:

> ʿMuḥammad b. Yaḥyā and Aḥmad b. Yūsuf told us ... on the authority of Thawbān who said: "The Prophet ... said: Three persons will fight

146 Ibn Abī Shayba, *al-Muṣannaf*, vol. 8, p. 679 (no. 198). Cf. Sulamī, *ʿIqd al-durar*, p. 168.

147 Nuʿaym b. Ḥammād, *Kitāb al-fitan*, p. 230.

148 Ibn Abī Shayba, *al-Muṣannaf*, vol. 8, p. 679 (no. 197). But see Elad, "The Struggle for Legitimacy ...", pp. 40–41 who adduces traditions hinting at the eschatological nature of the *mahdī* claims for Sulaymān b. ʿAbd al-Malik and ʿUmar b. ʿAbd al-ʾAzīz.

149 D. Cook, *Studies in Muslim Apocalyptic*, index under *al-nafs al-zakiyya*; Elad, *The Rebellion of Muḥammad al-Nafs al-Zakiyya*, pp. 28, 31, 34 and index; *idem*, "The Struggle for Legitimacy ...", p. 57.

150 Madelung, "ʿAbd Allāh b. al-Zubayr and the Mahdī"; Campbell, "ʿAbd Allāh b. al-Zubayr", *EI*[3], s.v.

> for your treasure. Each one of them will be son of a *khalīfa*, but none will take over [the treasure, i.e., the reign]. Then the black flags will appear from the East[151] and slaughter you an unprecedented slaughter." Then he said something which I do not remember. Then he said: "When you see him [their leader?], pledge allegiance to him even if crawling on the snow, because he is the caliph of God, the *mahdī*." (*ḥaddathanā Muḥammad b. Yaḥyā wa Aḥmad b. Yūsuf qālā: ... ʿan Thawbān qāla: qāla rasūl Allah ... yaqtatilu ʿinda kanzikum thalātha. kulluhum ibn khalīfa thumma lā yaṣīru ilā wāḥidin minhum thumma taṭlaʿ al-rāyāt al-sūd min qibal al-mashriq fa-yaqtulūnakum qatlan lam yuqtalhu qawm. thumma dhakara shayʾan lā aḥfaẓuhu. fa-idhā raʾaytumūhu fa-bāyiʿūhu wa law ḥabwan ʿalā al-thalj fa-innahu khalīfat Allah al-mahdī.*)[152]

It seems that the title of *mahdī* was conferred on people quite easily and according to one tradition "any virtuous person was called *mahdī*" (*idhā kāna al-rajul ṣāliḥan qīla lahu al-mahdī*).[153]

In his *Tadhkira*, the Andalusī scholar al-Qurṭubī (1214–1273 CE) includes passages in which traditions about the apocalyptic appearance of the *mahdī* are mixed – in a rather incoherent manner – with veiled references to events in the Maghrib and al-Andalus since the Arab conquest until al-Qurṭubī's times. The gradual *reconquista* of Spain seems to have aroused messianic expectations among the Muslims of al-Andalus and in some traditions the *mahdī* appears in direct response to the military successes of the Christians.[154]

The Prophet is said to have predicted both the Muslim conquest of al Andalus and the Muslim defeat at the hands of the infidels.[155] In an allusion to the Almohad *mahdī* Ibn Tūmart (d. 1130) – combined with elements from the classical traditions about the *mahdī* – al-Qurṭubī says that a person will emerge in the "farthest Maghrib" (*aqṣā al-maghrib*), in a coastal town called Māsa. Following his emergence, some people from al-Andalus will

151 For the significance of the black colour for the ʿAbbāsī movement, see Sharon, *Black Banners from the East*, vol. 2, pp. 79–93.

152 Ibn Māja, *Sunan, Kitāb al-fitan* 34 (vol. 2, p. 1367). This tradition has been analysed by Madelung, "Mahdī", in *EI²*, s.v.

153 Nuʿaym b. Ḥammād, *Kitāb al-fitan*, p. 230 *supra*. Cf. Suyūṭī, *al-ʿArf al-wardī*, p. 238 *infra*; al-Muttaqī al-Hindī, *al-Burhān*, vol. 2, p. 843.

154 Qurṭubī, *Tadhkira*, pp. 1206–1207.

155 Qurṭubī, *Tadhkira*, p. 1207.

cross to al-Maghrib and ask the *mahdī* to help al-Andalus which is being taken over by the infidels. The *mahdī* obliges, crosses the sea and reaches Seville where he delivers an eloquent sermon and subsequently conquers seventy Christian cities.[156]

According to another tradition – related on the authority of Abū Saʿīd al-Khudrī – the *mahdī* will emerge in 599 AH/1202–1203 CE when the Muslims will be in disarray, will cross to al-Andalus, rule it for nine years and also conquer seventy Christian cities.[157] His white and yellow flags will be inscribed with "the greatest name of God" (*ism Allah al-aʿẓam*) and he will never be defeated. He will first receive the oath of allegiance in the Maghrib and then, unwillingly, a second time in Mecca. Following this second oath, he will set out from Mecca to Syria in order to fight ʿUrwa b. Muḥammad al-Sufyānī and his Kalbī associates. He will seize ʿUrwa "on the highest tree at the Lake of Tiberias".[158]

Al-Qurṭubī plays here a double role as an apocalypticist and a historian. As an apocalypticist, he expects resounding victories for the *mahdī* who will roll back the Christian *reconquista*; as a historian, he has a gloomy outlook for the Muslims of Spain. He mentions two important battles which took place slightly before his birth. In the Battle of Alarcos (*al-Arak*) which took place in 1195, the Muslims won a resounding victory, took much booty and lived well until the Battle of ʿUqāb (known as Las Navas de Tolosa in Spanish history) in 1212.[159] In the latter battle their fortunes took a turn for the worse, and since their defeat in it

> they are in retreat. The enemy dominates them because of internecine struggles. Details would take [too] long. Only little remains of al-Andalus now. We seek refuge in God from the internecine struggles, defeat and conflict ... (*wa lam yazal al-muslimūn min tilka al-waqʿa bi-'l-Andalus yarjiʿūna al-qahqarā ilā an istawlā ʿalayhim al-ʿaduww wa ghalabahum bi-'l-fitan al-wāqiʿa baynahum wa al-tafṣīl yaṭūl wa lam yabqa al-ān min al-Andalus illā al-yasīr fa-naʿūdhu bi-'llāh min al-fitan wa al-khidhlān wa al-mukhālafa ...*)[160]

---

156 Qurṭubī, *Tadhkira*, pp. 1214–1215.
157 Qurṭubī, *Tadhkira*, p. 1221.
158 Qurṭubī, *Tadhkira*, pp. 1206–1207.
159 For a glowing description of the Muslim victory in Alarcos, see Maqqarī, *Nafḥ al-ṭīb*, vol. 1, p. 423. For a brief reference to the Muslim defeat in al-ʿUqāb, see ibid., p. 425; see also Marrākushī, *al-Muʿjib*, p. 265.
160 Qurṭubī, *Tadhkira*, p. 1222. See also Filiu, *Apocalypse in Islam*, pp. 34–37.

An approach which integrates eschatological events with actual history can also be found in the works of the fourteenth-century Syrian scholar Ibn Kathīr. In his rather incoherent introduction to his *Kitāb al-fitan wa al-malāḥim*, he promises to deal with the "Portents of the Hour" which were predicted by the Prophet, but immediately moves to describe the murder of ʿUmar b. al-Khaṭṭāb, ʿUthmān b. ʿAffān and ʿAlī b. Abī Ṭālib.[161] Ibn Kathīr does not explain this abrupt transition from the apocalypse to the deplorable events of early Muslim history, but it is clear that he implicitly continues the trend initiated by Nuʿaym b. Ḥammād who saw in the death of the Prophet the first of the "tribulations".[162]

IX CONTEMPORARY TRENDS

In recent times there has been a new surge of interest in the apocalyptic drama in contemporary Muslim literature. Dozens of books, large and small, were published during the twentieth century and beyond, indicating the extent to which apocalyptics continue to exercise the hearts and minds of contemporary Muslims. Many of these books are only collections of material from the Qurʾān and the *ḥadīth*. The relevant works can be divided into several genres. Some of them deal with the theological question of the nature of apocalypse in Islam without trying to relate it to contemporary struggles and situations. In contradistinction to these, we have also works written by various radical Muslim thinkers who usually embrace the classical apocalyptic vision in which Islam is transformed at the end of days into the only religion, while Judaism and Christianity are destroyed. In a substantial part of this literature, the actors in the apocalyptic drama are identified with modern political or social powers. On the other hand, there is also a genre which is ecumenical in purpose, striving to provide a religious substrate for improving the relationship between Islam and Christianity. In this genre, Jesus is the main protagonist. He is described as one of God's messengers, has a positive image as a model of Ṣūfī asceticism and sometimes as an outright Muslim. Naturally enough

161 Ibn Kathīr, *Kitāb al-fitan wa al-malāḥim*, pp. 9–15. For more information on Ibn Kathīr's use of apocalyptic material, see Filiu, *Apocalypse in Islam*, pp. 37–42.
162 See earlier, at notes 14–16. For the methodological problems of using apocalyptic material for historical research, see Alexander, "Medieval Apocalypses as Historical Sources".

for this type of literature, the apocalyptic role of Jesus as a destroyer of Christianity (and Judaism) is ignored or explained away.

One author who deals with the *mahdī* question on its own merits, refraining completely from ascribing to it any contemporary significance, is Aḥmad b. Muḥammad b. al-Ṣiddīq (d.1960),[163] who published in 1928 a book-length monograph entitled "Exposition of the error hidden in the words of Ibn Khaldūn" (*Ibrāz al-wahm al-maknūn min kalām Ibn Khaldūn*) and dedicated to the refutation of Ibn Khaldūn's criticism of the *mahdī* idea.[164] Ibn al-Ṣiddīq's book makes an attempt to validate the *mahdī* idea by using the traditional method of discussing the reliability or otherwise of the *ḥadīth* transmitters (*al-jarḥ wa al-taʿdīl*). In a way, it is a mirror image of the work of Ibn Khaldūn who used the same method in order to debunk the same idea. Ibn al-Ṣiddīq begins his book with a lengthy list of reputable scholars who supported the appearance of the *mahdī*.[165] He attacks Ibn Khaldūn for not being competent in the sciences of *ḥadīth* and sets out to refute his views.[166] One of his arguments is that if the Muslim *umma* accepts a weak *ḥadīth*, one must follow it.[167] In his view, *ijmāʿ* should prevail over other considerations. Similarly, sound traditions related by people with "deviant" ideas – some of which were rejected by Ibn Khaldūn – may be accepted. Al-Bukhārī and Muslim included in their collections traditions by Murjiʾīs, Qadarīs and Khawārij who were fervent believers. If the traditions of such transmitters are rejected, a tremendous number of valuable traditions would be lost.[168]

A scholar who wrote extensively on the *mahdī* question and belongs essentially to the same trend as Ibn al-Ṣiddīq is Muḥammad Aḥmad Ismāʿīl al-Muqaddam (1952–). A surgeon and psychiatrist by profession,

163 See Kaḥḥāla, *Muʿjam al-muʾallifīn*, vol. 1, p. 285 (s.v. Aḥmad b. al-Ṣiddīq). The title of the book is corrupted in Kaḥḥāla's work. *Pace* N. Matar ("The English Merchant ...", p. 50, at note 11) who maintains that this book was written around 1590. This is not possible because Ibn al-Ṣiddīq mentions at the beginning of his work (pp. 4–5) scholars such as al-Zurqānī (d. 1710), al-Saffārīnī (d. 1774), al-Shawkānī (d. 1839) and (Ṣiddīq Ḥasan Khān) Qannawjī (d. 1890).

164 See earlier, at notes 136–138.

165 Ibn al-Ṣiddīq, *Ibrāz al-wahm al-maknūn*, pp. 3–6.

166 Ibn al-Ṣiddīq, *Ibrāz al-wahm al-maknūn*, pp. 13–14.

167 Ibn al-Ṣiddīq, *Ibrāz al-wahm al-maknūn*, pp. 16–18.

168 Ibn al-Ṣiddīq, *Ibrāz al-wahm al-maknūn*, p. 38. Other modern scholars who criticized Ibn Khaldūn include al-Kattānī (*Naẓm al-mutanāthir*, p. 240, *supra*) and Natsha (*al-Mahdī masbūq bi-khilāfa islāmiyya*, p. 25).

he is said to have established the *salafī da ʿwa* in Alexandria, Egypt.[169] His first book on the *mahdī* question was published in the wake of the 1979 takeover of the Meccan sanctuary by Juhaymān al-ʿUtaybī.[170] In 2002 he published a greatly expanded version (running to 814 pages and hundreds of footnotes) under the title *al-Mahdī wa fiqh ashrāṭ al-sā ʿa* ("The *mahdī* and the jurisprudence of the Portents of the Hour"). The preparation of this work evidently required an enormous effort and a great investment of time. The main purpose of the book is to validate the belief in the eschatological appearance of the *mahdī* and, at the same time, to deny the claims of all *mahdī* pretenders who appeared in Muslim history. Another important purpose of al-Muqaddam is to make sure that the expectation of the *mahdī*, who will change the situation of Islam and Muslims for the better, will not cause lethargy and inaction in the Muslim community.[171] The book includes an extensive list of traditions supporting the *mahdī* idea, a list of scholars who wrote books on the subject, as well as a list of those who considered the *mahdī* traditions as undoubtedly authentic (*mutawātir*). There is even an attempt to find Qur ʾānic verses hinting at the eschatological appearance of the *mahdī*.[172] While the belief in the eschatological appearance of the *mahdī* is unquestionably valid in the eyes of the author, a substantial part of his book is dedicated to the debunking of *mahdī* pretenders throughout history. Naturally enough, al-Muqaddam debunks the *mahdī*s who appeared in the various Shī ʿī denominations and considers the twelfth imām of the Twelver Shi ʿa as "the *mahdī* of superstition" (*mahdī al-khurāfa*).[173] He adopted a similar attitude to several Sunnī pretenders. The North African *mahdī* Ibn Tūmart (d. 1130) receives considerable attention. He is said to have pursued earthly power rather than salvation in the hereafter, he is denounced for unjustly rebelling against the ruling Almoravid dynasty, for shedding blood without *shar ʿī* justification and for falsely accusing his rivals of various doctrinal deviations. His pretensions to have attained infallibility (*ʿiṣma*) are influenced by the Shī ʿa. He cannot be considered a *mahdī* or even a reformist because of the corrupt nature of his movement.[174] In a similar

169 https://ar.wikipedia.org/wiki/محمد_اسماعيل_المقدم. Accessed 20 August 2018.
170 *Al-Mahdī ḥaqīqa lā khurāfa* ("The *mahdī* is the truth, not a legend") which was not available to me.
171 Muqaddam, *al-Mahdī wa fiqh ashrāṭ al-sā ʿa*, pp. 598–599.
172 Muqaddam, *al-Mahdī wa fiqh ashrāṭ al-sā ʿa*, pp. 77–153.
173 Muqaddam, *al-Mahdī wa fiqh ashrāṭ al-sā ʿa*, pp. 375–386.
174 Muqaddam, *al-Mahdī wa fiqh ashrāṭ al-sā ʿa*, pp. 387–426.

way, al-Muqaddam denounced the Indian *mahdī* Sayyid Muḥammad Jawnpūrī (d. 1505).[175]

Al-Muqaddam's criticism of the Sudanese *mahdī* Muḥammad Aḥmad (d. 1885)[176] is much more nuanced. He is supportive of this *mahdī*'s struggle against the British, maintains that Muḥammad Aḥmad led the most important Islamic revolt in the nineteenth century, and is appreciative of his *jihādī* ideology, his praise of martyrdom, his upright character and his conception of an Islamic state. However, he makes a sharp distinction between these positive traits in Muḥammad Aḥmad's thought and his claim to be the *mahdī*. He attributes this claim to the influence of Ibn al-ʿArabī, and speaks derisively about the *mahdī*'s claims to have experienced "presences" (*ḥaḍarāt*) in which the Prophet and other grandees of Islamic history made an appearance. The abolition of the *madhāhib* by Muḥammad Aḥmad is also criticized and attributed to Ibn al-ʿArabī's influence.[177]

A wide-ranging debate by important thinkers in modern Islam on the second coming of Jesus was prompted in 1942 by a question addressed to al-Azhar by a certain ʿAbd al-Karīm Khān from the "General Command of Middle Eastern Armies". Judging by his name and the historical situation in the early 1940s, he must have been a Muslim – possibly an Aḥmadī – officer in the Indian units serving the Allies in the Middle East and North Africa. He asked:

> Is Jesus is alive or dead according to the Noble Qurʾān and the Pure *sunna*? What is the ruling concerning a Muslim who denies that he is alive? What is the ruling concerning someone who will not believe in him if we assume that he returned to earth for the second time?[178]

Al-Azhar forwarded the question to the major Egyptian religious scholar Maḥmūd Shaltūt (1893–1963) who later served as the *shaykh al-Azhar* (between 1958 and 1963).[179] Shaltūt responded in a series of articles in *al-Risāla*, asserting that there is no proof from the Qurʾān or the *sunna*

175 See Chapter 3.
176 See Chapter 4.
177 Muqaddam, *al-Mahdī wa fiqh ashrāṭ al-sāʿa*, pp. 439–556, especially pp. 462, 484, 550–556.
178 The text of the question is published in *al-Risāla* 10 (1942), p. 515.
179 Ende, "Shaltūt, Maḥmūd", in *EI*², s.v.; Zebiri, *Maḥmūd Shaltūt*.

that Jesus is alive, that his ascension was spiritual rather than bodily and meant only increase in rank; this is the usage in Qur'ān 94:4.[180] The traditions about the descent of Jesus are shaky (*muḍṭariba*). Furthermore, they were related by Wahb b. Munabbih and Kaʿb al-Aḥbār who were converted scriptuaries who cannot be relied upon. Furthermore, these are traditions related by individual transmitters (*ḥadīth āḥād*) and as such cannot be used to establish an article of faith (*lā tufīdu ʿaqīda*). Therefore, a Muslim who denies that Jesus is alive or denies the idea of his future descent cannot be denounced as an infidel.[181]

Muḥammad Shaltūt's articles did not remain unanswered. Muḥammad Zāhid Kawtharī (1879–1952), an Ottoman *ʿālim* who left Turkey after the Kemalist revolution and settled in Egypt,[182] launched a scathing attack on Shaltūt, asserting that "religion is not something that can be changed every day" (*wa laysa al-dīn mimmā yubaddalu kulla yawmin*) and accusing him of being influenced by the Aḥmadīs. He also attacked al-Azhar for not dissociating itself from Shaltūt's views.[183] One of his arguments is that the preposition *ilā* in the phrase "God raised him to Himself" precludes the possibility that the phrase means increase in rank as Shaltūt suggested.[184] He also adduces material which indicates that traditions of individual transmitters (*ḥadīth al-āḥād*) do establish certain knowledge and necessitate action.[185] In addition, Kawtharī repeats the classical arguments in favour of the interpretation that Jesus is alive and will descend to earth again.[186]

The literature which interprets the apocalyptic traditions as relating to modern powers and political situations is much more extensive and is related to the radical trends in contemporary Islam. Numerous apocalyptic treatises have been written in recent decades describing the purported Jewish control of the United States, of the entire world, and

180 "We exalted your fame" (*wa rafaʿnā laka dhikrak*).
181 Shaltūt, "Rafʿ ʿĪsā", pp. 515–517; *idem*, "Nuzūl ʿĪsā", p. 363. This is briefly referred to in Zebiri, *Maḥmūd Shaltūt*, p. 114, and in Filiu, *Apocalypse in Islam*, pp. 69–70.
182 For a laudatory biography of Kawtharī – which includes only a few basic facts about his life – see Abū Zuhra, "al-Imām al-Kawtharī ", pp. 11–17.
183 Kawtharī, *Naẓra ʿābira*, pp. 40–43. For the Aḥmadī view on the descent of Jesus, see Chapter 5, at notes 66–69. See also al-Kawtharī, "*Inkār nuzūl ʿĪsā ʿalayhi al-salām wa iqrār ʿaqidat al-tajsīm*", in *Maqālāt al-Kawtharī*, p. 215 where al-Kawtharī quotes an Aḥmadi publication which reported that "the Azhar acknowledged the death of the Nazarean messiah".
184 Kawtharī, *Naẓra ʿābira*, pp. 58–59.
185 Kawtharī, *Naẓra ʿābira*, pp. 67–68.
186 See earlier, at note 48 above.

Jewish conspiracies against Muslims. These treatises revive the classical traditions about the "Jewish connection" of the *dajjāl*, predict the *mahdī*'s arrival, his global conquests, his establishment of the caliphate and his destruction of America and Israel. One of the more interesting authors belonging to this genre is Muḥammad Munīr Idlibī[187] who devoted a whole book to a modern interpretation of the apocalyptic drama, concentrating on the *dajjāl*. His main point is that the *dajjāl* is not one person but rather a group of people. Their activity started in the seventeenth century – about one thousand years after the emergence of Islam – when the British started their presence in India. The British and the West in general are the *dajjāl* and act on behalf of the Jews and the State of Israel.[188] The literary genre to which Idlibī's work belongs has been extensively surveyed and analysed by David Cook.[189] It has also been studied by Filiu whose work successfully brings out the ubiquitous nature of the apocalyptic ideas in the contemporary Muslim world.[190]

Let us now address the ecumenical trend in the Muslim perceptions of Jesus. A leading thinker here is Tarif Khalidi. In *The Muslim Jesus*, he goes as far as calling the material about Jesus in Muslim literature as "the Muslim gospel". He considers it relevant for "historical and theological reconciliation" between Christianity and Islam.[191] He mentions that Jesus has an eschatological task in the Muslim tradition, but says nothing about its violent and anti-Christian nature.[192] Another scholar in this group is Sulaymān ʿAlī Murād. In the introduction to his edition of Ibn ʿAsākir's chapter on Jesus, Murād says that Jesus has a standing in Islamic religious jurisprudence (*al-tashrīʿ al-dīnī al-islāmī*) which is matched only by that of the Prophet.[193] This is a gross exaggeration – especially if one speaks of

187 Muḥammad Munīr Idlibī is a Syrian thinker (1949–) who joined the Aḥmadī movement in 1981.

188 Idlibī, *Intabihū*, pp. 149–153 and *passim*. For comparable ideas in modern Shīʿa, see Amanat, "Apocalyptic in Modern Islam", pp. 252–260.

189 See his *Contemporary Muslim Apocalyptic Literature*, *passim*, especially pp. 126–171, and *The Mahdī's Arrival ...*, *passim*.

190 Filiu, *Apocalypse in Islam*, *passim*, especially pp. 80ff.

191 Khalidi, *The Muslim Jesus*, pp. 3–6, 17–22. The quotation is on p. 5 *infra*.

192 Khalidi, *The Muslim Jesus*, pp. 25–26; see also his "The Role of Jesus in Intra-Muslim Polemics ..." where a similar approach can be discerned. Khalidi mentions (on pp. 147–148) that Jesus is a prominent figure in the *fitan* and *malāḥim* genre, but says nothing about his actions during the apocalypse. See also Abu Sway, "Jesus Christ: A Prophet of Islam", especially p. 26.

193 Murād, *Sīrat al-sayyid al-masīḥ*, p. 7.

"religious jurisprudence" – but it is characteristic of scholars whose purpose is to use the personality of Jesus in order to build an infrastructure for improving the relationship between Islam and Christianity. He adduces a *ḥadīth* in which Jesus is introduced into the *shahāda* and traditions about the intimate relationship between Jesus and the Prophet.[194] Murād mentions the apocalyptic role of Jesus in destroying Christianity and attributes it to the fact that Ibn ʿAsākir lived in the Crusaders' period; this position is totally untenable because these traditions appear in sources which are much earlier than the Crusaders and Ibn ʿAsākir only collected them from the classical sources of *ḥadīth*.[195]

Ata'ur-Rahim and Thomson note that Islam will be established throughout the world in the wake of Jesus' destruction of the *dajjāl*, but refrain from explicitly mentioning his destruction of Judaism and Christianity.[196] Since the unitarian Christianity of Jesus was corrupted into Trinitarianism, they are willing to go as far as to say that "the only way to follow Jesus today is by following Muḥammad".[197] It should be noted, however, that it is very difficult to find in the Islamic tradition support for the ecumenical tendencies close to the hearts of these well-meaning modern authors.

x SUMMING UP

It is now time to make sense of the plethora of traditions and interpretations surveyed in this chapter. The issue of the apocalyptic drama is intriguing for the traditional scholars because they have to contend with a complex situation in their sacred literature. The *mahdī* does not appear in the Qurʾān or in the ninth-century *ḥadīth* collections of al-Bukhārí and Muslim, but he does appear in other collections of *ḥadīth* from the same period and in countless books by Sunnī and Shīʿī scholars with unassailable classical credentials. Not all the Sunnī scholars who wrote about the eschatological appearance of the *mahdī* expressed an opinion on the various *mahdī* pretenders who appeared in historical times, but those who did systematically denounced these claimants and accused them of imposture. As

194 Murād, *Sīrat al-sayyid al-masīḥ*, pp. 12–13.
195 Murād, *Sīrat al-sayyid al-masīḥ*, p. 16.
196 Ata'ur-Rahim, *Jesus, Prophet of Islam*, p. 271. But see ibid., p. 275 where it is said that "God will end every religion and sect other than Islam and will destroy the *dajjāl*."
197 Ata'ur-Rahim, *Jesus, Prophet of Islam*, p. 276.

for Jesus, ʿĪsā b. Maryam, he appears in the Qurʾān many times, but as a prophet who had been sent to the Children of Israel in the past, rather than as a messianic figure expected to emerge at the end of days. In the *ḥadīth* he appears in his Qurʾānic role, but also as an eschatological figure who descends from heaven in order to play an active role in the apocalyptic drama. There is of course an intimate connection between *ḥadīth* and Qurʾānic exegesis and the classical commentators of the Qurʾān who did their best to vindicate the views of the *ḥadīth* compilers and to provide support for the idea that Jesus is alive in heaven and will descend to earth before the Day of Judgment; they did so by stretching the meaning of the relevant Qurʾānic verses to the best of their ability, especially by explaining away the meaning of death in the verb *tawaffā*.

Modern scholars are not of one mind discussing the issue. Some take up the classical idea of the eschatological cataclysm in which Islam will triumphantly emerge as the sole religion without relating it to specific events or actors in modern history. Many others try to find the fulfilment of classical prophecies in specific contemporary events and cultivate the hope that the triumph of Islam over its adversaries is imminent. The material analysed in this chapter makes it clear that the *mahdī* idea in its various ramifications is not restricted to the Shīʿa, but is rather a vibrant part of the Sunnī tradition as well. The following chapters will deal with Sunnī thinkers and leaders who took up the idea of the *mahdī* and initiated political and religious movements inspired by it.

2

Ibn Tūmart, the *mahdī* of the Almohads (al-*Muwaḥḥidūn*)[1]

1 BIOGRAPHY AND HAGIOGRAPHY

In the second half of the eleventh century and at the beginning of the twelfth, North Africa and parts of Spain came under the rule of the Almoravid (*al-Murābiṭūn*) dynasty. This was the first Berber dynasty to successfully establish an empire in the Muslim West. It included a large part of North-West Africa, from Awdaghust in the south to Tangier, Oran and Algiers in the north. Following the Christian conquest of Toledo in 1085, the Almoravid ruler Yūsuf b. Tashfīn received repeated requests from the Party Kings (*mulūk al-ṭawā'if*) to cross the straits and come to their aid against the Christian advances. After some initial hesitation, the Almoravids obliged and took hold of most Muslim cities of al-Andalus. In their empire, Mālikī jurists were given positions of responsibility and this became a major bone of contention between the Almoravids and their Almohad rivals.[2]

The Almoravids were the dynasty in power when Muḥammad b. Tūmart started his march to reform Maghribī society and government.

1 In writing this chapter, I am indebted to the extensive research on the Almohad movement by scholars such as I. Goldziher, E. Lévi-Provençal, J. F. P. Hopkins, M. Fierro, M. García-Arenal, A. Bennison and others.

2 This process has been extensively researched by numerous scholars. The most recent substantial work is Bennison, *The Almoravid and Almohad Empires*, especially pp. 24–54.

(As frequently happens with Muslim religious leaders, biography and hagiography are inextricably intertwined in the traditions related to his life.) He was born into a Maṣmūda Berber clan in what is today south-west Morocco, or al-Sūs al-Aqṣā in the language of the Arab chroniclers and geographers. The date of his birth is in dispute. Lisān al-Dīn Ibn al-Khaṭīb (d. 776/1374) maintains that he was born in 486/1093, but the later scholar Ibn Qunfudh (d. 810/1407) gives the date of 471/1078).[3] Ibn al-Qaṭṭān maintains that at the time of his death in 524/1130 he was around fifty years old; this would place his birth date in 474/1081.[4] Al-Zarkashī says that he set out for his travels at the age of eighteen.[5] Since our sources maintain that he travelled to the East in 500 or 501/1107–1108, Ibn al-Qaṭṭān's date seems to be close to the truth. This evidence also precludes the very late date given by Ibn al-Khaṭīb which would make Ibn Tūmart travel to the East when he was fourteen.

Despite his clear Berber provenance, Ibn Tūmart's biographers provided him with an Arab genealogy which connects him – through the Idrīsī dynasty – to Fāṭima, the daughter of the Prophet and the wife of ʿAlī b. Abī Ṭālib. According to one account, an ancestor of Ibn Tūmart came to the Maghrib with ʿUqba b. Nāfiʿ, the seventh-century Arab Muslim conqueror of the Maghrib.[6]

In his *Akhbār al-mahdī*, al-Baydhaq – a contemporary and close associate of Ibn Tūmart – provides two genealogies: one is purely Arab, while the other integrates two Berber names (Ugallīd and Yāmṣal) into the Arab pedigree. This composite – and very odd – genealogy is deemed to be the correct one by al-Baydhaq who doubts the purely Arab genealogy saying that it was not known to Ibn Tūmart's relatives.[7] Ibn Abī Zarʿ also doubts the Arab genealogy and says some people consider it false (*wa qīla huwa daʿiyyun fī hādhā al-nasab al-sharīf*). He also quotes a rather unknown historian Ibn Maṭrūḥ al-Qaysī who simply says that Ibn Tūmart was "a man from Hargha, from the Maṣāmida tribes, and is known as Muḥammad b. Tūmart al-Harghī. And some say that he was from the Chanfīsa. And God knows all these things better."[8] We can deduce from these statements that

3 Ibn al-Khaṭīb, *Raqm al-ḥulal*, p. 57; Ibn Qunfudh, *al-Fārisiyya*, pp. 99–100.
4 Ibn al-Qaṭṭān, *Naẓm al-jumān*, p. 74. Cf. Anonymous, *Mafākhir al-Barbar*, p. 258.
5 Zarkashī, *Taʾrīkh al-dawlatayn*, p. 4.
6 Ibn ʿAbd al-Ḥalīm, *Kitāb al-ansāb*, p. 257.
7 Al-Baydhaq, *Akhbār al-mahdī*, p. 21. See also a note by Lévi-Provençal, ibid. p. 31 of the French translation and cf. Ibn Khaldūn, *Kitāb al-ʿibar*, vol. 6, pp. 464–465.
8 Ibn Abī Zarʿ, *al-Anīs al-muṭrib ...*, pp. 217–218.

many Maghribī historians were far from uncritically believing in the odd Arab genealogies of Ibn Tūmart, but the emergence of these genealogies had good reasons: the lineage going back to Fāṭima complies with the classical requirements of a *mahdī* – who is expected to be a descendant of Fāṭima in accordance with the classical *ḥadīth* – while the added Berber element must have been helpful when Ibn Tūmart appealed to local tribal groups. It is noteworthy that Ibn Khaldūn provides a third genealogy which is mainly Berber and abruptly ends with a certain Khālid who appears also in the "purely Arab" genealogy.[9] We may remark in passing that Ibn Tūmart's presumed Arab lineage is compatible with the genealogical myth according to which the Berbers are related to the northern Arab tribal confederacy of Qays ʿAylān, or the southern Ḥimyar, but is in stark contrast with a contradictory myth which integrates the Berbers into the sacred history of mankind by saying that the Berbers are descendants of Ḥām who was awarded parts of Africa in a draw, conducted by angels after the Flood, between the sons of Noah. Alternatively, they are descendants of the army of Goliath who had to move to the Maghrib after King David killed their leader.[10]

Since the manuscript of al-Baydhaq's work is deficient at the beginning, we cannot glean from it details about Ibn Tūmart's early life. Laudatory biographies supporting the Almohads maintain that he was brave and generous, insisting on the truth, fearless of blame when acting in the cause of God.[11] During his youth he constantly attended the mosque, assiduously studying his slate. Since he was known as someone who was wont to light lamps in the mosque in order to read at night, he earned the Berber nickname *asafu*, which means torch.[12] As

9 Ibn Khaldūn, *Kitāb al-ʿIbar*, vol. 6, pp. 464–465.

10 These genealogical myths are described in Ibn ʿAbd al-Ḥalīm, *Kitāb al-ansāb*, pp. 18–30, 44–48 and elsewhere. See also Anonymous, *Mafākhir al-Barbar*, pp. 254–261. It is noteworthy that Ibn Ḥazm strongly rejects the Arab genealogies of the Berbers, but approvingly adduces their Hamitic genealogy. See Ibn Ḥazm, *ʿUqūd al-dhahab*, p. 404. For an analysis of these myths, see Shatzmiller, *The Berbers and the Islamic State*, pp. 17–27.

11 Cf. Qurʾān 5:54.

12 Dray, *Dictionnaire Berbère-Français*, s.v. Bel, *La religion musulmane en Berbérie*, p. 236 translates "flambeau de savoir". Taking care of, or contributing to lighting in mosques is a praiseworthy act in the Islamic tradition. See Zarkashī, *Iʿlām al-sājid bi-aḥkām al-masājid*, pp. 289, 401–402. *Pace* De Slane (Ibn Khaldoun, *Histoire des Berbères*, vol. 2, p. 163, note 1) who maintains that Ibn Tūmart received this nickname because he used to light candles in honour of saints.

one would say in English, he used to burn the midnight oil. He enjoyed studying *ḥadīth* as well as principles of jurisprudence and religion. Somewhat uncharacteristically for a devout Muslim, he is said to have also been an adept in geomancy (*ʿilm khaṭṭ al-raml*).[13] He is frequently described as being very eloquent in both Arabic and Berber. He did not engage in childish behaviour and was free of desire (*laysat lahu ṣabwa wa lā shahwa*). This may mean that he had no sexual drive or that he made up his mind to remain celibate. He did not touch women (*ḥaṣūr lā yaʾtī al-nisāʾ*), had neither wife nor concubine and begot no children.[14] Ibn Khallikān describes him as God-fearing, a recluse, ascetic, living roughly, wearing tattered clothing, taciturn, smiling in people's faces, assiduously performing commandments and having no earthly possessions except a walking stick and a drinking vessel (*kāna wariʿan mutaqashshifan mukhshawshinan mukhlawliqan kathīr al-iṭrāq muqbilan ʿalā al-ʿibāda lā yaṣḥabuhu min matāʿ al-dunyā illa ʿaṣan wa rakwa*).[15] He had three brothers and two sisters.[16] Strict asceticism and uncompromising enforcement of religious norms stood at the centre of his personality. He forbade slavish imitation in jurisprudence (*taqlīd*) as well as reading books promoting individual reasoning (*raʾy*). His biographers do not seem to perceive a contradiction between these two ideas. He studied everything profoundly.[17]

Historians of the Maghrib maintain that Ibn Tūmart travelled to the Middle East in 500 or 501/1107–1108. Though this was common practice among aspiring scholars in the Maghrib and al-Andalus,[18] some modern scholars doubt the historicity of this trip. According to the traditional accounts, he set out from Harghā in the Maghrib, crossed the sea into al-Andalus, and went to Cordova. There he spent a year studying with Ibn Ḥamdīn, the *qāḍī* who ordered the public burning of al-Ghazālī's *Iḥyāʾ*

13 Al-Marrākushī, *al-Muʿjib*, p. 156.

14 Ibn al-Qaṭṭān, *Naẓm al-Jumān*, p. 75 (ed. 1990, p. 124); Ibn Khaldūn, *Kitāb al-ʿibar*, part l, vol. 6, p. 471. Bel (*La religion musulmane en Berbérie*, p. 247) considers his celibacy a result of austere asceticism, but *ḥaṣūr* could also signify sexual dysfunction. See Lane, *Arabic-English Lexicon*, s.v. *ḥaṣūr*.

15 Ibn Khallikān, *Wafayāt al-aʿyān*, vol. 5, p. 46.

16 Ibn al-Qaṭṭān, *Naẓm al-Jumān*, p. 74.

17 Ibn al-Qaṭṭān, *Naẓm al-Jumān*, p. 38.

18 For instance, in many biographies of scholars assembled by Ibn Bashkuwāl we read the phrase "he travelled to the East" (*lahu riḥla ilā al-Mashriq*) or similar expressions. See Ibn Bashkuwāl, *Kitāb al-ṣila*, *passim*. Cf. Zniber, "L'iteneraire psycho-intellectuel d'Ibn Toumert", p. 21.

ʿulūm al-dīn.[19] According to some sources, he also went to al-Mahdiyya (in modern Tunisia) where he studied with the Mālikī scholar al-Māzirī.[20] Then he went to Almeria where he boarded a ship to the East – in search of knowledge in the great centres of Muslim learning in the Mashriq. On his way he stopped for some time in Alexandria where he studied with Abū Bakr al-Ṭurṭūshī (451/1059–520/1126),[21] whose denunciations of reprehensible innovations in religion might have influenced Ibn Tūmart's world view. It is noteworthy that al-Ṭurṭūshī's *Kitāb al-ḥawādith wa al-bidaʿ* includes passages against mingling of men and women as well as denunciation of men veiling their faces. Al-Ṭurṭūshī maintains that this fashion was spread among the people of the Maghrib.[22] As we shall see later, both issues became central in Ibn Tūmart's struggle against innovations in religion. In addition to al-Ṭurṭūshī, Ibn Tūmart is said to have studied principles of jurisprudence (*uṣūl al-fiqh*) and scholastic theology (*uṣūl al-dīn*) with Abū Bakr al-Shāshī in Baghdad.[23]

Some historians relate that Ibn Tūmart met Abū Ḥāmid al-Ghazālī (d. 505/1111) during his visit to Baghdad. This tradition became controversial since the beginning of modern research into the Almohad movement. As described by Ibn Qaṭṭān, the meeting took place in 503/1109–1110. Al-Ghazālī asked Ibn Tūmart about the fate of his *Iḥyāʾ ʿulūm al-dīn* in the Maghrib, and when he heard that the book was burned by the Almoravids in Cordova and elsewhere, he cursed them and invoked God to destroy their kingdom. Ibn Tūmart volunteered to perform the task.[24] According to

19 El Hour, "The Andalusian *qāḍī* in the Almoravid Period", pp. 74–75. Ibn Ḥamdīn had a bad reputation as a scholar and it is not clear what Ibn Tūmart could have learned from him. On the polemics against al-Ghazālī in Muslim Spain, see Serrano Ruano, "Why Did the Scholars of al-Andalus Distrust al-Ghazālī?"

20 Zarkashī, *Taʾrīkh al-dawlatayn*, p. 4. For al-Māzirī, see Brockelmann, *GAL S I*, p. 663.

21 See A. Ben Abdesselem, "Ṭurṭūshī", *EI²*, s.v.

22 Ṭurṭūshī, *Kitāb al-ḥawādith wa al-bidaʿ*, pp. 40–41, 66, 68–69, 141, For a study of al-Ṭurṭūshī and a Spanish translation of his work, see Fierro, *Kitāb al-ḥawādith wa al-bidaʿ*.

23 Ibn ʿIdhārī, *al-Bayān al-mughrib*, vol. 1, p. 312; Marrākushī, *al-Muʿjib*, p. 155; Ibn al-Qaṭṭān, *Naẓm al-jumān*, Rabāṭ n.d., p. 3. Abū Bakr Muḥammad b. Aḥmad al-Shāshī al-Qaffāl (429/1037 - 507/1113) was a Shāfiʿī jurist who taught in the Madrasa Niẓāmiyya in Baghdād between 504/1110 and his death. There is a biography of him in Subkī, *al-Ṭabaqāt al-Shāfiʿiyya al-kubrā* (vol. 6, pp. 70–78), but it does not include anything relevant to his connection with Ibn Tūmart. His major work is *Ḥilyat al-ʿulamāʾ fī maʿrifat madhāhib al-fuqahāʾ*.

24 Ibn al-Qaṭṭān, *Naẓm al-jumān*, pp. 16–18. In his extraordinarily careful edition of this work, Maḥmūd ʿAlī Makkī provides an exhaustive list of sources which mention

Ibn Abī Zarʿ, he studied with al-Ghazālī for three years.[25] Goldziher denied the historicity of this meeting on grounds of chronology: Ibn Tūmart set out for Baghdad in 500 or 501/1106–1107, while al-Ghazālī left it in 488/1095 and started teaching in Naysābūr in 499/1105.[26] Goldziher's view has been adopted by other scholars,[27] but has recently been challenged by M. Fletcher, though her work is based mainly on conjecture and on the many uncertainties in al-Ghazālī's biography rather than on any new evidence.[28]

Whether the meeting took place or not, some scholars consider Ibn Tūmart to be an indirect student of al-Ghazālī[29] and his presumed connection with such an illustrious personality became a powerful tool in the legitimacy struggle of the Almohad movement. We may note in passing that the connection between Ibn Tūmart and al-Ghazālī was still remembered in Tīnmallal when the traveller al-Zarhūnī visited the area in 1700.[30]

The sources describing Ibn Tūmart's journey back to the Maghrib are much more abundant. A tradition adumbrating his career as a strict follower of the *sharīʿa* and an uncompromising enforcer of religiously sanctioned behaviour maintains that he was trying to induce the sailors on his ship to pray and refrain from drinking wine. These religious demands infuriated the sailors to such an extent that according to one source they threw him overboard. However, he managed to stay afloat miraculously for half a day, swimming behind the ship; eventually a sailor was sent to rescue him from the waves.[31] This legend has been analysed in comparison to the biblical story of Jonah by D. Wasserstein,[32] and there certainly are comparable elements in the two stories: a dangerous storm breaks out because of the presence of a certain passenger on board. However, it

---

this meeting. Some affirm it, some doubt it and some deny that it ever occurred. See ibid., p. 16, note 5. Cf. Zarkashī, *Taʾrīkh al-dawlatayn*, p. 4.

25 Ibn Abī Zarʿ, *al-Anīs al-muṭrib ...*, pp. 218–219.

26 Goldziher, *Le Livre de Mohammed Ibn Toumert*, pp. 9–10.

27 See, for instance, García-Arenal, *Messianism and Puritanical Reform*, p. 163; Fierro, "The Legal Policies of the Almohad Caliphs", pp. 229–230, note 14.

28 Fletcher, "Ibn Tūmart's Teachers". Cf. Griffel ("Ibn Tūmart's Rational Proof for God's Existence", p. 755 note 7) who denies the historicity of the meeting by quoting a passage from *al-Munqidh min al-ḍalāl*, according to which Ghazālī was in Nishapur when Ibn Tūmart was in Alexandria.

29 Griffel, "Ibn Tūmart's Rational Proof for the Existence of God", p. 756.

30 Zarhūnī, *Riḥlat al-wāfid*, pp. 24–25, 120–121.

31 Al-Marrākushī, *al-Muʿjib*, p. 156; Ibn al-Qaṭṭān, *Naẓm al-Jumān*, pp. 39–40.

32 Wasserstein, "A Jonah Theme in the Biography of Ibn Tūmart".

should be noted that there is also a substantial difference between Jonah and Ibn Tūmart: Jonah was fleeing from the divine mission with which he was entrusted, while Ibn Tūmart was trying to make the sailors abide by the divine commandments. Jonah's ship incurred divine wrath because on board there was a passenger who disobeyed God's order, while Ibn Tūmart's one was in jeopardy because the sailors refused to heed the pious passenger's exhortations.

After the ship anchored on the North African coast,[33] Ibn Tūmart set out for his native region in "The Farthest Sūs" (*al-Sūs al-Aqṣā*). On his way there, he visited a number of cities. In some of them he built mosques; in all of them he engaged in "commanding right and forbidding wrong" (*al-amr bi-'l-ma'rūf wa al-nahy 'an al-munkar*) which meant in practice issuing various legal decisions, breaking musical instruments, spilling wine and preventing mingling between men and women. In Tilimsān he encountered a procession in which a bride was riding to her husband, sitting on a saddle, with a band playing music in front of her. He broke the drums, stopped the music and made her dismount.[34] Elsewhere he denounced women selling milk while wearing jewellery, "as if they were on their way to their husbands".[35] In some places he debated with local scholars and – according to the Almohad sources – he always had the upper hand. His ability to defeat his adversaries is explained by the fact that he was adept at the art of debate and knew "the principles of religion" (*al-uṣūl*) while his opponents knew only *ḥadīth* and positive law (*furū'*).[36] In some places he suffered various indignities, such as being beaten by the local riffraff and being expelled from towns.[37] For fear of being killed, he sometimes pretended to be a madman.[38] During his travels he went to Marrākush and had his first confrontation with the Almoravid ruler 'Alī b. Yūsuf. When he was told to salute the ruler as caliph he asked: "Where is the amīr – I see

33 Al-Baydhaq mentions first the city of Tunis, but the text is defective here and other cities may have been mentioned in the full text.

34 Al-Baydhaq, *Akhbār al-Mahdī*, p. 60; cf. Fromherz, *The Almohads*, p. 40. Classical Muslim attitudes to music and entertainment are not as negative as Ibn Tūmart would have it. See During, "Samā'". In "Exert yourselves, O Banū Arfida!", M. J. Kister draws attention to copious and variegated material on the attitudes to music and entertainment in general in the *ḥadīth* literature. Very lenient, even supportive, attitudes existed side by side with the most stringent denunciations.

35 Al-Baydhaq, *Akhbār al-Mahdī*, p. 61.

36 Ibn Abī Zar', *al-Anīs al-muṭrib* ..., p. 222.

37 Ibn Khaldūn, *Kitāb al-'ibar*, vol. 6, pp. 467–468.

38 Subkī, *Ṭabaqāt al-Shāfi'iyya al-kubrā*, vol. 6, p. 110.

only veiled slave-girls!" (*ayna al-amīr? innamā arā jawāriya munaqqabāt*).[39] He also denounced ʿAlī b. Yūsuf's sister for being unveiled.[40] This adumbrates Ibn Tūmart's opposition to the Almoravid custom according to which men veil their faces while women walk unveiled.[41] This became one of the main components of Ibn Tūmart's world view. All these issues will be addressed in more detail later in this chapter.[42]

Ibn Tūmart returned to his native region in 515/1121. He settled in Īgīlīz, a place not far from Marrākush, for three years during which he taught and preached to the tribes. Since he used to seclude himself there in a cave – apparently in emulation of the Prophet who hid in a cave during his *hijra* from Mecca to Medina – it became a place of pilgrimage for the Almohads after Ibn Tūmart's death.[43]

The next major event in his career was the proclamation of his mission and his acceptance of the oath of allegiance (*bayʿa*) from his supporters. It should be noted that the proclamation came only in the last ten years of his career, after he had already spent a few years propagating his religious ideas in numerous cities in the Maghrib. The exact date of the proclamation, as well as its location, are difficult to ascertain. Ibn al-Qaṭṭān gives three possible dates for it: 514, 515 or 516/1120–1122.[44] The ceremony took place either in Īgīlīz or in Tīnmallal,[45] both located in "The Farthest Sūs", in the vicinity of Marrākush. One of the participants in the ceremony was ʿAbd al-Muʾmin b. ʿAlī, whom Ibn Tūmart had met before and convinced to study with him instead of going to the East in search of knowledge. This is the way in which the Almohad tradition described the first meeting between Ibn Tūmart and ʿAbd al-Muʾmin who became the *mahdī*'s first *khalīfa*. Another prominent

39 Al-Baydhaq, *Kitāb akhbār al-mahdī*, pp. 67–68.

40 Ibn Khaldūn, *Kitāb al-ʿibar*, vol. 6, p. 468.

41 Al-Bakrī (*al-Masālik wa al-mamālik*, p. 294) gives a detailed description of the Almoravid face covering. It consists of *lithām* which seems to cover the lower part of the face; above it they wear the *niqāb* "so that only the sockets of the eye are visible" (*ḥattā lā yabdū minhu illā maḥājir ʿaynayhi*). Al-Bakrī also says that the face covering "sticks to them more that their [own] skin" (*wa ṣāra dhālika lahum alzama min julūdihim*). See the excursus at the end of this chapter.

42 See Section IV of this chapter.

43 For details about Īgilīz and a discussion of its etymology, see Āzāyku, *Namādhij*, pp. 25–27.

44 Ibn al-Qaṭṭān, *Naẓm al-jumān*, pp. 33, 74. Ibn Abī Zarʿ (*al-Anīs al-muṭrib* ..., p. 226) opts for 15 Ramaḍān 515/27 November 1121.

45 See Āzāyku, *Namādhij*, pp. 53–58. Some additional details about this place are given in Ibn Abī Zarʿ, *al-Anīs al-muṭrib* ..., p. 224, note 326.

participant was ʿAbd Allah b. Muḥsin al-Wansharīsī who later became the person responsible for the violent purging of suspected dissidents from the movement,[46] and who commanded the Almohad army in the disastrous Battle of al-Buḥayra and was lost there.[47] It is noteworthy that at the allegiance ceremony Ibn Tūmart released his followers from their loyalty to the Almoravid leader ʿAlī b. Yūsuf.[48] The Almoravids launched an attack on the Almohads, but were defeated, and in Shaʿbān 516/October 1122 the army of Ibn Tūmart laid an unsuccessful siege on Marrākush.[49] This first defeat of the Almoravids increased Ibn Tūmart's prestige and he conducted nine military operations against them. According to al-Baydhaq, all were successful due to Ibn Tūmart's superior tactics, to his ability to encourage his troops by religious exhortations, to predict favourable outcomes of the battles, and to miracles which he is said to have performed.[50]

Ibn Tūmart died on 25 Ramaḍān 524/1 September 1130. His body was moved to Tīnmallal where he had earlier erected a fortress in which he kept his property. The twelfth-century geographer al-Idrīsī says that the fortress had a high cupola, but it was left without any ornaments or decoration, according to the (Almohad) principle (*ʿalā ṭarīq al-nāmūs*) of simplicity in building. Tīnmallal became a place of pilgrimage for Ibn Tūmart's supporters and the burial place of the Almohad leadership.[51] Some historians make the unlikely claim that his death was concealed from the public, and ʿAbd al-Muʾmin, the first *khalīfa* of Ibn Tūmart, was therefore given the oath of allegiance in private. Ibn Tūmart's death was made public only several years later, at which time the oath of allegiance to ʿAbd al-Muʾmin was also publicized.[52]

Though Ibn Tūmart himself started military operations against the Almoravids, the major political and military expansion of his movement had to wait for the period of his first *khalīfa*, ʿAbd al-Muʾmin and his

46 Baydhaq, *Akhbār al-mahdī*, pp. 55–57, 73; ʿĀmilī, *al-Ḥulal al-mawshiyya*, pp. 174–175; Ibn al-Qaṭṭān, *Naẓm al-jumān*, p. 33.
47 Al-Baydhaq, *Akhbār al-mahdī*, pp. 27–28.
48 Ibn al-Qaṭṭān, *Naẓm al-jumān*, p. 29.
49 Ibn Abī Zarʿ, *al-Anīs al-muṭrib …*, pp. 227–228.
50 Al-Baydhaq, *Akhbār al-mahdī*, pp. 74–77.
51 Ibn al-Qaṭṭān, *Naẓm al-Jumān*, p. 126; Ibn al-Khaṭīb, *Raqm al-ḥulal*, p. 58. Idrīsī, *Nuzhat al-mushtāq*, vol. 1, pp. 229–230, Ibn Ṣāḥib al-Ṣalāt, *Kitāb al-mann bi-ʾl-imāma*, pp. 215–216; Ibn Abī Zarʿ, *al-Anīs al-muṭrib …*, p. 232.
52 Al-Baydhaq, *Akhbār al-mahdī*, p. 83; al-ʿĀmilī, *al-Ḥulal al-mawshiyya*, pp. 188–189; see a survey of the various views on the date on which the death of Ibn Tūmart was made public in Ibn al-Qaṭṭān, *Naẓm al-jumān*, p. 168, note 1.

successors. This expansion has been the subject of extensive research, but it is beyond the scope of this study. Suffice it to say that by the end of the twelfth century the Almohad empire ruled North Africa from Tangier, Bijāya and Tūnus in the north to Marrākush and Sijilmāsa in the south, as well as al-Andalus with the cities of Seville, Cordova, Murcia and Granada.[53]

II IBN TŪMART'S MANIFESTATION AS THE *MAHDĪ* AND HIS DENUNCIATION

In his claim to be the *mahdī*, Ibn Tūmart's was preceded by several Berber pretenders in the Maghrib and al-Andalus who claimed to be *mahdī*s and even prophets. The most notable of these figures were Ṣāliḥ b. Ṭarīf (eighth century) of the Barghawāṭa Berbers and Ḥā Mīm b. Mann Allah (tenth century) among the Ghumāra. Both of them produced a religion based on Islam, but included substantial changes in belief and ritual. Ṣāliḥ produced for the Berbers a book which the chronicles call "their Qur'ān", replaced Ramaḍān with Rajab as the month of fasting, imposed five prayers during the day and five during the night, allowed unlimited polygamy and used Berber formulae in prayer. Ḥā Mīm reduced the number of prayers to two, imposed fasting on Mondays and Thursdays (or Wednesdays) and allowed meat of female swine, claiming that only meat of male swine was forbidden in the Qur'ān. According to some accounts, he also abolished the *ḥajj* commandment. None of these two figures was politically as successful as Ibn Tūmart, but they did create an ambiance of religious fermentation among the Berbers which must have facilitated Ibn Tūmart's claim to be the *mahdī* and made the concept familiar to his audience.[54] According to the

53 The most recent description and analysis of the rise and eventual disintegration of the Almohad empire is Bennison, *The Almoravid and Almohad Empires*, pp. 62–117.

54 Goldziher seems to have been the first modern scholar who drew attention to these Berber movements. See his "Materialien zur Kentniss der Almohaden-bewegung in Nordafrica", pp. 51–55. See also Ferhat and Triki, "Faux prophètes et Mahdīs ...", *passim*. For Ṣāliḥ b. Ṭarīf's claim to be the *mahdī* and for the religious reforms introduced by him and his associates, see Anonymous, *Mafākhir al-Barbar*, p. 186; Anonymous, *Kitāb al-istibṣār*, pp. 197–200; al-Bakrī, *al-Masālik wa al-mamālik*, pp. 247–254; Ch. de la Veronne, "Ṣāliḥ b. Ṭarīf", *EI*[2], s.v. For Ḥā Mīm, see al-Bakrī, *al-Masālik wa al-mamālik*, pp. 200–202. See also R. le Tourneau, "Ḥā Mīm b. Mann Allah", in *EI*[2], s.v.; Bel, *La religion musulmane en Berberie*, pp. 170–188; García-Arenal, *Messianism and puritannical reform*, p. 58; Anonymous, *Mafākhir al-Barbar*, p. 225; Anonymous, *Kitāb al-istibṣār*, pp. 191–192; Ibn Abī Zar', *al-Anīs al-muṭrib*, pp. 164–166. For an analysis

anonymous chronicle *Mafākhir al-Barbar*, the standing of the Almoravid ʿAbd Allah b. Yāsīn among the Jazūla was the same as the standing of the *mahdī* among the Almohads.[55] Ibn Abī Zarʿ calls him *mahdī al-murābiṭīn* as if it were his standard appellation.[56] Maribel Fierro surveyed several messianic pretenders also in al-Andalus – such as Ibn al-Qiṭṭ at the beginning of the tenth century – though she thinks that the precariousness of the Muslim existence in al-Andalus and the expectation that it is bound to disappear sooner or later perhaps impeded the development of "mahdist geography" in al-Andalus.[57] However, we need to remember that this precariousness may work also in an opposite direction: we have seen that in the thirteenth century – when the "precariousness" of Muslim existence in Spain was certainly more acute – it did produce messianic expectations.[58]

In contradistinction to other *mahdīs*, whose assumption of the messianic title was legitimized by various types of divine or prophetic intervention, Ibn Tūmart's "appointment" as *mahdī* was simple and devoid of any supernatural elements. The descriptions of the oath of allegiance which he received vary. The earliest source which mentions it is Ibn Tūmart's contemporary al-Baydhaq who accompanied the *mahdī* on his travels. He only mentions that the ceremony took place in Tīnmallal, under a *kharūb* tree. ʿAbd al-Muʾmin, who became Ibn Tūmart's first *khalīfa*, and ʿAbd Allah b. Muḥsin al-Wansharīsī, who later ruthlessly purged the "dissidents" from the movement, pledged their allegiance on this occasion. Al-Baydhaq, the author of Ibn Tūmart's biography *Kitāb akhbār al-mahdī*, also belongs to this select group.[59]

The later author ʿAbd al-Wāḥid al-Marrākushī (d. 1228) has a more extensive account, giving details of Ibn Tūmart's preaching to the people of Tīnmallal. He aroused their interest in the *mahdī* idea by quoting relevant traditions and eventually declared that he was the *mahdī*. When this idea became established in their hearts, they pledged their allegiance to him. Though eschatology was not a central motif in Ibn Tūmart's literary

of this material, see Norris, *The Berbers in Arabic Literature*, pp. 2–104.

55 Anonymous, *Mafākhir al-Barbar*, p. 186. 192.

56 Ibn Abī Zarʿ, *al-Anīs al-muṭrib*, p. 167. See also ibid., p. 177 where the ruler of Maknāsa bears the title of *mahdī*. One gains the impression that even minor rulers could be called *mahdīs*.

57 Fierro, "Mahdisme et eschatologie", pp. 56ff, 64.

58 See Chapter 1, at note 156.

59 Al-Baydhaq, *Akhbār al-mahdī*, ed. Lévi-Provençal, p. 73; ed. Ḥājiyyāt, pp. 52–53. For biographical details about the first ten followers of Ibn Tūmart, Ibn Abī Zarʿ, *al-Anīs al-muṭrib …*, pp. 224–225.

output, he used the classical eschatological motifs during the initial stages of his activity as *mahdī*. He identified his followers with the group that was expected to conquer Persia and Byzance, kill the *dajjāl*, and an amīr from among them would lead the prayer after the descent of Jesus. These motifs are prominent also in a poem recited at Ibn Tūmart's grave during the reign of Abū Yaʿqūb Yūsuf, the successor of ʿAbd al-Muʾmin (r. 1163–1184).[60]

Ibn al-Qaṭṭān (mid-thirteenth century) and al-ʿĀmilī (d. between 1409 and 1417) provide a rather embellished description of the event. According to al-ʿĀmilī, Ibn Tūmart delivered in Ramaḍān 515/November–December 1121 a speech which reflected the classical traditions on the *mahdī*, but included also expressions which were his own additions, appropriate to his Maghribī milieu. The audience in front of whom he spoke included many Berbers. After praising God and the Prophet, and describing the *mahdī* who will fill the earth with equity and justice after it was full with wrongdoing and iniquity, he said:

> His [i.e., the *mahdī*'s] place will be the Farthest Maghrib, his time will be the end of time. His name is the name of the Prophet, his lineage is the lineage of the Prophet. The wrongdoing of the rulers is manifest and the land is full with corruption. This is the end of time, the name is the name, the lineage is the lineage and the deed is the deed. (*maqānuhu al-maghrib al-aqṣā, zamānuhu ākhir al-zamān, wa 'smuhu 'smun li-'l-nabī wa al-nasab nasab al-nabī wa qad ẓahara jawr al-umarāʾ wa 'mtalaʾat al-arḍ bi-'l-fasād wa al-ism al-ism, wa al-nasab al-nasab wa al-fiʿl al-fiʿl.*)[61]

Placing the *mahdī* in the Maghrib is not part of the classical tradition, but its significance is self-evident in our context. "The name is the name" is a reference to the classical tradition according to which the *mahdī* will bear the name of the Prophet as well as the name of his father: Muḥammad b. ʿAbd Allah. Similarly, the lineage of Ibn Tūmart reaches the Prophet's family, as required by the classical tradition. And his deeds – the establishment of justice and the struggle against infidels – are also deeds envisaged for the *mahdī* in the collections of *ḥadīth*.[62]

---

60 Al-Marrākushī, *al-Muʿjib*, pp. 161–162.
61 Ibn al-Qaṭṭān, *Naẓm al-jumān*, pp. 75–76. Cf. al-Āmilī, *al-Ḥulal al-mawshiyya*, pp. 175–176; García-Arenal, *Messianism and Puritanical Reform*, p. 171.
62 See Chapter 1, Section IV.

Ibn Tūmart was probably thinking of himself when he described the *mahdī* in these terms, and his first ten supporters followed suit. His future *khalīfa* ʿAbd al-Muʾmin asserted: "Only you fit this description, you are the *mahdī*"(*hādhihi al-ṣifa lā tūjadu illā fīka, fa-anta huwa al-mahdī*).[63]

The complete loyalty to Ibn Tūmart, and to his claim to be the infallible *mahdī*, continued during the reign of his first successors ʿAbd al-Muʾmin (r. 1130–1163), Abū Yaʿqūb Yūsuf (r. 1163–1184) and to a certain extent also during the time Abū Yūsuf Yaʿqūb al-Manṣūr (1184–1199). Abū Yaʿqūb Yūsuf is said to have been "an adept in the thought of the *mahdī*" (*kāna ... mutaqaddiman fī ʿilm al-imām al-mahdī*).[64] There are some indications to the effect that this unquestionable loyalty began to slacken during the time of al-Manṣūr (r. 1184–1199)[65] and the process came to fruition on the initiative of Abū al-ʿAlāʾ Idrīs al-Maʾmūn (1229–1232) who disowned the *mahdī*, denounced his religious claims and removed all symbols related to him from public life. Ibn Tūmart is thus the only *mahdī* discussed in the present work whose political or religious heirs disowned him about one hundred years after his death.

This unusual event in the history of Sunnī messianic movements should be understood against the background of the political situation in Spain. In the first half of the thirteenth century, the Christian *reconquista* was in full swing. Cordova fell into Christian hands in 1236 and Seville followed suit in 1248.[66] At the same time, internecine struggles plagued the Almohad dynasty. The Muslim defeat in the Battle of al-ʿUqāb (known in Spanish history as Las Navas de Tolosa) in 1212 was seen as a catastrophic turning point in the history of Islam in al-Andalus.[67]

Abū al-ʿAlāʾ Idrīs al-Maʾmūn (r. 624/1226 – 629/1232) assumed power under these adverse conditions. He was given the oath of allegiance in Seville, but the Almohads of Marrākush vacillated and eventually gave their support to Yaḥyā, the nephew of al-Maʾmūn. Facing the loss of the Almohad capital, al-Maʾmūn asked Fernando III of Castile for help. Against the background of Islamic traditions, asking help from a non-Muslim

63 ʿĀmilī, *al-Ḥulal al-mawshiyya*, p. 176. See a similar description in Ibn al-Qaṭṭān, *Naẓm al-jumān*, pp. 75–76.

64 Ibn Ṣāḥib al-Ṣalāt, *Kitāb al-mann bi-ʾl-imāma*, p. 233.

65 Bawwiz, *Dirāsa fī fikr al-mahdī*, p. 117.

66 Bennison, *The Almoravid and Almohad Empires*, p. 117.

67 See al-Qurṭubī's (d. 1372) gloomy assessment of this battle for the Muslims in Chapter 1, at notes 159–160.

ruler is a problematic move. On the basis of the Qurʾān and Muslim jurisprudence, it is easy to make a case against a Muslim leader who makes such a request – though there are also traditions according to which the Prophet received help from a Jewish group and gave them an equal share of the spoils.[68] In any case, it is problematic to ask for non-Muslim help even in a struggle against other non-Muslims, and it is even more so to seek such an alliance in an internecine struggle within a Muslim dynasty. This is especially true when the potential non-Muslim ally represents an independent, and in our case also powerful, political entity which is in the process of reducing the Muslim presence in Spain. However, seeking an alliance with this Christian power seems to have been al-Maʾmūn's only way to regain control of Marrākush, the Almohad capital. According to Ibn Abī Zarʿ's account, Fernando demanded a heavy price for his help: transferring ten frontier fortresses of his choice in al-Andalus to his control, building a church in Marrākush where Christians would enjoy complete freedom of worship (including sounding the *nawāqīs* calling to prayer), and forbidding Christian conversion to Islam while allowing Muslim conversion to Christianity. Al-Maʾmūn agreed to these conditions. When he entered Marrākush in 627/1230 with the help of the Christian troops, and soundly defeated his rebellious nephew Yaḥyā b. al-Nāṣir and killed large numbers of the Almohads, he mounted the pulpit, cursed Ibn Tūmart and said: "Do not call him the infallible *mahdī*, rather call him the contemptible profligate. Nobody except the prophets is infallible. There is no *mahdī* except Jesus" (*lā tadʿūhu bi-'l-mahdī al-maʿṣūm wa 'dʿūhu bi-'l-ghawī al-madhmūm fa-innahu lā maʿṣūm illā al-anbiyāʾ wa lā mahdī illā ʿĪsā*).[69]

68 The main proof text again collaboration with non-Muslim is Qurʾān 5:51: "O believers, take not Jews and Christians as friends; they are friends of each other. Whoso of you makes them his friends is one of them." In the *ḥadīth* literature there is a tradition according to which the Prophet refused an offer of a polytheist to fight on the side of the Muslims. See Muslim b. al-Ḥajjāj, *Ṣaḥīḥ*, vol. 3, pp. 1449–1450 (*Kitāb al-jihād wa al-siyar, bāb 51*); Ibn Māja, *Sunan*, vol. 2, p. 945 (*Kitāb al-jihād, bāb 27*); Mālik b. Anas, *al-Mudawwana al-kubrā*, vol. 3, pp. 40–41. For a survey of the various views on the matter in the books of law, see Friedmann, *Tolerance and Coercion*, pp. 36–37 and now also Yarbrough, "I'll not accept aid from a *mushrik*". For a contemporary discussion of the issue along traditional lines, see Ṭarīqī, *al-Istiʿāna bi-ghayr al-muslimīn*, pp. 72–75.

69 Ibn Abī Zarʿ, *al-Anīs al-muṭrib*, pp. 329–330; Ibn ʿIdhārī, *al-Bayān al-mughrib, Qism al-muwaḥḥidīn* pp. 284, 286, 444; Anonymous, *Mafākhir al-Barbar*, pp. 270–271. The aforementioned source notes the struggle between Yaḥyā and al-Maʾmūn, but has

This is a terse and rather enigmatic version of al-Ma'mūn's proclamation, especially as far as the sentence about Jesus is concerned. Fortunately, we have a longer and more intelligible version – addressing the leaders of the Almohad community and all its members – in al-ʿĀmilī's *al-Ḥulal al-mawshiyya*. After the customary preamble, the declaration reads:

> ... Be advised that we have discarded the falsehood and proclaimed the truth: there is no *mahdī* except Jesus the son of Mary, the spirit of God. Even if tongue[s] used to call someone *mahdī* instead of Jesus, he should not be so called.[70] He [i.e., Jesus] was called *mahdī* only because he spoke in the cradle (*mahd*). This is a blameworthy innovation which we removed. May God help us with this necklace which we wear. We have dropped the name of him whose infallibility was not proven. We have removed his trace. Let him be erased and fall. Let him not hold out.
>
> (*... li-taʿlamū annā nabadhnā al-bāṭil wa aẓharnā al-ḥaqq wa an lā mahdī illā ʿĪsā ibn Maryam rūḥ Allah wa in jarā maḥallahu al-lisān lā yusammā. Wa mā summiya mahdiyyan illā annahu takallama fī al-mahd.*[71] *Fa-tilka bidʿa qad azalnāhā wa Allah yuʿīnunā ʿalā hādhihi al-qilāda allatī taqalladnāhā. Wa qad asqaṭnā 'sma man lam tathbut lahu ʿiṣma fa-li-dhālika azalnā ʿanhu rasmahu fa-yumḥā wa yasquṭ wa lā yathbut.*)[72]

nothing to say about the denunciation of Ibn Tūmart or the help al-Ma'mūn received from the Christian ruler.

70 The phrase *wa in jarā maḥallahu al-lisān lā yusammā* is difficult and the suggested translation is not certain. I thank my colleagues Albert Arazi and Isaac Hasson for their assistance with understanding it. The version printed in Allouch's edition of *al-Ḥulal* (p. 137): *wa in jarā mā ḥallat al-lisān* is even more incomprehensible.

71 The Allouche edition (p. 137) has here *illā annahu lakum fī al-mahdī* which is incomprehensible and the editor placed a question mark after it. He also suggested an unsubstantiated emendation, reading *illā annahu lakum fī al-mahdī* [*iʿtiqād fāsid*], which led Le Tourneau ("La disparition de la doctrine Almohade", p. 195) to translate: "Il (sc. Ibn Tūmart) n'est nommé Mahdī que parce que vous avez une conviction erronée sur ce qu'est le Mahdī." *Pace* García-Arenal who translates "... there is no Mahdi other than ʿĪsā ibn Maryam, who alone was called al-Mahdi because he spoke of the good guidance ..." See García-Arenal, *Messianism and Puritanical Reform*, p. 198.

72 Al-ʿĀmilī, *al-Ḥulal al-mawshiyya*, pp. 248–249. It is noteworthy that the Tūnis 1909 edition of this work mentions this declaration and describes it as "well-known" (*shahīra*), but does not adduce the whole text (see p. 124). My thanks go to Prof. Ali Hussein of Haifa University for placing this rare edition of the book at my disposal. For an extensive discussion of the attribution of this work to al-ʿĀmilī (d. *c.* 1417) see the Beirut 2010 edition, pp. 5–8, 14.

According to another description of this episode, al-Maʾmūn also abolished holding the prayers in Berber and using the dictum *aṣbiḥ wa li-ʾllāhi al-ḥamd*[73] which was common practice since the beginning of the Almohad state.[74]

One of the main purposes of the denunciation of Ibn Tūmart is the removal of his legacy from public life, by removing his mention from the Friday sermon and from the currency. Furthermore, the passage intends to debunk the title of *mahdī* in general, by saying that Jesus was known as *mahdī* only because he was able to speak in the cradle (*mahd*), not because he was "rightly guided" and not because of any messianic assignment. In linguistic terms, this argument means that the term *mahdī* is derived from the root *m-h-d* rather than from *h-d-y*. The idea that Jesus was given by God the ability to speak while he was a newborn infant in the cradle is based on Qurʾān 3:46 and Qurʾān 5:110. In both verses God says to Jesus that he will speak to men both in the cradle and when he comes of age

---

Cf. also Ibn Khaldūn, *Muqaddima*, p. 301 (translation by Rosenthal, vol. 2, p. 185). Ibn Khaldūn does not mention this episode, but maintains, in general, that this interpretation was used to prevent the use of this tradition to support the *mahdī* idea.

73 The issue of praying in Berber was still alive in the times of al-Wansharīsī (d. 1508). He quotes an anonymous scholar who allowed those who did not know Arabic to pray in Berber because "God knows all languages" (*Allah aʿlam bi-kulli lugha*). See al-Wansharīsī, *al-Miʿyār*, vol. 1, p. 186. On the other hand, al-Wansharīsi (loc. cit. p. 278) considers *aṣbiḥ wa li-ʾllāhi al-ḥamd* an "ugly innovation which was introduced in the sixth century" (*bidʿa qabīḥa uḥdithat fī al-miʾa al-sādisa*). See also al-Shāṭibī, *Kitāb al-Iʿtiṣām*, vol. 2, p. 65 and *idem*, *Fatāwā*, p. 207.

I was also not able to find out the meaning of the apparently Berber words *suʿdūd* and *nārdī*. It is possible that the manuscript copyists who did not know Berber corrupted these words beyond recognition. The uncertainty concerning these words is evident from the fact that on p. 317 we have *sūdūt* instead of *suʿdūd*.

74 Ibn ʿIdhārī, *al-Bayān al-mughrib, Qism al-muwaḥḥidīn*, p. 286. Not everything in Ibn ʿIdhārī's description of the ritual changes introduced by al-Maʾmūn is clear. In addition to the abolition of prayers in Berber and of the aforementioned dictum, Ibn ʿIdhārī mentions that al-Maʾmūn *qaṭaʿa al-nidāʾ baʿd al-ṣalāt wa al-nidāʾ ʿalayhā bi-tāṣliyat al-islām wa hiya iqāmat al-ṣalāt bi-ʾl-lisān al-barbarī wa ka-dhālika suʿdūd wa nārdī wa aṣbiḥ wa li-ʾllāhi al-ḥamd wa mā ashbaha dhālika mimma kāna al-ʿamal ʿalā dhālika min awwal dawlat al-muwaḥḥidīn*. *Nidāʾ* is used in the Qurʾān in the sense of *adhān* (see Qurʾān 5:61, 62:9) and *qaṭaʿ... al-nidāʾ ʿalayhā bi-tāṣliyat al-islām* means the abolition of the call to prayer in Berber. It is however not clear what is the *nidāʾ* after the prayer is over. On p. 317 there is a more understandable version: *duʿāʾ* is used instead of *nidāʾ*. This version probably relates to the question whether a personal supplication (*duʿāʾ*) can be pronounced after the ritual prayer is completed. This is a disputed matter in the Islamic tradition. For an extensive survey of the various views, see Ādam ʿAlī, *al-Imām al-Shāṭibī*, pp. 89–103. See also al-Wansharīsī, *al-Miʿyār*, vol. 1, pp. 279–300.

(*yukallimu al-nās fī al-mahdi wa kahlan*). In the classical Qur'ānic exegesis, the ability of Jesus to speak in infancy was one of his miracles; he used it in order to exonerate his mother from accusations of sexual indiscretion[75] and it had nothing to do with his being the *mahdī*. The *ḥadīth* literature expands on the theme of infants speaking in the cradle, includes Jesus in this select group but, again, does not connect these miraculous abilities to the office of the *mahdī*.[76]

The denunciation of Ibn Tūmart was not agreed upon by all the Almohads and this discontent must have been one reason for the change of direction by 'Abd al-Wāḥid al-Rashīd (1232–1242), the successor of al-Ma'mūn. Al-Rashīd embraced a different approach to Ibn Tūmart and the Almohad doctrine. Ibn 'Idharī gives the impression that after al-Rashīd became the new caliph, "the souls longed to attract the Almohad community" (*wa qad kānat al-nufūs tatashawwaqu ilā istijlāb 'iṣābat al-tawḥīd*). The people of Marrākush are described as thrilled with this development which is described as a result of the changing balance of power between various groups, rather than by any development of doctrine like the one which accompanied the reform of al-Ma'mūn. In any case, the rules and customs of the Almohads were restored to what they had been before: after some delays, al-Rashīd saw to it that the name of Ibn Tūmart would be mentioned again in the Friday *khuṭba* and on the coins.[77] It is also noteworthy that the Almohad legacy was preserved in the Hafsid dynasty which ruled in Ifrīqiyā between 1229 and 1574.[78]

The denunciation of Ibn Tūmart and its description in our sources has baffled a number of scholars.[79] It is evident that al-Ma'mūn's intention is to deprive Ibn Tūmart of his *mahdī* title as well as his infallibility, both of which were part of his standard appellation "the infallible *imām* and the

75 See, e.g., Ṭabarī, *Jāmi' al-bayān*, vol. 3, p. 272, on Qur'ān 3:46. The story is also found in the "Tales of the Prophets" (*qiṣaṣ al-anbiyā'*) literature. See for instance, Tha'labī, *Qiṣaṣ al-anbiyā' al-musammā bi-'l-'arā'is*, pp. 269–270.

76 The most frequently quoted *ḥadīth* says that "only three [infants] spoke in the cradle" (*lam yatakallam fī al-mahdi illā thalātha*). See, e.g., Muslim, *Ṣaḥīḥ*, *Kitāb al-birr* 8 (vol. 4, pp. 1976–1977. For references to the attempt to connect *mahdī* with *mahd*, see Chapter 1, note 34.

77 Ibn 'Idhārī, *al-Bayān al-mughrib, Qism al-muwaḥḥidīn*, pp. 308, 309, 317–318.

78 Bel, *La religion musulmane en Berberie*, pp. 272–282; Brunschwig, *La Berberie orientale*, pp. 272–274.

79 See García-Arenal, *Messianism and Puritanical Reform*, p. 198; Le Tourneau, *La disparition de la doctrine almohade*, p. 195, note 1.

[well-]known *mahdī*" (*al-imām al-ma ʿṣūm wa al-mahdī al-ma ʿlūm*).[80] The infallibility of the prophets, which is referred to in the short version of the denunciation of Ibn Tūmart, is a well-known and extensively debated theme in Muslim theology not only with regard to the prophets in general, but also with regard to the Prophet Muḥammad. The best-known issue in the discussions related to Muḥammad's infallibility is the episode known as the Satanic verse, which is understood as a bona fide error on the part of the Prophet who did not immediately sense that Satan intervened in the divine revelation.[81]

III ORGANIZATION AND DISCIPLINE

The Muwaḥḥidūn were organized in a strict hierarchy, first analysed by J. F. P. Hopkins. At the top stood the people who joined the movement soon after Ibn Tūmart's proclamation, known as "the ten", "the fifty" and "the seventy". Some of the remainder were characterized by their respective tribal affiliations (such as the Hargha or the Hantāta), or by their tasks in the movement, such as the "warriors" (*ghuzāt*) or "naval warriors" (*ghuzāt al-baḥr*). It is not clear to what extent this hierarchy was observed in practice, and it is not clear whether the practice changed with the passage of time. It stands to reason that this structure could have been observed only as long as the first members of the movement were alive, but the sources do not tell us much about what happened after the generations changed. In the ideal descriptions of this structure, there was no mobility between the various groups.[82]

It seems that during his lifetime Ibn Tūmart maintained strict – even draconic – discipline in his movement. It is noteworthy that strict discipline and draconic punishments for transgressions large and small were also the hallmark of the Almoravids against whom Ibn Tūmart rose in rebellion.[83] Ibn Tūmart was constantly preaching to his followers. Attendance of his

80 Al-Baydhaq, *Kitāb akhbār al-mahdī*, ed. Lévi-Provençal, p. 21.
81 A very convenient source surveying the theological debate concerning the infallibility of prophets is al-Rāzī, *ʿIṣmat al-anbiyāʾ*. See ibid., pp. 93ff. for the discussion of the Prophet Muḥammad's infallibility. See also Madelung, "ʿIṣma", in *EI²*, s.v., with extensive bibliography. Cf. Ahmed, "Ibn Taymiyya and the Satanic Verses".
82 Hopkins, "The Almohade Hierarchy", *passim*; Ibn al-Qaṭṭān, *Naẓm al-Jumān*, p. 29.
83 See H. T. Norris, "New Evidence on the Life of ʿAbd Allah b. Yāsīn ...", p. 256; Ibn Abī Zarʿ, *al-Anīs al-muṭrib*, p. 169 *supra*; al-Qāḍī ʿIyāḍ, *Tartīb al-madārik*, vol. 3, pp. 780–82.

sermons was obligatory: whoever absented himself was punished; if he persisted, he was executed. He wrote for his followers a book on the unity of God (*tawḥīd*) in Berber. According to Ibn Abī Zarʿ, this book "was like the noble Qurʾān among the Maṣāmida". Whoever did not learn it by heart was considered an infidel.[84] Furthermore, every member was obliged to learn by heart a part (*ḥizb*) of the Qurʾān; whoever did not remember his part was whipped once or twice, and if he failed again, he was executed. The same fate was destined for anyone who deceived his kith and kin.[85] In general, "the command of the *mahdī* is a decree and whoever dissents will be killed" (*amr al-mahdī ḥatm man khālafahu yuqtal*).[86]

These are severe punishments of individuals for transgressions committed by them. However, strict discipline was maintained also on the tribal, collective level. The idea to punish whole tribes seems to have been the brainchild of ʿAbd Allah b. Muḥsin al-Bashīr al-Wansharīsī, one of the first ten members of Ibn Tūmart's movement.[87] Ibn al- Athīr relates that Ibn Tūmart thought that the tribes included numerous "evil and corrupt" people (*ahl al-sharr wa al-fasād*). No specific religious deviation is mentioned, but the remedy is, again, "commanding right and forbidding wrong". He summoned the tribal leaders who had pledged allegiance to him and instructed them to provide him with lists of these presumed villains. Those of "the evil and corrupt" who refused to repent were bound, placed at the left side of al-Bashīr al-Wansharīsī and each tribe was instructed to execute its own "miserables" (*ashqiyāʾ*).[88] These massacres seem to be a result of Ibn Tūmart's consternation of potential disloyalty in the tribes rather than of any organized resistance to his leadership.[89]

Al-Baydhaq's memoirs speak about mass executions of whole tribal groups without mentioning any specific transgression committed by them.

84 Ibn Abī Zarʿ, *al-Anīs al-muṭrib*, pp. 226–227.

85 Ibn al-Qaṭṭān, *Naẓm al-Jumān*, p. 29.

86 Ibn Tūmart, *Aʿazz mā yuṭlab*, p. 236.

87 For some details about him, see Ibn Abī Zarʿ, *al-Anīs al-muṭrib ...*, p. 224, note 328. Nuwayrī (*Nihāyat al-arab*, vol. 24, pp. 283–285) describes the way in which al-Wansharīsī convinced the *mahdī* that he was taught by God to distinguish between the "people of Paradise and the people of Fire".

88 Ibn al-Athīr, *al-Kāmil*' vol. 10, pp. 575–576. *Shaqī* (pl. *ashqiyāʾ*) is a Qurʾānic term for those destined to hell, contrasted with *saʿīd*. See Qurʾān 11:105. Placing the "miserables" on the left side is a clear reference to the Qurʾānic "people of the left" (*aṣḥāb al-shimāl*), destined for hell on the Day of Judgment.

89 *Pace* Le Tourneau ("Sur la disparition de la doctrine Almohade", pp. 193–194) who speaks about serious resistance to Ibn Tūmart during his lifetime.

Al-Bashīr al-Wansharīsī executed, for forty days in a row, people described as "dissidents, hypocrites, and filthy" (*mukhālifūn, munāfiqūn, khubathā'*). According to al-Baydhaq's account, five tribes (*qabā'il*) were executed in one place, while others met a similar fate elsewhere. Nothing is said about the way in which the alleged guilt of these groups was ascertained, there is nothing specific about this guilt and there is no hint as to the real reason for this massacre. The whole procedure is called in Almohad chronicles *al-mayz*, in the sense of "weeding out" or "purging" dissidents.[90] In other Arab chronicles the term *tamyīz* is used.[91] Le Tourneau maintains that these executions were a response to resistance to Ibn Tūmart, but the sources do not hint at such a possibility and create the impression that the executions resulted from Ibn Tūmart's unsubstantiated suspicions of disloyalty.[92] The policy of mass executions was continued under 'Abd al-Mu'min after the conquest of Wahrān, Tilimsān and other places. Sixty notables from Fez were executed when they came to surrender to the Almohads, asking for clemency.[93] All these events are good examples of the absolute obedience demanded by most messianic leaders discussed in the present work.

IV THE BELIEF SYSTEM OF IBN TŪMART

As Goldziher has said, "the Almohad movement is theological through and through".[94] Ibn Tūmart and his supporters considered themselves "unitarians, believers in the unity of God" (*al-muwaḥḥidūn*). This is of course a general Muslim tenet and, strictly speaking, all Muslims are "unitarians" in the sense that they believe in the oneness of God. It is therefore necessary to find out what are the peculiar issues which caused Ibn Tūmart to consider himself and his movement as *Muwaḥḥidūn*.

Ibn Tūmart starts his definition of *tawḥīd* with a *ḥadīth* according to which whoever dies while knowing that there is no god except Allah will enter Paradise. The rest of the passage includes the well-known tradition about the five pillars of Islam and the famous instructions concerning the

90 Al-Baydhaq, *Akhbār al-mahdī*, p. 78. Dozy (*Supplement aux dictionnaires arabes*, s.v. *mayz*) has *revue de soldats* but this is not meaningful in our context. For other uses of *tamyīz*, see Fromherz, *The Almohads*, pp. 96–100.
91 See Ibn al-Athīr, *al-Kāmil*, vol. 10, p. 575.
92 Le Tourneau, "Sur la disparition de la doctrine Almohade", pp. 193–194.
93 Ibn 'Idhārī, *al-Bayān al-mughrib, Qism al-muwaḥḥidīn*, pp. 22–23.
94 Goldziher, "Materialien zur Kentniss der Almohadenbewegung", p. 59.

conversion of Jews in Yemen which the Prophet is said to have given to Muʿādh b. Jabal when he sent him there. The chapter ends with a statement on the prerequisites of sound belief. All these are only marginally related to *tawḥīd*, and the whole passage seems incoherent and does not follow up or substantiate the initial sentence about the salvific power of *tawḥīd*.[95] It is also appropriate to indicate at this point that the idea that mere acknowledgment of God's oneness is sufficient to gain entry into Paradise is disputed in the Islamic tradition. According to some views, the belief in the oneness of God guarantees unqualified entry into Paradise, even for sinners; according to others, this belief guarantees salvation only after the sins of the person in question are atoned for by temporary stay in the Fire. Some scholars opined that *tawḥīd* is indeed the key to Paradise, but it will not open the gate without the wards on it; these wards are a metaphor for the commandments.[96] Performance of commandments is an essential condition for making the key operational.

Ibn Tūmart devotes much attention to the denial of anthropomorphism. Ibn Khaldūn explains that the people of the Maghrib were in isolation from the Ashʿarī tradition, and did not use figurative explanations of the "ambiguous" verses: "they understood them as they were" (*imrār al-mutashābihāt kamā jāʾat*). This seems to mean that they understood them literally. Ibn Tūmart therefore decided to introduce the Ashʿarī tradition into the Maghrib and cause the Maghribī scholars to adopt the Ashʿarī *taʾwīl*.[97] We shall see later that anthropomorphism was a main topic in his criticism of the Almoravids. Its denial is closely related to the belief in the existence of God who created the world. Nothing resembles something which does not belong to its category. The creator does not belong to the category of the created. If he did, he would be as incapable as the created things are and it would be impossible to countenance his deeds, the most important of which is the creation itself. These deeds are not open to doubt because creation necessarily needs a creator. Therefore, the creator bears no similarity to the created, in accordance with the

95 Ibn Tūmart, *ʿAqīda*, pp. 46–47; Ibn Tūmart, *Aʿazz mā yuṭlab*, pp. 213, 278; Ishbīlī, *Sharḥ Murshidat Muḥammad b. Tūmart*, p. 10.

96 Ibn Tūmart, *ʿAqīda*, pp. 46–47; *idem*, *Aʿazz mā yuṭlab*, pp. 213–214. For a convenient survey of the various relevant views, see al-Ḥanbalī, *Kalimat al-ikhlāṣ*, *passim*, and Friedmann, "Conditions of Conversion", pp. 99–100.

97 Ibn Khaldūn, *Kitāb al-ʿibar*, part 1, vol. 6, p. 466. Ibn Khaldūn is not aware of the fact that Ibn Tūmart plays on the common root of *tashbīh* and *mutashābih* in order to criticize anthropomorphists on the basis of Qurʾān 3:7. See note 102.

Qur'ānic verse "Is He who creates as he who does not create? Will you not remember?"[98]

The use of human intellect (*'aql*) and its limitations is another central issue in Ibn Tūmart's world view. He has no doubt that human intellect will necessarily lead to the acknowledgment of the existence of God. The very existence of human beings – who had been non-existent before creation – leads in the same direction. Ibn Tūmart uses the standard argument asserting that a deed must have a doer and since the world does exist, it must have a creator. In his view, this logical necessity is firmly established in the minds of all people with intellect. This is also the meaning of the Qur'ānic verse "Is there any doubt regarding God, the Originator of the heavens and the earth ... ?" (*a fī Allah shakkun fāṭir al-samāwāt wa al-arḍ ...* ?).[99]

While human intellect (*'aql*) has this absolutely necessary role in causing mankind to believe in the existence of God who created the world, it has little importance in other issues related to religion. This is correct both in theology and in the *sharī'a*. In theology, human intellect has limits which it cannot cross (*li-'l-'uqūl ḥaddun taqifu 'indahu lā tata'addāhu*). For instance, it is not able to describe the "modality" (*takyīf*) implied in Qur'ānic verses which speak about God in anthropomorphic terms. In other words, human intellect is not able to explain verses which describe God as sitting on His throne, descending in the last third of every night to the lower heaven and the like.[100] In Ibn Tūmart's view, any attempt to do this would necessarily lead either to anthropomorphism (*tajsīm*) or to an absolute denial of divine attributes (*ta'ṭīl*). Both these conclusions are in his view nonsensical and impossible (*muḥāl*).[101] It is noteworthy that Ibn Tūmart plays on the common root of *tashbīh* and *mutashābih* in order to use the Qur'ānic criticism of those who follow the *mutashābih* verses to criticize anthropomorphists. He does this although the classical exegesis does not see any connection between *tashbīh* in the sense

98 Ibn Tūmart, *'Aqīda*, pp. 51–52; *idem*, *A'azz mā yuṭlab*, pp. 216–217.

99 Ibn Tūmart, *'Aqīda*, pp. 47–49; *idem*, *A'azz mā yuṭlab*, p. 214; Qur'ān 14:11. For the standard argument about the logical necessity of God's existence, see, e.g., Ghazālī, *Iḥyā' 'ulūm al-dīn*, vol. 1, p. 138. See also Abrahamov, *Islamic theology*, pp. 32ff.

100 For an extensive analysis of this problem in various schools of Islamic theology, see the seminal work of Holtzman, *Anthropomorphism in Islam*. God's "sitting on His throne" is mentioned in several Qur'ānic verses, e.g., 20:5. His "descent to the lower heaven" is mentioned in the famous *ḥadīth al-nuzūl*; see, for instance, Bukhārī, *Ṣaḥīḥ*, vol. 1, p. 289 (*Kitāb al-tahajjud* 14). For an analysis of this *ḥadīth*, see Holtzman, op. cit, pp. 30–31 and elsewhere.

101 Ibn Tūmart, *'Aqīda*, pp. 52–54; *idem*, *A'azz mā yuṭlab*, p. 217.

of anthropomorphism and *mutashābih* in the sense of ambiguous or abrogated verses.[102]

Human intellect is also inutile in relation to the *sharīʿa*. This inutility is caused by the fact that from the scholastic point of view – which classifies things into necessary, impossible and possible – the commandments are neither necessary nor impossible. They are in the domain of the possible (*ḍarūrāt al-ʿaql thalāth: wājib wa jāʾiz wa mustaḥīl fa-'l-ʿibādāt laysat min qabīl al-wājib fī al-ʿaql wa lā min qabīl al-mustaḥīl fa-lam yabqa illā al-jāʾiz*). Some of them are as likely to be imposed as they are to be forbidden (*fa-laysa baʿḍuhā bi-awlā bi-'l-ibāḥa aw al-ḥaẓr min baʿḍ*). God rules His universe as He wishes, and the intellects have no say in this. This does not mean that there is no wisdom in the *sharīʿa* or that it is not operating according to rational rules. Those who think along these lines impugn religion and ignore God's wisdom. On the other side of the spectrum are people intent on deriving the *sharīʿa* using their intellects and on employing various types of analogy in deriving the law. Both approaches are wrong and a deviation from the truth.[103]

Like other *mahdī*s described in this work,[104] Ibn Tūmart believed in strict determinism. Whatever God decreed, will necessarily happen. Using the classical predestinarian formulation, he maintains that he who is (destined to be) happy, is already happy in his mother's womb and he who is (destined to be) miserable is already miserable in his mother's womb by God's decree (*al-saʿīd saʿīd fī baṭn ummihi wa al-shaqī shaqī fī baṭn ummihi kullu dhālika bi-qaḍāʾihi wa qadarihi*).[105] Human beings have thus little influence on their fate. God has absolute knowledge of every detail in his world;[106] He determined everything in advance and nobody can change such divine decisions.[107] One could argue that such an extreme predestinarian opinion is not suitable for a revolutionary movement such as the Almohads who wanted to introduce major changes in the Muslim

102 "The ambiguous verses which imply anthropomorphism" (*al-mutashābihāt allatī tūhimu al-tashbīh*); see Ibn Tūmart, *ʿAqīda*, p. 53. For the classical material on the *mutashābihāt*, see L. Kinberg, "*Muḥkamāt* and *mutashābihāt* ...", *passim*.

103 Ibn Tūmart, *Aʿazz mā yuṭlab*, p. 157. Cf. ibid., p. 44: "The intellect has no place in the law" (*idh al-ʿaql laysa lahu fī al-sharʿ majāl*).

104 See Chapter 3 at notes 117, 158–160; Chapter 4 at notes 4, 116.

105 Muslim b. al-Ḥajjāj, *Ṣaḥīḥ*, vol. 4, p. 2037 (*Kitāb al-qadar* 3; Ibn Māja, *Muqaddima* 7).

106 God's infinite knowledge is a major theme in Ibn Tūmart's *Murshida* and in its commentaries. See Ibn Tūmart, *Aʿazz mā yuṭlab*, p. 226, and al-Ishbīlī, *Sharḥ*, pp. 12–14.

107 Ibn Tūmart, *ʿAqīda*, pp. 57ff; *idem*, Ibn Tūmart, *Aʿazz mā yuṭlab*, p. 220.

belief system and society, but I have not seen a discussion of this problem in the relevant literature.

It is not possible in our framework to delve into all the "principles of religion" discussed in Ibn Tūmart's work. It is, however, necessary to give some attention to his views on analogy (*qiyās*), because of the conclusions which Ibn Tūmart derives from it. The guiding principle in his discussion is that *qiyās* must not be used when a relevant *ḥadīth* is available. The Companions of the Prophet did not employ rational analogy in matters of jurisprudence (*lā yaṣiḥḥu an yaqīsū bi-ʿuqūlihim fī al-sharʿ*). When they based their rulings on the public good (*maṣlaḥa*) or counsel (*mashwara*), they did not derive the law by employing their intellect, but rather on their understanding of what the Prophet said. The nature of Ibn Tūmart's views on *qiyās* can best be judged by the examples given by him. The Qurʾān instructs the believers "to be good to parents, whether one or both of them attain old age with you; say not to them 'Fie' neither chide them ..."[108] It is clear that this verse forbids not only chiding the parents, but also doing to them things which are more hurtful (*tanbīh bi-'l-adnā ʿalā al-aʿlā, a fortiori*). Similarly, the *ḥadīth* which forbids denying surplus water to others can be understood as forbidding the denial of all life necessities because the idea (*maʿnā*) behind the original prohibition was compassion (*muwāsāt*) and this is applicable not only to water.[109] Such use of *qiyās* is acceptable to Ibn Tūmart, apparently because there is no Qurʾānic verse or *ḥadīth* contradicting it and he agrees with the resulting ruling. In other cases he is very strict in investigating the nature of *qiyās* and finds reasons to reject the results if they are not acceptable to him. By way of example, he rejects the idea that female apostates should not be killed because from the grammatical point of view the *ḥadīth* demanding the execution of apostates uses the masculine form (*man baddala dīnahu fa-'ḍribū ʿunuqahu*), and is contradicted by another *ḥadīth* according to which it is forbidden to kill women. In his view, the ideas (*maʿānī*) behind the two injunctions differ from each other: the prohibition to kill women was issued in the context of *jihād* and was caused by their weakness and inability to fight, while the killing of apostates is a punishment and a deterrent and from this point of view there is no difference between men and women. Therefore, the analogy (*qiyās*) between these two rulings is

---

108 Qurʾān 17:23.

109 Bukhārī, *Ṣaḥīḥ*, *Kitāb al-shurb* 2, vol. 2, p. 75. For a discussion of this issue, see ʿAsqalānī, *Fatḥ al-bārī*, vol. 5, pp. 31–33.

unacceptable and female apostates must be treated in the same way as their male counterparts.[110] Another example of false *qiyās* is the denial of the necessity to perform ablution after touching the penis; the penis is one of the bodily organs, no ablution is necessary after touching them, and therefore there is no necessity to perform ablution after touching the penis. People who employ analogy in this false way "tear the religious law to shreds" (*mazzaqū al-shar'a kulla mumazzaqin*).[111]

Another central issue in Ibn Tūmart's belief system is the necessity of an *imām* in every age. He substantiates the idea by a Qur'ānic verse in which God made Abraham an *imām* for the people.[112] The *imām* must be infallible (*ma'ṣūm*).[113] Should there be any possibility that he commits an error, he would not be able "to command good and forbid wrong". Only absolute and unassailable virtue can eradicate its opposite. Ibn Tūmart gives endless examples of this binary view of the world: only absolute, incontestable truth can eradicate falsehood, only absolute justice can eradicate iniquity. The *imām* is the pillar which holds heaven and earth in their place. Should he be removed, the whole structure would crumble. Therefore, absolute obedience to his commands is essential. Ibn Tūmart gives a glowing description of the Companions of the Prophet and of their obedience to their leader.[114] Following the Prophet's death, Abū Bakr and 'Umar b. al-Khaṭṭāb followed suit and also demanded absolute obedience. Ibn Tūmart hints at the famous *ḥadīth* according to which Abū Bakr was determined to fight the rebellious Bedouins of the *ridda* wars if they dared to deny him even the smallest

110 For the different views on this issue in the early schools of law, see Friedmann, *Tolerance and Coercion*, pp. 135–139.

111 Ibn Tūmart, *A'azz mā yuṭlab*, pp. 165–167. The quotation is on p. 166. Goldziher adduces this passage from manuscript (*Materialien*, p. 90), but does not analyse its contents.

112 Qur'ān 2:124.

113 Ḥusayn Mu'nis (*Ta'rīkh al-Maghrib*, vol. 2, p. 71) gives a different interpretation of *ma'ṣūm*, arguing that this term does not mean infallibility from error – this belongs to God alone – but rather being protected by God from any harm so that he can accomplish his mission. He mentions that Almohad historians use the root *'-ṣ-m* to indicate cases in which God protected Ibn Tūmart from harm. It is true that this usage can be found in Almohad chronicles; however, in *A'azz mā yuṭlab* (p. 229) Ibn Tūmart says that "the *imām* must be protected from falsehood so that he can destroy falsehood, because falsehood cannot destroy falsehood, and he must be protected from error because error cannot eradicate error ... (*lā yakūnu al-imām illā ma'ṣūman min al-bāṭil li-yahdim al-bāṭil li-anna al-bāṭil lā yahdim al-bāṭil wa an yakūna ma'ṣūman min al-ḍalāl li-anna al-ḍalāl lā yahdimu al-ḍalāl*).

114 Ibn Tūmart, *A'azz mā yuṭlab*, pp. 229–231.

item which they used to give to the Prophet, and made up his mind to exterminate them (*qātala ʿalā ʿiqāl wa ʿalā al-qalīl wa al-kathīr wa qāma bi-'l-amr baʿda al-rasūl ḥattā arāda qawmun nizāʿahu wa raʾā min al-raʾy istīṣālahum*).[115] He evidently sees in the *ridda* wars a historical example to be followed, an example that justifies his massacres of real or imaginary dissidents. It may be noted in passing that the classical historians do not describe the *ridda* wars as resulting in the massacre of the vanquished Bedouins, but rather in their submission to the authority of Medina.[116]

The ideal period of Islam, the period of the four "righteous caliphs", also called *khilāfat al-nubuwwa*, lasted for thirty years (632–661). In Ibn Tūmart's view, the situation suddenly and dramatically changed for the worse after this period came to a close with the death of ʿAlī b. Abī Ṭālib. Nothing of the positive features of the first thirty years after the Prophet's death remained intact. These positive features were replaced by internecine struggles, dissension, lack of obedience, emergence of heretical views and an endless list of other negative phenomena. "The ornaments of this world became religion, ignorance became knowledge and falsehood became truth ..." (*ḥattā ṣāra zukhruf al-dunyā dīnan wa al-jahl ʿilman wa al-bāṭil ḥaqqan ...*). In Ibn Tūmart's description, this period has no redeeming features. It is *zamān al-ghurba*, "strange times";[117] this is a reference to a *ḥadīth* according to which "Islam began as a stranger and it will return to what it was. Blessed be the strangers" (*al-islām badaʾa gharīban wa yaʿūdu kamā badaʾa fa-ṭūbā li-'l-ghurabāʾ*).[118] This *ḥadīth* has usually been understood to mean that at the beginning of Islamic history – the Meccan period of the Prophet's activity is perhaps the best example – when Muslims were few and Islam barely existed, Islam and Muslims looked strange and outlandish in an alien, non-Muslim environment. According to a common interpretation of the *ḥadīth*, the "strangers" were people who left their as yet polytheistic tribes in order to perform

115 Ibn Tūmart, *Aʿazz mā yuṭlab*, p. 232. For a seminal analysis of the controversy concerning the treatment of the rebellion of the Bedouin tribes after the Prophet's death, see Kister, "... *ʾillā bi-ḥaqqihi* ...' A Study of an Early *ḥadīth*". *ʿIqāl* is a rope used to bind camels and serves here as an example of something having a very small value. For the standard tradition about Abū Bakr's determination to fight the rebellious tribes, see Muslim, *Ṣaḥīḥ*, *Kitāb al-īmān* 32 (vol. 1, pp. 51–52).

116 See, for instance, Shoufani, *Al-Ridda*, pp. 125–131 (on the Battle of ʿAqrabāʾ).

117 Ibn Tūmart, *Aʿazz mā yuṭlab*, pp. 233–234. Ibn Tūmart quotes this tradition in his general description of the apocalypse, without explicitly relating it to his own times. See ibid., pp. 296–297.

118 See Muslim, *Ṣaḥīḥ*, *Kitāb al-īmān* 232, 233 (vol. 1, pp. 130–131).

hijra to Medina and join Islam (*al-nuzzāʿ min al-qabāʾil*), or people who kept their virtue when everybody else became corrupt. The tenth-century scholar al-Ājurrī (d. 970–971) devoted a monograph to these "strangers", describing them as a literary and moral elite.[119] The "strangeness" of Islam will recur before the Day of Judgment when the "strangers" will flock to Jesus at his second coming.[120] Several medieval scholars used the *ḥadīth* also in order to bemoan the situation of Islam in their own times, and the same is true of some contemporary Muslim thinkers in whose view Islam suffers from decadence and weakness.[121]

Like the other *mahdī*s described in this work, Ibn Tūmart did not place the classical apocalypse at the centre of his thought, but the catastrophic situation expected in the *ḥadīth* to prevail just before the end of days is transposed into the twelfth-century Maghrib. Consistently with the style of *Aʿazz mā yuṭlab*, Ibn Tūmart provides a long list of negative features of his age: ignorant leaders, wicked kings, disregard of Qurʾānic injunctions, disunity and dissension, performing commandments without understanding their meaning and many more.[122] ʿAbd al-Muʾmin – who became Ibn Tūmart's first successor – describes the period in which Ibn Tūmart appeared as *zaman al-fatra*, a period without prophets.[123] From the traditional Muslim point of view, this is an odd description for the lifetime of Ibn Tūmart or for any other Muslim period: since Muḥammad is considered the last prophet, all times after his death are, in a sense, *zaman al-fatra*. If read in conjunction with Qurʾān 5:19 which speaks about the

119 Al-Ājurrī, *Kitāb al-ghurabāʾ*, *passim*.

120 Ājurrī, *Kitāb al-ghurabāʾ*, p. 55; Ibn Qayyim al-Jawziyya, *Tahdhīb madārij al sālikīn*, vol. 2, pp. 917– 924.

121 For instance, al-Fāsī (d. 1511) bemoans the pitiable features of the Muslim elites in the tenth century AH. See his *Bayān ghurbat al-islām*, *passim*, especially p. 37. The slightly later Indian Muslim Ṣūfī Shaykh Aḥmad Sirhindī (d. 1624) describes the deplorable situation of Islam in his days as reflected in our *ḥadīth*. See Friedmann, *Shaykh Aḥmad Sirhindī*, pp. 16–17. The contemporary scholar ʿAbd Allah b. Yūsuf al-Judayʿ makes an attempt to list all collections of *ḥadīth* in which this *ḥadīth* appears and gives some classical interpretations, but does not relate them to contemporary situations. Abū Muḥammad Mukhtār al-Jibālī, on the other hand, sees the contemporary woes of Muslim society, such as wine drinking and thinly clad women, as related to our *ḥadīth*. See the introduction to his *Ghurbat al-islām*, which is a separate publication of a relevant passage from the *Fatāwā* of Ibn Taymiyya. For a convenient survey of the relevant *ḥadīth* material, see al-Ḥanbalī's *Kashf al-kurba*, *passim*.

122 Ibn Tūmart, *Aʿazz mā yuṭlab*, pp. 240–241.

123 Al-Baydhaq, *Akhbār al-mahdī*, pp. 16–17.

coming of the Prophet Muḥammad,[124] ʿAbd al-Muʾmin's statement could reasonably be interpreted as hinting at Ibn Tūmart's prophetic qualities.[125]

The pitiable situation of the Muslims before Ibn Tūmart's coming needs immediate improvement. And, indeed, his appearance transforms the situation completely. Everything is suddenly done according to the *sunna*, truth prevails and falsehood is eradicated. But the main change as seen by Ibn Tūmart is the total obedience accorded to him. Everything is now done according to his wish and his wish is identical with the wish of God.[126] Belief in the *mahdī* is obligatory and anybody who doubts him is an infidel.[127] Therefore unconditional obedience is imperative and any dissent carries capital punishment.[128] Obedience is also a central motif in the speech in which Ibn Tūmart is said to have appointed ʿAbd al-Muʾmin as his successor.[129]

It is noteworthy that Ibn Tūmart is the only *mahdī* discussed in the present work who devoted substantial attention to questions subsumed under the title "basic principles of religion" (*uṣūl al-dīn*). Questions such as rules concerning the derivation of the law from its sources, the relationship between the principles of derivation and positive law, as well as theological issues such as the possibility of seeing God in this world or in the next are extensively discussed in *Aʿazz mā yuṭlab*. As we have seen, Ibn Tūmart bemoans the disunity of the Muslim community in his time and places great emphasis on the need to unite it. One of the ways to achieve this goal is, in his understanding, preferring the "basic principles" (*uṣūl*) of religion to the "details" (*furūʿ*) derived from them. The reasoning behind this preference is the understanding that the basic principles are agreed on by all Muslims, while the details create the possibility of dissension. In his view, there can be no contradiction between a basic principle and the details derived from it; a basic principle cannot be the basis for a contradictory one, nor the basis for a detail contradicting it (*inna al-aṣl lā tatanāqaḍu furūʿuhu wa lā yakūnu aṣlan li-mā naqīḍuhu aṣlun lahu wa lā aṣlan li-naqīḍi farʿihi*).[130]

Positive law as such is not a central issue in Ibn Tūmart's thought. In *Aʿazz mā yuṭlab* there are chapters about legal topics, such as ritual purity,

124 "People of the Book, now there has come to you Our messenger, making things clear to you, upon an interval between the messengers ..."
125 Al-Baydhaq, *Akhbār al-mahdī*, pp. 16–17.
126 Ibn Tūmart, *Aʿazz mā yuṭlab*, pp. 234–236.
127 Ibn Tūmart, *Aʿazz mā yuṭlab*, p. 238 *infra*.
128 Ibn Tūmart, *Aʿazz mā yuṭlab*, p. 236.
129 Marrākushī, *al-Muʿjib*, pp. 167–168.
130 Ibn Tūmart, *Aʿazz mā yuṭlab*, p. 32 *infra*.

division of spoils and plunder, wine drinking and levying the *jizya*,[131] but these chapters consist of quotations from the Qur'ān and the *ḥadīth* and the only contribution of Ibn Tūmart is the choice of the quoted passages. On the other hand, in Ibn Tūmart's biography there are a few anecdotes from which we can gauge his views on legal issues. On his way back from the Middle East to the Maghrib, he passed through Tunis. On a Friday, after the congregational prayer, there were funeral prayers. He noted that the people do not pray for a certain deceased person. When asked about the reason, he was told that the person was a Jew who used to pray (with Muslims). After numerous people testified to the veracity of this characterization, Ibn Tūmart organized a prayer for this deceased person.[132] This anecdote reflects a legal question: can an unequivocally Islamic behaviour – such as participation in Muslim prayer – be regarded as conversion to Islam even if the prospective convert did not utter the declaration of faith (*shahāda*) in front of witnesses and did not formally convert? This is a disputed matter between the schools of law. The Ḥanafīs ruled that an unequivocally Islamic behaviour can be accepted as indicating conversion and Ibn Tūmart ruled in favour of this view.[133]

Another, rather confused, story with legal implications, deals with a robber in Constantine who used to enter people's houses in order to kill them and take their property. It seems that at first someone flogged him, while Ibn Tūmart ruled that he should be executed rather than flogged, but the (mistaken?) flogging precludes the execution. Then someone apparently thought that the hand of the robber should be amputated for theft, but Ibn Tūmart ruled that it is not permissible to impose two *ḥadd* punishments for one offence (*lā yajūzu jamʿu ḥaddayn fī dhanb wāḥid*) and the flogging which the robber received precludes also the amputation. The text mentions the name of the *qāḍī* of the city, but he is not part of the story.[134]

131 Ibn Tūmart, *Aʿazz mā yuṭlab*, pp. 274–275

132 Al-Baydhaq, *Akhbār al-mahdī*, p. 50.

133 Al-Kāsānī, *Badāʾiʿ al-ṣanāʾiʿ*, vol. 7, p. 103, *infra*. Cf. Friedmann, "Conditions of Conversion ...", p. 105. *Pace* Lévi-Provençal who characterizes the deceased person as a "pseudo-musulman" (*Akhbār al-mahdī*, translation, p. 76, note 1). Ibn Tūmart's ruling is based on the classical *ḥadīth* in which we find the idea that someone who prays in the direction of the *qibla* and eats from what the Muslims slaughter is considered a Muslim. See Bukhārī, *Ṣaḥīḥ*, *Kitāb al-ṣalāt* 28 (vol. 1, pp. 110–111). See also Ibn Māja, *Sunan, Kitāb l-masājid 19*, vol. 1, p. 263: "If you see a man regularly frequenting the mosques, testify to his belief" (*idhā raʾaytum al-rajul yaʿtādu al-masājid fa-'shhadū lahu bi-'l-imān*).

134 Al-Baydhaq, *Akhbār al-mahdī*, p. 53.

Another legal issue which attracted Ibn Tūmart's attention was the method of inflicting capital punishment. On his way back from the East, he passed through Akarsīf and heard that a man was executed there by crucifixion. He ruled that crucifixion is not a method of execution: criminals should be executed and their corpses should then be crucified and put on display, to serve as warning to future culprits.[135]

An excellent example of the rigour with which the Almohads tried to implement the *sharīʿa* according to their understanding is the destruction and rebuilding of mosques in Marrākush because of their imprecise *qibla*. Ibn Tūmart did not raise this issue when he stayed in two mosques in Marrākush on his way back from the East.[136] But when the city was besieged and conquered by ʿAbd al-Muʾmin, the Almohads argued that Ibn Tūmart refrained from taking residence in the city because the *qibla* of its mosques was to the east rather than in the exact direction of the Kaʿba (*li-tashrīq masājidihā ʿan al-qibla al-mustaqīma*). Only after the mosques were destroyed and rebuilt, did the Almohads take up residence in Marrākush.[137] Prayer in the eastern direction was a controversial issue in the early period of Islam and it is surprising that it persisted in a city built as late as the eleventh century.[138]

V THE POLEMICS OF IBN TŪMART AND HIS *JIHĀD*

Ibn Tūmart defined the uncompromising tone of his polemics against the Almoravids in his first epistle to their leaders. Their leader ʿAlī b. Yūsuf has been "seduced by this world" (*al-maghrūr bi-dunyāh*)[139] The Almoravids are

> people whom Satan seduced and God visited them with His wrath, the vicious and tyrannical Lamtūnī[140] bunch. We command you what we command ourselves: fear of God and obedience to Him. This

135 Al-Baydhaq, *Akhbār al-Mahdī*, p. 62.

136 Al-Baydhaq, *Akhbār al-mahdī*, pp. 67–68.

137 Al-Baydhaq, *Akhbār al-mahdī*, p. 105. There is an extensive discussion of the difficulties in establishing the exact *qibla* in the Maghrib and al-Andalus in Ibn ʿAbd al-Ḥalīm, *Kitāb al-ansāb*, pp. 110–114.

138 For an extensive discussion of the eastern prayer direction in early Islam, see Bashear, "*Qibla musharriqa*", especially p. 269.

139 Al-Baydhaq, *Akhbār al-mahdī*, p. 11.

140 Lamtūna was the dominant tribe in the Almoravid empire.

> world was created for extinction. Paradise is for the God-fearing and torture in hell for those who rebel. You have duties towards us according to the *sunna*. If you discharge them, you will be fine; if not, we shall seek God's help to kill you and blot out whatever you leave behind. We shall destroy your abodes so that the inhabited places turn desolate and things which were new become worn out. This letter of ours is *iʿdhār* and a warning for you. He who gave a [fair] warning has absolved himself from responsibility [for what may happen if his warning is not heeded]. Peace be upon you. This is a greeting required by the *sunna*, not a greeting expressing satisfaction (*wa kitābunā hādhā ilaykum iʿdhār wa indhār wa qad aʿdhara man andhara wa al-salām ʿalaykum salāma 'l-sunna lā salāma 'l-riḍā*).[141]

When one considers accepted Muslim norms of etiquette, this is an exceedingly rude letter. It lacks the customary greeting at the beginning and the greeting at the end is deliberately downgraded, devoid of all significance. The coarse tone of the letter is understandable when we take into account the deep hostility of Ibn Tūmart to his Almoravid rivals and his intention to leave no place for compromise in this rivalry. Somewhat surprising is the fact that the accusation of anthropomorphism, which became the hallmark of Ibn Tūmart's polemics against the Almoravids, is left unmentioned.

A much more detailed polemical attack on the Almoravids is included in a special chapter of *Aʿazz mā yuṭlab*. Many of the accusations are inspired by classical *ḥadīth* which Ibn Tūmart interpreted to suit his polemical purposes. In the headline of the chapter, his enemies are described as "liars, the veiled ones, the anthropomorphists" (*al-mubṭilūn, al-mulaththamūn, al-mujassimūn*). Then we have several lists of defamatory details of various kinds. Some relate to the Almoravid provenance, appearance and attire, some to their intellectual and religious inferiority and others to their policies and morals. Even before they came from Kākudam,[142] their inferiority was apparent: they were barefooted, naked, destitute, shepherds of sheep and cattle and ignorant of divine commandments.[143] Most of these defamations speak for themselves, but the inclusion of herding sheep in the list of contemptible characteristics of the Almoravids requires a comment. In the

141 *Rasāʾil Muwaḥḥidiyya*, vol. 1, p. 43.
142 A city in the "farthest Maghrib" (*al-maghrib al-aqṣā*) which was known as the place from which the Almoravids came. See Yāqūt, *Muʿjam al-buldān*, s.v.
143 Ibn Tūmart, *Aʿazz mā yuṭlab*, p. 242.

Muslim tradition, there are various attitudes to raising cattle and agricultural work. While some prophetic traditions speak favourably about acquiring sheep and landed property, others denounce it because raising cattle, tilling the land and the agricultural rhythm in general could interfere with *jihād* and cause the defeat and humiliation of the Muslims.[144] This is probably the reason why Ibn Tūmart considered animal husbandry a blameworthy occupation.

More blameworthy characteristics of the Almoravids become apparent as they take over the country. They are kings and erect tall buildings (*yataṭāwalūna fī al-bunyān*), a practice regarded in classical Muslim political thought as characteristic of kings ('king' being a pejorative term, in contrast with '*imām*' or '*khalīfa*') and incompatible with the early Islamic ideal of simplicity and asceticism.[145] Furthermore, they have numerous slave girls and procreate with them. Figuratively, they are deaf and dumb because they do not listen to the (religious) truth and do not proclaim it. They have whips like tails of cows (*fī aydīhim siyāṭ ka-adhnāb al-baqar*) and beat the people with them. Ibn Tūmart pays particular attention to the attire and demeanour of Almoravid women. "Their heads are like humps of Bactrian camels" (*ruʾūsuhunna ka-asnimat al-bukht*), because they gather their hair on the top of their heads. They are dressed but look naked (*kāsiyāt ʿāriyāt*), probably because they wear transparent clothing; they deviate from the truth and cause others to do the same (*māʾilāt mumīlāt*);[146] they are angry in the morning and curse at night.[147] All these accusations are adapted from a classical *ḥadīth* which speaks of a group of men consigned to hell because they used to flog people unjustly, and a group of women of doubtful morals who engaged in seductive behaviour and therefore will never be admitted to Paradise.[148]

The attire of the Almoravids is another element in Ibn Tūmart's polemics against them. It is well known that Almoravid males used to veil their faces while Almoravid women were unveiled. The origins of this custom

144 Kister, "Land Property and *jihād*", *passim*.

145 *Al-taṭāwul fī al-bunyān* is an accusation levelled at ʿUthmān b. ʿAffān. See Ibn Qutayba, *al-Imāma wa al-siyāsa*, p. 50; cf. Crone, *Medieval Islamic Political Thought*, pp. 44–47.

146 This is Ibn Tūmart's explanation of this expression. In the classical *ḥadīth* it seems to have a more concrete meaning, such as coquettish gait and the like. For an extensive commentary on this *ḥadīth*, see Ibn al-Ḥājj, *al-Madkhal*, vol. 1, pp. 236–237.

147 Ibn Tūmart, *Aʿazz mā yuṭlab*, pp. 242–243.

148 Muslim, *Ṣaḥīḥ*, vol. 3, p. 1680 (*Kitāb al-libās wa al-zīna* 125), vol. 3, pp. 2192–2193 (*Kitāb al-janna* 52). See also al-Nawawī, *Sharḥ Ṣaḥīḥ Muslim*, vol. 14, pp. 356–357 and vol. 17, pp. 196–198 who gives more explanatory possibilities.

are not clear;[149] Ibn Tūmart considered it a blameworthy deviation from Islamic norms because of the *ḥadīth* in which the Prophet is said to have cursed "men who make themselves resemble women and women who make themselves resemble men" (*laʿana rasūl Allāh al-mutashabbihīn min al-rijāl bi-'l-nisāʾ wa al-mutashabbihāt min al-nisāʾ bi-'l-rijāl*).[150] This formulation is terse and certainly allows for Ibn Tūmart's interpretation, but it needs to be noted that the commentators on the *ḥadīth* understood it in much wider terms and included in the "resemblance" not only the veil, but also issues such as men being effeminate, wearing jewellery and speaking softly like women, and women wearing turbans (*amāʾim*) or shawls (*ṭayālisa*, sg. *ṭaylasān*) like men.[151]

ʿAbd al-Wāḥid al-Marrākushī (1185–1228), the historian who served the Almohad governor of Seville at the beginning of the thirteenth century – and whose book probably reflects views prevalent among the Almohads – considers the influential status of women under the Almoravids as the prime reason for the disintegration of their dynasty.[152] After mentioning the tyrannical rule of the Almoravids, the spread of blameworthy practices in their times and their unbridled haughtiness, he says:

> Women took charge of the situation and were entrusted with positions [of power]. Every woman belonging to influential people of

149 See the Excursus at the end of this chapter.

150 Ibn Tūmart, *Aʿazz mā yuṭlab*, p. 247; Bukhārī, *Ṣaḥīḥ*, vol. 4, p. 94 (*Kitāb al-libās* 61).

151 Al-ʿAynī, *ʿUmdat al-qāriʾ*, vol. 22, p. 41; al-Qasṭallānī, *Irshād al-sārī*, vol. 12, pp. 583–584; al-ʿAsqalāni, *Fatḥ al-bārī*, vol. 10, pp. 332–334. These three sources speak about the obligation of women to veil their faces, but do not explicitly mention the Almoravid custom of veiling the faces of men.

It is noteworthy that the controversy about the attire of the Almoravids continued long after their dynasty ceased to exist. In response to a question, al-Wansharīsī (d. 1508) (*al-Miʿyār*, vol. 1, p. 225) vindicated the veiling of men among them on the basis of Qurʾān 7:32 and 49:13 which he interprets as indicating that the existence of different tribes and their attires are God's doing and the Almoravids were therefore within their rights when they chose to veil their men. He also praises them for their struggle and *jihād* for the sake of Islam.

152 This prominence of women among the Almoravids may be the result of their tendency to compel women and youngsters to engage in gainful employment. See al-Bakrī, *al-Masālik wa al-mamālik*, p. 287: "The people of Sūs and Aghmāt are most eager to obtain gainful employment and most desirous of livelihood. They oblige their women and youngsters to learn a trade and make a living" (*wa ahl al-Sūs wa Aghmāt akthar al-nās takassuban wa aṭlabuhum li-'l-rizq yukallifūna nisāʾahum wa ṣibyānahum al-taḥarruf wa al-takassub*). Al-Bakrī wrote his description of the Maghrib in the mid-eleventh century, in the Almoravid period.

> Lamtūna and Masūfa had her scoundrel, villain and robber as well as wine seller and brothel owner. In this situation, the negligence of the *amīr al-muslimīn* [the title of the Almoravid ruler] increased, his weakness grew, he was satisfied with the title of ruler and with the taxes paid to him ... He completely neglected the affairs of the subjects ... (*wa 'stawlā* [sic] *al-nisā' 'alā al-aḥwāl wa usnidat ilayhinna al-umūr wa ṣārat kullu 'mra'a min akābir Lamtūna wa Masūfa mushtamila 'alā kulli mufsid wa shirrīr wa qāṭi' sabīl wa ṣāḥib khamr wa mākhūr wa amīr al-muslimīn fī dhālika kullihi yatazāyad taghāfuluhu wa yaqwā ḍu'fuhu wa qani'a bi-'smi imrat al-muslimīn wa bi-mā yurfa'u ilayhi min al-kharāj ... wa ahmala umūr al-ra'iyya ghāyat al-ihmāl*).[153]

The deviations of the Almoravids from true Islam as understood by Ibn Tūmart require that they be shunned, refused help and fought. It is not difficult for Ibn Tūmart to find appropriate verses and traditions to support this idea and adapt it to his own world view. The Prophet commanded Muslims to differentiate themselves from Jews, Christians, polytheists and Zoroastrians;[154] Ibn Tūmart adds anthropomorphists to the list of people to be shunned.

The conclusion from these harsh opinions on the Almoravids is the obligation to wage *jihād* against them. Ibn Tūmart starts the chapter on this by quoting Qur'ān 9:123: "O believers, fight the unbelievers who are near to you, and let them find in you a harshness ..."[155] It is noteworthy that he chose a verse directed at indeterminate unbelievers rather than verses enjoining *jihād* against Jews, Christians or polytheists (such as Qur'ān 9:5 or 9:29). This choice of verse is significant: it allows Ibn Tūmart to direct his *jihād* against Muslims whom he declared to be unbelievers rather than against adherents of religions other than Islam. Naturally enough, Ibn Tūmart uses numerous Qur'ānic verses and prophetic tradition (*ahādīth*) in order to convince his supporters of their obligation to wage *jihād* and promises them the rewards which await them in the hereafter. The verse which speaks about God who buys the lives and the property of the believers in exchange for Paradise, and the one which

153 Al-Marrākushī, *al-Mu'jib*, p. 154. This passage has already been noted by Dandash, *Aḍwā' jadīda*, p. 164.
154 For the classical material on this idea, see Kister, "Do not assimilate yourselves".
155 Ibn Tūmart, *A'azz mā yuṭlab*, p. 249.

promises eternal life for those who fall in battle, are the obvious proof texts for the idea of *jihād*. The *ḥadīth* in which the Prophet expresses his wish to fight, die in battle and be resurrected only in order to fight and die again and again figures prominently in Ibn Tūmart's epistle enjoining *jihād*.[156] Ibn Tūmart takes care to clarify that *jihād* against the Almoravids is a personal obligation and no believer has an excuse to abandon it (*fa-jihād al-kafara al-mulaththamīn qad ta'ayyana 'alā kulli man yu'min bi-'llāhi wa al-yawm al-ākhir lā 'udhra li-aḥadin fī tarkihi* ...).[157] The use of *ta'ayyana* here is significant: since Ibn Tūmart considers the Almoravids as destroying Islam in an Islamic area, the fight against them is in legal theory a personal obligation (*farḍ 'ayn*) rather than a communal one.[158]

VI NON-MUSLIMS IN IBN TŪMART'S THOUGHT

It is well known that the Almohads applied an intolerant policy towards Jews and Christians, abolishing their status as "protected communities" (*ahl al-dhimma*) whom Islamic law allowed to retain their religious beliefs if they abided by the relevant discriminatory rules included in it. These policies were initiated by the first successor of Ibn Tūmart, 'Abd al-Mu'min (r. 1130–1163).[159] We need to point out that Ibn Tūmart himself did not advise his followers in this direction. In his *A'azz mā yuṭlab*, he quotes the classical material about collecting the *jizya* from Jews, Christians, Zoroastrians and Berbers without any indication or hint that he intends to change anything in this approach. Even the reference to the Berbers did not elicit any remark on the part of Ibn Tūmart.[160] Payment of *jizya*

156 'Azzāwī, *Rasā'il Muwaḥḥidiyya*, vol. 1, pp. 45–46. See also Qur'ān 9:111 and 2:154. For the Prophet's desire for recurrent martyrdom, see Bukhārī, *Ṣaḥīḥ*, vol. 2, p. 201 (*Kitāb al-jihād* 7).

157 Ibn Tūmart, *A'azz mā yuṭlab*, p. 260; also in 'Azzāwī, *Rasā'il Muwaḥḥidiyya*, vol. 1, pp. 46 *infra* – 47.

158 For this distinction, see E. Tyan, "Djihād", *EI*², s.v.

159 For a survey of the Almohad persecution of the *dhimmīs*, see Hopkins, *Medieval Muslim Government in Barbary*, pp. 59–70 and the more recent and well researched article of Molénat, "Sur le rôle des Almohades dans la fin du Christianisme local au Maghreb et en al-Andalus". For a critical evaluation of this material, see Cherif, "Encore sur le statut des ḏimmī-s sous les Almohades".

160 Ibn Tūmart, *A'azz mā yuṭlab*, pp. 406–407. Cf. Cherif, "Encore sur le status des ḏimmī-s ...", pp. 65–66. On the tradition according to which 'Uthmān b. 'Affān took *jizya* from the Berbers, see Friedmann, *Tolerance and Coercion*, p. 84.

is of course the main symbol of *dhimma* status. It is also noteworthy that in his chapter on *jihād* he adduces passages about fighting against "innovators" (*ahl al-bidaʿ*), rebels (*man kharaja ʿalā jamāʿat al-nās*) and people who spread corruption on earth, but barely mentions the copious *ḥadīth* material about *jihād* against non-Muslims.[161] Jews and polytheists are mentioned only in a few passages quoted from the *ḥadīth*. Most of Ibn Tūmart's chapter on *jihād*, martyrdom (*shahāda*) and other issues related to *jihād* consists of quotations of relevant classical *ḥadīth*. There is no possibility to gauge Ibn Tūmart's interpretation of this material. The headlines which he (or ʿAbd al-Muʾmin) appends to the various passages give no clue to this. It seems that there are no additions or even emphases by Ibn Tūmart himself. Significantly enough, there are no quotations of the Qurʾānic verses – such as Qurʾān 9:5 or 9:29 – which command fighting against polytheists and "People of the Book". It seems clear that Ibn Tūmart's struggle is directed first and foremost against his Muslim opponents. To fight anthropomorphists is in his view a personal duty of every Muslim (*farḍ ʿalā al-aʿyān*) and is much more important than fighting the Christians.[162] The abolition of the *dhimma* and the subsequent persecution of the *dhimmīs* were the doing of Ibn Tūmart's successors and are therefore beyond the scope of this study.[163]

VII THE RECEPTION OF IBN TŪMART

It is now time to investigate the question how major Muslim thinkers perceived the thought and the activities of Ibn Tūmart. It seems that the first significant thinker who devoted substantial attention to him was Ibn

161 Ibn Tūmart, *Aʿazz mā yuṭlab*, pp. 420–421.

162 Al-Baydhaq, *Akhbār al-mahdī*, p. 9; Ibn Abī Zarʿ, *al-Anīs al-muṭrib* ..., p. 223. In classical law, *jihād* becomes a "personal duty" (*fard ʿayn*) when Muslims are under attack; otherwise it is a duty of the community (*farḍ kifāya*) in which only Muslims who are called upon by the ruler are obliged to participate.

163 See Molénat, "Sur le rôle des Almohades dans la fin du Christianisme ..." For a study which doubts the prevalent view of the Almohad treatment of the religious minorities, particularly Jews, see Cherif, "Encore sur le status des *ḏimmī*-s sous les Almohades". See also Fierro, "A Muslim land without Jews or Christians". Fierro (p. 243ff) gives five plausible – yet conjectural – reasons why a Muslim *mahdī* would want to abolish the *dhimma* pact and demand conversion of the *dhimmīs*. The first of her reasons are the apocalyptic traditions about the elimination of all religions except Islam by Jesus (in most traditions not by the *mahdī*) during his second coming; see Chapter 1, Section III.

Taymiyya (d. 1328) who discussed Ibn Tūmart both in his *Fatāwā* and in his *Minhāj al-sunna al-nabawiyya*. Ibn Taymiyya criticizes Ibn Tūmart on several counts. He accuses him of exploiting the ignorance of the Berbers and performing deceitful tricks in order to convince them to join his movement. He mentions the purge of dissidents,[164] calling it "the Day of Distinction on which he distinguished between the People of Paradise and the People of the Fire" (*yawm al-furqān farraqa fīhi bayna ahl al-janna wa ahl al-nār*) and made the blood of the latter licit. But the principal criticism directed by Ibn Taymiyya against Ibn Tūmart was doctrinal. He argues that the accusation of anthropomorphism levelled by Ibn Tūmart against his adversaries was false because they never asserted their support for this doctrine. He compares his doctrinal campaign against the Almoravids to the *miḥna* of the ʿAbbāsī caliph al-Maʾmūn against the opponents of the Muʿtazila. Ibn Tūmart should be denounced for calling his movement *muwaḥḥidūn*. All Muslims are *muwaḥḥidūn* and the *tawḥīd* of Ibn Tūmart is actually *taʿṭīl*, the denial of divine attributes which is the hallmark of the Muʿtazila. This is exactly what the Jahmiyya, the Muʿtazila and others say: "They call the denial of [divine] attributes *tawḥīd*" (*sammaw nafy al-ṣifāt tawḥīdan*).[165] Ibn Taymiyya also reproaches Ibn Tūmart for introducing his mention as "the infallible *imām* and the (well) known *mahdī*" into the Friday sermon. This resulted in the removal of the names of the four "righteous caliphs" therefrom, though they are undoubtedly more deserving to be mentioned there than Ibn Tūmart.[166] And, in general, he was not the *mahdī* whose coming the Prophet had predicted, he did not fill the earth with justice, and engaged in reprehensible matters though he also did good things (*fa-'ddaʿā annahu al-mahdī al mubashshar bihi wa lam yakun al-amr ka-dhālika wa lā malaʾa al-arḍ kullahā qisṭan wa lā ʿadlan bal dakhala fī umūr munkara wa faʿala umūran ḥasana*).[167] The "reprehensible matters" seem to be related to Ibn Tūmart's doctrine, while by "the good things" Ibn Taymiyya probably means his insistence on avoiding prohibited behaviour and assiduously performing the commandments. His disciple Ibn Qayyim al-Jawziyya (d. 1350) also does not mince words

164 See earlier, at notes 88–89 of this chapter.

165 Ibn Taymiyya, *Majmūʿ fatāwā*, vol. 11, pp. 477–479, 488. H. Laoust provided an annotated translation of this text in "Une *fetwā* d'Ibn Taymiyya sur Ibn Tūmart". See also Ibn Taymiyya, *Minhāj al-sunna al-nabawiyya*, vol. 3, pp. 296–297.

166 Ibn Taymiyya, *Minhāj al-sunna al-nabawiyya*, vol. 4, pp. 167–168.

167 Ibn Taymiyya, *Minhāj al-sunna al-nabawiyya*, vol. 4, pp. 98–99; vol. 8, pp. 258–259.

in his denunciation of Ibn Tūmart. He calls him a liar, a wrongdoer who took power on false pretensions, killed people, enslaved their progeny and "was worse for the Muslims than al-Ḥajjāj b. Yūsuf".[168]

Among the Maghribī historians, Ibn Tūmart encountered a mixed reception. *Akhbār al-mahdī* by al-Baydhaq, a contemporary and a close associate of the *mahdī*, is replete with laudatory material. Wherever he comes, he attracts students of Islam (*ṭalaba*) who flock to study with him. Al-Baydhaq describes him as someone who is assiduous in spreading his world view, is insistent on stopping practices which he considers reprehensible, is mostly successful in his endeavours and frequently succeeds in convincing local officials and *qāḍīs* that his demands are justified. He always has the upper hand in theological and legal debates.[169] Interpreters of dreams predict his greatness and foresee that he will establish a great empire.[170]

The *Naẓm al-jumān* by Ibn Qaṭṭān (d. mid-thirteenth century) belongs to the same laudatory genre. Maḥmūd ʿAlī Makkī, who wrote an extensive introduction to his edition of the book, calls it "a court history" (*tāʾrīkh balāṭī*) written by a historian who must have imbibed his father's enthusiasm for the Almohads since childhood.[171] Quoting classical *ḥadīth* – the connection of which to Ibn Tūmart is tenuous at best – together with some of Ibn Tūmart's exploits, he reaches the conclusion that Ibn Tūmart was indeed the *mahdī*.[172] He also includes in the book an epistle describing a visionary debate between "the evil-bidding soul" (*al-nafs al-ammāra bi-ʾl-sūʾ*) and "tranquil soul" (*al-nafs al-muṭmaʾinna*). These are concepts from Ṣūfī mystical psychology which deals with the various aspects of the human soul. In the debate the "tranquil soul", which represents the positive component in humans, convinces the "evil-bidding" one that Ibn Tūmart is indeed the *mahdī* and refutes all arguments to the contrary. Though the two protagonists in the debate are rooted in Islamic mysticism, the debate itself is totally removed from it: it discusses issues such as the compatibility of Ibn Tūmart's biography with

168 Ibn Qayyim al-Jawziyya, *al-Manār al-Munīf*, pp. 99–100.
169 See, e.g., al-Baydhaq, *Akhbār al-mahdī*, p. 51 where people in Constantine accept Ibn Tūmart's ruling on a legal issue. In Tilimsān, upon his instructions people construct a cistern near a mosque so that men do not perform their ablutions where women draw water. See al-Baydhaq, *Akhbār al-mahdī*, p. 61. See also ibid., p. 68.
170 Al-Baydhaq, *Akhbār al-mahdī*, p. 54.
171 Ibn al-Qaṭṭān, *Naẓm al-jumān*, pp. Rā-Sīn.
172 Ibn al-Qaṭṭān, *Naẓm al-jumān*, p. 49.

the classical *ḥadīth*, his administrative capabilities, the contradiction between his appearance in the Maghrib and the traditions which envisage the appearance of the *mahdī* in the East, and the compatibility of Ibn Tūmart's rule with the classical traditions according to which the *mahdī* will rule over Arabs.[173]

If we look at the assessment of Ibn Tūmart by Ibn Abī Zarʿ (died after 1326) who lived after the fall of the Almohad dynasty, we find it highly critical. He accuses Ibn Tūmart of using the ignorance of the Berbers who knew nothing about the world or about religion. He deceitfully enticed them and took hold of their minds by his eloquence and convinced them that he was the *mahdī*.[174] He had no compunction in shedding the blood of many in order to attain his goals. He was well versed in *ḥadīth* and principles of religion and cunningly prepared the way for his successor to establish a dynasty.[175]

The Andalusian Mālikī scholar al-Shāṭibī (d. 1388) belongs to the same trend of thought. In his *Kitāb al-Iʿtiṣām*, which is devoted to the denunciation of blameworthy innovations in religion (*bidaʿ*), al-Shāṭibī lists Ibn Tūmart's deviations from the prophetic *sunna*. Someone who claims for himself infallibility resembles him who claims prophethood, and if he claims that heaven and earth exist thanks to him, he exceeds even that claim.[176] He condemns Ibn Tūmart's baseless introduction of capital punishment for transgressions such as deception, disobedience of his orders, doubting his status as the *mahdī* or his *ʿiṣma*. All these rulings are based on his personal opinion (*raʾy*) though he claimed that he did not follow this method of deriving the law. This is a clear contradiction. Al-Shāṭibī concludes that Ibn Tūmart's claim to be the *mahdī* is false because the *mahdī* is Jesus.[177]

The mixed reception of Ibn Tūmart continued into the modern period. Several contemporary scholars provide very negative assessments. One

173 See Ibn al-Qaṭṭān, *Naẓm al-jumān*, pp. 50–67. According to Makkī (ibid., p. 50 note 1), the author of the epistle, Abū ʿAbd al-Raḥmān b. Ṭāhir, was a member of the ruling family of Murcia who died in 1178–1179. The author addressed the epistle to ʿAbd al-Muʾmin, Ibn Tūmart's first successor. For the two protagonists of the debate in Ṣūfī thought, see al-Sulamī, *ʿUyūb al-nafs wa mudāwātuhā*, pp. 70–72.

174 Ibn Abī Zar, *al-Anīs al-muṭrib bi-rawḍ al-qirṭās*, p. 227.

175 Ibn Abī Zar, *al-Anīs al-muṭrib bi-rawḍ al-qirṭās*, pp. 233–235.

176 Al-Shāṭibī, *Kitāb al-Iʿtiṣām*, vol. 2, p. 69.

177 Al-Shāṭibī, *Kitāb al-Iʿtiṣām*, vol. 2, pp. 64–65. On the identification of the *mahdī* with Jesus, see Chapter 1, Section II.

of them is the Moroccan historian ʿIṣmat ʿAbd al-Laṭīf Dandash. As a background for her view, she gives a glowing description of the Almoravid dynasty, even seeing it as a model of democracy.[178] Among their praiseworthy deeds, she mentions their successful *jihād* against polytheist Ghana and their endeavour to put an end to all anti-Sunnī sects in the Maghrib and give hegemony to the Mālikī school.[179] On the other hand, she accuses Ibn Tūmart of being a supporter, even a propagandist, of the Bāṭiniyya. His choice of Tīnmallal as his headquarters was in emulation of Alamūt: both places resemble each other in their inaccessibility.[180] She denies that his main objective was the cleansing of Maghribī Islam of beliefs and practices which contradict "pure" Islam according to his understanding. She systematically debunks essential components of Ibn Tūmart's Almohad hagiography, such as his defeat of the Marrākush *ʿulamāʾ* in debate, or his being persecuted because of "commanding right and forbidding wrong": the real reason for the persecution was his support of one Ismāʿīlī section against another.[181]

The Egyptian historian Ḥusayn Muʾnis (d. 1996) writes in a similarly critical vein. In his view, Ibn Tūmart put his scholarship in the service of his political aim of toppling the Almoravid dynasty. He posed as a religious reformer in order to attract attention and accused the Almoravids of things which were the norm in the whole Muslim world.[182] In order to achieve his aims, he interpreted Qurʾānic verses arbitrarily (*ʿalā hawāhu*) and spread mostly forged *aḥādīth*.[183] The theological accusations of anthropomorphism against the Almoravids are baseless: they were a fighting Sunnī group who were not discussing (theological matters), they did not write (theological treatises?) and their members did not have peculiar views on any of the basics of Islam (*kānū jamāʿatan sunniyya mujāhida taʿmal wa lā tatakallam aw taktub wa lam yakun li-afrādihā raʾy khāṣṣ fī ayyi rukn min arkān al-islām*).[184] And the *tamyīz* perpetrated by al-Bashīr on behalf of Ibn Tūmart was an atrocity.[185] Similar views are expressed by ʿAbd Allah Gannūn (Guennoun) (d. 1989) who asserts that Ibn Tūmart's

178 Dandash, *Aḍwāʾ jadīda*, p. 34.
179 Dandash, *Aḍwāʾ jadīda*, p. 13.
180 Dandash, *Aḍwāʾ jadīda*, pp. 26–27.
181 Dandash, *Aḍwāʾ jadīda*, p. 23.
182 Muʾnis, *Taʾrīkh al-Maghrib*, vol. 2, pp. 64–65.
183 Muʾnis, *Taʾrīkh al-Maghrib*, vol. 2, pp. 70–71.
184 Muʾnis, *Taʾrīkh al-Maghrib*, vol. 2, p. 66.
185 Muʾnis, *Taʾrīkh al-Maghrib*, vol. 2, p. 68.

claim to be the *mahdī* was not an integral part of his thought. He adopted it very late in his career and made it only to increase the numbers of his followers and to influence the minds of "the simpletons and the common people" (*li-takthīr al-atbāʿ wa al-anṣār wa al-taʾthīr ʿalā ʿuqūl al-sudhdhaj wa al-ʿawāmm*) after he decided to fight the Almoravids on the battlefield and establish a state of his own.[186]

Abd al-Majīd al-Najjār (1945–), a Tunisian scholar associated with the European Council for Fatwā and Research, promotes a rather positive view of Ibn Tūmart. He credits him with willingness not only to study what constitutes in his view "pure" Islam, but also to make a substantial contribution to put it into practice. He rejects the information about mass executions of dissidents (*tamyīz*) perpetrated by Ibn Tūmart, but admits that his life and the harsh treatment by the Almoravid amīr may have pushed him in the direction of violence which he used in his attempts "to command right and forbid wrong".[187] The main achievement of Ibn Tūmart in al-Najjār's view is the introduction of the Ashʿarī theology to the Maghrib; this undermined the anthropomorphistic views which had been prevalent in the region beforehand. Putting the "principles of religion" (*uṣūl al-dīn*) – Qurʾān, *ḥadīth* and well documented consensus (*ijmāʿ*) – at the centre stage of religion at the expense of knowledge based on speculation (*ilm zannī*), analogy (*qiyās*) and traditions transmitted by individual scholars (*akhbār al-āḥād*) is in al-Najjār's view also a major achievement. He credits Ibn Tūmart also with establishing "consultative government" (*niẓām shūrī*), though he criticizes the hereditary nature of succession in the Almohad dynasty after his death.[188] His polemics against the Almoravids are enhanced by comparing the lofty ideals of the Almohads to the concrete deeds of the Almoravids. This is a basic tool of many a polemicist.[189]

186 Kunūn, *ʿAqīdat al-Murshida*, pp. 105–106.
187 Al-Najjār, *Tajribat al-iṣlāḥ*, pp. 71–72.
188 Al-Najjār, *Tajribat al-iṣlāḥ*, pp. 99–100, 138.
189 Al-Najjār, *Tajribat al-iṣlāḥ*, pp. 102–103.

Excursus

The face covering of the Almoravids[1]

Since Ibn Tūmart presented the face covering (*lithām*) of the Almoravid males and the unveiling of their women as a major reason for his struggle against them, it is perhaps appropriate to add here a note about the traditions relating to the origins and the significance of this attire among them. Some of these traditions are mythical. In his *al-Ḥulal al-mawshiyya*, Ibn Simāk al-ʿĀmilī adduces a tradition about the origins of the *mulaththamūn*. After giving details about their tribal affiliation with the Lamtūna and the Ṣinhāja and their nomadic way of life in the desert, he states that "the Ṣinhāja relate themselves to the Ḥimyar and there is no relationship between them and the Berbers except the womb" (*wa Ṣinhāja yarfaʿūna nasabahum ilā Ḥimyar wa laysa baynahum wa bayna al-Barbar illā al-raḥim*). This means that genealogically they belong to Ḥimyar – this is to say the southern Arabs – and their relationship with the Berbers is based only on marrying local women after they arrived in the Berber region. Their migration to the Maghrib was caused by a change in the religious character of the government in their native Yemen. One of the kings was informed by a Jewish sage (*baʿḍ aḥbārihim*) about the revealed divine books and about "the seal of the prophets" (*khātam al-anbiyāʾ*) who is about to be sent by God. The king believed in this and promised to support this Prophet when he arrives.[2] However, when this king died,

1 I am indebted to my friends and colleagues Professor Yoram Bilu and Professor Frank Stewart of the Hebrew University for a very helpful discussion of this issue.

2 This is a common motif in the classical descriptions of the emergence of Islam: adherents of pre-Islamic religions are said to have predicted the coming of the Prophet and promised to support him if they are alive when he manifests himself. Students of early Islam will remember, for instance, the Christian *ḥanīf* Waraqa b. Nawfal who made a similar promise. See Bukhārī, *Ṣaḥīḥ*, vol. 1, pp. 5–6 (*Kitāb badʾ al-waḥy* 3).

his successors reneged on this promise, reverted to infidelity and started persecuting the previous king's followers. The latter "donned the veil like their women" (*talaththamū ka-fiʿli nisāʾihim*) and fled for their lives, wandering from country to country until they reached the Farthest Maghrib (*al-maghrib al-aqṣā*) and settled there.[3] According to another myth, the custom originated when the Lamtūna encampment was attacked while their warriors were out on a raid and the encampment was without a defending force. The elders instructed the women to don male attire, put on turbans and cover their faces with veils to create the illusion of a large fighting force. This stratagem resulted in the retreat and eventual defeat of the attackers. Since then, the male Almoravids followed the custom of covering their faces.[4]

These foundational myths of the Almoravids can explain their uncompromising attachment to their face covering, but it does not explain the unveiling of the Almoravid women which is presented as one of the main causes of strife with the Almohads. The eleventh-century geographer Abū ʿUbayd Allah al-Bakrī gives the following description of the Almoravid's attire:

> All the desert tribes don the *niqāb* which is worn above the *lithām*, so that only the sockets of the eyes are visible. They do not abandon this under any condition. None of them recognizes a relative or a friend unless he dons the *niqāb*. The same is true in battles: if one of them is killed and his face covering falls off, he is not recognized until the face covering is put back [on his face]. The face covering sticks to them more strongly than their skins. They call all people whose attire differs from theirs "mouths of flies" in their language (*wa jamīʿ qabāʾil al-ṣaḥrāʾ yaltazimūna al-niqāb wa huwa fawqa al-lithām ḥattā lā yabduwa illā maḥājir ʿaynayhi wa lā yufāriqūna dhālika fī ḥālin min al-aḥwāl wa lā yumayyizu al-rajul minhum waliyyahu wa lā ḥamīmahu illā idha tanaqqaba wa ka-dhālika fī al-maʿārik idh qutila minhum al-qatīl wa zāla qināʿuhu lam yuʿlam man huwa ḥattā ʿāda ʿalayhi al-qināʿ wa ṣāra dhālika lahum alzama min julūdihim wa hum yusammūna man khālafa ziyyahum hādhā min jamīʿ al-nās afwāh al-dhubbān fī lughatihim*).[5]

3 Al-ʿĀmilī, *al-Ḥulal al-mawshiyya*, pp. 62–63. This tradition has already been analysed by Bennison, *The Almoravid and Almohad Empires*, pp. 123–124.

4 Al-Nuwayrī, *Nihāyat al-arab*, vol. 24, pp. 263–264.

5 Al-Bakrī, *al-Masālik wa al-mamālik*, p. 294.

It is thus clear that medieval chroniclers tend to explain the veiling of Almoravid males by quasi-historical anecdotes. Only rarely one finds an explanation saying that "they use the veil because of the extreme heat and cold, like the desert Arabs" (*yatalaththamūn li-shiddat al-ḥarr wa al-bard ka-mā yafʿal al-arab fī al-barriyya*).[6] Modern ethnographers who described the face covering custom of the Berber tribes insist that the custom is not a hygienic device related to the harsh climatic conditions in the desert, but rather a status symbol. They substantiate this interpretation by the fact that slaves and women do not wear the veil and men put it on in a ceremony when they are around twenty-five years of age and have already girded the sword. It is a rite of passage from adolescence to manhood.[7] Also, they report that when a man has to lift the veil in order to eat, he holds his hand in front of his mouth so that no one can see it. This indicates that the mouth is considered a private or impure organ which must be concealed at all times.[8] According to some anecdotes, they considered covering the face more important than covering the pudenda.[9]

The interpretation of the veil as a status symbol of the Almoravid male which is denied to the Almoravid woman would be natural in a society in which males enjoy unquestionable superiority. However, our sources include a significant amount of material about the strong position of the Almoravid woman in society. Some of the Almohad writers even explained the disintegration of the Almoravid empire by the superior position of women in their society.[10] The interpretation of the veil as a status symbol should therefore be subjected to further scrutiny.

6 Al-Nuwayrī, *Nihāyat al-arab*, vol. 24, p. 263. See also al-Dimashqī, *Nukhbat al-dahr*, p. 352.

7 Keenan, "The Tuareg Veil", p. 4.

8 Rodd, *People of the Veil*, pp. 140, 286–290. There is a survey of the various interpretations of this custom in Maḥmūd, *Qiyām dawlat al-murābiṭīn*, pp. 49–51.

9 Nuwayrī, *Nihāyat al-arab*, vol. 24, p. 264.

10 See earlier, at note 152 of this chapter.

3

The Mahdawī movement in India

1 HAGIOGRAPHY AND HISTORY

The province of Gujarāt came under the rule of the Delhi Sultanate at the end of the thirteenth century. During the latter part of the fourteenth century, the grip of the Sultanate over its province weakened and a provincial governor was able to assert his independence. During most of the fifteenth century (1394–1495), Gujarāt was under the rule of the Sharqī dynasty, one of the so-called "succession states" of the Delhi Sultanate. Its capital Jawnpūr, which was founded in 1359, became a renowned centre of culture, the dynasty engaged in intense building activity and saw in the construction of mosques a symbol of political prestige. Ṣūfī orders such as the Chishtiyya had an established presence in it. Consequently, the town came to be known as the "Abode of Bliss" (*Jawnpūr dār al-surūr*).[1]

When a baby boy was born in Jawnpūr in October 1440 (14 Jumādā al-ūlā 847 AH), a voice from an invisible source (*hātif-i ghaybī*) exclaimed: "The truth has come, and falsehood has vanished away; surely falsehood is ever certain to vanish" (*jā'a al-ḥaqq wa zahaqa al-bāṭil inna al-bāṭila kāna zahūqan*).[2] In the city temples, the idols tumbled from their pedestals. The boy was born clean of all impurities and upon birth covered his pudenda with both hands. A seal of sainthood (*muhr-i wilāyat*) was seen on his back. The Prophet informed the father in a dream that he had bestowed

1 For an extensive discussion of the mosques and of other structures of Jawnpūr, see Ilāhābādī, Khayr al-Dīn Muḥammad, *Ta'rīkh-i Jawnpūr*. BL Ms. Or. 188; cf. Rieux, vol. 1, p. 311. See also "Sharḳīs", *EI*[2], s.v. (K. A. Nizami).

2 Qur'ān 17:81.

his own name on the boy who was hence named Muḥammad. He was also called Abū al-Qāsim, the Prophet's own epithet (*kunyā*). When Shaykh Dāniyāl, the head of the Chishtī Ṣūfīs in the city, was appraised of all this, he determined that the boy was the "promised mahdī" (*mahdī-yi maw'ūd*) because his birth was similar to that of the Prophet.

The name of Muḥammad Jawnpūrī's parents is a subject of controversy: in historical sources the names are given as Sayyid Khān (or Sayyid Buddh Uwaysī) and Bībī Āghā Malik, but the Mahdawīs assert that their names were 'Abd Allah and Bībī Āmina,[3] in order to make Jawnpūrī's name and pedigree compatible with the classical traditions concerning the name and pedigree of the *mahdī* expected at the end of days.[4] The question of Jawnpūrī's parents' name has been used in anti-Mahdawī polemics long after the *mahdī*'s death.[5] Though the Mahdawī movement can by no means be considered Shī'ī, Shī'ī imāms, such as 'Alī, al-Ḥusayn, Zayn al-'Ābidīn, Muḥammad Bāqir, Ja'far al-Ṣādiq and Mūsā al-Kāẓim appear in Jawnpūrī's traditional lineage and create a genealogical connection between him and the Prophet. The genealogical connection between Sunnī *mahdī*s and Shī'ī imāms is not peculiar to the Mahdawīs; other Sunnī *mahdī*s also claim such genealogy.[6]

A significant feature of Jawnpūrī's hagiography is his connection with al-Khiḍr. Al-Khiḍr was present when Jawnpūrī started his religious studies, at the *bismillāh* ceremony. He greeted him as the *imām* of latter days (*'alayka al-salām yā imām ākhir al-zamān*) and the caliph of God, gave him a date from which the Prophet had eaten in the past,[7] declared his belief in him and asked Dāniyāl to do likewise.

As for Jawnpūrī's own achievements, they were also remarkable. At the age of seven he committed the Qur'ān to memory; at the age of twelve he completed the entire *madrasa* curriculum and was publicly given the title

3 Badāyūnī, *Najāt al-Rashīd*, p. 77; Raḥmān 'Alī, *Tadhkira*, p. 198, ll. 5–7; Ansari, "Sayyid Muḥammad Jawnpūrī ...", pp. 44–45.

4 See Chapter 1, at note 102; Abū Dāwūd, *Sunan*, Cairo 1983, vol. 2, p. 460.

5 See Walī b. Yūsuf, *Inṣāf Nāma*, pp. 26–28, 37.

6 See, e.g., Chapter 2, at notes 6, 9.

7 See 'Alī, *Siyar-i Mas'ūd*, p. 14. This is a custom attested in the classical tradition as *taḥnīk*. The Prophet used to rub the palate of someone, usually a newborn child, with the pulp of a date which he had chewed, with salutary effect on the child's health and well-being. See Bukhārī, *Ṣaḥīḥ*, vol. 3, p. 41 (*Kitāb manāqib al-anṣār* 45) where the Prophet is described doing *taḥnīk* for 'Abd Allah b. al-Zubayr, "the first child born in Islam". See also Kister, "The Struggle Against Musaylima", p. 43.

of "the lion of scholars" (*asad al-ʿulamāʾ*).[8] Mahdawī hagiography thus attributes to him signs of future greatness from early childhood.

Little is known about Jawnpūrī's early years. We are told that he married his cousin Bībī Ilāhdētī in 866/1461–2, at the age of nineteen. One year after the marriage, the couple had a daughter; in 869/1464–5, they had a son named Sayyid Maḥmūd who was to become the *mahdī*'s successor, the "second *mahdī*" (*thānī mahdī*) in Mahdawī parlance. In 891/1486, a second son, Sayyid Ajmal, was born.[9]

Despite the principle of dissociation from the ruling circles which is strongly supported in the Mahdawī tradition, Mahdawī hagiography maintains that Jawnpūrī had connections with the Sultans. Ḥusayn b. Maḥmūd, the last ruler of the Sharqī dynasty of Jawnpūr (r. 1458–1500), is said to have been one of his followers. The hagiographers assert that Jawnpūrī encouraged Ḥusayn to wage war against a non-Muslim ruler of Bengal and even tipped the battle in favour of the Muslims, but some scholars question the historicity of this and maintain that this is only an attempt to embellish Jawnpūrī's biography with initiating *jihād* against a non-Muslim ruler.[10] We are also told that the Sultan provided Jawnpūrī with a *madad-i maʿāsh* of seven localities, but Jawnpūrī tore the document to shreds.[11] This anecdote is compatible with the Mahdawī principle of opposing connection with the rulers, let alone accepting gifts from them. "Flies in the privy are better than jurisprudents at the gate of Sultans," the Mahdawīs used to say.[12]

In 887/1482, when Jawnpūrī was forty years old – the age at which the Prophet Muḥammad was called to prophethood – he received a divine command to migrate from Jawnpūr and to summon people to God's way.[13] This was the first Mahdawī *hijra*, leaving one's place of residence; the obligation to do this eventually became one of the leading ideas of the Mahdawī movement. Jawnpūrī left the city accompanied

8 Sikandarābādī, *Sawāniḥ-i mahdī-yi mawʿūd*, p. 11; ʿAlī, *Siyar-i Masʿūd*, pp. 13–15.
9 ʿAlī, *Siyar-i Masʿūd*, pp. 15, 28.
10 ʿAlī, *Siyar-i Masʿūd*, pp. 15–17; Qamaruddin, pp. 33–34; Ansari, "Sayyid Muḥammad Jawnpūrī ...", pp. 45, 47.
11 ʿAlī, *Siyar-i Masʿūd*, pp. 17–18.
12 Gujarātī, *Majālis*, p. 48. Criticism of *ʿulamāʾ* who frequent the residences of Sultans can be found in classical *ḥadīth* (see, e.g., Ibn Ḥanbal, *Musnad*, vol. 1, p. 357 and elsewhere), but I was not able to find the peculiar formulation mentioned previously in *ḥadīth* collections, though Gujarātī explicitly attributes this saying to the Prophet. Were people in the ninth/fifteenth century still inventing *aḥādīth*?
13 ʿAlī, *Siyar-i Masʿūd*, p. 19.

by seventeen followers and visited several places in Gujarāt. Mahdawī hagiography maintains that he stayed in each place for a considerable period of time and preached to large crowds. His preaching was highly effective and his listeners were mesmerized; some completely changed their way of life ("left this world" in Mahdawī parlance), became ascetics and joined Jawnpūrī. The stay in Chāpānēr is particularly significant for the Mahdawīs: it was there that Jawnpūrī's preaching came to the attention of Sulṭān Maḥmūd Bēgaṙhā, though he was prevented from meeting him by the court *ʿulamāʾ*. They opined that if the Sultan meets Jawnpūrī, he will be influenced by him, leave his kingdom and become a *faqīr*. Since Gujarāt is full of polytheists and rebels, such an abdication would be detrimental to Islam.[14]

While in Chāpānēr, Jawnpūrī suffered a personal loss: in 891/1486 his wife died at the age of thirty-six. Slightly later, in Manḋū, his younger son, Sayyid Ajmal, suffered the same fate as a result of a domestic accident.[15] At Paṫn Nahrwālā, Jawnpūrī married his second wife Bībī Malkān, and his son and successor Sayyid Maḥmūd married for the first time.[16]

In 901/1495 Jawnpūrī boarded a boat in Dabhul on his way to perform the pilgrimage to Mecca. By that time, the number of his followers reached three hundred and sixty. In accordance with the principle of absolute reliance on God (*tawakkul*), he instructed his followers not to take with them any provisions and leave even the water bags empty. The hagiographical tradition maintains that the ship owners provided food and drink for a few days. When provisions ran out, the passengers went without food for a few days. Then a ship was seen from the distance and quickly drew near to Jawnpūrī's boat. Some people boarded the boat and asked whether there are some "reliers" on the ship (*is jihāz mēñ koʾī mutawakkil lōg hayñ?*). Everybody pointed to Jawnpūrī and his associates. Those who boarded Jawnpūrī's boat said that whatever is on their ship was sent by God for Jawnpūrī. They unloaded their cargo of food and drink and went on their way. Nobody knew their identity. Jawnpūrī accepted the gift, saying that it was "absolutely permissible" (*ḥalāl-i ṭayyib*).[17]

14 See *EI²*, s.v. (Mohhibbul Hasan); ʿAlī, *Siyar-i Masʿūd*, p. 26; Sikandarābādī, *Sawāniḥ-i mahdī-yi mawʿūd*, p. 22.
15 ʿAlī, *Siyar-i Masʿūd*, pp. 28–29.
16 ʿAlī, *Siyar-i Masʿūd*, pp. 62–63.
17 ʿAlī, *Siyar-i Masʿūd*, p. 38. For the Mahdawī concept of "permissible" gifts, see later, at notes 162–166.

After the boat anchored in Jedda, Jawnpūrī and his associates went to Mecca. One day, during circumambulation of the Kaʿba, Jawnpūrī abruptly exclaimed between the Kaʿba corner (*rukn*) and the place (*maqām*) (of Ibrāhīm) that he was the *mahdī* and said that whoever follows him is a believer. This happened in 901/1495. Three persons, one of whom is said to have been al-Khiḍr disguised as a Bedouin, immediately pledged allegiance to him.[18] Following his declaration, Jawnpūrī intervened in the resolution of a legal question. During prayer time, a Ḥanafī group pronounced the *basmala* and the *āmīn* silently, while a Shāfiʿī group did the same in a loud voice. God brought forth the spirits of Abū Ḥanīfa and of al-Shāfiʿī; both presented their arguments and suggested they invoke the spirit of the Prophet in order to make a decision. Before this could be done, Jawnpūrī declared both to be right.[19] This hagiographic description adumbrates the disregard of differences between the legal schools (*madhāhib*) in Mahdawī thought.[20] Such disregard is characteristic of other messianic movements as well.[21]

When Jawnpūrī made preparations to go to Medina (apparently to visit the Prophet's tomb), the Prophet's spirit appeared to him, told him that he will be always with him, that there is therefore no necessity to go to Medina and that he should go back to Gujarāt to start his mission (*daʿwa*). Non-Mahdawī sources see his departure in a different light and say that he was ordered to leave Mecca because of his claim to be the *mahdī*.[22] Thus, after a sojourn of several months in Mecca, Jawnpūrī set out for his return journey to India. Mahdawī hagiography speaks about several miracles performed by him during the voyage from Jedda to Gujarāt.[23]

Settling in the city of Aḥmadābād, Jawnpūrī made his residence in one of the city mosques. Commenting on the splendour and prosperity of the city, he remarked that "this town is the donkey's paradise; it is the paradise of the world-seekers, situated in a tavern" (*yih shahr jannat al-ḥimār hay. yaʿnī ṭalibān-i dunyā kī jannat hay jō kada mēñ hay*).[24] This observation is well in line with the classical ascetic idea according to

18 ʿAlī, *Siyar-i Masʿūd*, p. 40; Walī b. Yūsuf, *Inṣāf Nāma*, pp. 25–26.
19 ʿAlī, *Siyar-i Masʿūd*, p. 40 *infra*; cf. Sikandarābādī, *Sawāniḥ-i mahdī-yi mawʿūd*, p. 34; Raḥmān ʿAlī, *Tadhkira*, p. 200.
20 Cf. ʿAlī, *Siyar-i Masʿūd*, pp. 72 *infra* – 73.
21 See Chapter 4, at notes 148–150.
22 Badāyūnī, *Najāt al-Rashīd*, p. 79; Qamaruddin, *The Mahdawī movement*, p. 36.
23 ʿAlī, *Siyar-i Masʿūd*, pp. 41–42; Sikandarābādī, *Sawāniḥ-i mahdī-yi mawʿūd*, p. 35.
24 ʿAlī, *Siyar-i Masʿūd*, p. 44 *infra*.

which this world is prison for the believer and paradise for the infidel.[25] In 903/1497, sometime after reaching Aḥmadābād, Jawnpūrī renewed his claim to be the *mahdī*. His sermons attracted large crowds. Non-Mahdawī sources describe him as a "man of ecstasy" (*dhū ḥāl*) who addressed the masses as if they were the elite, disregarding the principle that people should be addressed according to their ability to undertstand.[26] Mahdawī hagiography, on the other hand, concentrates on the extreme effectiveness of his preaching. Soldiers and their commanders inclined towards him.[27] Whoever listened to him abandoned this world and became an ascetic. This is why the wazīrs of Sultan Maḥmūd tried to prevent the Sultan from going to see Jawnpūrī: they feared that Jawnpūrī's words would "remove the Sulṭān from his place" and affairs of state would be neglected.[28] In Mahdawī hagiography, the event is seen in a different light: the high officials of the kingdom supported Jawnpūrī, but the *ʿulamāʾ* feared the loss of their worldly power, lodged a complaint against Jawnpūrī with the Sultan and obtained from the Sultan an order to expel the *mahdī* from Aḥmadābād. Jawnpūrī protested his innocence and declared that all his preaching conformed to Muslim law.[29]

One day Jawnpūrī promised the people that he could enable them to see God with their own eyes. This prompted some *ʿulamāʾ* to demand his execution. Eventually he left Aḥmadābād for a village called Baŕhlī, near Nahrwālā Patan. There he renewed his claim of being the *mahdī*. According to Mahdawī hagiography, this was done on express divine orders, and the wording was more expansive than the Mecca declaration:

> I am the promised *mahdī* and the seal of Muḥammadan sainthood. I am the caliph of God and the follower of the Prophet. Whoever obeys me is a believer, and whoever rejects me is an infidel.[30]

Many people accepted his claim and pledged their allegiance. Following this new assertion of his claim to be the *mahdī*, Jawnpūrī made visits to

25 See Ibn Māja, *Sunan*, vol. 2, p. 1378 (*Kitāb al-zuhd, bāb* 3).
26 Makkī, *Ẓafar al-wālih*, p. 35; Sikandar b. Muḥammad, *Mirʾāt-i Sikandarī*, p. 137.
27 ʿAlī, *Siyar-i Masʿūd*, pp. 44–45, 51.
28 Sikandar b. Muslim, *Mirʾāt-i Sikandarī*, p. 137; cf. Raḥmān ʿAlī, *Tadhkira*, p. 199 *infra*.
29 ʿAlī, *Siyar-i Masʿūd*, pp. 51–52.
30 ʿAlī, *Siyar-i Masʿūd*, p. 65 *infra*. In Nuṣrat's *Kuḥl al-jawāhir*, fol. 16a, l. 6, this became the third principle of the Mahdawī creed.

numerous places in India. According to the hagiographic tradition, these visits resulted in substantial increases in the numbers of the Mahdawīs. Jawnpūrī eventually left India, and set out for Afghanistan. In Qandahār, he initially received rough treatment, but after explaining a few verses from the Qur'ān, the governor apologized to him and honoured him.[31] Jawnpūrī's stay at Farah is described in a similar manner. Initially he was treated with hostility; his claim to be a *mahdī* was then thoroughly investigated and, naturally enough, found to be true. Jawnpūrī died in Farah in 910/1505. The Mahdawīs maintain that he died a natural death, while others describe his death as murder.[32]

Jawnpūrī was succeeded by his son Sayyid Maḥmūd, who came to be known in Mahdawī circles as "the second *mahdī*" (*thānī mahdī*). He stayed in Farah for one year after his father's death. Returning to Gujarāt, he engaged in propagating the Mahdawī doctrines and establishing Mahdawī institutions, which came to be known as *dā'iras*. His activities were strenuously opposed by the *'ulamā'* of Gujarāt, at whose insistence he was imprisoned. He died in prison in 919/1513. The persecution of the Mahdawīs continued under Sayyid Khwāndmīr (1481–2/1524), Jawnpūrī's second successor and son-in-law who was killed in a battle against the armies of Sultan Muẓaffar II of Gujarāt. Nevertheless, it appears that the number of Mahdawīs increased during his time. Shāh Ni'mat, Shāh Niẓām and Shāh Dilāwar were the third, fourth and fifth successors. After the death of the latter in 944/1537, there seems to be no record of further successors.[33] Nevertheless, some people continued to consider themselves as Mahdawīs and were even willing to suffer for their beliefs. Celebrated cases were those of 'Abd Allāh Niyāzī who was severely flogged in 955/1548 9 for refusing to abjure his belief in Jawnpūrī, and Shaykh 'Alā'ī who was put to death for the same reason in 957/1550.[34] About the same time, 'Alī b. Ḥusām, known as al-Muttaqī al-Hindī (d. 1567) and famous as the author of *Kanz al-'ummāl*, included in his *al-Burhān fī 'alāmāt mahdī ākhir al-zamān* fatwās issued by the *muftī*s of the four schools of law in Mecca, denouncing the Mahdawīs and their leader and declaring them

31 'Alī, *Siyar-i Mas'ūd*, pp. 102–103.

32 Makkī, *Ẓafar al-wālih*, p. 36; Sikandar b. Muḥammad, *Mir'āti-Sikandarī*, pp. 137–138; 'Alī, *Siyar-i Mas'ūd*, pp. 104ff; Raḥmān 'Alī, *Tadhkira*, p. 201.

33 Ansari, "Sayyid Muḥammad Jawnpūrī ...", pp. 63–65; Qamaruddin, *The Mahdawī Movement ...*, pp. 106–116.

34 Qamaruddin, *The Mahdawī Movement ...*, pp. 134, 138.

apostates because of their beliefs.[35] All this must have caused a serious setback for the Mahdawīs, but the movement continued to exist. There are reports about Mahdawī risings in the Deccan 1821–1822, and about clashes between Mahdawīs and non-Mahdawīs because of doctrinal differences in the same period.[36] In 1876 an anti-Mahdawī author was murdered in Ḥaydarābād (Deccan), apparently for writing a refutation of the Mahdawī doctrines.[37]

The literature of the Mahdawī movement, as well as the polemical treatises against it, are enormous in size and run to thousands of pages.[38] Only a part of both was used for the preparation of this chapter. It seems that the *mahdī* himself did not write a book, but in the century following his death we have major works which are essential for the elucidation of Mahdawī beliefs, their relationship with mainstream Islam, their conception of the *mahdī* and their place in the history of Muslim thought in general. Two of these works were written soon after the *mahdī*'s death and contain numerous traditions attributed to him. The first, entitled *Inṣāf Nāma,* is by Walī b. Yūsuf who reports in the beginning of the book that he spent a year with Sayyid Maḥmūd, the *mahdī*'s son and first successor; later he kept company for ten years with Sayyid Khwāndmīr (1481–1524), the *mahdī*'s second successor. He kept a record of their sayings and recorded also numerous utterances of the *mahdī* which he heard from them. All this material is preserved in the *Inṣāf Nāma.*[39] Slightly later is the *Majālis,* written by Shaykh Muṣṭafā Gujarātī (d. 1577),[40] which describes a religious disputation between the Mahdawī author and some mainstream *ʿulamāʾ* at Akbar's court; the same author's *Jawāhir al-taṣdīq* was written in order to prove that Jawnpūrī was a *mahdī.*[41] All three works are written from a Mahdawī perspective and enable us to study the main elements of Mahdawī beliefs in the century that followed Jawnpūrī's death.[42] Another major Mahdawī work was written in the nineteenth

35 Al-Muttaqī al-Hindī, *al-Burhān,* vol. 2, pp. 865–877.
36 See Storey, *Persian Literature,* p. 759 (11); Shurreef, *Qanoon-e-Islam,* pp. 259–260.
37 Storey, *Persian Literature,* vol. 1, part 2, p. 1155 (no. 1619).
38 For an extensive bibliography, see Qamaruddin, *The Mahdawī Movement,* pp. 239–247.
39 Walī b. Yūsuf, *Inṣāf Nāma,* p. 3.
40 See Qamaruddin, *The Mahdawi Movement,* p. 148.
41 Gujarātī, *Jawāhir al-taṣdīq,* p. 1.
42 Mahdawī works are not easy to obtain. Even the British Library, which probably has the best collection of material concerning Indian Islam, lacks numerous titles mentioned in Mahdawī literature. The reason seems to be the inward-looking nature

century by Sayyid Nuṣrat Mahdawī (1841–1911) under the title *Kuḥl al-jawāhir li-arbāb al-baṣā'ir*.[43]

II THE NATURE OF JAWNPŪRĪ'S RELIGIOUS CLAIM

When Jawnpūrī made his declaration in 901/495, he only said that he was the *mahdī* and that whoever believed in him was a believer.[44] This became the basis for the Mahdawīs' repudiation of all those who rejected their leader. At this point, Jawnpūrī did not provide any further explanation of his objectives. His followers, however, were constantly asked about the significance of his mission and how it fitted into the classical traditions about the *mahdī*. Among the most frequently asked questions was whether the appearance of Jawnpūrī precluded the coming of the *mahdī* at the end of days. Jawnpūrī himself – at least in one utterance ascribed to him – envisaged the appearance of *mahdī*s after him (*pas az man tā qiyāmat mahdī shawand*), in the same way as saintly people (*awliyā'*), such as Bāyazīd Bisṭāmī, Ibrāhīm-i Adham, Shiblī and Junayd appeared after Muḥammad. This is another case in which the *mahdī* creates an affinity between himself and the Prophet. The comparison between those who will follow the *mahdī* and those who followed the Prophet is not complete; while the mystical self-awareness of the four saintly figures just mentioned (and especially that of al-Bisṭāmī) was hardly modest, they are not considered *mahdī*s. As for those who will come after the *mahdī*, they are Sayyid Maḥmūd, Sayyid Khwāndmīr and all the close associates (*muhājirān*) of the *mahdī*.[45] Of these, Sayyid Maḥmūd was considered a "second *mahdī*"; and the general statement of Jawnpūrī quoted earlier indicates that he did not completely exclude the possibility of another *mahdī* appearing after him. At least, he did not deem it necessary to deny such a possibility categorically. Later Mahdawīs held much more decisive views on this issue, which comes up

of the movement and its desire to keep some of its ideas hidden from outsiders.

43 British Library MS. Or. 6653, 337 folios, incomplete at the end. It was written in response to the anti-Mahdawī *Hadiyya Mahdawiyya* by Abū Rajā Muḥammad Zamān Khān (d. 1876). I am indebted to the late Mr Qāḍī Maḥmūd al-Ḥaqq of the British Library who drew my attention to this as yet uncatalogued manuscript. Only a small part of it has been used in the preparation of the present work.

44 'Alī, *Siyar-i Mas'ūd*, p. 40; Raḥmān 'Alī, *Tadhkira*, p. 200, ll. 2–3; Walī b. Yūsuf, *Inṣāf Nāma*, pp. 25–26.

45 Walī b. Yūsuf, *Inṣāf Nāma*, pp. 395–396.

a few times in the *Kitāb al-majālis*. When Gujarātī asserts that the perfect qualities of Jawnpūrī make it clear that he was the *mahdī*, Emperor Akbar asks what will happen if another person with the same qualities appears in the future: will he be recognized as the *mahdī*? Gujarātī responds that this will never happen. Nevertheless, should it happen, the treatment should be the same as would be awarded to a prophetic claimant. This clearly means that any messianic pretender in the future must be summarily rejected. In a striking comparison with the Prophet, Gujarātī says: "The seal of the prophets and the seal of the saints – both came and departed" (*khātam-i anbiyā' ham āmad o gudhasht wa khātam-i awliyā' ham āmad o gudhasht*). This statement is part of the constant tendency of the Mahdawīs to create an affinity between Jawnpūrī and the Prophet and to undermine the idea that another *mahdī* may appear in the future.[46] On other occasions, Gujarātī gave the same response.[47] The formula saying that "the promised *mahdī* has come and departed" (*mahdī-yi maw'ūd āmad o gudhasht*) became the classic formulation of the Mahdawī attitude and is also the reason why the Mahdawīs are sometimes designated as *ghayr mahdī*, people who do not believe in a *mahdī* expected to appear at the end of days. It is probably the clearest formulation of the disengagement of the Sunnī idea of the *mahdī* from its eschatological roots[48] and also the main reason for the hostile relationship between the Mahdawīs and mainstream Islam. We can see from a description of the Mahdawīs in the early nineteenth century that the statement about the *mahdī*'s coming and departure became a credal statement, sort of a *shibboleth*, for the Mahdawīs.[49]

The explicit disengagement of the *mahdī* idea from the eschaton was one of the serious bones of contention between the Mahdawīs and their rivals, and placed them in a disadvantageous position in their polemical encounters with representatives of mainstream Islam. As seen in Chapter 1, the classical *mahdī* is part of an eschatological drama well attested in the prophetic tradition, even if details differ between the various versions. A person claiming to be the *mahdī* is therefore immediately exposed to

46 Gujarātī, *Majālis*, pp. 26–27.

47 Gujarātī, *Majālis*, pp. 3, 7, 43, 49.

48 See "Ghair Mahdī", in *Encyclopaedia of Religion and Ethics*, s.v. (I. Goldziher). It is, however, noteworthy that later Mahdawīs seem to have developed a more catholic attitude, and were willing to say that the views of the Sunnīs and the Shī'īs were also correct and belief in a "*mahdī* about to come" (*āyanda mahdī*) is also obligatory and his denial is infidelity. See Nuṣrat, *Kuḥl al-jawāhir*, fol. 16a, ll. 6–9.

49 Shurreef, *Qanoon-e-Islam*, pp. 259–260.

questions concerning the compatibility of his claim and achievements with the classical tradition. In Jawnpūrī's case, this issue was prominent in the disputations between the Mahdawīs and their opponents, and on some occasions caused clashes between the Mahdawīs and other Muslims. Anti-Mahdawī *fatwās* were issued and some Mahdawīs were put to death because of their belief that the *mahdī* had come and departed.[50]

It was clear that the classical tradition did not provide for a *mahdī* who was born in Jawnpūr, received his calling in Gujarāt and died in Afghanistan.[51] Furthermore, the Mahdawīs could not point to any wondrous natural phenomena (*ashrāṭ al-sā'a*) expected to herald the coming of the *mahdī* according to the relevant traditions. Contrary to the classical *ḥadīth* which indicates that the *mahdī*'s father will be called 'Abd Allāh, Jawnpūrī's father was Sayyid Khān and it took some effort on the part of the Mahdawīs to spread the idea that his original name was, indeed, 'Abd Allāh, while Sayyid Khān was his epithet or title (*'urf, khiṭāb*). This was not easy, and in some disputations concerning this Jawnpūrī was compelled, in desperation, to suggest that his opponents ask God why He appointed the son of Sayyid Khān as *mahdī*. He also pointed out that the father of the Prophet was a polytheist, so how was he called 'Abd Allāh?[52] The real Servant of God (*'Abd Allāh*) is the Prophet and the same is true for the *mahdī*.[53] It was also not easy to discern any compatibility between the classical idea according to which the *mahdī* "will fill the earth with equity and justice, even as it had been replete with wrong and iniquity"[54] and Sayyid Muḥammad Jawnpūrī's meagre achievements. On the contrary, the Mahdawīs suffered one defeat after another, were expelled from city after city and their opponents could easily claim that divine support for the Mahdawī movement was sadly lacking.

The Mahdawīs responded to these challenges in various ways. Since the very idea of the *mahdī* originated in the *ḥadīth* literature, they found fault with the relevant traditions, arguing that some are unreliable while others contradict each other. Some traditions say that the *mahdī* and Jesus will

50 Gujarātī, *Majālis*, pp. 7, 19.
51 Gujarātī, *Majālis*, pp. 3–4.
52 Since Allah was an important – though not the sole – deity in the Jāhiliyya, this is not a difficult question to answer.
53 'Alī, *Siyar-i Mas'ūd*, pp. 6, 69; Walī b. Yūsuf, *Inṣāf Nāma*, p. 26; Badāyūnī, *Najāt al-Rashīd*, p. 77; Raḥmān 'Alī, *Tadhkira*, p. 198, ll. 5–7; Ansari, "Sayyid Muḥammad Jawnpūrī ...", pp. 44–45.
54 See Chapter 1, Section IV.

meet, while others indicate that they will come at different times. Some say that the "false messiah" (*dajjāl*) will be coterminous with the *mahdī*, while others assert that he will come after the *mahdī*'s departure. Similarly, there are disparate opinions about the *mahdī*'s birth, his sending and his burial; therefore the *ʿulamāʾ* agreed only that the *mahdī* will be "a just *imām* from the descendants of Fāṭima ... whom Allah will create whenever He wants and will send him to support His religion" (*imām ʿādil min wuld Fāṭima ... yakhluquhu Allāh matā shāʾa wa yabʿathuhu nuṣratan li-dīnihi*). In general, these traditions are unreliable. Those dealing with the signs (*ʿalāmāt*) of the *mahdī*'s coming are reported by single transmitters (*āḥād*); as such, they cannot be followed in matters of belief.[55] The Mahdawī attitude in this matter is understandable: since the classical traditions place the *mahdī* squarely in the eschatological realm, the Mahdawīs had to undermine them in order to bolster their own messianic claim.

Responding to mainstream Muslim attacks on account of their earthly failures, which were described as incompatible with the classical *mahdī*'s status as an *imām* and with the prophetic dictum according to which "truth prevails" (*al-ḥaqq yaʿlū*), the Mahdawīs argued that even prophets were commonly rejected by their communities and, therefore, military or political failure cannot be construed as a reason to invalidate Jawnpūrī's claim. As an example of a religious leader's failure, they mention Shuʿayb, the prophet of Midyan, whose two daughters were his only supporters; nevertheless, Qurʾān 7:85 mentions the "reform" (*iṣlāḥ*) of Shuʿayb.[56] Even more significant is the case of Noah. He lived for hundreds of years, spread the message constantly, but only a very small number of people (various traditions speak of eighty, forty or seven) believed in him. Earthly victories are not a condition of being a prophet or a *mahdī*. It is in this sense that the endeavour of Jawnpūrī can be considered successful.[57] The classical statement that the *mahdī* will fill the earth with justice is to be understood only in the sense of spreading justice among his followers. Similarly, obedience of the people is not a condition for being an *imām*: obedience is the people's obligation, but if they rebel – this does not impugn the status of

55 Gujarātī, *Majālis*, pp. 9–10.

56 "Do not spread corruption in the land after it has been set right" (*wa lā tufsidū fī al-arḍ baʿda iṣlāḥihā*). Ṭabarī (*Tafsīr*, vol. 8, p. 238) attributes this "setting right", or "reform" to Shuʿayb.

57 Gujarātī, *Majālis*, pp. 11–14, 20–21, 30–34, 36–39; Gujarātī, *Jawāhir al-taṣdīq*, pp. 33–35.

the *imām*. The Prophet himself did not command obedience in the early (Meccan?) period of Islam, the infidels rebelled against him, but this did not annul his status as a prophet and a messenger. He was sent as "mercy to the worlds" (*wa mā arsalnāka illā raḥmatan li-'l- ʿālamīn*, Qurʾān 21:107), but most people initially did not take advantage of this prophetic mercy. He said that if humanity rejects him, he will address the Arabs; if the Arabs do not accept him, he will try Quraysh; if they refuse, he will address the Banū Hāshim; and if the Banū Hāshim refuse, he will remain alone. Even in this situation his prophetic status will not be diminished: the only task of a prophet is to deliver the message.[58] The *mahdī*'s case is similar.[59]

III SAYYID MUḤAMMAD JAWNPŪRĪ AND THE PROPHET

The hagiographical traditions which we surveyed at the beginning of this chapter clearly attempt to create a close affinity between Jawnpūrī and the Prophet. We are told that Jawnpūrī, the Prophet and Abraham were once seen together and no one could distinguish between them.[60] The statement that Jawnpūrī was born clean of all impurities probably means that he was born circumcised; this is another way to indicate the similarity between Jawnpūrī and the Prophet who is also said to have been born circumcised and no one was allowed to see his pudenda at birth.[61] The Prophet and the *mahdī* are placed together in a paraphrase on a Qurʾānic verse which reads: "If the Prophet and the *mahdī*, peace be upon them, willed, whoever is in the earth would have believed, all of them, all together, without any doubt" (*wa law shāʾa al-nabī wa al-mahdī ʿalayhimā al-salām an yuʾmina man fī al-arḍ kulluhum jamīʿan la-āmana kulluhum wa lā rayba fīhā*).[62] The Qurʾānic verse reads: "And if your Lord had willed, whoever is in the earth would have believed, all of them, all together."[63] To transfer Allah's abilities to the Prophet and the *mahdī* is an extremely audacious step in the Islamic tradition. Yet the most striking step in the same direction is to say "... and we shall pray for the two Muḥammads, the two seals, may Allah

58 Cf. Qurʾān 5:102.
59 Gujarātī, *Jawāhir al-taṣdīq*, pp. 41, 69, 71–72.
60 Sikandarābādī, *Sawāniḥ-i mahdī-yi mawʿūd* p. 10.
61 Kister, "... 'And he was born circumcised' ...", p. 12.
62 Gujarātī, *Jawāhir al-ṣidq*, p. 68.
63 Qurʾān 10:99.

bless both of them and their families ..." (*wa nuṣallī ʿalā muḥammadayn al-khātamayn ṣallā Allāhu ʿalayhimā wa ālihimā*),[64] or to speak about "explaining the Qur'ān by the tongues of the two Muḥammads, the Prophet and the *mahdī*, may God bless both of them and grant them peace (*bayān al-Qur'ān bi-lisān al-Muḥammadayn fa-humā al-nabī wa al-mahdī ṣallā Allah ʿalayhimā wa sallam*).[65] Using the formula *ṣallā Allāh ʿalayhi wa sallam* for anyone else than the Prophet barely exists in the Muslim tradition, and this rather standard Mahdawī usage is a clear indication of the distance the Mahdawīs are willing to go in order to raise the standing of their leader and make his rank as close as possible to that of the Prophet.[66]

Sayyid Muḥammad Jawnpūrī based his messianic claim on divine appointment. God informed him that he was the *mahdī* of latter days (*mahdī ākhir al-zamān*) and the inheritor of the Prophet (*wārith nabī al-Raḥmān*).[67] The Mahdawīs have made systematic efforts to attribute to their leader similarities with the Prophet. Bazmee Anṣārī quotes Jawnpūrī's statement that he is "synonymous with Muḥammad ibn ʿAbd Allah, the Messenger of God".[68] In the view of his followers, Jawnpūrī called to God in exactly the same way as the Prophet did. He made his claim to be the *mahdī* because his essence became identical with the Muslim declaration of faith (*lā ilāha illā 'llāhu*); this is explained as a reflection of his perfect following of the Prophet. The Mahdawīs quote a prophetic *ḥadīth* according to which the *mahdī* "follows me and does not err" (*yaqfū atharī wa lā yukhṭi'*). Moreover, all his rulings are according to what he received from the angel on God's behalf; this is exactly the manner in which revelation was bestowed on the Prophet. Jawnpūrī's rulings therefore represent the

64 Sikandarābādī, *Sawāniḥ-i mahdī-yi mawʿūd*, p. 2. The "two seals" are the "seal of prophethood" (the Prophet Muḥammad), and the "seal of sainthood", an epithet bestowed by the Mahdawīs on Jawnpūrī. See later, at notes 81–86 of this chapter.

65 Walī b. Yūsuf, *Inṣāf nāma*, p. 309; Shāh Dilāwar, *Khaṣāʾiṣ*, pp. 9–10; Gujarātī, *Jawāhir al-taṣdīq*, p. 69 *supra*.

66 See also the following statement at the beginning of a nineteenth-century Mahdawī manuscript which reads: "Praise be to God who illuminated the day and night by the two moons; and blessing and peace upon the two seals who were sent for the guidance of men and *jinn* and upon their guiding families and their rightly guided companions" (*al-ḥamd li-'llāh alladhī nawwara al-malawayn bi-'l-qamarayn wa al-ṣalāt wa al-salām ʿalā ʿal-khātamayn alladhayn buʿithā li-'htidā' al-thaqalayn wa 'alā ālihimā al-hādīn wa aṣḥābihimā al-muhtadīn*). Nuṣrat, *Kuḥl al-jawāhir*, fol. 2a, ll. 1–2.

67 Walī b. Yūsuf, *Inṣāf Nāma*, pp. 25, 328.

68 Anṣārī, "Sayyid Muḥammad Jawnpūrī", p. 51. The quotation is from a Mahdawī source (*al-Qawl al-maḥmūd*) which was not available to me, and I do not know what original term Anṣārī translates as "synonymous".

true law of Muḥammad; Muḥammad would have ruled in the same way had he been alive in Jawnpūrī's days. The Prophet was infallible according to Qur'ān 53:3–4 (*wa mā yanṭiqu ʿan al-hawā, in huwa illā waḥyun yūḥā*) and Jawnpūrī, as his perfect follower, is also infallible.[69]

Both the *mahdī* himself and his followers insisted on the unequivocal recognition of his messianic status and considered all deniers as infidels. They also invested considerable effort in supporting Jawnpūrī's claim to messianic status by promoting the idea that the names of his parents were ʿAbd Allāh and Āmina, as required by the classical traditions. Nevertheless, the Mahdawī teachings have extremely little to do with the messianic idea in its classical form; the *mahdī* and his followers occasionally spoke about the end of times, but did not fill this concept with any specific meaning. Neither the *mahdī* nor his followers predicted the imminent enactment of the eschatological drama which plays such an important part in the relevant classical traditions. Their efforts went in other directions. The Mahdawīs did their utmost to invest their leader with a status superior to the pre-Islamic prophets, superior to the most illustrious figures of early Islam – such as Abū Bakr and ʿUmar – and equal with that of the Prophet Muḥammad or, at least, closely connected with him in the spiritual sense.[70] He is said to have been "a perfect follower" of the Prophet, but at the same time his equal in rank (*Sayyid Muḥammad Jawnpūrī agar chih tābiʿ-i tāmm hayñ Muḥammad kē, lēkin rutbe mēñ ān-ḥaẓrat kē barābar hayñ*).[71] Elsewhere we are told that "Muḥammad the messenger of Allah and, secondly, Muḥammad *mahdī* the desire of Allah" (*yakī Muḥammad rasūl Allāh thānī Muḥammad mahdī murād Allāh*) are the two (perfect) Muslims in the world.[72] In a similar vein, Walī b. Yūsuf speaks about explaining the Qur'ān by the "tongue of the two Muḥammads" meaning the Prophet and Sayyid Muḥammad Jawnpūrī (*bayān al-Qurʾān bi-lisān al-Muḥammadayn fa-humā al-nabī wa al-mahdī ṣallā Allāh ʿalayhimā wa sallam*). The striking usage of *ṣallā Allāh ʿalayhimā wa sallama* – an honorific formula normally used exclusively for the Prophet – for both the Prophet and for Jawnpūrī clearly indicates that the Mahdawīs' veneration for Sayyid Muḥammad Jawnpūrī was no less than their veneration for the Prophet himself.[73] In

69 Walī b. Yūsuf, *Inṣāf Nāma*, pp. 315–316; Shāh Dilāwar, *Khaṣāʾiṣ*, pp. 5–6.
70 Shāh Dilāwar, *Khaṣāʾiṣ*, p. 2.
71 Nuṣrat, *Kuḥl al-jawāhir*, fol. 17b, lines 7–8.
72 Walī b. Yūsuf, *Inṣāf Nāma*, p. 322.
73 Walī b. Yūsuf, *Inṣāf Nāma*, p. 309; Shāh Dilāwar, *Khaṣāʾiṣ*, p. 10. Cf. Shāh Qāsim,

one place the text may be interpreted as using this formula for Jawnpūrī alone.[74] Wherever the sainthood of the Prophet is sealed, the people who are responsible for that place are prophets (*qā'im-maqām-i ān-jā anbiyā' bāshand*).[75] Furthermore, the Prophet predicted the existence of people whose standing with God resembles his own; though they are neither prophets nor martyrs, both the prophets and the martyrs envy them because of their standing in God's eyes.[76] The essential parity between the Prophet and the *mahdī* is also reflected in the statement that the Prophet explained certain aspects of the Qur'ān while the *mahdī* explained the others. It is also significant to observe that Walī b. Yūsuf approvingly quotes a tradition according to which the *mahdī* will "destroy whatever was before him and launch Islam afresh (*yahdim mā qablahu kamā ṣana'a rasūl Allāh wa yasta'nif al-islām jadīdan*).[77] In emulation of a famous saying attributed to the Prophet, Jawnpūrī is reported to have said that if someone quotes a tradition from him, it should be compared with the Qur'ān: if it accords with it, it is genuinely his; if it does not accord, it did not originate with him.[78] It is hardly possible to imagine a clearer hint at Jawnpūrī's affinity and even equality with the Prophet. Furthermore, those who did not have the good fortune of being guided by the Prophet, will be guided by the *mahdī* at the end of days. This seems to indicate that the mission of the Prophet had remained in some sense unfinished and was completed by the *mahdī*. The divinely initiated transformation of Sayyid Muḥammad Jawnpūrī into an unlettered (*ummī*) man is another broad hint at his affinity with the Prophet whose illiteracy has become a Muslim article of faith.[79] Then there is also a spiritual pedigree starting with Adam and concluding with the *mahdī*:

> Adam the sincere friend (*ṣafī*) of God sowed the wheat, Noah the confidant (*najī*) of God watered the field, Abraham the friend

---

al-Ḥujja, p. 3, where the expression *ṣallā Allāhu 'alayhimā wa 'alā ālihimā* is used for the Prophet and for Jawnpūrī.

74 Walī b. Yūsuf, *Inṣāf Nāma*, p. 12 *infra*.

75 Walī b. Yūsuf, *Inṣāf Nāma*, p. 379.

76 Walī b. Yūsuf, *Inṣāf Nāma*, p. 384.

77 Walī b. Yūsuf, *Inṣāf Nāma*, p. 68; cf. Shāh Qāsim, *al-Ḥujja*, p. 18. The same idea is expressed in classical *ḥadīth*: "Islam cuts off whatever was before it and the *hijra* cuts off whatever was before it" (*inna al-islām yajubbu mā kāna qablahu wa inna al-hijra tajubbu mā kāna qablahā*). See Ibn Hanbal, *Musnad*, vol. 4, p. 199.

78 Walī b. Yūsuf, *Inṣāf Nāma*, pp. 4–5; Shāh Qāsim, *Ḥujja*, p. 33. Cf. al-Jāḥiz, *Kitāb al-bayān wa al-tabyīn*, Cairo 1968, vol. 2, p. 28.

79 See Section VII of the present chapter.

> (*khalīl*) of God cleaned the field and removed the rubbish, Moses the interlocutor (*kalīm*) of God reaped, Jesus the spirit (*rūḥ*) of God trashed the wheat, Muḥammad the messenger (*rasūl*) of God prepared the flour, baked the bread, tasted it and kept it for the son; the son is the *mahdī* who allowed those who performed the *hijra* [with him] and Sayyid Khwāndmīr to taste it.[80]

It is noteworthy that all links in this pedigree, except Jawnpūrī and Sayyid Khwāndmīr, are prophets; and though no prophetic claim is made for Jawnpūrī explicitly, one probably can interpret his inclusion in this line of spiritual descent as a subtle hint at his quasi-prophetic status.

The ideas described previously create a close affinity between the Prophet and the *mahdī*, and sometimes include subtle hints at the latter's superiority. Qāsim Shāh refers to a view held by Ibn Sīrīn (d. 728), according to whom the *mahdī* is superior to some prophets. He is explicitly described as superior to the Prophet's Companions, including Abū Bakr and ʿUmar.[81]

The spiritual standing of Jawnpūrī is further enhanced by his description as *khātam wilāyat Muḥammad* or *khātam al-wilāya al-muḥammadiyya*.[82] As mystical concepts, sainthood (*wilāya*) and its seal (*khātam al-awliyāʾ*) have a long history in Ṣūfī thought. In Ṣūfī literature, sainthood is commonly discussed in conjunction with prophecy (*nubuwwa*). The two concepts describe, as Hermann Landolt has formulated it in reference to the thought of ʿAlāʾ al-Dawla al-Simnānī, "the double experience of the Prophet Muḥammad – his *wilāya* or mystical experience and his *nubuwwa* or prophetic authority".[83] Closely related is another pair of concepts, "the seal of prophethood" (*khātam al-nubuwwa*) or "the seal of the prophets" (*khātam al-anbiyāʾ*),[84] and "the seal of sainthood" (*khātam al-wilāya*) or "the seal of the saints" (*khātam al-awliyāʾ*).[85] Al-Ḥakīm al-Tirmidhī (died between 905 and 910)[86] was probably the earliest thinker to discuss these

80 Walī b. Yūsuf, *Inṣāf Nāma*, pp. 309–310.
81 Shāh Qāsim, *al-Ḥujja*, p. 31; Shāh Dilāwar, *Khaṣāʾiṣ*, p. 2.
82 Walī b. Yūsuf, *Inṣāf Nāma*, pp. 13–14; Shāh Dilāwar, *Khaṣāʾiṣ*, p. 11.
83 "Walāya", *The Encyclopaedia of Religion*, s.v.
84 See Friedmann, "Finality of Prophethood ..." (= *idem, Prophecy Continuous*, pp. 49–82).
85 For a comprehensive analysis of this concept, see Chodkiewicz, *Seal of the Saints*.
86 Radtke and O'Kane, *The Concept of Sainthood ...*, p. 2; cf. "Al-Tirmidhī, Abū ʿAbd Allāh Muḥammad b. ʿAlī al-Ḥakīm", *EI*², s.v. (Y. Marquet).

two concepts in juxtaposition to each other. Prophecy is (divine) speech (*kalām*) which derives from Allah by way of (prophetic) inspiration (*waḥy*), coming together with divine spirit. Sainthood (*wilāya*) is the domain of those with whom God communicates (*waliya Allāh ḥadīthahu*) in other ways, and this communication comes together with divine presence (*sakīna*).[87] In contradistinction to those who reject prophecy, those who reject saints do not become infidels. The saints are also called *muḥaddathūn*, "those who are spoken to" (by God or by an angel). Tirmidhī continues saying:

> The *muḥaddathūn* have [different] ranks. Some of them were given a third of prophethood, some half of it and some more than that. He who has the greatest share in this is the seal of the saints (*man lahu khatm al-wilāya*).[88]

As Tirmidhī says elsewhere, the seal of the saints "is close to the prophets, almost attaining their rank" (*dhālika min al-anbiyāʾ qarībun yakādu yalḥaquhum*).[89] From the vantage point of mainstream Islam, the belief in the seal of the saints thus treads a perilous path: it may be interpreted as infringing upon the dogma of the finality of Muḥammad's prophethood.

The concept of the seal of the saints was discussed in the most elaborate manner by Ibn al-ʿArabī who considered himself to hold this position. In his *ʿAnqāʾ mughrib*, he says that "a noble messenger of my Lord came to me, assigning the sealing of the saints (*furāniqu*[90] *rabbī qad atānī mukhabbiran / bi-taʿyīni khatmi al-awliyāʾi karīmu*).[91] Some later Muslim scholars claimed that there have been many "seals": Chodkiewicz mentions among them ʿAbd al-Ghanī al-Nābulsī (d. 1731) and Aḥmad Tījānī (d. 1815).

87 See I. Goldziher, "Über den Ausdruck '*Sakīna*'", in *Abhandlungen zur arabischen Philologie*. Leiden: E. J. Brill, 1896, pp. 177–204; cf. "Sakīna", *EI*², s.v. (T. Fahd).
88 Tirmidhī, *Khatm al-wilāya*, p. 367. Cf. Friedmann, *Prophecy Continuous*, pp. 86–92 and the literature quoted there.
89 Tirmidhī, *Khatm al-awliyāʾ*, p. 367.
90 The Cairo edition has *f-rā-f-q*, but this does not make sense. For the reading *furāniq*, see Elmore, *Islamic Sainthood*, p. 229, note 17. Some commentators quoted by Elmore (p. 230, note 18) suggest that the appointee is Jesus, but in the text there is no hint pointing in this direction. I am indebted to my friend and colleague Professor Sara Sviri for bringing Elmore's book to my attention.
91 Ibn al-ʿArabī, *ʿAnqā mughrib*, p. 3, line 2 from bottom. For a comprehensive discussion of Ibn al-ʿArabī's claim, see Chodkiewicz, *The Seal of the Saints* pp. 128–146.

The Shīʿī scholar Ḥaydar Āmulī (d. 1385) maintains that the seal of the Muḥammadan sainthood is the *mahdī*.[92]

We have seen in Chapter 1 that the Shīʿī commentators looked in the Qurʾān for references to the *mahdī*, and their Sunnī counterparts did the same for the second coming of Jesus. In a similar vein, and with full awareness of the Ṣūfī traditions discussed earlier, the Mahdawīs are wont to interpret Qurʾānic verses as referring to their leader as the *mahdī* and as the seal of Muḥammadan sainthood (*khātam al-wilāya al-muḥammadiyya*). Qurʾān 5:57, which speaks of people whom God loves and who love God, is used in this manner. The phrase "And what of him who stands upon a clear sign (*al-bayyina*) from his Lord ..." in Qurʾān 11:17 – which was understood by the classical exegetes as a reference to the Prophet Muḥammad – is understood by the Mahdawīs as referring to Jawnpūrī's messianic status. The "clear sign" is understood as the *wilāya muḥammadiyya*; the conclusion is that the Qurʾān itself hints at Jawnpūrī as the "Seal of Muḥammadan Sainthood" (*khātam al-wilāya al-muḥammadiyya*) and as the *mahdī* of latter days.[93] It goes without saying that this is a totally anachronistic interpretation, but this is not an unsurmountable obstacle for the Mahdawīs who insist that their master was, indeed, "the seal of the saints" and use the Qurʾān to substantiate this assertion.

The theme of the seal of the saints is systematically used by the Mahdawīs in order to bestow upon Sayyid Muḥammad Jawnpūrī, as the seal of the saints, an extremely elevated status. The thrust of the argument is to prove that the *mahdī* – now identical with the seal of the saints – is superior to Abū Bakr and ʿUmar. He is a *khalīfa* by divine appointment, while Abū Bakr and ʿUmar were elected by (less authoritative) community councils; *hijra* with the *mahdī* is obligatory, while this is not the case with other *awliyāʾ*, even Abū Bakr and ʿUmar; on the Day of Judgment, the *awliyāʾ* will assemble under the banner of the *mahdī*, the seal of the saints, in the same way as the prophets will assemble under that of Muḥammad, the seal of the prophets. Here comes a very subtle and complex argument – based on the thought of Muḥyi al-Dīn Ibn al-ʿArabī (d. 1240) – which results in a somewhat veiled conclusion: sainthood (*wilāya*) is, in a certain sense, superior to prophethood (*nubuwwa*). All messengers take their knowledge from Muḥammad who is the seal of the prophets. This is reasonably

92 Chodkiewicz, *The Seal of the Saints*, p. 136.
93 Walī b. Yūsuf, *Inṣāf Nāma*, pp. 13–14.

straightforward, though it may raise some difficulties if one takes into account the belief in the finality of Muḥammad's prophethood. More striking is the statement that the seal of the prophets takes his knowledge from his "inner self" (*bāṭin*) (rather than from divine revelation as main-stream Muslims would probably state). He does this because he is also the seal of the saints, though he cannot manifest himself in this capacity because the nature of being a messenger prevents him from doing so. At some unspecified time in the future, when he reveals his inner aspect as *khātam al-awliyā'*, it will become clear that all messengers and saints take their knowledge from the niche (*mishkāt*) of the seal of the saints (*al-rusul kulluhum ya'khudhūna al-'ilm min khātam al-rusul wa khātam al-rusul ya'khudhuhu min bāṭinihi min ḥaythu annahu khātam al-awliyā' lakin lā yuẓhiruhu li-anna waṣf risālatihi yamna'uhu fa-idhā aẓhara bāṭinahu fī ṣūrat khātam al-awliyā' yuẓhiruhu fa-'l-ḥāṣil anna al-rusul wa al-awliyā' kullahum ya'khudhūna al-'ilm min mishkāt khātam al-awliyā'*).[94] "This proves that the 'journey' (*sayr*) of the Prophet to God and beholding His essence and attributes finds its fulfilment and perfection in the *mahdī*, and not in any other *walī*, even if he is Abū Bakr" (*yadullu 'alā anna sayr al-nabī 'alayhi al-salām ilā Allāh wa ru'yat dhātihi wa ṣifātihi lahu al-tamām fī al-mahdī lā fī ghayrihi min sā'ir al-awliyā' wa in kāna Abā Bakr*).[95] This seems to indicate that the spiritual perfection of the Prophet depends in this sense on the *mahdī*; there could hardly be a more manifest way to express the boundless veneration of the Mahdawīs for their leader. It is even possible to conclude from this argument that in a certain sense the *mahdī* is in their view superior to the Prophet.[96]

Jawnpūrī's exalted status bestows major spiritual benefits on himself and may do the same for his followers. In an imaginary discussion with God, Jawnpūrī asserted that he saw God with the eye of the heart, with the eye of the head and with every hair in his body. This is an extraordinary achievement: even the Companions of the Prophet who were unsurpassed in all other respects were not privileged with seeing God.[97]

When seen against the background of Islamic thought, Jawnpūrī's statement is rather audacious. The possibility of seeing God has been a controversial issue since the beginning of Muslim theology. The Mu'tazilīs

94 Dilāwar Shāh, *Khaṣā'iṣ*, pp. 12–13.
95 Shāh Dilāwar, *Khasā'iṣ*, p. 13.
96 Shāh Dilāwar, *Khaṣā'iṣ*, pp. 7–19.
97 Walī b. Yūsuf, *Inṣāf Nāma*, p. 315.

rejected the possibility that God may be seen with the eyes, but some of them thought that He may be seen with the heart. The prevalent Sunnī position speaks of seeing God only in the afterlife. Some scholars say that in order to make this possible, God will create (in the believers?) a special, sixth sense on the Day of Resurrection.[98] Seeing Him with "the eye of the heart" is less objectionable: it may refer to mystical experience and may fall within the framework of acceptable beliefs. However, seeing Him with "the eye of the head" means seeing Him in a concrete manner in this world and carries anthropomorphistic implications. Yet the controversial nature of this belief did not prevent Jawnpūrī from telling a *mullā* (who denied the possibility of seeing God in this world) that he chose the way of the blind, while the Mahdawīs chose the way of those who see.[99] God deserves to be seen with the "eyes of the head" and one should see Him in this way (*Khudāy-rā bi-chashm-i sar dīdanī ast bāyad dīd*). Aspiring to see Him is a duty of every man and woman. Seeing Him with the eyes of the head, the eye of the heart or in a dream is in Jawnpūrī's view a prerequisite of belief, but he concedes that someone who sincerely aspires to attain the sight of God and turns his heart away from anything except Him – is also considered a believer.[100]

IV RELIGIOUS EXCLUSIVITY AND *HIJRA*

In the previous section we discussed the idea of "the seal of the saints" which places the Mahdawīs in close connection with the Ṣūfī movement. Ṣūfī ideas permeate Mahdawī literature and Ṣūfī principles are used in order to substantiate various beliefs in Mahdawī thought. This is done at times in a rather unexpected manner. Surprisingly enough, Ṣūfī concepts are used in order to dissociate the Mahdawīs from all other Muslims and declare all non-Mahdawī Muslims as infidels. When Shaykh Muṣṭafā Gujarātī (d. 1577), who argued the Mahdawī case at the court of Akbar, was asked why he insists, in daring contradiction to the views of the *ʿulamāʾ*, that Jawnpūrī was the *mahdī*, he responds that in the Ṣūfī movement – to whom

98 See "Ruʾyat Allāh", *EI²*, s.v. (D. Gimaret); J. van Ess, *Theologie und Gesellschaft*, vol. 4, pp. 411–415; about the "sixth sense", see Ashʿarī, *Maqālāt al-islāmiyyīn*, ed. Ritter, Istanbul 1929, p. 216, ll. 3–5.
99 Walī b. Yūsuf, *Inṣāf Nāma*, p. 323.
100 Walī b. Yūsuf, *Inṣāf Nāma*, pp. 306–307.

he and his predecessors belong – it is forbidden to reject the words of a *walī*.[101] Moreover, such a rejection is tantamount to infidelity, as is clear from a *ḥadīth qudsī* in which Allah says: "Whoever is inimical to one of my saints, is inimical to me; and whoever is inimical to me, will enter the Fire" (*man ʿādā waliyyan min awliyāʾī fa-qad ʿādānī wa man ʿādānī dakhala al-nār*).[102] Since the Mahdawīs consider Jawnpūrī both as the seal of the saints and as the *mahdī*, the two claims reinforce each other and enable the Mahdawīs to consider all opponents of Jawnpūrī's messianic claim as infidels. Qurʾān 11:17 says that "whoever disbelieves in it, being one of the partisans (*aḥzāb*), his appointed place is the Fire". According to most classical commentators the object of disbelief in this verse is the Qurʾān, but the Mahdawīs understand it as a reference to those who reject their leader. Walī b. Yūsuf discusses the prophetic authority (*nubuwwa*) and the mystical experience (*wilāya*) of the Prophet, asserting that both must be accepted. Prophetic authority is Muḥammad's outward aspect and sainthood is the inner one; disbelief in any of them is tantamount to infidelity. Whoever believes in Muḥammad's prophethood but not in his sainthood in all its details is an infidel. And since Jawnpūrī has been made the seal of Muḥammadan sainthood, belief in him is mandatory:

> Accept Muḥammad the *mahdī*, so that you may succeed. Whoever does not accept Muḥammad the *mahdī*, does not accept Muḥammad the messenger of God" (*fa-taqabbalū Muḥammadan al-mahdī laʿallakum tufliḥūn wa man yam yataqabbal Muḥammadan al-mahdī fa-innahu lam yataqabbal Muḥammadan rasūl Allāh*).[103]

Moreover, since the *mahdī* was appointed by God and all his rulings have a divine origin, anyone who denies him, *ipso facto* denies God himself.[104] Thus, non-recognition of Sayyid Muḥammad Jawnpūrī as the *mahdī* is

101 Gujarātī, *Majālis*, pp. 4, 8–9.

102 Walī b. Yūsuf, *Inṣāf Nāma*, p. 34. Cf. Bukhārī, *Ṣaḥīḥ, Kitāb al-riqāq*, no. 38 (ed. Krehl, vol. 4, p. 232). This idea can sometimes be found also in Ṣūfī orders. In Sammān's *Azāhīr al-riyāḍ*, describing the thought of Aḥmad al-Ṭayyib who introduced the Sammānī order into the Sudan at the beginning of the nineteenth century, there is a whole chapter devoted to traditions which denounce those who mistreat or deny the Ṣūfīs; they are considered infidels. The chapter also includes another version of the tradition quoted earlier: "Whoever hurts a friend of mine, I shall fight him" (*man ādhā li waliyyan fa-qad ādhantuhu bi-ḥarb*). See Sammān, *Azāhīr al-riyāḍ*, pp. 134–135.

103 Walī b. Yūsuf, *Inṣāf Nāma*, pp. 15, 39–40, 365.

104 Walī b. Yūsuf, *Inṣāf Nāma*, pp. 34–35, 37–42.

tantamount to disbelief in God and in His Prophet. Qāsim Shāh adduces a passage from *Naqliyyāt ʿAbd al-Rashīd* according to which "denial of the *mahdī* is denial of Muḥammad, the denial of Muḥammad is denial of the Qurʾān, and the denial of the Qurʾān is the denial of God".[105] Therefore, non-Mahdawī Muslims must be considered infidels.

Mahdawīs were, of course, not very numerous, and the paucity of their numbers was occasionally considered as an argument against them. But they stood their ground: in his arguments at Akbar's court, the Mahdawī Shaykh Muṣṭafā Gujarātī maintained that the few Mahdawīs were right while their numerous opponents were wrong. To bolster his argument, Gujarātī mentions Joseph who was one but truthful, while his eleven brothers were liars. It is the same with other prophets: as a rule, many people reject them and only a few believe in them. Hence, the paucity of the Mahdawīs cannot be used as an argument against them and cannot refute the idea that the *mahdī* came and departed.[106]

The controversy concerning the significance of the paucity of the Mahdawīs continued well into the nineteenth century. The anti-Mahdawī writer Abū Rajāʾ argued with thinly disguised cynicism that according to the Mahdawīs "Muslims are only a few Mahdawīs, Deccanīs, Hūndārīs and Gujarātīs; the Muslim community has contracted to such an extent 380 years ago" (*Musalmān faqaṭ yihī: chand Mahdawī o Dakhanī o Hūndārī o Gujarātī hayñ awr ummat-i muḥammadiyya tīn saw assī baras sē isī qadr ikhtiṣār par hō gaʾī hay*). In other words, the appearance of Jawnpūrī brought about the dramatic dwindling of the Muslim community.[107] The nineteenth-century Mahdawī writer Sayyid Nuṣrat responded by saying that the paucity of believers and the large number of unbelievers has been the human condition since time immemorial and is clear from numerous Qurʾānic verses, such as 11:40 which describes the paucity of believers during the time of Noah.[108] And, indeed, the *mahdī* is like Noah's ark: those who embark on it will be saved while the rest will drown.[109] The latter are derisively called "carrion-eaters" (*murdār-khwār*),[110] people who do not observe even the

105 Shāh Qāsim, *al-Ḥujja*, p. 32, note 1. *Naqliyyāt ʿAbd al-Rashīd* is not available to me.

106 Gujarātī, *Majālis*, pp. 36–39.

107 Abū Rajāʾ, *Hadiyya Mahdawiyya*, p. 17.

108 Nuṣrat, *Kuḥl al-jawāhir*, fol. 16a, line 15 - fol. 17a, line 4. Qurʾān 11:40 reads: "... Only a few believed with him" (i.e., with Noah).

109 Walī b. Yūsuf, *Inṣāf Nāma*, p. 22.

110 Walī b. Yūsuf, *Inṣāf Nāma*, pp. 76, 212.

most basic tenets of Islam. It is noteworthy that Jawnpūrī's first assertion of his being the *mahdī*, as preserved in Mahdawī hagiography, points in the same direction: "I am the promised *mahdī*. Whoever follows me is a believer."[111] Hence, those who do not follow him are infidels.

This stringent attitude had serious ritual and social consequences. The *mahdī* forbade his followers to pray behind a non-Mahdawī *imām*, and instructed them not to go to places where this may be inevitable. If someone did pray under the leadership of a non-Mahdawī – he must repeat his prayer because it was invalid. If Mahdawīs go to a town, they have to pray in their own congregation even if they are very few in number.[112] Jawnpūrī's attitude to non-Mahdawīs can best be gauged from a tradition according to which he raised his sword and said that "this is the only thing that remains for them" (*bā īshān īn mānda ast*), and declared them to have the status of unprotected inhabitants of enemy territory against whom war may legitimately be waged (*ḥarbīs*). According to Islamic law, such persons are not eligible to pay the *jizya*; Jawnpūrī nevertheless expressed his desire to levy *jizya* from them should God issue an order to this effect and give him the power to implement it.[113] In other words, he was willing to use the most unequivocal language in order to demonstrate that non-Mahdawīs cannot be considered Muslims. Without any hesitation, Jawnpūrī asserts that his attitude to non-Mahdawīs is based on the Qur'ān and nothing of it is based on his own views.[114]

As we have seen, Sayyid Muḥammad Jawnpūrī received at the age of forty a divine command to migrate from Jawnpūr and to summon the people to God's way. In emulation of Jawnpūrī's compliance with this command, and drawing inspiration from Qur'ānic verses such as 4:88 and 8:72,[115] performing the *hijra* became an essential test of a Mahdawī's commitment to the movement. The time of the *hijra* is important: those who performed it early are better than the latecomers and may serve as their spiritual guides (*murshid*).[116] The *mahdī* declared the *hijra* to be an

111 ʿAlī, *Siyar-i Masʿūd*, p. 40.
112 Walī b. Yūsuf, *Inṣāf Nāma*, pp. 44–47.
113 Walī b. Yūsuf, *Inṣāf Nāma*, pp. 48–49; cf. ʿAlī, *Siyar-i Masʿūd*, p. 95.
114 Walī b. Yūsuf, *Inṣāf Nāma*, p. 97.
115 Qur'ān 8:72 reads: "Those who believe, and have emigrated and struggled with their possession and their selves in the way of God, and those who have given refuge and help – those are friends one of another. And those who believe, but have not emigrated – you have no duty of friendship towards them till they emigrate ..."
116 Walī b. Yūsuf, *Inṣāf Nāma*, pp. 200–201.

individual duty (*farḍ ʿayn*)[117] and gave it a definition which goes far beyond the obligation to move away from one's place of residence. In addition to the physical move, it involves complete reliance on God and resignation to His will (*tawakkul o taslīm*), an abandonment of desire to receive anything from human beings (*az khalq bē ṭamaʿ*), abandonment of gainful employment (*taʿayyun*),[118] considering both benefit and harm as coming from God (*nafaʿ o żarar-rā az khudā-yi taʿālā bīnad*), living in seclusion (from non-Mahdawīs?) and other ascetic qualities.[119] It also entails cutting any emotional ties with relatives who were left behind. For example, if someone left Gujarāt and moved to Khurāsān but remained emotionally attached to his relatives in Gujarāt, he is considered a wrongdoer (*ẓālim*).[120]

Considering the non-Mahdawīs as infidels is only one indication of the extreme exclusivity characteristic of the Mahdawī movement. Mahdawī literature tends to employ strict criteria of classification to groups with whom Mahdawīs came into contact. In contradistinction to classical Muslim tradition which devoted much attention to classifying the non-Muslims,[121] but was reasonably inclusive with regard to various Muslim groups, the Mahdawīs concentrate on classifying their Muslim coreligionists according to their attitudes to Sayyid Muḥammad Jawnpūrī and his movement. Naturally enough, the Mahdawīs are the most important group in this classification. Wholehearted acceptance of Jawnpūrī's claim to be the *mahdī* is an indispensable condition for being recognized a "true" Mahdawī and Muslim, but is not sufficient in itself. Further conditions are necessary in order to remove any doubt concerning the absolute fidelity of a person to the Mahdawī movement. The first and foremost of these is the *hijra*, leaving one's place of residence and moving to the *mahdī*'s camp or, later, to a Mahdawī institution (*dāʾira*). Only those who do this are considered true believers. The terms used for them are *muʾminān*, *muhājirān*, *muhājirān-i mahdī*, or *muṣaddiqān*.

117 *Farḍ ʿayn* is contrasted with *farḍ kifāya*, a collective duty, which is not incumbent on every individual if a sufficient number of community members perform it. For a basic explanation of the two concepts, see "Farḍ", *EI*², s.v. (Th. W. Juynboll).

118 *Taʿayyun* literally means "being appointed to a position". The word was probably pronounced *taʿyīn*, or even *taʿīn*. See Steingass, *Persian–English Dictionary*, s.v.

119 Walī b. Yūsuf, *Inṣāf Nāma*, p. 335.

120 Walī b. Yūsuf, *Inṣāf Nāma*, p. 187.

121 See Friedmann, "Classification of Unbelievers in Sunnī Muslim Law and Tradition", *Jerusalem Studies in Arabic and Islam* 22 (1998), pp. 163–195 (*Tolerance and Coercion in Islam*, pp. 54–86).

Hijra is, therefore, not only a means to gather Mahdawīs outside their regular habitats in order to build the human resources for the movement; it is also a symbol of a substantial social change. Numerous traditions about the *mahdī* and his successors indicate that for the Mahdawīs, family relationships must be replaced by membership in the Mahdawī community. This is the reason for the cases in which members of the movement who stayed in a Mahdawī institution (*dā ʾira*) were instructed not to socialize with their relatives in neighbouring towns. An extreme example of this attitude speaks about a Mahdawī who requested permission from the *mahdī* to respond positively to his mother's invitation to pay her a visit. Jawnpūrī instructed the man to tell his mother that he was dead. From the mother's vantage point, he was, indeed, dead: the relationship between mother and son came to an end when the latter joined the movement while she remained outside it. Similarly, when a Mahdawī died, his inheritance was distributed equally between the members of the *dā ʾira*; nothing was given to his sons or daughters if they were not members of the movement. Again, blood relationships were rendered inconsequential and non-Mahdawīs were excluded from inheritance like any other unbelievers according to Islamic law.[122]

Hijra is, of course, a well-known concept from classical Islamic literature. In a recent article,[123] Patricia Crone surveyed the various ideas related to it and suggested a new conceptual framework for their analysis. The Qurʾānic *muhājirūn* are closely associated with *jihād*. The "classical" or "closed" concept, as she calls it, is based on prophetic traditions according to which "*hijra* ceased after the conquest (of Mecca), but *jihād* and intention (remain); when you are called up, go forth."[124] Crone's "open-ended" concept of *hijra* is best epitomized by the tradition saying that

> there will be a *hijra* after the *hijra*. The best people [will go] to the place where Abraham moved ... The worst people will remain in the land. Their land will seize them ... and they will be resurrected with apes and pigs.[125]

122 Walī b. Yūsuf, *Inṣāf Nāma*, pp. 196–198. For the various views in Islamic law on inter-religious inheritance, see Friedmann, *Tolerance and Coercion*, p. 57.
123 Crone, "The First-Century Concept of the *Hiǧra*".
124 Ṣanʿānī, *Muṣannaf*, vol. 5, p. 309 (no. 9711); cf. Crone, loc. cit., p. 371.
125 Cf. Ibn Ḥanbal, *Musnad*, vol. 2, p. 84 and elsewhere (see Wensinck, *Concordance* ..., s.v. *hijra*); cf. Crone, loc. cit, p. 356.

The same purpose is served by abundant material advocating migration to the garrison cities long after the Prophet's death. In contradistinction to the traditional view and to the views of several modern scholars, Crone maintains that the "open-ended" concept preceded the "closed" one. Whatever the historical sequence may have been, it is clear that the "open-ended" concept of *hijra* gained the upper hand. Traditions such as "there is no *hijra* after the conquest (of Mecca)[126] never stood in the way of Muslims who intended to make the *hijra* an element of their religious thought and practice. Later Muslim thinkers were able to explain this tradition in a way which maintained the legitimacy of *hijra* and its relevance to their times.[127] *Hijra* in a certain sense became an important component of the Sudanese *mahdī*'s thought,[128] and thousands of Indian Muslims performed it when they left British India in 1920 in order to live in the Muslim-ruled country of Afghanistan.[129] Jawnpūrī himself was able to circumvent the closure of the *hijra* by referring to contradictory traditions reflecting its open-ended nature, envisaging "*hijra* after the *hijra*". These traditions allowed Jawnpūrī to conclude that the *hijra* was as valid at the end of times as it had been in the early days of Islam: the obligation to perform it has not been abrogated.[130] It also allowed him to transform the *hijra* into an essential element in the beliefs of his movement. Even minor children and women were required to perform it. The *mahdī*'s closest associates are referred to in Mahdawī literature as *muhājirān*, those who performed the *hijra* with him.[131] The importance of the *hijra* among the Mahdawīs can be gauged from the story about a certain Mahdawī called Bandagī Malik Maʿrūf who fell seriously ill in Nahrwālā. God kept him alive for a year; when the year elapsed, he performed *hijra* to Jālōr and died there. Sayyid Khwāndmīr, the second successor of Jawnpūrī, observed that God prolonged his life on

126 See Ṣanʿānī, *Muṣannaf*, vol. 5, p. 309 (no. 9712) and Wensinck, *Concordance ...*, s.v. *hijra*.

127 ʿUthmān b. Fūdī, *Kitāb bayān wujūb al-hijra ʿalā al-ʿibād wa bayān wujūb naṣb al-imām wa iqāmat al-jihād*, ed. Fatḥī Ḥasan al-Miṣrī, Khartūm and Oxford, 1977, especially pp. 18–20 where the tradition according to which "there is no *hijra* after the conquest (of Mecca)" is explained; see also Wansharīsī, *Asnā al-matājir*; Miller, "Muslim Minorities and the Obligation to Emigrate ..."; Qureshi, "The ʿ*ulamā*ʾ of British India.

128 See Chapter 4, at notes 101–102.

129 See Qureshi, "The ʿ*ulamā*ʾ of British India ..."

130 Walī b. Yūsuf, *Inṣāf Nāma*, pp. 113–114. The text quoted here seems to be corrupt in a few places. Cf. Ibn Ḥanbal, *Musnad*, vol. 2, p. 84 and elsewhere (see Wensinck, *Concordance ...*, s.v. *hijra*).

131 Walī b. Yūsuf, *Inṣāf Nāma*, pp. 35–36, 39, 44–45, 173, 182–183, 207.

purpose, so that Malik Maʿrūf could perform the *hijra* before his death.[132] Conversely, there is a tradition according to which the *mahdī* considered people who performed the *hijra* and later returned to Gujarāt as apostates, though after reflection he seems to have softened his position at least with regard to his closest associates.[133]

Thus, acceptance of Jawnpūrī's messianic claim and performing the *hijra* are the two indispensable conditions for becoming a full Mahdawī. However, the Mahdawī literature mentions additional groups which are related to the Mahdawīs, but did not attain full membership in the movement. These groups are designated by names known from the formative period of Islam. First, we have the "hypocrites" (*munāfiqān*). These are people who accepted Jawnpūrī's messianic status, but refrained from performing the *hijra*. *Hijra* is thus the criterion by which real believers are distinguished from the half-hearted ones. God commanded the Prophet to perform it so that his obedient followers are distinguished from the hypocrites (*ay Muḥammad, az Makka bi-Madīna hijrat kun tā muṭīʿān o munāfiqān paydā shawand*).[134] These "hypocrites" are equal to "nominal" Mahdawīs (*lisānī*): persons who support the *mahdī* by word, but not by deed. And they are destined for "the lowest reach of the Fire" (*fī al-darak al-asfal min al-nār*).[135]

Both the *muhājirān* and the *munāfiqān* are groups well known from the period of the Prophet and using these terms is intended to create an affinity between that period and the period of the *mahdī*. Yet there is one important group from the prophetic period whose existence in the period of the *mahdī* is explicitly denied: these are the helpers of the Prophet in Medina (*anṣār*). This group does not exist in the period of the *mahdī*, because the only helper of the *mahdī* is Allah himself.[136] This is a significant deviation from the general tendency to depict the two periods as similar to each other, and can easily be interpreted as a thinly veiled hint that in a certain sense the *mahdī*'s status in the eyes of God is higher than that of the Prophet himself: the Prophet needed help from humans, while Jawnpūrī was in a position to dispense with it.

132 Walī b. Yūsuf, *Inṣāf Nāma*, pp. 182–183.

133 Walī b. Yūsuf, *Inṣāf Nāma*, p. 132.

134 Walī b. Yūsuf, *Inṣāf Nāma*, pp. 175–183, 207, 219, 343, 346 *infra*. The quotation is on p. 181. The Qurʾān includes verses supporting *hijra*, but this very specific divine injunction and this purpose of the *hijra* seems to be Mahdawī in its origins.

135 Walī b. Yūsuf, *Inṣāf Nāma*, pp. 171, 177 *infra*, 202; cf. Qurʾān 4:144.

136 Walī b. Yūsuf, *Inṣāf Nāma*, p. 207.

Both *munāfiqān* and *lisāniyān* have a pejorative ring and it is therefore easy to use these terms in a negative sense. Yet the Mahdawī literature uses also the term "assenters" (*muwāfiqān*) for those who accepted Jawnpūrī's messianic claim but did not perform *hijra* and did not join a *dā'ira*. Though this is essentially a positive term, in Mahdawī parlance it designates those who must be shunned because their acceptance of Jawnpūrī was merely verbal and did not entail the willingness to leave their social milieu and replace it with total immersion in Mahdawī society. The Mahdawīs were forbidden to have meals at the homes of these "assenters"; the *mahdī* used to say that if the assenters want to spend in the way of God, they should support those Mahdawīs who practise absolute reliance on God (*tawakkul*) and are not asking assistance of anyone (*istighnā' karda and*). The assenters will not receive any reward if they host poor Mahdawīs at their homes and should refrain from doing it. They waste their money and place the Mahdawī guests in a humiliating situation. Furthermore, having meals at the assenters' homes may become a habit, creating a sense of economic security which is not compatible with absolute reliance on God.[137] Any relationship with the assenters was to be shunned: Sayyid Maḥmūd, the *mahdī*'s son and first successor, refused to exchange greetings with them and wept profusely when he received a letter from a noble lady who belonged to this group. Mentioning his name by a non-Mahdawī was a cause of shame and grief.[138]

The most despicable group according to the Mahdawī classification are the world-seekers (*ṭālib-i dunyā*) or the world-possessors (*dunyā-dār*). These are the wealthy people explicitly designated as infidels (*ṭālib-i dunyā kāfir*).[139] This group will be discussed in greater detail during our discussion of the ascetic thought of the Mahdawī movement.

On the social level, declaring non-Mahdawīs as infidels resulted in a demand to refrain from any relationships with them. This included a prohibition on visiting their homes for any purpose. In order to sanction this social segregation, Walī b. Yūsuf frequently mentions traditions from the early Muslim period, as well as Qur'ānic verses which forbid forging alliances with Jews and Christians. Since non-Mahdawīs are considered infidels – and as such are at par with Jews and Christians – these verses are considered relevant for determining the relationship between the

137 Walī b. Yūsuf, *Inṣāf Nāma*, p. 132; cf. ibid., p. 213.
138 Walī b. Yūsuf, *Inṣāf Nāma*, pp. 214–215.
139 Walī b. Yūsuf, *Inṣāf Nāma*, pp. 171, 343, 346 *infra*.

Mahdawīs and other Muslims. Qur'ān 3:118 in particular served as a source of inspiration for the Mahdawīs. The verse urges Muslims not to enter into intimate relationships with those who do not belong to their faith; it was interpreted as a reproach to those companions of the Prophet who maintained ties with their relatives among the so-called "hypocrites" and shared secrets with them. ʿUmar b. al-Khaṭṭāb who used this and other verses in order to justify his firm refusal to appoint a Jew as an accountant – and caned a governor who repeatedly attempted to advance this appointment – serves as a model for Jawnpūrī and his associates.[140]

In a similar vein, there was strong opposition to giving Mahdawī girls in marriage to non-Mahdawīs and to the affluent. A novice coming to a *dā'ira* was not allowed to marry a Mahdawī girl before he spent a year in the *dā'ira* and proved that he was, indeed, a sincere "seeker of God"; when he was eventually given a girl in marriage, it was stipulated that she may not go out of the *dā'ira* and mingle with "world seekers". In theory at least, poor suitors were preferred to affluent ones. When a prominent Mahdawī gave his daughter in marriage to a poor man and was rebuked for not observing the marital compatibility rules (*kafā'a*),[141] he responded by quoting the Qur'ānic verse according to which "the most noble among you in the eyes of God are the most pious", implying that a husband's piety and religiosity can easily compensate for his poverty.[142]

V EXTREME ASCETICISM

Ascetic ideas abound in classical Islam. It is not difficult to find in the Qur'ān, in the prophetic *ḥadīth* and in ascetic (*zuhd*) literature passages expressing disdain and contempt for this world and for hoarding worldly possessions, together with unequivocal statements about the merits of the hereafter and the necessity to strive for it rather than aspire to the acquisition of worldly wealth. Some of the most prominent Muslims of the early period, such as Ḥasan al-Baṣrī, were well known for promoting this world view. However, these uncompromising ideas were tempered by other statements frowning on excessive asceticism, encouraging family

140 Walī b. Yūsuf, *Inṣāf Nāma*, pp. 51–55. Other verses quoted are Qur'ān 4:89 and 68:8.

141 See "Kafā'a", *EI*², s.v. (Y. Linant de Bellefonds).

142 Walī b. Yūsuf, *Inṣāf Nāma*, pp. 207–209; Qur'ān 49:13.

life, promising the believers spoils in this world and happiness both here and in the hereafter. One can easily substantiate the idea that in classical Islam, asceticism and worldliness were vying for precedence and the relative weight given to each differed between individuals, social groups and literary genres.

Mahdawī thought, on the other hand, is characterized by the most extreme and unmitigated asceticism. A favourite tradition reflecting their approach says that "this world is a carcass and its seekers are dogs" (*al-dunyā jīfa wa ṭālibuhā* (sic) *kilāb*).[143] The fifth chapter of the *Inṣāf Nāma* starts with a striking statement by Jawnpūrī who said that "the existence of worldly life is infidelity" (*wujūd-i ḥayāt-i dunyā kufr ast*). He then goes on to enumerate the usual components of earthly life, such as women, children, property, animals, sown fields, buildings, clothing and foods; he defines those who aspire to possess these things as infidels. And those who socialize with such persons or befriend them, "do not belong to us, do not belong to the Prophet Muḥammad and do not belong to God".[144]

Jawnpūrī concludes his introductory remarks to this chapter by quoting an allegedly prophetic utterance which says: "This world is for you, the next world is for you, and God is for me". Jawnpūrī expands his tradition by saying that "this world is for you, O infidels; the next world is for you, O deficient believers, and God is for me and for those who follow me" (*al-dunyā lakum yā ayyuhā al-kāfirūn wa al-ʿuqbā lakum yā ayyuhā al-muʾminūn al-nāqiṣūn wa al-mawlā lī wa li-man ittabaʿanī*).[145] This is a rather implausible explanation and the text does not include the slightest indication that this might have been the Prophet's intention; it is a far-fetched attempt to explain away a tradition which indicates that success and prosperity in this world are legitimate pursuits for Muslims and do not harm their prospects to gain entry into Paradise.

The controversy on this issue has a long history in the Muslim tradition. The Qurʾān contains numerous verses which deprecate this world and threaten seekers of wealth with dire punishment. In classical exegesis, these verses were subject to diverse explanations. Some commentators

143 Gujarātī, *Majālis*, p. 51.

144 Walī b. Yūsuf, *Inṣāf Nāma*, p. 56.

145 Walī b. Yūsuf, *Inṣāf Nāma*, p. 58; cf. ʿAlī, *Siyar-i Masʿūd*, pp. 139–141. Searching for the *al-dunyā lakum* ... tradition in several data bases did not yield any results, but Jawnpūrī's attitude in the matter is clear even if the *ḥadīth* quoted does not appear in the searchable collections. The "deficient" believers seem to be those who accepted Jawnpūrī's claim to be the *mahdī*, but failed to perform *hijra* and join him.

maintained that these threats are directed against non-Muslims only, while others argued that they hold true for Muslims and non-Muslims alike. The latter view was held by ascetics who wanted to further the ideal of a simple lifestyle for Muslims and opposed the opulence which spread among some of them in the wake of the great conquests of the seventh century. The controversy between the early ascetic Abū Dharr (d. 32/652–653) and Muʿāwiya concerning Qurʾān 9:34 is a case in point. The verse threatens "those who hoard gold and silver and do not spend them in the way of God" with painful punishment. Muʿāwiya maintained that the threat is directed against the People of the Book only, while Abū Dharr al-Ghifārī argued that hoarding of wealth is forbidden for Muslims as well.[146]

The Mahdawīs come down squarely on the side of the most extreme asceticism. A discussion between Jawnpūrī and a certain *ʿālim* called Rukn al-Dīn closely resembles the aforementioned controversy between Muʿāwiya and Abū Dharr al-Ghifārī. The discussion revolves around Qurʾān 11:15–16 which reads:

> Those who desire the life of the present world and its adornment, we will pay them in full for their deeds therein and they shall not be defrauded there. Those are they for whom in the world to come there is only the Fire; their deeds there will have failed, and void will be their works.

Rukn al-Dīn refers to (unnamed) commentators who maintained that the verse speaks about infidels only, while Jawnpūrī argues that the unrestricted formulation of the verse does not lend itself to such an interpretation and must be understood as referring to Muslims and non-Muslims alike. Hence a Muslim who is desirous of the present world ceases to be a Muslim. Provocatively, Rukn al-Dīn declares that the characteristics described in Qurʾān 11:15–16 fit him, fit the king, the *qāḍī* and all the *ʿulamāʾ*. Undaunted by the severe implications of Rukn al-Dīn's sweeping statement, Jawnpūrī declares him an infidel. His denunciation implicitly applies also to the king, to the *qāḍī* and to the *ʿulamāʾ*.[147]

Discussions of asceticism in Mahdawī literature are frequently related to the question whether gainful employment is legal for the Mahdawīs.

146 "Abu Dharr al-Ghifārī", *EI*², s.v. (J. Robson); Bukhārī, *Ṣaḥīḥ, Kitāb al-zakāt*, 4 (ed. Krehl, vol. 1, p. 355); cf. Ṭabarī, *Jāmiʿ al-bayān*, vol. 10, pp. 121–122.
147 Walī b. Yūsuf, *Inṣāf Nāma*, pp. 58–59.

Again, the issue has been extensively discussed in classical Islamic thought.[148] A positive attitude to gainful employment seems to have been prevalent in classical *ḥadīth*. The early Ḥanafī author Muḥammad b. al-Ḥasan al-Shaybānī (132–189/750–805)[149] seems to have been the first author to give the subject a systematic treatment in his *Book of Earning* (*Kitāb al-Kasb*). A frequently quoted prophetic *ḥadīth* adduced at the beginning of his work states that "seeking gain is incumbent on every Muslim" (*ṭalab al-kasb farīḍa ʿalā kulli Muslim*). According to another one, "Seeking lawful [gain] is like fighting the heroes [in *jihād*]; whoever spends the night fatigued by seeking lawful [gain], he spends it being forgiven [by God]" (*ṭalab al-ḥalāl ka-muqāraʿat al-abṭāl wa man bāta kāllan min ṭalab al-ḥalāl bāta maghfūran lahu*). And ʿUmar b. al-Khaṭṭāb went so far as to prefer dying while riding in pursuit of gain to dying in *jihād*.[150] Al-Shaybānī then adduces Qurʾānic verses and prophetic traditions used by "ignorant ascetics" (*juhhāl ahl al-taqashshuf*) to prove that seeking gain is prohibited; this is followed by an extensive refutation of these views. Particularly relevant to our discussion is his denial of any contradiction between seeking lawful gain and absolute reliance on God (*tawakkul*).[151]

In Ṣūfī works, the views expressed are diverse. Al-Kalābādhī devotes a short chapter to the question of earning one's livelihood and maintains that the Ṣūfīs agreed on the permissibility to acquire earnings from trade, commerce or agriculture, provided care is exercised to avoid things of doubtful legality. They maintain that it is incumbent on a man to earn a living if he has dependants. Others think that it is permissible but not necessary to earn, provided that the person's trust in God is not impaired or his religion affected. "It is, however, more proper and right to occupy oneself with one's obligations to God, and it is a prior duty to turn away from all acquisition, in perfect trust and faith in God." Sahl al-Tustarī (d. 283/896) said that "it is not proper for those who put all their trust in God to acquire, except for the purpose of following the *sunna*; and for others

148 For basic information, see "Kasb", *EI*², s.v. (Cl. Cahen). This article concentrates on the positive attitudes to gainful employment and almost completely disregards the ascetic thinking on the issue. For the ascetic views, see "Tawakkul", *EI*², s.v. (L. Lewisohn).

149 See "al-Shaybānī, Abū ʿAbd Allāh Muḥammad b. al-Ḥasan b. Farqad", *EI*², s.v. (E. Chaumont).

150 Shaybānī, *Kasb*, pp. 71–72.

151 Shaybāni, *Kasb*, pp. 81–95.

it is not proper except for the purpose of mutual assistance".[152] Abū Ṭālib al-Makkī (d. 386/998) devotes a chapter in his *Qūt al-qulūb* to the issue of gainful work. He quotes Qur'ānic verses which seem to view earning with favour.[153] The first two traditions in the chapter read: "Being active and doing gainful work does not harm him whose reliance [on God] is sound, does not impair his [spiritual] standing and does not diminish his [spiritual] condition ..." The most licit food eaten by a man is what he gained by his hand or by a sinless sale" (*wa lā yaḍurru al-taṣarruf wa al-takassub li-man ṣaḥḥa tawakkuluhu wa lā yaqdaḥu fī maqāmihi wa lā yanquṣu min ḥālihi ... aḥallu ma akala al-ʿabd min kasbi yadihi wa kulli bayʿ mabrūr*).[154] Al-Sulamī (d. 412/1021) asserts that the Ṣūfīs do not plan for the future, do not work for their livelihood and behave as passively as they would if they were in their mother's womb, in their grave or on the Day of Judgment.[155] Al-Ghazālī mentions the prophetic *ḥadīth* which favours seeking gain and bemoans the fact that it is not followed in his times, because many people say that except for water and plants growing on uncultivated land (*mawāt*), everything is tainted with corruption and does not belong to things which are permissible (*ḥalāl*) and may be legitimately sought after by Muslims.[156] Abū al-Najīb al-Suhrawardī (d. 563/1168) maintains that seeking lawful gain is a duty and that the Ṣūfīs agreed on the permissibility of earning by engaging in commerce and crafts in a morally upright way, without considering this to be the (real) reason to gain livelihood (*min ghayri an yarā dhālika sababan li-'stijlāb al-rizq*); this apparently means that the Ṣūfī must always be aware of God, the real Provider.[157]

Having seen the variety of pertinent views in classical Ṣūfī literature, we can now return to Mahdawī views on gainful employment. While the thrust of Mahdawī thinking is totally opposed to it, there are indications that these extreme attitudes were for obvious reasons difficult to enforce and, consequently, traditions in which the *mahdī* did not frown

152 Kalābādhī, *al-Taʿarruf li-madhhab ahl al-taṣawwuf*, pp. 102–103; translation by A. J. Arberry, *The Doctrine of the Ṣūfīs*, p. 73.

153 Qur'ān 7:10 ("We have established you in the earth and there appointed for you livelihood ...") and 78:8–11 ("And We created you in pairs, and We created your sleep for a rest; and We appointed night for a garment, and We appointed day for a livelihood").

154 Makkī, *Qūt al-qulūb*, vol. 2, pp. 29. Translation in Gramlich, *Die Nahrung der Herzen*, vol. 2, p. 330.

155 Sulamī, *Jawāmiʿ*, pp. 36–37 (no. 86).

156 Ghazālī, *Iḥyāʾ ʿulūm al-dīn*, vol. 2, p. 158.

157 Suhrawardī, *Kitāb ādāb al-murīdīn*, pp. 5–6.

upon gainful employment came into being. In one instance, Jawnpūrī is quoted as explicitly permitting it (*mu'min-rā kasb ḥalāl ast*), and Walī b. Yūsuf declares that he never heard from the *mahdī*'s associates that the *mahdī* determined time and again that acceptance of fixed income is reprehensible. Neither did he hear from his associates that Jawnpūrī told someone not to accept gainful appointment and "eat fixed income" because it is reprehensible (*wa īn banda bā aṣḥāb-i kibār ham na-shanīda kih kasī-rā amrī kardand kih ta'īn* (sc. *ta'yīn*) *bi-khwarīd la'īn ast*). When followers asked his permission to leave their employment, he evaded the request and told them, in a rather enigmatic way, to ask God instead. In a similar vein, there are reports of conciliatory attitudes expressed by the *mahdī*'s second successor Bandagī Miyāñ Sayyid Khwāndmīr to questions of gainful employment (*waẓīfa*) and fixed income. When asked to prevent members of the movement from acting against Jawnpūrī's teachings (and, presumably, accepting gainful employment), he asserted that his task was to explain the Qur'ān, not to act as a chief of police (*kōtwāl*) who is responsible for enforcing the law.[158]

These statements seem to express ambivalent attitudes to the issue of gainful employment. On the other hand, we are told – in the same source – that in his public addresses the *mahdī* always declared fixed income as reprehensible and used to condemn those who had it.[159] He instructed a follower to stop grinding corn, pay someone to do the work instead of him and use his time for worship. Bandagī Miyān expelled from a *dā'ira* in Sind women who made a living from embroidery, saying that the donations used in the *dā'ira* are for those who dedicate themselves to God.[160] If someone cannot endure poverty, he should beg and satisfy his hunger. This is better than to go and earn a farthing, because whoever embarks on the way of earning, he will want to earn even more the next day.[161] Those who go about in search of livelihood and have gainful appointments are not entitled to the charitable payments mentioned in Qur'ān 2:272–273;[162] these are restricted to those who "are confined in the way of God".[163]

158 Walī b. Yūsuf, *Inṣāf Nāma*, pp. 64, 222.
159 Walī b. Yūsuf, *Inṣāf Nāma*, pp. 223.
160 Walī b. Yūsuf, *Inṣāf nāma*, pp. 282–283.
161 Walī b. Yūsuf, *Inṣāf Nāma*, p. 62.
162 "... whatever good you expend ... is for the poor who are restrained in the way of God, and are unable to journey in the land" (in search of livelihood).
163 Walī b. Yūsuf, *Inṣāf Nāma*, pp. 70–71.

The only source of income explicitly permitted in Mahdawī thinking is unsolicited donations (*futūḥ*). Discussions about this type of income have a long history in Ṣūfism; the problem has been to ensure that accepting donations will not impair the recipient's absolute reliance on God (*tawakkul*). The Mahdawīs developed this perception in the most extreme direction and gave highly restricted definitions to the term "unsolicited". They did this by creating an additional category of permissibility. A permissible thing (*ḥalāl*) is something judged permissible in Muslim law; "absolutely permissible" (*ḥalāl-i ṭayyib*), a category inspired by Qur'ānic verses in which this expression occurs,[164] is something "that comes one by one, without thought or volition (of the person receiving it), immediately contemplating God. 'Absolutely permissible' things are unlimited" (*ḥalāl-i ṭayyib ān ast kih yakāyak bē gumān o bē ikhtiyār bi-rasad fī al-ḥāl naẓar bar khudā-yi taʿālā āyad wa ḥalāl-i ṭayyib-rā ḥisāb nīst*).[165] This means that one must not accept many donations simultaneously and that one must not think about them or want them to come. The statement that "absolutely permissible" things are unlimited is probably meant to imply that it is possible to survive while strictly observing the rule that only things fitting this definition may be accepted. Strict and sophisticated criteria were developed in order to make this distinction. The "absolutely permissible" differs from the "permissible" not in itself, but rather in the mental attitude of the person receiving it and in the manner in which the donation is delivered. For instance, if someone sits in his room, hears the sound of steps and thinks that someone is bringing him a donation – this is incompatible with *tawakkul*. The mental attitude of the recipient who hoped that a donation was on the way impaired his reliance on God; the clear implication is that in such circumstances the donation must not be accepted, though the text does not explicitly say so. This attitude can also be found in classical asceticism (*zuhd*): al-Makkī refers to an ascetic who used to reject a donation if he received it after he had looked forward to it; others did not touch such a donation as a punishment for their (greedy) soul (*wa qad kāna baʿḍuhum idhā jāʾahu al-sabab*

164 Qur'ān 2:168, 5:88, 8:69. "Absolutely permissible" is, of course, not a literal translation of *ḥalāl-i ṭayyib*, but it conveys the meaning intended by the Mahdawīs precisely enough.

165 Walī b. Yūsuf, *Inṣāf Nāma*, p. 157. This idea is inspired by Qur'ān 3:37 according to which God provided provisions to Mary without reckoning (*bi-ghayri ḥisāb*).

baʿda taṭalluʿin ilayhi raddahu. wa minhum man kāna yukhrijuhu wa lā yatanāwalu minhu ʿuqūbatan li-nafsihi).[166]

In another case, Jawnpūrī refused to accept a donation because of the manner in which it was delivered. He stayed in a city which was home to a merchant sympathetic (*muwāfiq*) to the Mahdawiyya. Miyān Sayyid Salām Allāh, a Mahdawī, went to town on an errand and involuntarily passed near that merchant's door. The merchant sent 80,000 tankas for Jawnpūrī who refused to accept them. When Salām Allāh argued that the donation was sent and delivered by God, Jawnpūrī responded: "Why, then, have *you* brought it? It cannot be said that this was delivered by God. This is called permissible, but not absolutely permissible" (*shumā chi-rā āwardīd? īn-rā rasānīda-yi Khudāʾ namī-gūyand. īn-rā ḥalāl mī-gūyand, fa-ammā ḥalāl-i ṭayyib na-gūyand.*)[167] In this case, a Mahdawī's active participation in the delivery rendered the donation unacceptable. In a similar vein, Sayyid Khwāndmīr refused to send Mahdawīs to a village in order to bring a gift of maze. "Servants of God will not go from village to village for the sake of grain; whatever has been decreed, will arrive without (our) intervention (*bē-wāsiṭa*) and you will take it," he said.[168]

In another case, a certain Fatḥ Khān gave Sayyid Maḥmūd, Jawnpūrī's son and successor, 30 tankas. A month later, he gave him the same sum again. When he tried to make the donation for the third time, Sayyid Maḥmūd refused, saying: "Perhaps Fatḥ Khān regards us as (permanent) employees (*magar Fatḥ Khān mā-rā taʿayyun gardānad*).[169] In this case, the recurrence of the donation is the invalidating factor. Permanence of income is considered injurious to reliance on God: if someone is certain that his livelihood is assured, his feeling of total dependency on God is bound to be impaired.

We have said earlier that in Mahdawī thinking membership in the community must replace family relationships. This stringent principle has implications also for acceptance of donations. The brothers of Bībī Kad Bānū sent some money to Sayyid Maḥmūd. He refused to accept, saying that they sent it for the sake of their relatives; if they wanted to send it for the sake of God, they would have sent it to some other *dāʾira* in need.

166 Makkī, *Qūt al-qulūb*, vol. 2, p. 36 *infra*.
167 Walī b. Yūsuf, *Inṣāf Nāma*, p. 156; cf. ibid., pp. 239–240.
168 Walī b. Yūsuf, *Inṣāf Nāma*, p. 236. For other cases of a similar nature, see ibid., pp. 237–238.
169 Walī b. Yūsuf, *Inṣāf Nāma*, p. 224.

Eventually, the brothers gave the money to Bībī Kad Bānū without Sayyid Maḥmūd's knowledge and she spent it. When Sayyid Maḥmūd learned of this, he expelled the lady from the *dā'ira* and told her: "Go to your brothers' house and eat there."[170] Kinship between donor and recipient rendered the gift illicit and its acceptance was considered sufficient reason for expelling a Mahdawī from the movement.

VI MAHDAWĪ *JIHĀD*

The impression gained from Mahdawī sources is that during the times of Jawnpūrī and his son Sayyid Maḥmūd the movement did not offer military resistance to its enemies. Jawnpūrī is quoted as saying that he has no territorial aspiration and does not want to rule a state of his own.[171] The Mahdawīs were repeatedly persecuted and expelled from town after town, but only during the reign of Sayyid Khwāndmīr (1513–1524) did the movement acquire a semi-military character. In a letter to certain *'ulamā'*, Sayyid Khwāndmīr warned that from now on the Mahdawīs will meet force with force. Attempts at reconciliation failed and Sayyid Khwāndmīr was killed in a battle against Sultan Muẓaffar's armies in 1524.[172]

The addition of a military aspect to the movement resulted in the development of Mahdawī thinking on *jihād* and caused some debate: the question was raised whether it was legal to fight against Muslim rulers who rejected Sayyid Muḥammad Jawnpūrī's messianic claim but, of course, did not renounce Islam. Like on other issues, Mahdawī thinking on *jihād* reflects a sustained effort to create an affinity between the period of the *mahdī* and early Islam. At the same time, it is influenced by Ṣūfī perceptions of *jihād* as a struggle against one's "evil-bidding" soul. In the Qur'ānic context, *jihād* is closely associated with *hijra* and the connection between the two is prominent in Mahdawī thought as well. Jawnpūrī and his followers were expelled from Nahrwālā, Champanēr and Khānbīl;[173] Jawnpūrī's interpretation of these events is inspired by the Qur'ān and by the migration (*hijra*) of the Prophet and his Companions from Mecca to Medina. Contextualizing Qur'ān 3:195, he says that the

170 Walī b. Yūsuf, *Inṣāf Nāma*, p. 239.
171 Anṣārī, "Sayyid Muḥammad Jawnpūrī", p. 51.
172 Qamaruddin, *The Mahdawī Movement*, pp. 106–116.
173 Walī b. Yūsuf, *Inṣāf Nāma*, pp. 29, 166, 363; 'Alī, *Siyar-i Mas'ūd*, pp. 51–52.

Mahdawīs already "migrated and were expelled from their habitations" and "suffered hurt in My way"; it still remains for them to fight and be killed (*wa qātalū wa qutilū mānda ast*). Military *jihād* is clearly meant in this interpretation. Support for military *jihād* is strengthened by Qur'ānic verses which differentiate between believers who fight in the way of God and those "who sit (at home)" (*al-qā'idūn*), promising more reward for the former.[174] Nevertheless, spiritual meanings of *jihād* and *hijra* are also present when Jawnpūrī interprets Qur'ān 3:195 differently and explains that the migration is not only from one's habitat, but also from one's bad deeds and wicked character; *jihād* is waged with both body and soul. Those who were expelled from their habitations left the natural world for the World of (mystical) Reality (*'ālam al-ḥaqīqa*) in order to get close to God. Echoes of the classical transformation of the *hijra* into a spiritual one, expressed in traditions such as "the migrant is he who abandons what Allah has forbidden" (*al-muhājir man hajara mā nahā Allah 'anhu*),[175] are clearly discernible in this description. These "spiritual migrants" who were afflicted while seeking God, suffered from a variety of woes, fought against their evil-bidding souls and were "killed" with the sword of truth – God will acquit them of their evil deeds in the same way as He acquits those who fought and were slain in military *jihād*. This spiritual or "greater" *jihād*, mentioned in the prophetic tradition according to which "we have returned from the smaller *jihād* to the greater *jihād*", should continue until military struggle begins. Then, when the warriors encounter the enemy, they should stand firm and remember God frequently. Until the battle is joined, the warriors should fight their evil-bidding souls. Remembering God constantly is essential for military struggle. Jawnpūrī derives this from Qur'ān 8:46: "When you encounter a fighting force, stand firm and remember God frequently ..."[176] This verse makes a connection between fighting and *dhikr* and is therefore very appropriate for the point that Jawnpūrī wants to make.

The military *jihād* in which the Mahdawīs were involved is presented as a response to their oppression by mainstream Muslims. Jawnpūrī encouraged and even commanded his followers to fight whenever they were oppressed and wronged. Naturally enough, Qur'ān 22:39–40, in which the early Muslims were given permission to fight because they had been

174 Walī b. Yūsuf, *Inṣāf Nāma*, pp. 176–177, 360. Cf. Qur'ān 4:94.

175 Bukhārī, *Ṣaḥīḥ*, *Kitāb al-īmān*, 4 (vol. 1, p. 11).

176 Walī b. Yūsuf, *Inṣāf Nāma*, p. 361.

wronged and expelled from their habitations, is brought to bear on the Mahdawīs. When the "army of the accursed" (*lashkar-i mal'ūnān*) started attacking the Mahdawīs, burning their mosques and houses, branding their faces and killing them, Sayyid Khwāndmīr sent some Mahdawīs to kill *mullās* who were issuing *fatwās* to kill Mahdawīs. In such a situation, he thought, *jihād* becomes an individual duty of every believer, be they man or woman, slave or free.[177]

This attitude was not accepted without opposition. Some Mahdawīs were not sure whether it was licit to fight against people who pronounced the Muslim declaration of faith (*kalima gūyān*). This debate is reminiscent of a controversy which erupted in the Muslim community in the wake of the Prophet's death. Abū Bakr (r. 632–634 CE) decided to fight the rebellious Arab tribes who refused to pay taxes to the nascent Muslim state but did not renounce Islam. 'Umar b. al-Khaṭṭāb, who eventually became Abū Bakr's successor, argued that it was illegal to fight those who pronounced the Muslim declaration of faith (*shahāda*) and must therefore be considered Muslims.[178] When Sayyid Khwāndmīr started preparing for war, some of the closest associates of the *mahdī* argued that it was illegal to fight Muslims. These associates maintained that they followed the Prophet, the *mahdī* and the Qur'ān. Fighting Muslims and declaring them infidels is not permissible and amounts to the abrogation of the Qur'ān and of the *sharī'a*. The Qur'ān enjoins Muslims "not to say to him who offers you a greeting 'You are not a believer'",[179] and the Prophet asserted that those who pray in the direction of the *qibla* and eat from what Muslims slaughter is a Muslim.[180] The *ḥadīth* according to which the Prophet was commanded to wage war until the enemy says that there is no god except Allah is also relevant to this discussion: the Mahdawīs' enemies must be considered people who fulfilled this condition. If the non-Mahdawīs were infidels, it would be permissible to take their daughters without proper

177 Walī b. Yūsuf, *Inṣāf Nāma*, pp. 362–363, 369. For the distinction between *jihād* as a communal duty (*farḍ kifāya*) and as an individual duty (*farḍ 'ayn*), see "Djihād", *EI²*, s.v. (E. Tyan).

178 See M. J. Kister, "... *illā bi-ḥaqqihi* ... A study of an early *ḥadīth*", *JSAI* 5 (1984), 33–52.

179 Qur'ān 4:94.

180 Bukhārī, *Ṣaḥīḥ*, vol. 1, p. 111 (*Kitāb al-ṣalāt* 28). For a similarly catholic approach to the community boundaries, see Muslim, *Ṣaḥīḥ*, vol. 1, p. 79 (*Kitāb al-īmān* 111); Bukhārī, *Ṣaḥīḥ*, vol. 4, pp. 136–137 (*Kitāb al-adab* 73–74). See also Friedmann, "Conversion, Apostasy ...", p. 146.

marriage, and to plunder their property. This is illicit and even amounts to infidelity. After further deliberations, however, all agreed that in view of the atrocities perpetrated by the enemies of the Mahdawīs, *jihād* against them had become justified.[181]

Those Mahdawīs who supported military *jihād* against their opponents placed the emphasis elsewhere. They stressed that the Qur'ān and the *ḥadīth* speak harshly against those who reject the *mahdī*. According to a peculiar interpretation of Qur'ān 11:17, those who reject the *mahdī* are destined for Hell.[182] According to a *ḥadīth*, anyone who rejects the *mahdī* is an infidel (*man ankara al-mahdī fa-qad kafara*). It would be better to forgive, endure or reach an agreement with those who consider the religion of the *mahdī* as a reprehensible innovation and threaten to expel those who support it from their habitat. At the same time, it is essential to command right (*al-amr bi-'l-ma'rūf*) and this is done by hand, tongue and soul. If none of these means helps and the enemies place themselves beyond the pale of the *sharī'a* (by rejecting the *mahdī*), then it is legal to fight them. Eventually, all agreed that this was the right way.[183] Like in the seventh-century controversy between Abū Bakr and 'Umar, the Mahdawīs resolved that belonging to the Muslim community simply by pronouncing the declaration of faith was not sufficient: in the seventh century the poor tax had to be paid in order to belong, while in the Mahdawī period one could not be spared the fury of *jihād* without recognizing the messianic status of Sayyid Muḥammad Jawnpūrī and performing *hijra* to his camp.

VII RELIGIOUS KNOWLEDGE VERSUS MYSTICAL ECSTASY

Since the very beginnings of Islamic thought, Muslims have discussed the nature of knowledge and made distinctions between its various types.[184] Ṣūfī thinkers were not an exception and many of them included definitions

181 Walī b. Yūsuf, *Inṣāf Nāma*, pp. 363–365.

182 The verse reads in part: "... Whosoever disbelieves in it [or in him], being one of the partisans, his promised land is the Fire." In the mainstream interpretation, this verse is directed against the non-Muslims who reject the Qur'ān or the Prophet, but the Mahdawīs interpret it as a reference to Jawnpūrī.

183 Walī b. Yūsuf, *Inṣāf Nāma*, p. 366.

184 For a seminal study of this field, see F. Rosenthal, *Knowledge Triumphant*, Leiden: E. J. Brill, 1970.

of knowledge in their works. Abū Naṣr al-Sarrāj (d. 378/988), who wrote a very early manual of Ṣūfism, speaks about three kinds of knowledge: the knowledge of prophetic tradition, the knowledge of the religious law and the knowledge of the Ṣūfīs. In his view, these three branches are of equal validity and al-Sarrāj considers scholars belonging to them as heirs of the prophets who are upholding justice. The Ṣūfīs, though, enjoy a certain advantage: they accept the views and rulings of the scholars of *ḥadīth* and of the jurists, but they are more sincere in observing the commandments, do not seek ways to circumvent them by allegorical explanations and do not seek worldly pleasures. Furthermore, among the scholars who deal with the "external", legal facets of religion (*ʿilm al-ẓāhir*) there are some who denounce Ṣūfī knowledge while they themselves do not know from the Qurʾān and the prophetic tradition anything except legal topics which they use to overcome their opponents and obtain prominent positions in society. The knowledge of the Ṣūfīs, on the other hand, belongs to the spiritual elite which shuns worldly success and therefore has an advantage over the others.[185] Al-Hujwīrī (d. 456/1063–1064) also devotes the first chapter of his *Kashf al-Maḥjūb* to the various types of knowledge. He first quotes the famous prophetic dictum according to which "seeking knowledge is incumbent on every Muslim" (*ṭalab al-ʿilm farīḍa ʿalā kulli muslim*). When discussing the various types of knowledge, he says that the exoteric and the esoteric cannot exist without each other. "The exoteric aspect of the Truth without the esoteric is hypocrisy, and the esoteric without the exoteric is heresy" (*ẓāhir-i ḥaqīqat bī bāṭin nifāq wa bāṭin-i ḥaqīqat bī ẓāhir zandaqa*).[186] Abū al-Najīb al-Suhrawardī (d. 563/1168) is also appreciative of legal knowledge and asserts that the Ṣūfīs must learn the injunctions of the *sharīʿa* so that their practice is compatible with them. While he maintains that Ṣūfī religiosity is superior, he accords the jurists an essential role and does not denounce them for holding lucrative positions of leadership in Muslim society.[187] He mentions prophetic traditions in praise of knowledge, quotes the famous saying according to which the *ʿulamāʾ* are heirs of the prophets (*al-ʿulamāʾ warathat al-anbiyāʾ*) and divides humanity into the learned, the learners and riffraff.[188] It is evident

185 Al-Sarrāj, *Kitāb al-Lumaʿ*, pp. 4–15.
186 Hujwīrī, *Kashf al-maḥjūb*, pp. 14–15; translation by Nicholson, *Kashf al-Maḥjūb*, p. 14.
187 Al-Suhrawardī, *Kitāb ādāb al-murīdīn*, pp. 13–15.
188 Al-Suhrawardī, *Kitāb ādāb al-murīdīn*, p. 22.

that the mainstream of Ṣūfī thought takes a balanced view on the relationship between knowledge acquired by learning and mystical knowledge bestowed by God.

Nevertheless, there is sufficient evidence to suggest that among the Ṣūfīs there was also a significant group who viewed knowledge acquired by learning with contempt. They used to define the knowledge of *ḥadīth* or *fiqh* as originating with a mere human being, meaning the Prophet; Ṣūfī, mystical knowledge emanates from the immortal God (*naḥnu naʾkhudhu ʿilmanā min al-ḥayy alladhī lā yamūt wa antum taʾkhudhūnahu min ḥayyin yamūt*). Some denounced Ṣūfīs who related traditions from the Prophet and even said that such type of knowledge is "a veil between the heart and God the Exalted".[189] In his famous denunciation of Ṣūfism, Ibn al-Jawzī speaks of Ṣūfīs who think that

> the objective [of the mystical quest, i.e., God] is too exalted to be attained by knowledge. It can be attained by grace bestowed on man, not by his seeking it. [Satan] closed in front of these Ṣūfīs the gate of salvation which is the pursuit of knowledge, and they began hating the term "knowledge" in the same way as the Shīʿī hates the names of Abū Bakr and ʿUmar. They said: "Knowledge is a veil and the *ʿulamāʾ* are veiled from the objective by knowledge" (... *wa anna al-maqṣūd ajallu min an yunāla bi-'l-ʿilm wa innamā al-ẓafar bihi rizq yusāq ilā al-ʿabd lā bi-'l-ṭalab fa-sadda ʿalayhim bāb al-najāt alladhī huwa ṭalab al-ʿilm fa-ṣārū yubghiḍūna ism al-ʿilm kamā yubghiḍ al-rāfiḍī ism Abī Bakr wa ʿUmar wa yaqūlūn: al-ʿilm ḥijāb wa al-ʿulamāʾ maḥjūbūn ʿan al-maqṣūd bi-'l-ʿilm*).[190]

Sayyid Muḥammad Jawnpūrī neatly fits the group described in the last two passages. He held an extremely negative view on the role of the *ʿulamāʾ* and on the way in which his followers should relate to Muslim jurisprudence and other "external" varieties of knowledge. Knowledge, disparagingly described by him as "knowledge of hypocrisy and disputation", is the greatest veil concealing God. Knowledge is ugly and ignorance is beautiful (*qāla al-muḥaqqiqūn: al-ʿilm ḥijāb Allāh al-akbar; wa fī al-Kāfī: al-ʿilm qabīḥ wa al-jahl ḥasan, ay ʿilm al-riyāʾ wa al-mubāḥatha*).[191] Jawnpūrī's

189 Ibn Qayyim al-Jawziyya, *Madārij al-sālikīn*, vol. 2, p. 179.
190 Ibn al-Jawzī, *Talbīs Iblīs*, p. 352.
191 Walī b. Yūsuf, *Inṣāf Nāma*, p. 252.

denunciation of the "external" *ʿulamāʾ* is harsh and uncompromising: they acquired their knowledge in order to obtain positions of leadership, such as judgeship, being professional witnesses in courts (*shahāda*),[192] inspecting the markets (*ḥisba*) and teaching. Their hearts are like those of wolves, God has no need of them and they are the enemies of the *mahdī*.[193] This view of the *ʿulamāʾ* has ramifications on the Mahdawī attitude to learning. A whole chapter in the *Inṣāf Nāma* deals with Jawnpūrī's prohibition to learn or read, and with his injunction to concentrate exclusively on *dhikr*, the ecstatic repetition of a divine name. Mahdawīs were not permitted to read even during siesta time; this should be used for sleeping. And it should be clear that when Jawnpūrī denounces reading and learning, he does not mean learning non-religious subjects as one might be inclined to expect; surprisingly enough, his prohibition relates to reading books of religion, and even the Qurʾān. He explicitly prohibited reading the Qurʾān and studying *ʿilm*, presumably meaning subjects such as *ḥadīth* or *fiqh*.[194] He told a certain judge that if he read Qurʾānic exegesis, he will not be allowed to behold God. In a similar vein, Bandagī Miyāñ Sayyid Khwāndmīr said that even if someone reads the Qurʾān – and reads it as it should be read[195] – a veil of light comes between him and God; only *dhikr* tears the veil and, presumably, restores the intimacy between God and believer. Shāh Niʿmat once asked permission to read something, but the *mahdī* refused to grant it and said that if he read and learned, he would not recognize Jawnpūrī's messianic status. Jesus was able to treat the sick, but was not able to treat a fool who was engaged in study, albeit for a short period of time only. On one occasion Jawnpūrī quoted a verse of poetry according to which "you cannot reach a deep understanding of divine attributes until you do not learn the commandments" (*tā ʿilm-i farīża-rā na-khwānī / taḥqīq-i ṣifāt-i ḥaqq na-dānī*), but immediately continued saying that if someone learns too much, he will be tempted to seek worldly pleasures and will be

192 These are not witnesses in a particular case, but rather court employees who perform various auxiliary functions, assisting the *qāḍī*. See "Shāhid", *EI*², s.v. (R. Peters); Tyan, *Histoire de l'organisation judiciaire*, pp. 236–252; Tsafrir, *The History of an Islamic School of Law*, p. 68.

193 Walī b. Yūsuf, *Inṣāf Nāma*, pp. 20–21.

194 Walī b. Yūsuf, *Inṣāf Nāma*, p. 281. Cf. the views of Muḥammad Aḥmad, the Sudanese *mahdī*, who allowed reading only the Qurʾān, saying: "Leave alone all books except the Qurʾān, because they are a veil [hindering] the comprehension of its meaning." See *al-Āthār al-kāmila*, vol. 7, p. 82.

195 Alluding to Qurʾān 2:121, but this verse of course praises those who read the book properly.

humiliated thereby.[196] The negative attitude to religious learning brought about a situation in which outsiders got the impression that the Mahdawīs do not know even how to pray properly. Eventually, Jawnpūrī conceded that "indispensable knowledge" (*ʿilm-i lā buddī*) is necessary, so that prayer, fasting and similar commandments are properly performed. Nevertheless, he continued to argue that the "light of faith" (*nūr-i īmān*) is sufficient to understand the meanings of the Qurʾān when they are explained. He instructed his son Sayyid Maḥmūd to abandon reading the *Tamhīdāt* of ʿAyn al-Quḍāt al-Hamadānī,[197] saying that he should concentrate his efforts on *dhikr* in order to create the spiritual condition for understanding the Qurʾān. For a long time, Jawnpūrī prevented Shāh Niẓām from reading the *Mīzān*;[198] only much later, when the *mahdī* and his close associates went to Khurāsān prior to the *mahdī*'s death, did he allow him to read *ḥadīth*. Walī b. Yūsuf explains that only when a person is (spiritually) perfect, such learning will not cause him harm.[199]

The denunciation of the so-called "external" sciences, as developed in Mahdawī thought, stood in stark contrast with Jawnpūrī's own hagiography according to which he had been a precocious student who committed Qurʾān to memory at the age of seven, completed the regular curriculum at the age of twelve and had been given the title of "a lion among the *ʿulamāʾ*" as a token of appreciation for his achievements precisely in these "external" sciences. Initially a source of pride for his family and community, this detail in Jawnpūrī's biography later became something of an embarrassment. Mahdawī tradition maintains that after making the messianic claim and after receiving from God mystical knowledge (*ʿilm-i ladunī*) in great abundance, Jawnpūrī asked God what was the purpose of bestowing upon him all this "external" (and now apparently useless) knowledge; God responded that this was done so that the "external" *ʿulamāʾ* are also compelled to believe in him. In any event, before he became *mahdī*, God cleansed Jawnpūrī of the external knowledge and bestowed upon him the mystical one. This cleansing was essential because God bestows mystical knowledge only on the unlettered (*ummī*). The hearts of such people

196 Walī b. Yūsuf, *Inṣāf Nāma*, p. 249.

197 See "ʿAyn-al-Qożāt Hamadānī, EIr, s.v. (G. Bövering) and cf. Walī b. Yūsuf, *Inṣāf Nāma*, p. 199, *infra*.

198 The book is not identified. From the end of the story, one gains the impression that some book of prophetic traditions is meant, such as *Mīzān al-ʿamal* by al-Ghazālī.

199 Walī b. Yūsuf, *Inṣāf Nāma*, pp. 243–245.

are pure and nothing is written on them; therefore, whatever they hear clings to their hearts permanently. If someone whom God chooses for His purpose does not belong to the category of the unlettered, He transforms him into a *jaʿlī ummī*, a person who had been learned in the past, but God "delettered" him and made him forget his learning. To reinforce his praise for the unlettered, Jawnpūrī quotes Qurʾān 62:2 which states that God sent to the unlettered a messenger from among them. This verse is conventionally explained as relating to the Prophet's mission to the Arabs who had not received a heavenly book before him and were unlettered in this sense, but this conventional interpretation does not deter Jawnpūrī from using it for his denunciation of learning. Finally, if a Mahdawī started reading and writing, some of the *mahdī*'s associates denounced him as a hypocrite and accused him of preparing to flee the *dāʾira*.[200]

This negative attitude to learning reflects a prominent anti-intellectual streak in Mahdawī thought. Mahdawī religiosity does not encourage learning, religious or other; it rather places nearly exclusive stress on *dhikr*, the ecstatic repetition of a divine name, a ritual conducive to mystical ecstasy. *Dhikr* is a well-known Ṣūfī ritual[201] and its existence among the Mahdawīs who draw most of their inspiration from Ṣūfī lore is to be expected. The centrality of *dhikr*, the precise rules of its performance and the demand to engage in it to the exclusion of any other religious activity for most of the day are salient characteristics of the Mahdawī movement. Constant remembrance of God is a duty incumbent on Muslims, male and female. The obligation to perform *dhikr* can be derived from numerous Qurʾānic verses in which remembrance of God is enjoined. These verses range from general injunctions "to remember God often", through a more specific command to "remember your Lord in your soul, humbly and fearfully, not loud of voice, mornings and evenings", to dire threats against those "whose hearts are hardened against the remembrance of God".[202] During the remembrance, the worshipper must be in a state of ritual purity, wear pure clothing and be in a pure place. He should sit cross-legged, facing Mecca, placing his hands on his thighs, or the palm of his right hand on the back of the left one. He should say *lā ilāha illā 'llāh* with his heart in the presence of God, watching his voice, and closing his eyes.[203]

---

200 Walī b. Yūsuf, *Inṣāf Nāma*, pp. 242–252.
201 See "Dhikr", *EI*², s.v. (L. Gardet).
202 Qurʾān 7:204; 33:41; 39:22.
203 Walī b. Yūsuf, *Inṣāf Nāma*, pp. 254–256.

We have seen that *dhikr* is considered central in Mahdawī thought. In Mahdawī literature we also find instructions concerning the amount of time which has to be devoted to *dhikr*. In general, one must not waste time without *dhikr*. Jawnpūrī instructed his followers to perform "abundant *dhikr*", according to Qur'ān 33:41. He defined the duration of "abundant *dhikr*" as fifteen hours a day and specified the times of day when it must be performed. *Dhikr* lasting nine hours is defined as insufficient and is considered the *dhikr* of the hypocrites, according to Qur'ān 4:142. Those who perform *dhikr* for twelve hours are condemned even more severely: they are engaged in remembering God for half a day and give equal time to ungodly activities. This means that their love of God equals their love of Satan; their *dhikr* is that of *mushrikūn* who "take to themselves compeers apart from God, loving them as God is loved".[204] Behaviour during *dhikr* time was strictly regulated. No two persons were allowed to sit together and if someone left the room ahead of time, he was expelled from the *dā'ira* and his room was torn apart.[205]

VIII THE MAHDAWIYYA: GENERAL CONSIDERATIONS

The late Professor Muhammad Mujeeb, who seems to have been one of the first modern scholars to devote substantial attention to the Mahdawīs, considered the movement "an active and assertive social force in Indian Muslim society", a movement for moral and social reform.[206] "Reform" is a positive term in modern parlance; but in our case the positive features of Jawnpūrī's thought and activities are not self-evident. The exclusivity of the movement, the denunciation of Muslims who did not join it, the demand to sever family relationships with non-Mahdawīs, the opposition to gainful employment in order to promote total dependence on God, the anti-intellectual tendency reflected in the opposition to studying even the sacred literature of Islam – all these are not ideals of moral and social reform in the modern sense.

Sayyid Muḥammad Jawnpūrī's movement represents a rather unusual combination of asceticism, Ṣūfism, mysticism and militancy. When saying this, I do not mean to imply there is an inherent, necessary contradiction

204 Qur'ān 2:165.
205 Walī b. Yūsuf, *Inṣāf Nāma*, pp. 271–273.
206 Mujeeb, *The Indian Muslims*, p. 101.

between asceticism, Ṣūfism and *jihād*. Students of early Islam will remember that the early group of ascetics, known as *ahl al-ṣuffa*, "the homeless" of the first generation of Muslims who lived near the Prophet's mosque in Medina in extreme poverty, and never left their places except for waging *jihād*. The unusual feature of our case is the seamless integration of asceticism, Ṣūfism and militancy into Mahdawī thought. The ascetic component is self-evident: the prevalent opposition to gainful employment, the preference of begging to earning a livelihood, the principle of giving Mahdawī girls in marriage only to poor grooms, the social boycott of the "world-seekers" as the rich are called in Mahdawī parlance – all these reflect the insistence on extreme asceticism and glorification of poverty in the movement.

The Ṣūfī element in Mahdawī thought is also prominent, though the Mahdawīs do not call themselves Ṣūfīs. The main component of their identity is fidelity to Jawnpūrī, unquestionable acceptance of his messianic claim and fighting for the cause by word and sword. Nevertheless, the centrality of *dhikr* certainly connects the Mahdawī movement to Ṣūfī practices. Furthermore, much of the material used to edify the members of the movement is taken from what we normally call the Ṣūfī tradition. Figures such as Bāyazīd Bisṭāmī, Ibrāhīm-i Adham, Abū Bakr Shiblī, and Junayd are mentioned as *awliyā'* who came after the Prophet Muḥammad.[207] And Jawnpūrī's claim to be the *khātam al-awliyā'* certainly derives from Ṣūfī lore. Mysticism in the sense of striving for "an intensified experience of the sacred"[208] figures prominently and is best exemplified by Jawnpūrī's aspiration to see God as its fulfilment.[209]

During the lifetime of Jawnpūrī, militancy and glorification of military *jihād* were restricted to the theoretical level. Jawnpūrī explained relevant Qur'ānic verses and considered them relevant to the situation of the Mahdawīs who were persecuted and oppressed by the rulers of Gujarāt. Only after Jawnpūrī's death did the Mahdawīs engage their adversaries in battle, but they were soundly defeated in 1524. This military defeat and the paucity of the Mahdawīs in general became something of an embarrassment for them: it was difficult to explain the stark difference between the persecuted Jawnpūrī and the defeated Mahdawīs on the one hand and the victorious *mahdī* of the eschaton on the other. The sophisticated Mahdawī system of thought did not prevent the earthly failures of the movement.

207 Walī b. Yūsuf, *Inṣāf Nāma*, pp. 395–396.
208 See Sviri, *Perspectives on Early Islamic Mysticism*, p. 24.
209 Cf. Qamaruddin, *The Mahdawī Movement*, pp. 66–67.

4

Muḥammad Aḥmad, the Sudanese *mahdī*

1 BIOGRAPHY

Muḥammad Aḥmad b. ʿAbd Allāh was born in 1844 on the Labab island in the Sudanese province of Dongola to a family of boat-builders. He had three brothers and a sister. When he was still a child, the family migrated to the Kharṭūm area where the father, ʿAbd Allah, had a better opportunity to engage in his trade. ʿAbd Allah died in Kararī, north of Kharṭūm, and was buried there. Muḥammad Aḥmad's brothers continued in their father's trade; Muḥammad Aḥmad, on the other hand, displayed since early childhood an inclination and aptitude for religious studies. He learned the Qurʾān in *madrasas* in Kararī and Kharṭūm, and expanded his traditional upbringing by studying Arabic grammar, Islamic jurisprudence and Ṣūfism. His principal teacher in his early teens was Muḥammad ʿAbd Allah Khūjalī, whom he later honoured by naming him Muḥammad al-Khayr. This was the period in which the extreme asceticism of Muḥammad Aḥmad expressed itself for the first time: the traditional account maintains that since Muḥammad al-Khayr was receiving financial support from the government, Muḥammad Aḥmad refused to consume the food provided by him. In keeping with the time-honoured principle of many Muslim ascetics, he opined that government money must have been obtained by oppression and illegal taxation. Therefore, when he did not receive food from his family, he lived on fish which he himself caught in the Nile.[1]

1 Shuqayr, *Taʾrīkh al-Sūdān*, vol. 3, p. 115.

In 1861, when Muḥammad Aḥmad was seventeen years old, he joined the Sammāniyya Ṣūfī order[2] and became a disciple of Muḥammad Sharīf b. Nūr al-Dā'im who lived at Umm Marḥī (north of Omdurman),[3] near the grave of his grandfather al-Shaykh al-Ṭayyib (who introduced the Sammānī order into the Sudan around 1800).[4] He stayed with him for seven years during which he distinguished himself again by his ascetic way of life. He did work normally done by slaves and slave-girls, such as hewing wood, carrying water, grinding and cooking – though he was not obliged to do all these things. In the best tradition of the early Muslim ascetics, he is said to have wept excessively, "so that he made the earth wet with his tears" (*ḥattā yuballil al-arḍ bi-dumūʿihi*).[5] This way of life was well appreciated by Muḥammad Sharīf who made him a *shaykh* and gave him permission to spread the order wherever he wanted. He went to Khartūm, stayed with his brothers and used his time to propagate the Sammāniyya.

In 1871 Muḥammad Aḥmad's brothers went to Jazīrat Aba where timber was plentiful for boat construction. He went with them and built there a mosque and a school (*khalwa*). It seems that the 1870s were of great importance in the development of Muḥammad Aḥmad's career. He became famous and the number of his followers increased. One of them was ʿAlī Wadd Ḥilw who later became his second *khalīfa*. His cordial relationship with Muḥammad Sharīf continued until 1878. Muḥammad Aḥmad used to visit his former teacher on holidays, expressing his reverence for him by humble, even abject, behaviour.

In 1878 Muḥammad Aḥmad's relations with Muḥammad Sharīf deteriorated. Naʿūm Shuqayr, whose *History and geography of ancient and modern Sudan*[6] is a veritable treasure trove of information on the Mahdiyya, gives two accounts of the break between the two persons. According to the first,

---

2 For the Sammāniyya order, see Karrar, *The Ṣūfī Brotherhoods*, pp. 43–55.

3 See Karrar, *The Ṣūfī Brotherhoods*, p. 44.

4 For a hagiography of Aḥmad al-Ṭayyib, see al-Sammānī, *Azāhīr al-riyāḍ*.

5 Shuqayr, *Taʾrīkh al-Sūdān*, vol. 3, p. 115. On the early "weepers" (*bakkāʾūn*) in the Muslim tradition, see "Bakkāʾ", in *EI*[2], s.v. (F. Meier).

6 *Taʾrīkh al-Sūdān al-qadīm wa al-ḥadīth wa jughrāfiyyatuhu*, Cairo 1903. Naʿūm Shuqayr (1864–1922) was born in Beirut. In 1883 he graduated from the Syrian Protestant College (*al-Kulliyya al-Injīliyya al-Sūriyya*), transformed in 1920 into the American University in Beirut. After graduation, he moved to Cairo where he worked for military intelligence. A biography of Naʿūm Shuqayr by Muḥammad Ibrāhīm Abū Salīm is found in Shuqayr's *Amthāl al-ʿawāmm fī Miṣr wa al-Sūdān wa al-Shām*, Beirut: Dār al-Jīl, 1995. For an appreciation of *Taʾrīkh al-Sūdān*, see Powell, *Brothers along the Nile*, pp. 176–178. See also Hill, *Biographical Dictionary*, p. 293.

Muḥammad Aḥmad grew haughty because of his increased popularity, claimed to be the *mahdī* and impudently suggested that Muḥammad Sharīf, his mentor, become his *wazīr* and counsellor. Muḥammad Sharīf scolded him and instructed him to desist. After Muḥammad Aḥmad disregarded this warning, Muḥammad Sharīf organized an assembly of local notables and repeated his demand. He even promised Muḥammad Aḥmad half of his property if he desisted from advancing his messianic claim. When Muḥammad Aḥmad refused, Muḥammad Sharīf expelled him from the order. In a poem written in 1882, Muḥammad Sharīf describes the development of his relationship with Muḥammad Aḥmad and mentions that eventually he declared him an infidel (*aftaytu fīhi bi-'l-ḍalāli wa 'l-kufri*), denounced him as being guided by Satan and asked the local governor to put him in jail.[7]

This account of the break between Muḥammad Aḥmad and Muḥammad Sharīf has been disputed. As Holt has pointed out, there is no other evidence for Muḥammad Aḥmad declaring himself as *mahdī* before 1881. Furthermore, Muḥammad Sharīf's account was communicated to Shuqayr after the defeat of the Mahdist state in 1898 and may have been intended "to curry favour with the Anglo-Egyptian conquerors".[8] The alternative, Mahdist explanation of the break between the two personalities highlights the growing popularity of Muḥammad Aḥmad which hurt Muḥammad Sharīf's pride, aroused his jealousy and caused him to denounce his rival. The Mahdists also accused Muḥammad Sharīf of engaging in behaviour which Muḥammad Aḥmad considered un-Islamic: kissing women in his assemblies and allowing them to kiss his hands. When Muḥammad Sharīf celebrated the circumcision of one of his sons, he invited many people and allowed them to dance and sing. This was denounced by Muḥammad Aḥmad who was present and asserted said that such entertainment is not allowed by the *sharīʿa*; consequently, Muḥammad Sharīf expelled him from his order and denounced him by saying that he was "a devil clad in human skin" (*al-Danqalāwī shayṭān mujallad bi-jild insān*).[9] If we take into account the future *mahdī*'s extreme asceticism and his stringent attitude to women, this explanation of the break has a ring of truth. It is noteworthy that Muḥammad Aḥmad did not stop communicating with Muḥammad Sharīf after the break. He wrote him at least two conciliatory letters in

7 Shuqayr, *Taʾrīkh al-Sūdān*, vol. 3, pp. 114–117.
8 Holt, *The Mahdist State in the Sudan*, p. 39.
9 Shuqayr, *Taʾrīkh al-Sūdān*, vol. 3, p. 118; Holt, *The Mahdist State in the Sudan*, pp. 39–40.

which he urged him to join the Mahdiyya and promised him safety despite what had transpired between them in the past.[10]

After the break with Muḥammad Sharīf, and despite the latter's opposition, Muḥammad Aḥmad established a relationship with Shaykh al-Qurashī, another prominent Sammānī leader who lived near al-Musallamiyya on the Blue Nile. The frugality of Muḥammad Aḥmad's lifestyle grew in intensity and for a period of time he mortified himself by living in an underground cave. This increased his prestige and gave him much publicity; people started coming to him, giving him presents and asking for his blessing. When al-Qurashī died in 1880, many considered Muḥammad Aḥmad as the new head (*wārith*) of the Sammānī order. This resulted in increasing the prestige of Muḥammad Aḥmad.[11]

Muḥammad Aḥmad devoted the following months to extensive travel, calling the people to repent. These travels allowed him to form an opinion about the extent of the people's disillusionment with the government and their desire to get rid of it. He got the impression that many were hoping for the appearance of the *mahdī* who would save them from their predicament; some were willing to recognize as such anyone who possessed superior intelligence and devotion to religion. During this period, he was visited by ʿAbd Allah al-Taʿāyishī who displayed extreme humility towards him and fainted twice in his presence. He affirmed that he discerned in him the signs of the *mahdī* which had been intimated to him by his father before his death. ʿAbd Allah pledged allegiance to Muḥammad Aḥmad and both went to the Abā island. Muḥammad Aḥmad started studying the traditions concerning the *mahdī*, and in March 1881 he made his claim. First, he did it in confidence to ʿAbd Allah al-Taʿāyishī, who later became his *khalīfa*, and then to his closest associates. Then he embarked on a tour of various areas in the Sudan, accompanied by a number of his followers. Everybody wore the patched garment (*jubba muraqqaʿa*), symbolizing in Ṣūfī orders poverty and simplicity, carried a rosary (*sabḥa*), a staff (*ʿukkāz*), and an earthen jug (*ibrīq al-fakhkhār*). He confided his claim to various notables on the way. When he returned to the Abā island on 29 June 1881, he started making his claim to a wider audience, in letters to notables, tribal chiefs and leaders of Ṣūfī orders.[12] This is considered to

10 *Al-Āthār al-kāmila*, vol. 1, pp. 420–423; vol. 5, pp. 285–286,

11 Shuqayr, *Taʾrīkh al-Sūdān*, vol. 3, p. 119.

12 Shuqayr, *Taʾrīkh al-Sūdān*, vol. 3, pp. 120–121. For the prophetic command concerning the patched garment, see *Al-Āthār al-kāmila*, vol. 5, pp. 456, 458.

be the date of his manifestation. Mahdist thinkers note that this happened before Muḥammad Aḥmad reached the age of forty as would have been expected, according to the age at which Muḥammad the Prophet had his first revelation. This is explained as a special favour to Muḥammad Aḥmad's successor ʿAbdullāhi.[13]

Muḥammad Raʾūf Bāshā, the governor of the Sudan, was notified of Muḥammad Aḥmad's now public claim to be the *mahdī*, and summoned him to Kharṭūm, but Muḥammad Aḥmad refused to comply asserting that it is the *mahdī* who should be obeyed rather than the governor. A subsequent military attempt to arrest Muḥammad Aḥmad in August 1881 was repulsed by the Mahdists.[14] Understanding that the government would not cease its attempts to arrest him, Muḥammad Aḥmad called upon his followers to make *hijra* to Jabal Qadīr, asserting that this was an explicit order given to him by the Prophet.[15] As we shall see later, the commandment to make *hijra* became one of the cardinal principles of the Mahdiyya.

The following years saw a great number of battles in which Muḥammad Aḥmad's troops engaged the Egyptian forces, frequently led by British officers. Noteworthy among these is the defeat of Colonel Hicks' expedition at Shaykhān on 5 November 1883; this was considered by Muḥammad Aḥmad as the starting point of his reign (*ḥulūl al-mahdiyya*) at which Islamic laws, such as the collection of alms (*zakāt*), were to be implemented.[16] Very much like starting the Islamic era with the *hijra* to Medina rather than with the Prophet's birth or the proclamation of his prophethood, the *mahdī* formally inaugurated his state after the first major political and military success. The subsequent capture of al-Ubayyiḍ on 12 November 1883 signalled the collapse of the Egyptian administration in western Sudan and enabled Muḥammad Aḥmad to establish his administration in Kordofān. The most famous among Muḥammad Aḥmad's battles is the conquest of Kharṭūm in January 1885 and the killing of General Charles Gordon, the British official appointed as governor general of the Sudan. The *mahdī* died of fever on 22 June 1885, but the state established by him

13 Al-Kordofānī, *Saʿādat al-mustahdī*, p. 94. The book was written upon the instructions of ʿAbdullāhi and during his incumbency; this is the probable reason for Kordofānī's statement. See Shaked, *The Life of the Sudanese Mahdī*, p. 25. The transliteration ʿAbdullāhi does not follow my usual system, but this is the form which is used for this person everywhere and any other form would create confusion.

14 Shuqayr, *Taʾrīkh al-Sūdān*, vol. 3, pp. 128–129.

15 Shuqayr, *Taʾrīkh al-Sūdān*, vol. 3, p. 130.

16 *Al-Āthār al-kāmila*, vol. 5, pp. 197–199.

continued until 1898. Following the defeat of the Mahdiyya in that year, the tomb of Muḥammad Aḥmad was destroyed.[17]

According to Shuqayr, Muḥammad Aḥmad had five wives, known as "mothers of the believers" (*ummahāt al-mu'minīn*). One of them died before he married her sister, so he did not have more than four wives simultaneously. He also had sixty-three concubines. Of his ten sons, seven died in battle or of disease; only three survived their father. He also had ten daughters, one of whom married his *khalīfa* 'Abdullāhi. His three brothers (Muḥammad, Ḥāmid and 'Abd Allah) died in battle.[18] His associates were graded according to the time when they joined the movement: the most honourable were "the disciples" (*talāmidha*) who had been with him before he made his messianic claim; then "the helpers of Abā" (*anṣār Abā*) who helped him on the Abā island; then "the helpers of Qadīr" (*anṣār Qadīr*) who migrated to him when he came to Qadīr in October 1881, and so on.[19] This is inspired by the principle of seniority (*sābiqa*) in classical Islam; there the payments from the treasury were determined by the date of conversion.[20]

The movement of the Sudanese *mahdī* attracted tremendous attention in England and in some parts of Europe. The news about Muḥammad Aḥmad also reached India and his uprising is mentioned in the eschatological works of Ṣiddīq Ḥasan Khān.[21] Because of the *mahdī*'s military successes against the British army, the conquest of Kharṭūm and the killing of General Gordon in 1885, the political and military interest in him is understandable. But the Europeans did not restrict themselves to the political and military descriptions. For the Polish writer Henryk Sienkiewicz, Muḥammad Aḥmad's movement served as a background for his children's novel *W pustyni i w puszczy* ("In desert and wilderness") which was translated into many languages and became a classic of children's literature. Karl May

17 Holt, *The Mahdist State in the Sudan*, p. 241. Since the purpose of our study is an analysis of the *mahdī*'s religious thought, I have given only a skeletal account of the relevant political and military events; for most of it I am indebted to Shuqayr's and Holt's works.

18 Shuqayr, *Ta'rīkh*, vol. 3, pp. 363–364; *Al-Kordofānī, Sa'ādat al-mustahdī*, p. 211.

19 Shuqayr, *Ta'rīkh*, vol. 3, p. 372.

20 See, for instance, Ṭabarī, *Ta'rīkh al-rusul wa al-mulūk*, ed. de Goeje, series I, pp. 2412–2414 (Translation by Y. Friedmann, *The History of al-Ṭabarī*, Albany: SUNY Press, 1992, vol. 12, pp. 200–203).

21 See Ṣiddīq Ḥasan Khān, *Iqtirāb al-sā'a*, p. 2; *idem*, *Ḥadīth al-ghāshiya*, p. 340.

wrote a trilogy entitled *Im Lande des Mahdi*, consisting of *Menschenjäger, Der Mahdi* and *Im Sudan*. His work has recently been the subject of a collective volume of literary analysis.[22] In England, *An illustrated narrative of the war in the Sudan*, published in 1885, gave the British public an opportunity to gain immediate knowledge of the events from the British point of view.[23] One year earlier, H. Sheridan Patterson acquainted the British reading public with the Muslim messianic traditions.[24] A short play in verse, rather sympathetic to the *mahdī*, was published in 1910.[25] In 1930, Alice F. Jackson published a literary account entitled *With Mahdi and Khalifa*. In some cases, travelogues and works of literature which had only tenuous connection to the *mahdī* revolt were given titles mentioning him; this was apparently expected to arouse the interest of potential readers.[26] Jurjī Zaydān wrote a novel entitled "The prisoner of the messianic pretender" (*Asīr al-mutamahdī*).[27] There are also memoirs of people who travelled to the Sudan or were the *mahdī*'s prisoners.[28] And, of course, numerous works by academic historians have been written.[29] In the Sudan, there has been tremendous interest in the *mahdī*'s movement; many works of research have been dedicated to its various aspects, in addition to the publications of the *mahdī*'s collected works in seven volumes.[30]

The political and military history of the Mahdiyya was surveyed and analysed by numerous scholars. The focus of this chapter is, rather, on the religious thought of the *mahdī*, on his ideas concerning the organization of Muslim society, on the manner in which he related to the classical Islamic tradition and on his place in the history of messianic thought in Islam. We shall also see that in a certain sense the Mahdiyya movement

22 Sudhoff, Dieter and Voller, Hartmut, eds, *Karl Mays "Im Lande des Mahdi". Literatur- und Medienwissenschaft, 92*, Oldenburg: IGEL Verlag, 2003.

23 For countries other than England, see Garçon, *Guerre du Soudan (le mahdī)*; van Balen, *De Dadels van Khartoem* (not seen); De Maurceley, *L'armée du mahdī*.

24 Patterson, *The Imām Mahdī, passim.*

25 Lyle, *The mahdī* and other poems.

26 See Graham, *Three Months on the Nile Defying the Mahdī*.

27 Beirut: Dār al-sharika li-'l-kitāb, n.d.

28 Such as Slatin, Rudolf, *Fire and Sword in the Sudan*, and many others.

29 See, for instance, the works by Holt and Searcy in the bibliography.

30 Muḥammad Ibrāhīm Abū Salīm made a singular contribution to scholarship by publishing the epistles of Muḥammad Aḥmad in seven volumes. In addition to Muḥammad Aḥmad's letters, the volumes contain also letters of his associates, responses of some addressees and Arabic versions of letters sent to Muḥammad Aḥmad by General Gordon. The seventh volume includes the *Majālis* in which Muḥammad Aḥmad's associates recorded the utterances of their leader, and several useful indices.

foreshadows the thinking of some radical Muslim movements of the twentieth century.

II MUḤAMMAD AḤMAD'S RELIGIOUS THOUGHT

The world view of Muḥammad Aḥmad is a synthesis of ideas derived from classical Muslim asceticism (*zuhd*), strict ethics in the relationships among the members of the movement, demands for stern implementation of several *shar'ī* principles and, most important, placing the duty to perform *hijra* and to wage *jihād* at the centre of a believer's religious obligations. Like other Muslim religious reformers, Muḥammad Aḥmad maintains that his appearance was made necessary by the serious decline which Islam has suffered. The legitimization of Muḥammad Aḥmad's messianic claim is provided in numerous visionary encounters with the Prophet, the first four caliphs, the mythical al-Khiḍr and other cardinal figures from Islamic history and mythology. Descriptions of these encounters are included time and again in Muḥammad Aḥmad's letters and he repeatedly uses them in order to convince the addressees of the veracity of his messianic claim. It is significant to observe that both political and spiritual leaders are present in these encounters. Each encounter is called a "presence" (*ḥaḍra*).[31] The first such encounter is mentioned in a letter from the beginning (*ghurra*) of Sha'bān 1298/end of June 1881:[32]

> A prophetic presence occurred to us. Our friend *al-faqīh* 'Īsā was there. The Prophet ... came, sat down next to me and said to the

31 Shaked (*The Life of the Sudanese Mahdī*, p. 45, note 65) maintains that "in the Mahdist usage the emphasis is not on the visual appearance of the Prophet but on the message he communicates". The purpose of the Prophet's appearance is, of course, his message. However, in many cases the descriptions of his appearance are very concrete: he sits next to the *mahdī* or makes him sit on his chair. See the next passage and also *Al-Āthār al-kāmila*, vol. 5, p. 223. Holt noted that the word *ru'yā* is not used in Muḥammad Aḥmad's descriptions. The reason probably is that *ru'yā* is usually used for a dream, while the encounters of the *mahdī* with the Prophet are said to have occurred with all protagonists in full wakefulness. See Holt, *The Mahdist State in the Sudan*, p. 105, note 1.

32 I have not found in Muḥammad Aḥmad's letters a substantiation of Holt's assumption that the date of Muḥammad Aḥmad's manifestation was influenced by the approaching end of the thirteenth century AH which occurred on 11 November 1882. See Holt, "The Sudanese Mahdia ...", p. 276.

> aforementioned brother: "Your *shaykh* is the *mahdī*." [ʿIsā] said: "I believe in it." Then the Prophet said: "He who does not believe in his being the *mahdī*, denies God and His Prophet." He said this three times. The brother mentioned above said: "Oh my master, Oh Messenger of God, the *ʿulamāʾ* mock us and we are also afraid of the Turks." The Prophet said: "By God, by God, by God – the power of your certitude [means] that if you indicate [that you desire even] the smallest straw, it will be given to you." (*inna quwā yaqīnikum in ashartum bi-adnā qashsha tanqaḍī* [sic] *ḥājatukum*)."[33]

Thus, Muḥammad Aḥmad is appointed *mahdī* by the Prophet himself. The Prophet declares that rejection of Muḥammad Aḥmad's messianic claim is tantamount to the denial of God and of His Prophet; the clear implication is that these deniers are infidels. In the same way as God made a compact with the Children of Israel and demanded that they follow the Prophet Muḥammad when he appears, the Prophet made a compact with his community and demanded that they follow the *mahdī*.[34] The Prophet also instructs two mythical figures to accompany the *mahdī* at all times: the first is ʿAzrāʾīl, the angel of death; the second is the figure of al-Khiḍr, whose characteristics include longevity and even immortality. The placement of both figures in the *mahdī*'s entourage seems to signify the defeat and death to be suffered by the enemies and the longevity to be enjoyed by the *mahdī* and his supporters. The famous Ṣūfī ʿAbd al-Qādir al-Jīlānī is also present at the *ḥaḍra*; his appearance may be explained by the *mahdī*'s membership in a Ṣūfī order.[35] In other descriptions of the appointment session, the Prophet tells the *mahdī* that he was created from the light of the Prophet's heart (*innaka makhlūq min nūr ʿinān qalbī*), that his name was changed from Muḥammad Aḥmad to Muḥammad al-Mahdī by the Prophet, and that the mole on his right cheek – reminiscent of the "seal of prophethood" between the Prophet Muḥammad's shoulders – is a symbol of his being the *mahdī*. In a similar vein, the Prophet extracted the *mahdī*'s heart from his chest, rinsed it and placed it back – in emulation of the

33 *Al-Āthār al-kāmila*, vol. 1, pp. 77–78; cf. ibid., pp. 98–99; vol. 5, pp. 223, 457. Muḥammad Aḥmad uses the term "Turks" for the rulers of Sudan because they used Turkish as their language. See Shaked, *The Life of the Sudanese Mahdī*, pp. 201–204; and Holt, *The Mahdist State in the Sudan*, p. 14.

34 *Al-Āthār al-kāmila*, vol. 7, pp. 25–26.

35 *Al-Āthār al-kāmila*, vol. 1, pp. 80–81, 379; vol. 3, pp. 322–323.

"chest opening" (*sharḥ al-ṣadr*) performed by angels in order to cleanse the Prophet's heart when he was a child.[36] ʿAzrāʾīl is designated as the commander of his army, holding in his hands a flag of light which is the flag of victory and a guarantee against defeat. A place where the *mahdī* or a successor of his is present will never be destroyed. The Prophet seats the *mahdī* several times on his chair and girds him with his sword.[37] Elsewhere he washes him with his hand. The four "righteous" caliphs, leaders of the Ṣūfīs (*aqṭāb*), al-Khiḍr, the ten angels and sixty thousand deceased saints are present. Elsewhere, the *mahdī* is supported by 240,000 Ṣūfīs, the *quṭb*, the "People of the Cave" and the messengers of the ten angels.[38] In addition to this, Muḥammad Aḥmad is the successor of the Prophet (*khalīfat rasūl Allāh*) and the "great *khilāfa*" (*al-khilāfa al-kubrā*) was bestowed upon him by God and His Prophet; this honour is apparently inspired by Qurʾān 2:30 and 38:26, where Adam and David were appointed God's *khalīfa*s on earth.[39] It is noteworthy that the relationship between the *mahdī* and the Prophet is not only spiritual. The *mahdī* is genealogically related to the Prophet: his father's parents were descendants of al-Ḥasan b. ʿAlī, the Prophet's grandson; this is clearly intended to make Muḥammad Aḥmad's genealogy compatible with the classical descriptions of the *mahdī*'s forefathers. His mother was also al-Ḥasan's descendant on her mother's side.[40] The Prophet determines that ʿAbdullāhi (al-Taʿāyishī) is the *mahdī*'s son and will be his successor. Paraphrasing a frequently quoted tradition, the Prophet is made to declare that "whoever hurts the *khalīfa* ʿAbdullāhi, hurts the *mahdī*; whoever hurts the *mahdī*, hurts me; and whoever hurts me, hurts Allah."[41] He intervenes in appointments of the *mahdī*'s deputies and in tactical military matters: for instance, he informs the *mahdī* that he will conquer al-Ubayyiḍ and that General Gordon's expedition is doomed.[42] There is also a speech (in rather non-classical Arabic) in which

36 *Al-Āthār al-kāmila*, vol. 1, p. 422. For the tradition speaking about the cleansing of the Prophet's heart, see Suhaylī, *al-Rawḍ al-unuf*, vol. 2, pp. 168–169; Guillaume, *The Life of Muḥammad*, p. 72.

37 For the sword symbolism, see Searcy, *The Formation of the Sudanese Mahdist State*, pp. 57–59.

38 *Al-Āthār al-kāmila*, vol. 1, pp. 83, 97–98, 175–176, 210–213, 221; vol. 7, pp. 116–117.

39 *Al-Āthār al-kāmila*, vol. 1, pp. 175, 210, 236, 255, 291 and in numerous other places.

40 *Al-Āthār al-kāmila*, vol. 1, pp. 93, 99, 339; cf. Shuqayr, *Taʾrīkh al-Sūdān*, vol. 3, p. 114.

41 *Al-Āthār al-kāmila*, vol. 5, pp. 449–450; vol. 7, p. 75. The classical *ḥadīth* reads "whoever hurts ʿAlī (or al-ʿAbbās), hurts me ..." See Wensinck, *Concordance*, s.v. *ādhā*.

42 *Al-Āthār al-kāmila*, vol. 1, p. 350; vol. 4, pp. 155–156; vol. 5, p. 458.

the Prophet promises victory over the Hicks expedition.[43] The *mahdī*'s contacts with the Prophet are not restricted to the explicitly mentioned *ḥaḍarāt*: he receives prophetic instructions and divine inspiration on a continuous basis. However, like the mission of the Prophet Muḥammad, his spiritual standing was to be kept secret until God decided to make it public.[44] Muḥammad Aḥmad feels – on the basis of a prophetic communication – that his mission will be easier than that of the Prophet: the Prophet had to face opposition of kings, Jews and Christians, while the Muslim community will follow Muḥammad Aḥmad without the effort which the Prophet himself had to invest.[45] It is noteworthy that in a rather late "presence", an angel brings down a green crown, describes it as the crown of victory and asks the Prophet to bestow it upon Muḥammad Aḥmad. A crown is not a Muslim symbol and its use by a leader whose source of inspiration is the classical Muslim tradition is rather surprising. The bestowal of the crown – rather than a sword as in earlier encounters – has been interpreted as a symbol that the wars of the *mahdī* have been successfully completed and a Mahdist state has been established.[46]

In most cases, Muḥammad Aḥmad's appointment as the *mahdī* is described as effected by the Prophet. It is noteworthy, however, that in the late years of his career, after the great military successes and the consequent growth in his self-assurance, we find a statement in which God himself is presented as making the appointment. Three times God is quoted as telling the Prophet: "This is your *khalīfa*, O Muḥammad" (*hādhā khalīfatuka yā Muḥammad*).[47] Furthermore, on the night of 6 Shawwāl 1301/30 July 1884, while in the state of full wakefulness, Muḥammad Aḥmad heard God greeting him. "I understood," he says

> that it was not an angel, nor a messenger, nor a prophet, because I heard Him with all my body, no letter or sound, [from] no direction or place, not with the known organ [sc. the ear], neither whispering nor audible, [coming] neither from near nor from far, in a manner without modality... (*fa-ʿinda dhālika fahimtu annahu laysa malak*

43 *Al-Āthār al-kāmila*, vol. 2, pp. 145–146.
44 *Al-Āthār al-kāmila*, vol. 1, pp. 71–72.
45 *Al-Āthār al-kāmila*, vol. 1, p. 177; vol. 7, p. 119 *infra*.
46 *Al-Āthār al-kāmila*, vol. 5, p. 448 and the editor's note on the same page. For a different description of Muḥammad Aḥmad's world view, see Holt, *The Mahdist State in the Sudan*, pp. 105–107.
47 *Al-Āthār al-kāmila*, vol. 5, pp. 455, 457.

> *wa lā rasūl wa lā nabī li-annī samiʿtuhu bi-jamīʿ badanī, bi-lā ḥarf wa lā ṣawt wa lā jiha min al-jihāt wa lā makān min al-amkina wa lā bi-'l-jāriḥa al-maʿlūma wa lā yūṣaf bi-'l-sirr wa lā bi-'l-jahr lā bi-'l-qurb wa lā bi-'l-buʿd wa bi-ḥālin lā yukayyaf*).[48]

And Muḥammad Aḥmad's admirers assert that his communication with Allah amounts to *waḥy*, which is used in the Muslim tradition for prophetic inspiration only.[49]

The wording of the pledge of allegiance (*bayʿa*) which Muḥammad Aḥmad used for sealing agreements with individuals and groups who wanted to join his movement is another indication of his systematic attempt to shape his movement according to the model of early Islam. As Holt has already recognized, the wording of this pledge is "clearly modelled upon the first Pledge of al-ʿAqaba, given by twelve Anṣār of Yathrib to the Prophet".[50] While Holt's observation is essentially correct and the Mahdist pledge is in part identical with the first pledge of al-ʿAqaba, there are also significant differences between the two documents. The Mahdist pledge reads:

> We have sworn allegiance to God and His apostle, and we have sworn allegiance to you, in asserting the unity of God, that we will not associate anyone with Him, we will not steal, we will not commit adultery, we will not bring false accusations and we will not disobey you in what is good (*maʿrūf*). We have sworn allegiance to you in renouncing this world and abandoning it, and being content with what is with God, desiring what is with God and the world to come, and we will not flee from *jihād*.[51]

The main difference between this text and the first pledge of al-ʿAqaba is the addition of the renunciation of this world and of the obligation not

48 *Al-Āthār al-kāmila*, vol. 7, p. 125; vol. 3, p. 189. The negative sentences are designed to preclude any anthropomorphistic interpretation of the passage. This passage has already been noted by Layish, *Sharīʿa and the Islamic State in 19th-Century Sudan*, p. 41.

49 Zahrāʾ, *al-Āyāt al-bayyināt*, p. 13. The proof text for this claim is Qurʾān 42:51. See also ibid., pp. 13 *infra* -14 where the spirit of Muḥammad Aḥmad's pronouncements is described as "the speech of God" (*kalām Allah*) which must be obeyed.

50 Holt, *The Mahdist State in the Sudan*, p. 117.

51 Translation by Holt, *The Mahdist State in the Sudan*, p. 117 (with minor modifications).

to flee from *jihād*; these elements are not included in the first pledge of al-ʿAqaba, but the obligation to support the Prophet in war was added in the second pledge.[52] As we shall see later, the inclusion of the warlike elements from the second pledge in the Mahdist text reflects the central place of *jihād* (and asceticism) in the world view of Muḥammad Aḥmad. It is also significant to observe that the classical battle cry "kill, kill" (*amit, amit*) was used by Muḥammad Aḥmad's warriors in their military engagements.[53]

Like other leaders of revivalist movements, Muḥammad Aḥmad explained that the need for his mission is rooted in the decline which Islam has suffered. Even before making his messianic claim, he asserted that Islam was, in his times, in an inferior situation: illegal innovations (*bidaʿ*) are rampant and, what is worse, they are endorsed by the scholars of religion (*ʿulamāʾ*). Following the correct path and commanding right depends on the abandonment of the current, accepted custom (*tark al-maʾlūf ittibāʿ al-maʿrūf*).[54] Muslims suffer from internal divisions; as the prophetic tradition predicted, they are divided into seventy-three sects of which only one will be saved. "Nothing remained of Islam except its name and nothing remained of the Qurʾān except its script" (*mā baqiya min al-islām illā ʾsmuhu wa min al-Qurʾān illā rasmuhu*).[55] The decline of Islam has been caused mainly by the length of time which has elapsed since the Prophet's death (*indirās al-dīn bi-ṭūl ʿahd nabiyyinā Muḥammad*).[56] This is a reflection of the classical idea according to which the ideal period of Islam was the time of the Prophet; after his death, a progressive decline set in. The formulation of this idea in the *ḥadīth* reads: "The best of my community is the generation in which I was sent, then those who follow them, then those who follow them" (*khayr ummatī al-qarn alladhī buʿithtu fīhi thumma alladhīna yalūnahum thumma alladhīna yalūnahum*).[57] Shaykh

52 For the two "Pledges of al-ʿAqaba", see Ibn Hishām, *al-Sīra al-nabawiyya*, ed. Muṣṭafā al-Saqqāʾ et alii, Beirut 1990, vol. 2, pp. 57, 63–64, 67 (translation by A. Guillaume, *The Life of Muḥammad*, pp. 199, 203–205); Ṭabarī, *Taʾrīkh*, ed. de Goeje, series I, pp. 1213, 1220–1222 (translation by W. Montgomery Watt and M. V. McDonald, *The History of al-Ṭabarī*, vol. 6, Albany: SUNY Press 1988, pp. 127, 133–134).

53 Zahrāʾ, *al-Āyāt al-bayyināt*, p. 10. For this battle cry in its classical context, see Abū Dāwūd, *Sunan*, vol. 3, p. 46 (*Kitāb al-jihād, bāb 79*); Dārimi, *Sunan*, vol. 3, p. 1593 (*Kitāb al-siyar* 15).

54 *Al-Āthār al-kāmila*, vol. 7, p. 239.

55 *Al-Āthār al-kāmila*, vol. 1, p. 69; vol. 2, p. 29; vol. 5, p. 247.

56 *Al-Āthār al-kāmila*, vol. 4, pp. 16, 29; vol. 5, p. 222.

57 Bukhārī, *Ṣaḥīḥ*, vol. 2, p. 416 (*Kitāb faḍāʾil aṣḥāb al-nabī, bāb* 1). Similar formulations can be found in many collections of *ḥadīth*; see Wensinck, *Concordance*, s.v. *qarn*.

Aḥmad Sirhindī (971/1564–1034/1624), who lived in India at the turn of the second millennium of Muslim history, developed an elaborate theory on the inferior status of the Muslim community during his lifetime, connected it to the passage of one thousand years since the death of the Prophet and used it to substantiate the need for the revivalist mission of "the renewer of the second millennium" (*mujaddid-i alf-i thānī*).[58] Muḥammad Aḥmad does not have such an elaborate theory on this, but his sense of the decline of Islam is the same. Like other Muslim revivalists, he maintains that the remedy of this situation lies in recreating the conditions which prevailed in the ideal, prophetic period. He refers to the famous tradition in which the Prophet commands Muslims:

> Follow my custom and the custom of the virtuous and rightly guided caliphs after me; hold to it with your teeth and beware of innovations, because every innovation is an error and every error is [leading] into the Fire (*ʿalaykum bi-sunnatī wa sunnat al-khulafāʾ al-rāshidīn al-mahdiyyīn min baʿdī; ʿuḍḍū ʿalayhā bi-'l-nawājidh wa al-aḍrās wa iyyākum wa muḥdathāt al-umūr fa-inna kulla muḥdathatin ḍalāla wa kulla ḍalālatin fī al-nār*).[59]

The attempt to accomplish this has apparently been successful: "God has restored for us the past, the time of the Companions" (*wa qad aʿāda lanā Allah al-zaman al-māḍī, zaman al-ṣaḥāba*);[60] the *mahdī*'s lifetime is integrated with the period of the Prophet (... *li-anna zamananā mundarij fī zamanihi*)[61] and is sometimes explicitly called "prophetic" because of Muḥammad Aḥmad's appearance as a successor of the Prophet (*hādhā al-zaman al-nabawī bi-ḥuḍūrī fīhi khalīfatan li-nabiyyinā* ...). In a vision seen by the *khalīfa* ʿAbdullāhi, the Prophet describes Muḥammad Aḥmad as "the spirit of Muḥammad" (*rūḥ Muḥammad ṣallā Allah ʿalayhi wa sallam*).[62] The *mahdī*'s miracles resemble those of the prophets. If an *ʿālim* follows him, he becomes like a "prophet sent" (by God) (*fa-ammā al-ʿālim al-tābiʿ lī fī mahdiyyatī fa-huwa ka-'l-nabī al-mursal*); if he opposes

58 See Friedmann, *Shaykh Aḥmad Sirhindī*, pp. 13–21.

59 *Al-Āthār al-kāmila*, vol. 6, pp. 167–168; cf. vol. 5, p. 318. For the *ḥadīth* in the original context, see Abū Dāwūd, *Sunan, Kitāb al-sunna*, vol. 4, p. 281.

60 *Al-Āthār al-kāmila*, vol. 1, p. 157.

61 *Al-Āthār al-kāmila*, vol. 2, pp. 29, 269; vol. 4, p. 443; vol. 5, p. 227; vol. 7, pp. 116–117, 120.

62 *Al-Āthār al-kāmila*, vol. 7, p. 124.

him, he is like Pharaoh.[63] Similarly, it is routinely stated that the *mahdī*'s companions have the standing of the Prophet's companions: at times he addresses them as "emigrants and helpers" (*al-muhājirūn wa al-anṣār*). He was told by the Prophet that the *ṣaḥāba* are like the companions of Muḥammad Aḥmad and the families of both are also similar (*aṣḥābuka ka-aṣḥābī wa āluka ka-ālī*).[64] Muḥammad Aḥmad's companions should therefore behave like those of the Prophet: they should not raise their heads or their voices in his presence out of humility and respect. Similarly, they should not enter the house of their leader or touch his body without permission; this is in compliance with Qur'ān 33:53 which gives the same instruction to the companions of the Prophet.[65] On the other hand, even the humble among Muḥammad Aḥmad's companions have the standing of 'Abd al-Qādir al-Jīlānī in the eyes of God.[66] In a vision seen by the first *khalīfa*, the Prophet himself is asserting the affinity of the *mahdī*'s successors with those of the Prophet: Muḥammad Aḥmad's *khalīfa* 'Abdullāhi al-Ta'āyishī has the standing of Abū Bakr al-Ṣiddīq, the first of the "righteous" caliphs, and must be obeyed. 'Alī b. Muḥammad Ḥilw had the standing of 'Umar b. al-Khaṭṭāb and Muḥammad Sharīf b. Ḥāmid that of 'Alī b. Abī Ṭālib. The idea to appoint Muḥammad al-Mahdī al-Sanūsī as a "successor" of 'Uthmān b. 'Affān was rebuffed by the latter's refusal, but it is clear that these appointments constitute a sustained attempt to recreate the prophetic period to the greatest extent possible. Those who join the *mahdī* early will be especially privileged: the first 12,000 will have the standing of God's helpers (*anṣār Allāh*).[67] This term evokes the Anṣār of early Islamic Medina.[68]

---

63 *Al-Āthār al-kāmila*, vol. 5, p. 418; cf. vol. 2, pp. 296–297 for a lengthy exhortation to follow the *mahdī*.

64 *Al-Āthār al-kāmila*, vol. 1, pp. 157, 185, 214, 222; vol. 2, pp. 30, 80, 173, 181, 227, 269, 295, 305; vol. 5, pp. 421, 455; vol. 7, p. 175.

65 *Al-Āthār al-kāmila*, vol. 7, pp. 202–204. Qur'ān 33: 53 reads: "O believers, enter not the houses of the Prophet, except if leave is given you for a meal ..." Cf. Qur'ān 49:2–3: "O believers, raise not your voices above the Prophet's voice and be not loud in your speech to him ..."

66 *Al-Āthār al-kāmila*, vol. 1, p. 422.

67 *Al-Āthār al-kāmila*, vol. 1, p. 157; vol. 7, pp. 123–124, 251. Holt, *The Mahdist State in the Sudan*, p. 103. For more material on the similarities between the Prophet and Muḥammad Aḥmad, see Shaked, *The Life of the Sudanese Mahdī*, pp, 218–224. For the failed attempt to appoint the Sanūsī as the counterpart of 'Uthmān, see later, at notes 238–240.

68 Cf. Searcy, *The Formation of the Sudanese Mahdist State*, pp. 53–54.

Furthermore, in some passages Muḥammad Aḥmad creates an impression of close affinity between himself and Muḥammad. In emulation of Muḥammad's call to prophethood, he should have been appointed *mahdī* after reaching the age of forty, but his appointment was made earlier (at the age of thirty-seven) as a miracle (*karāma*) for the *khalīfa* ʿAbdullāhi.[69] When Muḥammad Aḥmad encourages a poet to write poems in praise of the Prophet and of himself, he says that "praising me is like praising him (i.e., the Prophet); moreover, it is the same (*bal huwa huwa*)".[70] Strikingly enough, he quotes Qurʾān 9:26[71] while replacing "His messenger" by "His caliph" which is a clear reference to himself. To introduce the *mahdī* in this way into a Qurʾānic verse speaks volumes concerning the distance which Muḥammad Aḥmad was willing to go in order to portray himself as having almost the same standing as the Prophet.[72] In a sense the *mahdī* is even more privileged than the Prophet had been: while Muḥammad had to face the opposition of kings, Jews and Christians, the Muslim community will follow the *mahdī* willingly and he will not need to invest the effort which the Prophet had to invest in obtaining widespread support.[73] On the other hand, the enemies of the *mahdī* are described as representatives of the Jāhiliyya, the pagan period preceding the rise of Islam.[74] Muslims must abandon worldly enjoyment, hoarding property or perpetuating feuds originated before the *mahdī*'s appearance: all this belongs to the Jāhiliyya and must be terminated.[75] Furthermore, those who do not accept the *mahdī* resemble the Jewish and Christian sages of old who knew well that the Prophet was expected, but when he made his appearance they rejected him for fear of losing their position.[76]

Some of Muḥammad Aḥmad's followers took the affinity between their leader and the Prophet a step further. Ḥusayn Ibrāhīm Zahrā, known in Mahdist circles as "the sage of the Mahdiyya" (*ʿālim al-Mahdiyya*), uses

69 *Al-Āthār al-kāmila*, vol. 7, p. 120 *infra*.
70 *Al-Āthār al-kāmila*, vol. 4, p. 117.
71 "Then God sent down upon His messenger His Schechina, and upon the believers ..."
72 *Al-Āthār al-kāmila*, vol. 7, p. 206. Muḥammad Aḥmad's supporters also considered their leader as the *khalīfa* of the Prophet; see Zahrāʾ, *al-Āyāt al-bayyināt*, p. 5.
73 *Al-Āthār al-kāmila*, vol. 1, pp. 177, 422.
74 *Al-Āthār al-kāmila*, vol. 4, p. 152. Thus, the description of one's opponents as belonging to the Jāhiliyya has been used long before Sayyid Quṭb, the famous leader of the Muslim Brethren, adopted it as such an important component of his world view.
75 *Al-Āthār al-kāmila*, vol. 3, pp. 7–9.
76 *Al-Āthār al-kāmila*, vol. 2, p. 58.

in his description of Muḥammad Aḥmad a verse used in the Qur'ān for describing the Prophet: "... your comrade is not astray, neither errs, nor speaks he out of caprice. This is naught but a revelation revealed ..."[77] When Muḥammad Tātāy, who compiled one of Muḥammad Aḥmad's *Majālis*, explains his decision to collect his utterances, he describes them as

> the speech of a man who is in possession of the most perfect qualities and is superior to some prophets; this was determined by outstanding personalities. It is either the speech of the Exalted King, or of his Eminent Messenger, or of the Angel of Inspiration. It is the reception of wisdom known to God, manifesting the innermost wisdom known to the Majestic Lord. He must be continuously emulated in his words, in his actions, in what he tacitly approves of and in his movements – because he is the manifestation of God's names, His attributes and His essence ... (*innahu lammā khaṭara bi-'l-bāl tadwīnu mā yutawallā samā'uhu min kalām man inṭawā 'alā akmal al-khiṣāl wa faḍala ba'ḍa 'l-anbiyā' kamā jazama bi-dhālika fuḥūl al-rijāl li-annahu immā kalām al-maliki 'l-muta'āl aw rasūlihi al-mifḍāl aw malak al-ilhām alladhī huwa al-talaqqī min bāṭinihi li-ẓāhirihi li-ḥikmatin ya'lamuhā dhū al-jalāl. fa-ṣāra yuqtadā bihi fī aqwālihi wa af'ālihi wa sukūtihi wa ḥarakātihi 'alā al-tawāl idh huwa maẓhar asmā' Allāh wa ṣifātihi wa dhātihi* ...)[78]

This wording goes a long way to create an essential identity between Muḥammad Aḥmad and the Prophet. It clearly creates a new *sunna*, an obligation to follow the custom of the *mahdī* in the same way as the classical tradition obliged Muslims to follow the custom of the Prophet. Despite the fact that Muḥammad Aḥmad claimed to be an assiduous follower of the Prophet and of his *sunna*, it is still an audacious statement which could be easily denounced by mainstream Muslims as an unacceptable innovation.

While discussing the affinity created between the Prophet and Muḥammad Aḥmad, we should also devote some attention to the way in

77 Qur'ān 53:2–4; cf. Zahrā', *al-Āyāt al-bayyināt*, p. 27.

78 *Al-Āthār al-kāmila*, vol. 7, p. 17.

which the latter described the transformation effected by the Mahdiyya in the lives of his followers. Before the emergence of the Mahdiyya, they were disunited and neglected the Qur'ān and the *sunna* of the Prophet. Their lives were full of injustice and oppression and they engaged in corruption and senseless killing.[79] This is strikingly similar to the famous description given by the Muslim emigrants to the Abyssinian king after their migration to his country before the Prophet's migration to Medina: they were people of the Jāhiliyya, who were steeped in abominations, who mistreated their relatives and among whom the strong used to devour the weak.[80] In the same vein, Muḥammad Aḥmad demanded that whoever wanted to join him must "renew his Islam after performing a full ablution (*ghusl*)" and by pronouncing the declaration of faith (*shahāda*); "This is better for him than to maintain his Islam from the Jāhiliyya" (*hādhā khayrun lahu min an yuqīma bi-islāmihi alladhī maḍā fī al-jāhiliyya*).[81] It is clear that in Muḥammad Aḥmad's perception a new, Islamic, era was inaugurated after he made his claim, while the period that preceded him was an un-Islamic, *jāhilī*, period.

It is significant to observe that some of Muḥammad Aḥmad's followers treated the legacy of their leader in the same way as early Muslims treated the legacy of the Prophet Muḥammad: they collected his utterances in the form of *ḥadīth*. In the seventh volume of Muḥammad Aḥmad's collected works, there are five such collections, called the *Majālis*. The utterances are introduced by a number of formulae, such as "I heard him, peace be upon him, saying" (*sami'tuhu 'alayhi al-salām yaqūl*), or "The *imām mahdī*, peace be upon him, said" (*qāla al-imām al-mahdī 'alayhi al-salām*). In the third *majlis*,[82] collected by an anonymous compiler, the formula is much bolder: "The caliph of God and His messenger, the expected *imām* Muḥammad *al-mahdī*, may God be pleased with him, said" (*qāla khalīfat Allah wa rasūluhu al-imām Muḥammad al-mahdī al-muntaẓar, raḍiya Allah 'anhu*). This is as close as one can get to declaring Muḥammad Aḥmad as a messenger of God and may easily be interpreted as contradicting the

79 *Al-Āthār al-kāmila*, vol. 7, p. 205.

80 Ibn Hishām, *al-Sīra al-nabawiyya*, Saqā', Ābyārī, Shalabī, eds, Damscus: Dār al-Khayr, 1990, vol. 1, 265 (translation by W. Guillaume, *The Life of Muḥammad*, London: Oxford University Press, 1955, p. 151).

81 *Al-Āthār al-kāmila*, vol. 7, pp. 207–208. It is not possible to ascertain when did Muḥammad Aḥmad introduce this demand. In contradistinction to his letters which are dated, the *Majlis* in which this demand is found bears no date.

82 *Al-Āthār al-kāmila*, vol. 7, pp. 187–208.

dogma of the finality of Muḥammad's prophethood (*khatm al-nubuwwa*). A more implicit way to create affinity between Muḥammad Aḥmad and the Prophet is to describe him by expressions which had been used for the Prophet in the classical literature. Zahrā incorporates in his description of Muḥammad Aḥmad a passage which echoes the famous *ḥadīth* in which Khadīja tries to allay the fears of the Prophet following the first revelation which he received: "... he bears the burden (of the poor), strengthens the weak rightfully, entertains the guest, helps in the fulfilment of recurrent obligations, does what he says and says what he knows ..." (*yaḥmil al-kall, yuqawwī al-ḍa ʿīf fī al-ḥaqq wa yaqrī al-ḍayf wa yu ʿīn ʿalā nawā ʾib al-ḥaqq yaf ʿal mā yaqūl wa yaqūl mā ya ʿlam ...*).[83] In his *Sa ʿādat al-mustahdī*, Kordofānī speaks in a similar vein.[84]

The *Majālis* deal with Muḥammad Aḥmad's interpretations of selected Qur ʾānic verses, prophetic traditions which he quoted, his own statements, his exhortations and prayers. Some of them are quoted on the authority of one of Muḥammad Aḥmad's successors. The statements and exhortations are not arranged in any recognizable order and it is not possible even to ascertain whether they were uttered before his manifestation as *mahdī* or after it. Some use standard literary Arabic, while others are written in colloquial.

At this stage of research into the Mahdiyya, there is no way to vouch for the genuineness of this material as coming from Muḥammad Aḥmad himself; however, the utterances are essentially compatible with views expressed in Muḥammad Aḥmad's works and may therefore be used to enrich our description and analysis of his views.

III ASCETICISM AND *HIJRA*

According to Shuqayr's biography, Muḥammad Aḥmad exhibited ascetic tendencies from a young age. True to the classical ascetic tradition, he refused to consume food offered to him by his mentor Muḥammad al-Khayr who was receiving a salary from the government; Muḥammad Aḥmad considered this money illegitimate because it was wrongfully

83 Zahrā ʾ, *al-Āyāt al-bayyināt*, p. 8. For the *ḥadīth* in its original context, see Bukhārī, *Ṣaḥīḥ*, vol. 1, p. 5 (*Kayfa kāna bad ʾ al-waḥy ilā rasūl Allah bāb 3*) and Kister, "God will never disgrace thee", *passim*.

84 Kordofānī, *Sa ʿādat al-mustahdī*, p. 80.

gained (*māl al-ẓulm*). Therefore, when he did not receive food from his parents, he lived on fish which he himself had caught in the Nile. When he went in 1861 to study with Muḥammad Sharīf, Muḥammad Aḥmad again distinguished himself by his frugal way of life. He harshly criticized his shaykh Muḥammad Sharīf Nūr al-Dā'im for holding an ostentatious party celebrating the circumcision of his son, a party in which there was sumptuous food, intermingling of men and women, song and dance. Muḥammad Aḥmad's criticism of this event is seen by some as the reason for his expulsion from the Sammānī order by Muḥammad Sharīf. In a later period, after the break with Muḥammad Sharīf and during his association with al-Shaykh al-Qurashī, Muḥammad Aḥmad lived for some time in an underground cave; this gave him plenty of publicity and prestige in ascetic circles.[85]

Muḥammad Aḥmad's world view can be described as a synthesis between extreme determinism inspired by classical Muslim ascetics and a strong determination to attain the goals of the Mahdiyya. The combination between the conviction that man can do nothing in order to change his preordained destiny, the disdain for all things worldly and the determination to engage in *jihād* has been present among Muslim ascetics since the earliest period of Muslim history. A prophetic *ḥadīth* which does not seem to be attested in the canonical collections but is attributed to the Prophet in Ṣūfī literature reads: "I have two professions: poverty and *jihād*" (*lī ḥirfatāni al-faqr wa al-jihād*).[86] It is therefore not surprising that Muḥammad Aḥmad finds complete compatibility between his advocacy of extreme frugality, his belief in divine predestination and the wide-ranging political and military objectives of the Mahdiyya; he is able to integrate these two elements seamlessly into his thinking. The stage for this integration is set in a visionary encounter attended by the Prophet and al-Shaykh Aḥmad al-Ṭayyib (d. 1824) who introduced the Sammānī Ṣūfī order into the Sudan.[87] In this encounter, the Mahdiyya is compared to the Ṣūfī way (*ṭarīqa*). The Ṣūfī way includes humility, brokenness (of spirit?), paucity of food and drink, endurance and visitation of Ṣūfī leaders. The Mahdiyya includes all these, but adds to them war, prudence, determination, reliance on God and doctrinal unity. Only

85 Shuqayr, *Ta'rīkh al-Sūdān*, vol. 3, pp. 115, 118–119; Abū Salīm, *al-Khuṣūma* ..., p. 160.
86 Hujwīrī, *Kashf al-Maḥjūb*, p. 275. For an expanded version of this tradition, see Ghazālī, *Iḥyā' 'ulūm al-dīn*, vol. 5, p. 53. Cf. *Al-Āthār al-kāmila*, vol. 7, pp. 174, 179.
87 See "Aḥmad al-Ṭayyib b. al-Bashīr", in *EI*[3], s.v. (N. Grandin).

the Mahdiyya integrates all these elements and this is the source of its strength.[88]

Ascetic motifs are very frequent in Muḥammad Aḥmad's letters and he draws systematically on relevant material in the classical Muslim tradition. The reward of the poor in the hereafter is much greater than that of the rich. Love of money, love of life and parsimony are characteristics of the Jews and the idolaters.[89] The worthlessness of this world in comparison with the everlasting pleasures promised to Muslims in the hereafter is repeatedly stressed. Gluttony and carnal desire (*shahwat al-baṭn wa al-farj*) are two sharp swords used by the (evil-bidding) soul against otherwise perfect men. When reading this, we need to keep in mind that Muḥammad Aḥmad had four wives and dozens of concubines. The four cardinal sins as perceived by Muḥammad Aḥmad are fear of human beings, loving the pursuit of livelihood, loving this world and forgetting the next.[90] He recalls the classical tradition according to which the Prophet was offered by the Meccans kingship and wealth if he agrees to desist from his monotheistic preaching, but resolved to reject all worldly wealth and become a prophet and a slave (of God) instead.[91] Expanding on the early Muslim attitudes heaping scorn on the pomp and splendour of the Persian and Byzantine courts, Muḥammad Aḥmad addresses his followers saying that "you are not like the Persian emperors or the Byzantine emperors or the Pashas or the governors – so that we become conceited, adorn ourselves and enjoy (a good life)" (*innakum lastum fī kisrawiyya wa lā qayṣariyya wa lā bāshawiyya wa lā fī sanjakiyya ḥattā nazhū wa natazayyan wa natana* ʿ*am*). The Mahdiyya does not promise earthly positions and mundane ranks; its followers should train themselves to endure hunger and adversity. Quoting Qurʾān 28:83,[92]

88 *Al-Āthār al-kāmila*, vol. 1, p. 78.

89 The Qurʾān criticizes the Children of Israel and the idolaters for their love of life; see Qurʾān 2:96: "You will find them (sc. the Children of Israel) the eagerest of men for life. And of the idolaters, there is one of them who wishes to be spared a thousand years." See also the early Mahdist author al-ʿIbādī, *al-Anwār al-saniyya*, p. 14: "Fear of death is a Jewish characteristic" (*al-khawf min al-mawt akhlāq yahūdiyya*).

90 *Al-Āthār al-kāmila*, vol. 7, pp. 174–175, 212, 215.

91 *Al-Āthār al-kāmila*, vol. 2, pp. 32–33, 139. This is, of course, only one description of the Prophet's attitude to worldly wealth. For the controversy on the question whether poverty is part of the Islamic ideal and whether the Prophet died as a poor man or as a rich man, see Ibn Qutayba, *Kitāb taʾlīf mukhtalaf al-ḥadīth*, pp. 208–211.

92 "That is the Last Abode; we appoint it for those who do not desire grandeur in the earth, nor corruption."

Muḥammad Aḥmad affirms that Paradise is promised only to those who do not aspire to high positions and earthly prestige. And, in any case, livelihood is apportioned by God and no one can change His decisions: what was apportioned to someone will not elude him, even if he lies passively on his bed, and what eluded him was not destined to reach him. A man's livelihood is like his shadow, never leaving him alone. Muḥammad Aḥmad therefore instructs his followers not to hoard victuals because providing livelihood is God's responsibility. He praises a certain Aḥmad al-Fādinī who refused a commander's rank and asserts that love of leadership severs the relationship between the believer and his God.[93] Those whose exclusive goal is God, who are truthful in their religion and obedient to God do not aspire to earthly position or wealth. They should not have any possessions in their homes: neither money, nor livestock, nor servants nor any other worldly things. They should wear tattered robes and clothe their women in shabby garments. This type of attire is of particular importance for Muḥammad Aḥmad. It symbolizes the similarity of his followers to the People of Purity (*ahl al-ṣafā'*), meaning the Ṣūfīs; it instils fear in the hearts of the enemy; it inspires the prophets and saints who were present at Muḥammad Aḥmad's appointment ceremony (*ahl al-ḥaḍra*)[94] to respect his followers, and it prevents the risk of falling into dubious matters, probably meaning expensive clothing and other types of luxury.[95]

The demeanour of the Mahdists should always be modest: they should not ride between their houses and if they are not able to walk, they should preferably ride on donkeys. This is more compatible with modesty. Horses should be ridden only in *jihād* or in preparation for it.[96] A corollary of this is the injunction not to socialize with the rich; their company can result in spiritual death.[97]

This world (*dunyā*) is the enemy of Allah and the enemy of His friends. One must pass through it, but refrain from building in it.[98] It is the Paradise of the *mahdī*'s opponents who are deprived of divine mercy. It is the abode of those who have no abode (*al-dunyā dāru man lā dāra lahu*), meaning the miserable abode of those who attach themselves to

93 *Al-Āthār al-kāmila*, vol. 2, p. 76; vol. 5, pp. 306, 314, 363–364; vol. 7, pp. 162, 245, 248.
94 See earlier, at notes 35, 37.
95 *Al-Āthār al-kāmila*, vol. 7, p. 206.
96 *Al-Āthār al-kāmila*, vol. 2, p. 27.
97 *Al-Āthār al-kāmila*, vol. 7, p. 184.
98 *Al-Āthār al-kāmila*, vol. 3, p. 212.

this transitory world and are deprived of the eternal abode of Paradise. Following the ideas and even the exact formulations of early Muslim ascetics, Muḥammad Aḥmad scornfully describes this world as a carcass and its seekers as dogs (*al-dunyā jīfa wa ṭullābuhā kilāb*). The best man is he who ruins this world and builds the next. If the world weighed in the eyes of God more than a mosquito's wing, he would not allow the unbelievers even one sip of water from it. One should never delight when this world brings him something nor grieve when something of it turns away.[99] All worldly enjoyment and entertainment, such as music, must be abandoned.[100] Life must focus on God alone.

Naturally enough, such a single-minded devotion to God has ramifications on all aspects of the devotee's life. Family life may lead to betrayal of God and his Prophet; it must not be allowed to interfere with the duties of the *mahdī*'s supporters who have resolved to abandon their selves, their families, their children, their aspirations and their offspring (*baqāyā*). All these must be renounced in order to obtain what God has to offer. The *mahdī* sought inspiration for these ideas in ascetic passages such as Qur'ān 9:24 which inveighs against those early Muslims for whom God and *jihād* for His sake were less important than their families, property, commerce and habitats.[101] Qur'ān 9:24 reads: "Say: 'If your fathers, your sons, your brothers, your wives, your clan, your possessions that you have gained, commerce you fear may slacken, dwellings you love – if these are dearer to you than God and His Messenger and *jihād* in His way, then wait till God brings His command; God guides not people who are ungodly.'" Conversely, Paradise is the place in which preference is given to those who are poor and humble (*wa qad ustuʾthirat al-janna bi-'l-ḍuʿafāʾ wa al-masākīn*), they will enter it before all others and the Muslim community will be succoured by them (*tunṣaru hādhihi al-umma bi-ḍuʿafāʾihā*.[102]

Asceticism in the sense of frugal living is, however, not sufficient in Muḥammad Aḥmad's view. Like his predecessor Sayyid Muḥammad Jawnpūrī, Muḥammad Aḥmad demanded also *hijra*, leaving one's place of

99 *Al-Āthār al-kāmila*, vol. 1, pp. 91, 385–388, 415–416; vol. 2, p. 125; vol. 4, pp. 392, 438–439; vol. 5, pp. 290–291, 309, 344, 356, 369; vol. 7, p. 247. The two quotations are in vol. 2, p. 33 and vol. 4 p. 489 *infra*. These ideas are common in early Muslim asceticism.

100 *Al-Āthār al-kāmila*, vol. 1, p. 398; vol. 7, p. 217.

101 *Al-Āthār al-kāmila*, vol. 1, pp. 418–419; vol. 3, pp. 83, 338.

102 *Al-Āthār al-kāmila*, vol. 5, p. 370.

residence in order to join the *mahdī*'s camp. We have discussed the classical background of this idea in Chapter 3 and it is not necessary to delve into the details again. Suffice it to say here that the demand to perform *hijra* is repeated in Muḥammad Aḥmad's letters with great frequency. Even before declaring himself a *mahdī*, he encouraged *hijra* by saying that "whoever escapes with his religion from one land to another will earn Paradise" (*man farra bi-dīnihi min arḍ ilā arḍ istawjaba lahu al-janna*). It is easy to support this idea by indicating the rich rewards which accrued to Islam in general and to the Prophet in particular as a result of his leaving Mecca and migrating to Medina.[103] The *hijra* must be more than physical: whoever migrates from his habitat but his heart remains with his family, the door of Paradise will be closed to him and the door of the Fire will be flung open.[104] The principle of abandoning family relationships in favour of a new brotherhood of faith in the Mahdiyya is less prominent in the thought of Muḥammad Aḥmad than in that of Muḥammad Jawnpūrī, but it does exist: this new brotherhood is based on the idea that the young among the *mahdī*'s associates should be treated as sons, the elders as fathers and those of middle age as brothers of each other.[105] Qur'ān 9:23 which enjoins the believers not to take their fathers and brothers to be their friends if they prefer unbelief to belief is quoted in Muḥammad Aḥmad's letters as well.[106]

A general observation concerning the *hijra* idea is placed here, because its implications are far-reaching on the social level. In contemporary terms, the *hijra* advocated by Muḥammad Aḥmad was mobilization of thousands in order to organize a military force. On the social, human level it meant abandonment of home, livelihood, wife and children. This is a difficult proposition in any society and was equally difficult for the potential supporters of Muḥammad Aḥmad. The difficulties which he must have encountered in his mobilization efforts explain the countless exhortations in which he promised unlimited rewards and eternal pleasures in Paradise to those who will respond to his call, join the movement, fight for its cause and perhaps die in battle. There is of course no difficulty in finding material supporting this idea in the sacred sources of Islam. At the same time

103 *Al-Āthār al-kāmila*, vol. 1, pp. 69–70; cf. vol. 4, p. 86.
104 *Al-Āthār al-kāmila*, vol. 1, p. 209.
105 Ḥammūda, *Aḥmad Sulaymān* ..., p. 13; *Al-Āthār al-kāmila*, vol. 4, p. 622.
106 *Al-Āthār al-kāmila*, vol. 1, p. 254. Cf. Walī b. Yūsuf, *Inṣāf nāma*, pp. 187–188; see also pp. 195–196.

– albeit with less frequency – he tried to devalue family life and describes women and conjugal life in the rudest of terms. He does this despite the fact that he had four wives, numerous concubines and fathered ten sons and ten daughters.[107] In a letter replete with praising *jihād* and debunking earthly life and rank, he says:

> As for your wife, her beauty and [your] intimacy with her – let us assume that she is the most beautiful of women and the best of her time. Is it not true that her beginning is a putrid drop and her end a squalid corpse and in between she is a carrier of faeces? Your separation from her is foreordained either by death or during lifetime [by divorce?]. This is well known. If she is one of the depraved, separation from her now is better than in the future. And if she is one of the virtuous, you will be joined in the Gardens of Paradise where her ugly, contemptible features will be transformed into attributes of goodness and beauty. You will find her in the hereafter better, more beautiful, more gorgeous and more perfect. (*wa ammā zawjatuka wa jamāluhā wa qurbuhā wa wiṣāluhā fa-'friḍ annahā ajmal al-niswān wa aḥsan ahl al-zamān. fa-hal awwaluhā illā nuṭfatun madhira wa hal ākhiruhā illā jīfatun qadhira wa hiya fīmā baynahumā taḥmilu al-ʿadhira. fa-firāquka lahā maḥtūm immā bi-'l-mawt wa immā bi-'l-ḥayāt wa hādha amr maʿlūm. fa-in kānat min al-ṭāliḥāt fa-firāquha al-ān khayrun mimmā huwa ātin wa in kānat min al-ṣāliḥāt fa-sa-tajmaʿu baynakumā rawḍāt al-jannāt wa tatabaddalu qabāʾiḥuhā al-radhīla bi-'l-awṣāf al-ḥasana al-jamīla fa-tajiduhā fī al-ākhir(a) aḥsana wa ajmala wa ajalla awṣāfan wa akmal*).[108]

Like Muḥammad Aḥmad's appointment to be the *mahdī*, the order to perform *hijra* to Jabal Qadīr was given to him by the Prophet. Muḥammad Aḥmad says time and again that *hijra* is a commandment included both in the Qurʾān and in the prophetic *sunna*. Economic or social reasons cannot serve as an excuse for refraining from performing it. Quoting Qurʾānic verses and prophetic traditions, Muḥammad Aḥmad asserts that the existence of dependants cannot be used as a reason to stay at

107 See earlier, at note 18.
108 *Al-Āthār al-kāmila*, vol. 5, p. 409.

home: the *muhājir*'s family who stays behind will be taken care of by God himself.[109] Tending a field cannot serve as an excuse either, because "with God are things that are better and more lasting" (*mā ʿinda Allāh khayrun wa abqā*) (than any agricultural produce). And, indeed, the *mahdī*'s economic conditions improved greatly after his *hijra* to Qadīr and God provided for him abundantly. Furthermore, the pain caused by the separation from the family is less than the divine punishment inflicted on those who refrain from performing the *hijra*. Nevertheless, if nothing else is feasible, it is permissible to perform the *hijra* together with the family.[110]

IV RELIGIOUS EXCLUSIVITY AND *JIHĀD*

Like in the Qurʾān and in the prophetic tradition, the *hijra* in Muḥammad Aḥmad's thought is intimately related to *jihād* which he frequently describes as the most meritorious of commandments.[111] *Jihād* is a war against non-Muslims and it was therefore essential for Muḥammad Aḥmad to declare his opponents as infidels. Time and again he declares that whoever denies his claim to be the *mahdī* belongs to this category. He routinely asserts that the Prophet himself had affirmed that whoever rejects the *mahdī* is an infidel. In asserting this, Muḥammad Aḥmad follows in the footsteps of Ibn Tūmart and Sayyid Muḥammad Jawnpūrī who also adopted stringent attitudes to Muslims who did not join their movements or denied their messianic claims.[112]

Muḥammad Aḥmad asserts in numerous letters that his followers must engage in *jihād*, that the commandment to wage it was issued to him by

109 Qurʾān 63:9 enjoins the believers not to be distracted by their children from remembering God, while Qurʾān 64:14 describes property and children as a "temptation" (*fitna*). Qurʾān 65:3 which says that "whoever puts his trust in God, He shall suffice him" is also understood as a promise to take care of the *muhājir*'s dependants. The tradition quoted reads: "O God, you are the companion for travel and the substitute (taking care) of the family" (*allāhumma anta al-ṣāḥib fī al-safar wa al-khalīfa fī al-ahl*). Muslim b. b. al-Ḥajjāj, *Ṣaḥīḥ*, vol. 2, p. 978 (*Kitāb al-ḥajj*, 425). For further occurrences, see Wensinck, *Concordance*, s.v. *khalīfa*.

110 *Al-Āthār al-kāmila*, vol. 1, pp. 313, 346, 379–380, 421; vol. 2, pp. 43–44, 58, 153–154; vol. 3, pp. 40–42, 81–85, 194–197, 220, 319–320; vol. 4, p. 86, 178–181; vol. 5, pp. 4–5, 225–226.

111 *Al-Āthār al-kāmila*, vol. 1, p. 301; vol. 3, p. 58 and countless other places in the *Āthār*.

112 See Chapter 2, note 127; Chapter 3, Section IV; see also Chapter 1, notes 30, 101.

the Prophet himself and its abandonment is tantamount to abandoning religion itself.[113] Pertinent Qur'ānic verses and prophetic traditions are repeatedly quoted in order to give legitimacy to this demand. Pride of place belongs to the verses in which the Qur'ān denounces those contemporaries of the Prophet who refrained from joining the *jihād*.[114] This is another opportunity to create an affinity between Muḥammad Aḥmad and the Prophet. Furthermore, those who claim to be supporters of the *mahdī* but refrain from joining the *jihād* are hypocrites (*munāfiqūn*) and must be shunned.[115] According to a famous *ḥadīth*, *jihād* is the monasticism (*rahbāniyya*) of the Muslim community and whoever abandons it will be humiliated by God.[116] In particular, being engaged in agriculture cannot be used as an excuse for avoiding *jihād*. Only women, children and servants who do not participate in war may till the land. On this matter, Muḥammad Aḥmad invokes a frequently quoted classical tradition which says that "if you hold to the tails of cows and become content with abandoning *jihād*, God will inflict on you humiliation and will not remove it from you" (*idhā akhadhtum adhnāb al-baqar wa raḍītum bi-'l-qu'ūd 'an al-jihād sallaṭa Allāh 'alaykum dhullan lā yanza'uhu minkum*). Thus, gainful employment and economic considerations must not be allowed to interfere with the supreme duty to engage the enemy in battle and one must make do with what God provides. In matters of livelihood, Muḥammad Aḥmad takes an extremely deterministic stand and asserts that livelihood is in the hands of God; He will provide it even if men run away from it: "If a man rides the wind to run away from his livelihood, the livelihood will ride the lightning to catch up with him" (*law rakiba al-'abd al-rīḥ hāriban min rizqihi la-rakiba al-rizq al-barq ḥattā yalḥaqahu*). After all, says the Qur'ān (39:36), "shall not God suffice His servant?"[117] Muḥammad Aḥmad asserts that he

113 *Al-Āthār al-kāmila*, vol. 1, p. 177; vol. 7, p. 165.

114 Qur'ān 9:38–39, 120; *Al-Āthār al-kāmila*, vol. 1, pp. 104, 181–182, 191–192, 211.

115 *Al-Āthār al-kāmila*, vol. 1, p. 196; vol. 7, p. 170.

116 *Al-Āthār al-kāmila*, vol. 1, pp. 262–263; vol. 7, p. 165. According to another tradition, Muslim monasticism is sitting in the mosques; see *Al-Āthār al-kāmila*, vol. 7, p. 182.

117 *Al-Āthār al-kāmila*, vol. 1, p. 310; cf. vol. 2, p. 280; vol. 3, p. 133; vol. 5, pp. 262–263; vol. 7, p. 165. For an exhaustive treatment of this tradition in the *ḥadīth*, see Kister, "Land property and *jihād*", pp. 276–280. It is noteworthy that the *ḥadīth* literature contains also traditions in favour of agriculture which reflect the situation of the Muslim community after the wave of conquests in the first century and the acquisition of agricultural land in the occupied territories. See Kister, op. cit., pp. 290ff.

received permission even to abandon the prayer for the Prophet and the recitation of the Qurʾān in order to engage in *jihād*, though his followers should continue to perform their prayers with devotion.[118] Even the opening of a school which would teach Qurʾān to Muslim children must not bring about the abandonment of *jihād* by the teacher.[119] Naturally enough, martyrdom (*shahāda*) is also highly regarded. In addition to Qurʾān 3:169 which is the *locus classicus* for praising the martyrs, Muḥammad Aḥmad quotes also the *ḥadīth* in which the Prophet expressed his desire to die in *jihād* and to be resurrected, only in order to die in the same circumstances again and again.[120] He also affirms that he was in contact with martyred members of his movement and reports that they are totally satisfied with their pleasurable life in Paradise.[121] Mahdist historians follow suit: according to al-Kordofānī, for the Mahdists, "death is sweeter than honey" (*fa-inna al-mawt ʿindahum aḥlā min al-ʿasal*).[122]

Women's participation in *jihād* is obligatory, but not all women are required to wage military *jihād*. Mature or elderly women after whom men do not lust any more must wage military *jihād*, "with their hands and feet"; young women, on the other hand, must stay at home, fighting their (evil-bidding) souls (*fa-man ṣārat qāʿidatan wa 'nqaṭaʿa ʿanhā arab al-rijāl fa-yujāhidna bi-yadayhā wa rijlayhā; ammā al-shābbāt fa-yujāhidna nufūsahunna wa yaskunna fī buyūtihinna* ...).[123] "*Jihād* against the [evil-bidding] soul" (*jihād al-nafs*) is thus a mandatory substitute for military *jihād* with regard to young women. Preserving female chastity is more important than incorporating women in the fighting force, but once their chastity is no longer in danger, women ought to make their contribution on the battlefield.

We have had the opportunity to demonstrate that Muḥammad Aḥmad derives many of his ideas from the classical Muslim tradition. However, his views on women's participation in *jihād* do not seem to belong to this category. While both in the *ḥadīth* and in the historical literature one

118 *Al-Āthār al-kāmila*, vol. 5, p. 367.
119 *Al-Āthār al-kāmila*, vol. 4, p. 212.
120 *Al-Āthār al-kāmila*, vol. 4, pp. 493. Qurʾān 3:169 reads: "Count not those who were slain in God's way as dead, but rather living with their Lord, by Him provided, rejoicing in the bounty that God has given them and joyful in those who remain behind and have not joined them ..." For the *ḥadīth*, see Bukhārī, *Ṣaḥīḥ*, vol. 2, p. 201 (*Kitāb al-jihād*, 7).
121 *Al-Āthār al-kāmila*, vol. 5, p. 287.
122 Al-Kordofānī, *Saʿādat al-mustahdī*, p. 204.
123 *Al-Āthār al-kāmila*, vol. 1, p. 302.

can find material on women performing auxiliary tasks in warfare (such as carrying water to the warriors, treating the Muslim wounded, bringing the bodies of the fallen back to camp, giving the *coup-de-grâce* to the enemy wounded), the Prophet is reported to have said that women are not expected to fight and that a woman's *jihād* is the pilgrimage (*ḥajj*). This is said to have been his response when ʿĀʾisha and other wives of his asked him whether to participate in *jihād*.[124]

A common theme in Muḥammad Aḥmad's discussion of *jihād* is the question of spoils. Muslim tradition knows legal spoils, divided according to the rules established in the Qurʾān and in the *ḥadīth* (*maghānim*), and illegal spoils, or plunder (*ghulūl*), taken without regard to these rules before the leader distributes the spoils. This is not the place to delve into the details of the Muslim law of spoils, but a general picture is essential in order to place Muḥammad Aḥmad's thinking and actions into proper perspective. Qurʾān 8:41 rules that "whatever spoils you take, the fifth of it is God's, and the Messenger's, and the near kinsman's, and the orphan's, and for the needy, and the traveller ..." Elsewhere (Qurʾān 8:69) it allows Muslims "to eat whatever you have taken as spoils, such as is lawful and good ..." The standard interpretation of these two verses is that one fifth of the spoils belongs to the Prophet and the four groups mentioned in the verse, while the other four fifths belong to the warriors. According to another verse (Qurʾān 59:7), "whatever spoils of war God has given to His messenger from the people of the cities belongs to God, and His messenger, and the near kinsman, orphans, the needy and the traveller ..." This can be interpreted as meaning that in certain cases all the spoils belong to the Muslim treasury. Plunder, on the other hand, is forbidden and "whoever plunders, will bring the fruits of his plunder on the Day of Resurrection" (Qurʾān 3:161), apparently as a proof of his transgression. The prophetic tradition expands on this theme and speaks of the frightful punishments which will be inflicted on the plunderers on the Day of Judgment.

The question of spoils and plunder was of major importance because of the numerous victories achieved by the Mahdists and is repeatedly

124 Bukhārī, *Ṣaḥīḥ*, vol. 1, p. 386 (*Kitāb al-ḥajj*, 4); vol. 2, pp. 218–220 (*Kitāb al-jihād*, 62–68); Ṭabarī, *Taʾrīkh*, series I, p. 2363. The necessity to prevent intermingling of women with men is mentioned by some commentators as the reason for this attitude, but they also mention that the *ḥadīth* does not mean that women cannot volunteer for *jihād*. See al-ʿAsqalānī, *Fatḥ al-bārī*, vol. 6, p. 76. For the problem of intermingling between men and women during the pilgrimage, see Bukhārī, *Ṣaḥīḥ*, vol. 1, p. 308 (*Kitāb al-ḥajj*, 64).

mentioned in Muḥammad Aḥmad's letters. Muḥammad Aḥmad insisted that no spoils must be appropriated by the warriors before the legal distribution takes place. No spoils – including slave girls – may be enjoyed before victory is assured. Sometimes he demands that the spoils be gathered and preserved at a safe place near the battlefield until they can be distributed properly. In some letters he instructed the local commanders to send one fifth of the spoils to the treasury and distribute the rest to the warriors. This seems to have been the case with the spoils taken when Kharṭūm was conquered. It seems, however, that the method preferred by Muḥammad Aḥmad was to dispatch the spoils to the treasury (*bayt al-māl*). It is noteworthy that there was a significant exception to this rule and the spoils were not distributed in the same manner to everyone. For full time warriors there was no individual taking of spoils; they would receive their needs from the treasury in which the spoils had been deposited. On the other hand, warriors who join the *jihād* only for a limited period of time and have other professions to which they are expected to return after the battle – may take the four fifths of their spoils directly after giving one fifth to the treasury. This must have been a powerful incentive for merchants, artisans and peasants to participate in the Mahdist *jihād* on an occasional basis.

Certain types of spoils, such as cities which were taken over without fighting, belong to the treasury in their entirety, according to an interpretation of Qur'ān 59:7.[125] Firearms are also not subject to distribution and all of them must be sent to the treasury. Similarly, free women must be sent to the treasury and must not be enslaved by their captors except if they are Turkish: the Turks, male and female, are considered spoils (and therefore may be enslaved). Plunder is repeatedly and severely condemned. Referring to pertinent classical materials, Muḥammad Aḥmad considers it a result of worldly desires and threatens the plunderers with awful punishment in the hereafter. In some letters he also threatens them with earthly punishment: decapitation and enslavement of their children. The Prophet himself told Muḥammad Aḥmad that whoever hides anything from the spoils ought to be killed; in some formulations, the Prophet himself promised to do the killing. If someone brings to the treasury spoils which he has in his possession willingly, without being intercepted and searched, he will receive

125 "Whatever spoils of war God has given to His messenger from the people of the cities belongs to God, and His messenger, and the near kinsman, orphans, the needy and the traveller, so that it be not a thing taken in turns among the rich of you."

a share from them; otherwise, they will be taken from him and he will be punished. Also, in accordance with a classical *ḥadīth*, it is forbidden not to inform on a plunderer.[126] While enjoying legally distributed spoils is legitimate, Muḥammad Aḥmad maintained that on the level of principle, one should not covet spoils; if he does – he will not be allowed to have them. He expressed this view as part of his ascetic world view and this principle did not have much practical significance when the spoils were distributed.[127]

The *jihād* of Muḥammad Aḥmad was directed against the "Turko-Egyptian" regime, established in the Sudan after Muḥammad ʿAlī's invasion of 1820. Peter Holt has explained why this "clumsy adjective ... best describes both the conquest and the administration that followed".[128] As far as Muḥammad Aḥmad is concerned, he viewed the administration which he fought as consisting mainly of "Turks", who were supported by the British. Time and again he asserts that Allah ordered the Muslims to fight them and that "the Prophet has called the Turks infidels" who strive to extinguish the light of God, and feels no qualms when he invokes Qurʾān 9:5 and 9:14 – which enjoin killing polytheists – in this context. They are enemies of God who must not be obeyed, whose houses must not be entered and whose customs must not be emulated. No excuse will be accepted from those who associate with them.[129] In some places he calls the Turks "apostates" (*murtaddūn*), who cannot be reformed by preaching, only purified by sword. Since he invokes Qurʾān 9:5[130] and Qurʾān 9:14 in this context, one can conclude that he also considers them polytheists, albeit only by implication. Apostates and polytheists are, of course, the most abhorrent words in Muslim parlance.[131] He also accuses the Turks of perpetrating atrocities, of changing the *sharīʿa* of the Prophet and, strangely enough, of imposing *jizya* on Muslims. Using the term *jizya* – which in Islamic law denotes a tax imposed on non-Muslim subjects of a Muslim state – for taxes levied by the "Turko-Egyptian" government on

126 *Al-Āthār al-kāmila*, vol. 1, pp. 181–182, 197, 228–229, 343–344, 439; vol. 2, pp. 9–11, 18, 53, 163–164, 222; vol. 4, pp. 54, 62, 75–76, 263, 291–292, 379, 422–423, 425; vol. 5, pp. 36, 72–73, 75, 422, 459; vol. 6, pp. 229–232; vol. 7, p. 199.

127 *Al-Āthār al-kāmila*, vol. 7, p. 87.

128 Holt, *A Modern History of the Sudan*, p. 37.

129 *Al-Āthār al-kāmila*, vol. 1, pp. 191, 196, 397–398; vol. 2, p. 216.

130 "Then, when the sacred months are drawn away, slay the polytheists wherever you find them ..."

131 *Al-Āthār al-kāmila*, vol. 1, pp. 108, 204.

the Sudanese is a powerful tool to denounce the government as engaging in religiously illegitimate practices.[132]

This view of the Turks calls for comment. Muḥammad Aḥmad says that Allah ordered the Muslims to fight the Turks. Allah could have issued such an injunction only in the Qur'ān or in the "sacred *ḥadīth*" (*ḥadīth qudsī*), the utterances which the Prophet is reported to have received from God during his nocturnal journey to heaven (*mi'rāj*). It goes without saying that neither source includes any injunction to fight the Turks. In the prophetic *ḥadīth*, on the other hand, the situation is different. Here Muḥammad Aḥmad could have referred to a time-honoured tradition according to which a war against the Turks will be one of the Portents of the Hour. In the *Sunan* of Abū Dāwūd we read that "the Hour will not arrive until the Muslims will fight the Turks, whose faces are like forged shield, wearing hair".[133] Many other traditions describe the Turks as extremely hostile to Muslims, sometimes serving as instruments of divine vengeance. Together with the Jews, they are mentioned as supporters of the false messiah (*dajjāl*).[134] It is noteworthy that Muḥammad Aḥmad, who routinely quotes classical material in order to support his exhortations, does not normally avail himself of these traditions; it is possible that they were not part of his religious upbringing and did not command his attention. His failure to refer to this material is also an indication of the extent to which the idea of the *mahdī* has become independent of its eschatological origins and became part of historical, non-apocalyptic times.

In his attempts to raise the morale of the troops, Muḥammad Aḥmad frequently asserts that the victory of his warriors is predetermined. God is with the Muslims, the enemies are effeminate and cannot win:

> Do you not know that the armies of the heretics are [destined to be] shattered even if they are great in number? The hosts of the obstinate are in retreat even if their minds planned their advance. The determination of the erring is effeminate and diminished even if their selves are puffed up; therefore Allah the Exalted enabled one Muslim to overcome two of them, in the same way as a male

132 *Al-Āthār al-kāmila*, vol. 1, pp. 180, 269–270; vol. 2, pp. 170 *infra*; 281.
133 See Chapter 1, at note 6.
134 Abū Dāwūd, *Sunan*, vol. 4, p. 160 (*Kitāb al-malāḥim* 9). For a thoughtful analysis of the apocalyptic war against the Turks and of the image of the Turks in apocalyptic literature, see D. Cook, *Studies in Muslim Apocalyptic*, pp. 84–91, 99, 169.

> is allotted the share of two females.[135] The text of His clear Book affirms all this. God the Exalted said: "... and your host will avail you nothing though it be numerous; and God is with the believers." (*a-mā ta'lamūna anna jumū'a dhawī al-ilḥād mukassara wa in kānat bi-'l-ta'dād mukaththara wa juyūsh ulī al-'inād mudbira wa in kānat bi-'uqūlihim muqdima mudabbara wa 'azamāt rijāl al-ḍalāl mu'annatha muṣaghghara wa in kānat dhawātuhum mukabbara wa li-dhā ja'ala Allāh ta'ālā kulla Muslimin yaghlibu minhum ithnayn kamā anna li-'l-dhakar mithla ḥaẓẓi 'l-unthayayn wa yu'akkidu hādhā kullahu naṣṣu kitābihi al-mubīn. qāla ta'ālā: wa lan tughniya 'ankum fi'atukum shay'an wa in kathurat wa inna Allāh ma'a al-mu'minīn.*)[136]

Muḥammad Aḥmad is not the first to suggest that true faith is "masculine" while its opponents are "feminine" or "effeminate". The history of Ṣūfism knew numerous female ascetics and mystics, but the equation of the ideal Ṣūfī with manhood (*mard, jawānmard, fatā*) and the equation of the despised "world" (*dunyā*) with woman has a long history in Ṣūfism. Muṣṭafā Gujarātī, a sixteenth-century adherent of the Mahdawī movement in India, divides humanity into three groups from the religious point of view: the seekers of this world who are effeminate, the seekers of the next world who are feminine and the seekers of God who are masculine (*ṭālib al-dunyā mukhannath ṭālib al-'uqbā mu'annath wa ṭālib al-mawlā mudhakkar*).[137] Gujarātī's division is not the same as Muḥammad Aḥmad's, but the thrust of the passage is identical: manhood is an essential component of true religiosity.

During his whole messianic career, Muḥammad Aḥmad was engaged in military *jihād* and most references to *jihād* in his letters relate to warfare. Only rarely he mentions *jihād* in the sense of internal struggle (*jihād al-nafs*) and performance of commandments or good deeds; he calls these "the greater *jihād*" (*al-jihād al-akbar*). In another passage he mentions four types of *jihād*: *jihād* of the heart by means of which the saints adorn themselves with praiseworthy qualities; *jihād* of the ascetics in order to

135 A reference to Muslim law of inheritance; cf. Qur'ān 4:10, 175.

136 Qur'ān 8:19; *al-Āthār al-kāmila*, vol. 1, pp. 312, 346.

137 Gujarātī, *Majālis*, p. 60; see also MacLean, "Real Men and False Men ...", pp. 206–207. For relevant material in classical *taṣawwuf*, see Schimmel, *Mystical Dimensions of Islam*, pp. 427–435.

abandon everything except God; *jihād* of the scholars in order to make the truth manifest; and *jihād* of the warriors in order to kill the infidel enemies of God (*al-jihād ʿalā arbaʿa: jihād al-awliyāʾ bi-'l-qalb li-'l-taḥliya* [sic] *al-akhlāq al-marḍiyya; wa jihād al-zuhhād bi-tarki mā siwāhu; wa jihād al-ʿulamāʾ bi-iẓhār al-ḥaqq; wa jihād al-ghuzāt bi-qatl aʿdāʾ Allāh al-kafara*).[138]

V MUḤAMMAD AḤMAD, HIS ASSOCIATES AND GENERAL GORDON

Al-Āthār al-kāmila, the collected epistles of Muḥammad Aḥmad, include an exchange of letters between General Gordon and Muḥammad Aḥmad. Gordon started his correspondence with Muḥammad Aḥmad soon after his arrival in the Sudan in January 1884.[139] His first letter is dated 13 February 1884. Though the uprising of Muḥammad Aḥmad was already in full swing and his warriors have already achieved significant victories, the letter is written in a friendly, polite and dispassionate style. Gordon notifies Muḥammad Aḥmad that he was appointed governor of the Sudan, declares his desire to maintain friendly relations with him and expresses his friendship and compassion for the Muslims. The Arabic version of this letter reads as if it were written by a Muslim leader. He addresses Muḥammad Aḥmad in the following words: "The pride of honourable *amīr*s, the exemplar of virtuous saints, (Your) Excellency our Lord and Master, Muḥammad Aḥmad b. ʿAbd Allāh, may God protect him, Amen" (*fakhr al-umarāʾ al-mukarramīn wa qudwat al-awliyāʾ al-ṣāliḥīn ḥaḍrat sayyidinā wa mawlānā al-sayyid Muḥammad Aḥmad b. ʿAbd Allāh ḥafiẓahu Allāh, Āmīn*). The letter then stresses Gordon's desire to prevent further bloodshed and pacify the country. It also offers to Muḥammad Aḥmad the governorship of Kordofān – which was already in Muḥammad Aḥmad's hands – and asks him to send an ambassador of his to Kharṭūm. He also mentions the need to repair the communications system which was destroyed by the Bedouins (*ʿawāmīd wa sulūk al-tilighrāf li-tajdīd mā sabaqa itlāfuhu bi-wāsiṭat al-ʿurbān*).[140]

Muḥammad Aḥmad responded to the letter on 9 March 1884. His first letter is rather polite when compared with the later one. He asserts that

---

138 *Al-Āthār al-kāmila*, vol. 7, p. 164.
139 I was not able to find out who prepared the Arabic version of Gordon's letters.
140 *Al-Āthār al-kāmila*, vol. 2, pp. 244–245.

he is the *mahdī* and repeats several times his preference for the hereafter over this world, his love of poverty and the poor, and his disdain for earthly wealth and positions. In accordance with this ascetic stance, he rejects Gordon's offer to assume the governorship of Kordofān. He also returns a gift he received from Gordon because he is not after worldly possessions. He asks Gordon to embrace Islam, promises him salvation according to Qur'ān 5:68[141] and pledges to appoint him to some unspecified position and enter into alliance with him. To make this offer credible, he gives details about Sudanese notables who received appointments after they had submitted to him – as if appointments of Sudanese notables could serve as a precedent for the appointment of a converted British general.[142] In another letter, he notifies Gordon that he is sending him a garment worn by the members of his movement (*jubba*) and other parts of their attire, in expectation of Gordon's conversion and enrolment in his movement.[143] It is hard to believe that Muḥammad Aḥmad really believed in this possibility, but the letter does not lend itself to any other interpretation.

Having received the letters in which his peace overtures were uncompromisingly rejected, Gordon completely changed the tone of his discourse with Muḥammad Aḥmad. Instead of the lavish honorifics employed in the first letter, he now calls Muḥammad Aḥmad a "messianic pretender" (*mutamahdī*), characterizes his letter as "poor in style and meaningless" (*al-rakīk al-ʿibāra al-ʿārī ʿan al-maʿnā*), proving his ill intentions. He places the responsibility for any future bloodshed squarely on Muḥammad Aḥmad's shoulders.[144]

The following letters of Muḥammad Aḥmad and his associates to Gordon also become more and more acrimonious in tone. He speaks with a passion and an unshakable conviction that he has a divine mission to perform, that the triumph of Islam at his hands is inevitable and imminent, that this world is transitory and worthless and that the British and their allies are doomed. His letters are replete with threats and ultimatums, asserting that Gordon's only hope is submission and conversion to Islam which will bestow upon him honour in this world and in the next. Some of them deal with the military successes

141 "But had the People of the Book believed and been godfearing, We would have acquitted them of their evil deeds and admitted them to Gardens of Bliss."

142 *Al-Āthār al-kāmila*, vol. 2, pp. 246–253.

143 *Al-Āthār al-kāmila*, vol. 2, p. 254.

144 *Al-Āthār al-kāmila*, vol. 2, p. 258. This letter is not dated.

of Muḥammad Aḥmad. One notifies Gordon that the *mahdī*'s warriors captured a British boat, killed those who refused to embrace Islam and recognize the *mahdī* and gives details of the important correspondence which they found on the boat. He repeats his demand that Gordon surrenders.[145] The letters of ʿAbd al-Raḥmān al-Nujūmī and ʿAbd al-Qādir, Muḥammad Aḥmad's associates, repeatedly stress the fact that Muḥammad Aḥmad explained time and again that Gordon must submit and convert to Islam if he wants to escape imminent death and eternal damnation. The formula "submit and be safe" (*sallim taslam*) is repeatedly used in the letters.[146] Previous defeats of the British, such as the Hicks expedition, are used to boost the pressure on Gordon. This is psychological warfare; it is also in keeping with the classical Muslim idea according to which enemies must be given ample opportunity to convert before *jihād* is waged against them.[147]

The exchange of letters between Muḥammad Aḥmad and General Gordon enables us to gain a rare insight into the unbridgeable gap between the ways in which these two protagonists of the Sudanese drama viewed their respective roles. Some letters end with a backhanded greeting used in correspondence with unbelievers: "Peace be upon those who follow the straight path" (*al-salām ʿalā man ittabaʿa al-hudā*), implying that there will be no peace upon those who reject the Muslim "straight path".[148] This formula was used in letters attributed to the Prophet, demanding the conversion to Islam of contemporary potentates, such as the Byzantian and Persian emperors.[149]

---

145 *Al-Āthār al-kāmila*, vol. 4, pp. 8–13. An English version of this letter is printed in Hake, *The Journals of General Gordon*, pp. 360–366.

146 See, e.g., *Al-Āthār al-kāmila*, vol. 4, p. 155. This formula is slightly different from the classical "embrace Islam and be safe" (*aslim taslam*) used in the Prophet's letters to the potentates of the prophetic period. See also ibid., p. 207, where the formula *sallimū taslamū wa aslimū* is used in a letter to British troops after the fall of Kharṭūm.

147 *Al-Āthār al-kāmila*, vol. 3, pp. 211–217; vol. 4, pp. 45, 155, 201–202, 207–208, 243–244.

148 *Al-Āthār al-kāmila*, vol. 2, p. 257 *infra* (a letter by one of Muḥammad Aḥmad's associates); vol. 3, p. 217; vol. 4, pp. 13, 45, 244. For another description of Gordon and Muḥammad Aḥmad's correspondence, see Holt, *The Mahdist State in the Sudan*, pp. 111–112.

149 See, e.g., Ṭabarī, *Taʾrīkh, series* I, vol. 3, p. 1565.

VI LEGAL PRONOUNCEMENTS AND SOCIAL ISSUES

Muḥammad Aḥmad made a large number of pronouncements pertinent to legal matters. His collected works also include a few judgments which he made in specific cases. Most of these have also some social import and it seems therefore advisable to consider both topics together. Aharon Layish has shown that Muḥammad Aḥmad enjoined his followers time and again to observe the Qurʾān and the *sunna*, while disregarding the schools of law (*madhāhib*).[150] Shuqayr asserts, probably with a great deal of exaggeration, that Muḥammad Aḥmad "burned all books of the *sunna* and of Qurʾānic exegesis and all the religious and scholarly books, so that no book remained in the Sudan except the Qurʾān, (Muḥammad Aḥmad's) proclamations and his *rātib*."[151] Yet the general thrust of Shuqayr's description can be corroborated by Muḥammad Aḥmad's own writing. When discussing the meaning of "today I have perfected your religion for you ..." (Qurʾān 5:4), he concludes that all laws are to be derived from the Qurʾān and the *sunna* rather than from *fiqh*. Whoever belongs to a legal school, has a text in which he believes or a *shaykh* whom he follows, let him leave all these behind because they are of human provenance and are far removed from the prophetic light. All knowledge which one possessed before the emergence of the Mahdiyya must be abandoned; no one can reform himself without following this path.[152]

It is also significant that Muḥammad Aḥmad describes the *sharīʿa* as related to this world and is therefore liable to extinction, while gnosis goes with the believer to the hereafter (*wa ʿilm al-sharīʿa yabqā hunā li-annahu muʿallaqa* [sic] *bi-ʾl-fanāʾ wa ammā ʿilm al-maʿrifa fa-yadhhabu maʿahu ilā al-ākhira*).[153] In a similar vein, knowledge is of two types: mystical (*ladunī*) and acquired (*ḥādith*). Mystical knowledge comes from the heart and is therefore pure like water coming from a living spring; on the other

150 Layish, "The Sudanese Mahdī's Legal Methodology ...", *passim*.
151 Shuqayr, *Taʾrīkh al-Sūdān*, vol. 3, p. 364. In his *al-Āyāt al-bayyināt* (pp. 20–22), Zahrāʾ mentions Muḥammad Aḥmad's order to destroy the books of *fiqh*. He speaks favourably of their authors, but maintains that these books are only "impressions" (*āthār*) of the "original" (*ʿayn*) or "essence" of religion. This essence is the *mahdī* and the *fiqh* books are no longer necessary after his manifestation. For a discussion of the opposites *athar* and *ʿayn*, see Lane, *Lexicon*, s.v *athar*.
152 *Al-Āthār al-kāmila*, vol. 4, p. 485; vol. 7, pp. 24, 239.
153 *Al-Āthār al-kāmila*, vol. 7, pp. 176, 189, 239.

hand, knowledge acquired by reading is like water flowing on the ground and is malodorous and dirty.[154] Following some Ṣūfī exegetes, he also sees significance in the fact that the Qur'ān starts with a *bā'* and ends with a *sīn*; these two letters form the Persian word *bas* ("enough"), indicating that the Qur'ān is sufficient for all purposes.[155] Shuqayr characterized his legal approach as his own *ijtihād*.[156]

Despite his recurrent demands to abandon the schools of law, and despite his statements which seem to demote the *sharī'a* to the status of an earthly phenomenon, Muḥammad Aḥmad made numerous legal pronouncements which have been the subject of the important work of Aharon Layish and sometimes are in contradiction to the accepted laws of the *madhāhib*.[157] Muḥammad Aḥmad also gave instructions regarding the equality with which a *qāḍī* should treat litigants coming before him and stated that in difficult cases he himself would instruct the judge how to rule.[158] The pride of place among his rulings belongs to morality and penal law, especially those relating to women whom he considers the weakest in understanding among human beings.[159] His rules pertaining to women are harsh. Injunctions to beat women are ubiquitous in Muḥammad Aḥmad's epistles. This harshness is caused mainly by the idea that he considers women and family as "a trial, a calamity and a seduction" (*miḥna, baliyya, fitna*) which may deflect the believers from performing their religious duties – particularly *jihād* – and do not bring them closer to God. Great caution must therefore be exercised when choosing a wife: she must resemble her husband in her views and must not seek the pleasures of this world, lest she influences her husband adversely. The danger of such influence is very real, according to the prophetic dictum saying that "a man believes in the religion of his friend" (*al-mar'u 'alā dīn khalīlihi*). A woman who is disobedient to her husband (*nāshiza*) must be imprisoned in caves (*awkār*) or in darkened houses until she repents or dies (in disgrace) as a prostitute. If a wife prevents her husband from joining the *jihād*, her property becomes spoils for her husband, and if he supports her (and refrains from joining the *jihād*), his property becomes spoils for the

154 *Al-Āthār al-kāmila*, vol. 7, p. 246.
155 *Al-Āthār al-kāmila*, vol. 7, pp. 17–18, 24. Cf. ibid., vol. 3, pp. 319–320; vol. 4, p. 485. Cf. al-Alūsī, *Rūḥ al-ma'ānī*, vol. 30, p. 287.
156 Shuqayr, *Ta'rīkh al-Sūdān*, vol. 3, p. 364.
157 Layish, *Sharī'a and the State in 19th-Century Sudan*, *passim*.
158 *Al-Āthār al-kāmila*, vol. 7, p. 249.
159 *Al-Āthār al-kāmila*, vol. 6, p. 208.

Muslims. Both must be boycotted by the community: they should not be visited when sick, no one should participate in their funeral and no one should assist them in adversity.[160] Only rarely does Muḥammad Aḥmad instruct his followers not to beat their wives, and if this stricture is too difficult for them, let them beat them symbolically with the turban's edge.[161] This is similar to some classical commentators on Qur'ān 4:33 who explain that the wife beating enjoined in this verse should be done with a tooth pick or an implement of similar size.[162]

Despite the harsh views on women expressed in his letters, Muḥammad Aḥmad found ways to accommodate numerous women in his household and claims to have received divine support to fulfil this desire. Shuqayr reports that when young women were taken captive and sent to the treasury, he used to choose some for himself and to send the rest to his subordinates.[163] This can be corroborated by Muḥammad Aḥmad's sermons. After the conquest of al-Ubayyiḍ, some slave girls were brought to him. He says that he was afraid of the "seduction by women" (*fitnat al-nisā'*) and thought of expelling them from his household. At this point in the story, the supernatural intervened: a voice from an unseen source (*hātif*) told him that he is allowed to keep fifteen girls as the Prophet was wont to do. He was particularly apprehensive (of potential infatuation and distraction?) when he saw a particular girl. But the *hātif* spoke again, trying to address his concerns by saying that there is no objection to this relationship and that he was chosen for her according to the custom of the Prophet (*lā ḥaraja ʿalayka fīhā fa-innamā 'ṣṭafāka lahā ʿalā sikkat rasūl Allah*). His fears did not disappear until the *hātif* spoke for the third time, describing the girl as the booty of the Prophet (*hādhihi ghanīmat al-nabī*) and until one of his companions physically placed her hand in his. Even then, he asked for his companions' consent to keep the girls for himself. No objection seems to have been raised and this sermon goes a long way to corroborate Shuqayr's statement that Muḥammad Aḥmad had four legal wives and sixty-three concubines.[164]

---

160 *Al-Āthār al-kāmila*, vol. 5, pp. 389, 422.
161 *Al-Āthār al-kāmila*, vol. 7, p. 253.
162 Ṭabarī, *Jāmiʿ al-bayān*, vol. 4, pp. 68–69 (on Qur'ān 4:34).
163 Shuqayr, *Taʾrīkh*, vol. 3, p. 300.
164 The syntax of the sentence does not make clear who did the choosing; there are also other difficult places in this passage. See *Al-Āthār al-kāmila*, vol. 3, p. 62; cf. Shuqayr, *Taʾrīkh*, vol. 3, p. 363 and Layish, *Sharīʿa and the State in 19th-Century Sudan*, pp. 72–73.

Seclusion of women from strangers is essential. The best women are those who do not leave their homes except when it is absolutely necessary.[165] Muḥammad Aḥmad quotes a prophetic tradition according to which whenever a man is together with a strange woman, Satan is the third of them. Elsewhere he quotes Fāṭima who said that the best situation for a woman is not to see a (strange) man and not to be seen by him. He specifies punishments for the infringement of women's seclusion. Men must not greet a woman who is alone, but may greet women who are in a group.[166] A man who shakes hands with a strange woman should be punished with a hundred lashes; he who hugs her, fifty lashes, and two months of fasting or the manumission of a slave.[167] If a man knows that his slave girl is with a man illegally and does not inform on her, some say he must be killed, some favour imprisonment and some say his property becomes spoils. Muḥammad Aḥmad does not decide between these alternatives.[168]

Women's clothing was of particular interest to Muḥammad Aḥmad. This can be gauged from the fact that as early as in his appointment scene, Muḥammad Aḥmad is told by al-Shaykh al-Ṭayyib that when he makes the *hijra* to Qadīr, the women should be covered rather than unveiled like the (women of the) Baqqāra (tribe)[169] (*al-nisāʾ takūnu mustatira lā yankashifna ka-'l-baqqāra*).[170] Those who do not comply and do not cover their bodies and their heads should be given a hundred lashes. If a woman stands uncovered only for a minute, or speaks with a loud voice, she should receive twenty-seven lashes. If she speaks in vile language, her punishment is eighty lashes. Parents who do not properly cover a girl five years of age (and above?) are also flogged. As a rule, women must stay at home and should not even participate in funeral processions. Nevertheless, women of humble circumstances who have no one to serve them may go out on errands if no man lusts after them (because they are elderly?) and there is no fear of seduction (*fitna*), but even then they must cover their bodies

165 *Al-Āthār al-kāmila*, vol. 7, p. 165.

166 *Al-Āthār al-kāmila*, vol. 7, p. 253. The tradition about Fāṭima is taken from classical Shīʿī literature; see Ibn Sharāshūb, *Manāqib Āl Abī Ṭālib*, vol. 3, p. 341; Majlisī, *Biḥār al-anwār*, vol. 43, p. 84 *infra*. I am indebted to my friend and colleague Etan Kohlberg for these references.

167 *Al-Āthār al-kāmila*, vol. 3, p. 109.

168 *Al-Āthār al-kāmila*, vol. 1, p. 305.

169 See Braukämper, Ulrich, "Baggara", *EI²*, s.v.

170 *Al-Āthār al-kāmila*, vol. 1, p. 79.

properly.[171] Certain customs widespread among women are considered by Muḥammad Aḥmad as un-Islamic and must be eliminated. A woman who wails for the dead, mourns for a man other than her husband, blackens the door (as a sign of mourning), wails so much that her eyes become inflamed (*taskhīn*)[172] and slaughters an excessive quantity of cattle (*dhabḥ al-amwāl sarafan*) to entertain the mourners must be beaten and shunned until she repents.[173]

Women's transgressions are not the only ones mentioned in Muḥammad Aḥmad's writings. Drinking wine, even in minimal quantity, is punished with eighty lashes and seven days imprisonment. An accessory to this transgression receives the same punishment. A smoker's punishment is eighty lashes and the burning of his tobacco which is deemed worse than wine. Subsequent transgressions may be punished also by imprisonment or taking the transgressor's property as spoils. Trading in tobacco is punished by twenty-seven lashes. Stealing, even if the stolen object is of small value, is punished with the amputation of the hands; strictly speaking, this is harsher than in classical law which speaks about the amputation of one hand only if the stolen object is worth more than a certain minimal value. Abandonment of prayer should be punished by beating. In one place Muḥammad Aḥmad says that abandonment of prayer is seen by some as apostasy which carries the death penalty.[174] Elsewhere he explicitly says that whoever abandons prayer or performs it carelessly should be executed. Furthermore, someone who knows about such transgression but does not inform on the transgressor is punished by eighty lashes and seven days' imprisonment. Cursing a fellow believer by calling him a dog, a pig, a Jew, a pimp (*muʿarraṣ*), a pimp of his own wife (*dayyūth*), a sinner (*fājir*), a thief, a fornicator, a traitor (*khāʾin*), an accursed, an infidel, a Christian, a Sodomite – each of these curses is punished by eighty lashes and seven days' imprisonment.[175] Swearing by someone other than God is punished by forty lashes; if someone wants to mention in his oath a human being, he must say "by the Lord of so-and-so" (*wa rabbi fulān*). Players of games

171 *Al-Āthār al-kāmila*, vol. 1, p. 114, 276, 305; vol. 3, pp. 71, 109; vol. 5, pp. 318, 336, 389–390, 408–409, 419; vol. 7, p. 21. Cf. Layish, *Sharīʿa and the State in 19th-Century Sudan*, pp. 208–209.

172 For this meaning, see Lane, *Lexicon*, s.v. *s-kh-n*.

173 *Al-Āthār al-kāmila*, vol. 5, p. 418.

174 *Al-Āthār al-kāmila*, vol. 1, pp. 304–305. Cf. Ibn Māja, *Sunan*, vol. 1, p. 342 (*Kitāb Iqāmat al-ṣalāt* 77).

175 *Al-Āthār al-kāmila*, vol. 1, p. 303.

known as *manqala*, *ṭāwila* and *ṭāb* should receive discretionary punishment.[176] False testimony should be punished by beating till death. Another capital offence is irresponsible use of firearms which results in someone's death; if the firing was by error, only blood-money (*diya*) is imposed.[177]

In the *Majālis* it is reported that a man who had homosexual relations with a minor was decapitated "in order to purify him" (*taṭhīran lahu*); the boy was let off because of his age. Muḥammad Aḥmad issued a proclamation containing the details of his verdict.[178] A woman who married during the "waiting period" (*ʿidda*) after her husband had died, was stoned to death.[179]

In his legislative capacity, Muḥammad Aḥmad issued several decisions relating to slavery. We need to discuss these issues because they constitute a part of Muḥammad Aḥmad's intellectual and religious profile. It is well known that in the nineteenth century, slavery was an important branch of economic activity in the Sudan. The British had made several attempts to abolish the slave trade, and in 1877 they reached an agreement to this effect with Khediw Ismāʿīl. According to the Khediw's proclamation, the implementation of the agreement in Egypt was determined to start seven years after its conclusion, while its implementation in the Sudan was to wait for twelve years. Yet at the beginning of 1884, General Gordon declared that the treaty would not be implemented.[180] Thus, when the Mahdist movement broke out, slavery and the slave trade were flourishing and, according to one scholar, the Mahdist state "made slavery the mainstay of the northern [Sudanese] economy".[181] In Muḥammad Aḥmad's letters, slavery is taken for granted and is discussed as an institution that

---

176 *Al-Āthār al-kāmila*, vol. 4, p. 109 *infra*. For *manqala* and *ṭāwila*, see Dozy, *Supplement*, s.v. For more details about all three games, see Lane, *Manners and Customs*, pp. 344–352.

177 *Al-Āthār al-kāmila*, vol. 1, pp. 113–114, 276, 280–281, 303–305; vol. 2, pp. 263–264; vol. 3, 109; vol. 5, pp. 318, 336, 389–390; vol. 7, pp. 108, 129, 133, 135, 200, 230. 231, 254.

178 *Al-Āthār al-kāmila*, vol. 7, p. 129; Layish, *Sharīʿa and the State in 19th-Century Sudan*, pp. 212–213.

179 *Al-Āthār al-kāmila*, vol. 7, pp. 135, 231. Cf. Layish, *Sharīʿa and the State in 19th-Century Sudan*, p. 205.

180 Gordon, *Journals*, p. 137, note 9; Holt, *The Mahdist State in the Sudan*, p. 86; Mowafi, *Slavery, Slave Trade ...*, p. 83.

181 Jok, *War and Slavery in Sudan*, p. 75. For a survey of slavery in the Sudan and some contemporary views concerning it, see Hennerbert, *The English in Egypt*, pp. 23–31; Mowafi, *Slavery, Slave Trade ...*, p. 83.

must be managed rather than as a problem that must be solved. It is also noteworthy that Muḥammad Aḥmad, who is wont to quote the Qurʾān and the prophetic tradition on every occasion, barely quotes prophetic utterances which enjoin humane treatment of slaves.[182] The matter-of-fact, non-judgmental and non-moralistic attitude to slavery is characteristic of Muḥammad Aḥmad's letters and sermons. It can be gauged, for example, from a letter in which Muḥammad Aḥmad instructs the addressees to return stray animals and slaves to their masters for free, or send them to the treasury. In a similar vein, he instructs his lieutenants to return to the people of Bāra – except the Turks and their followers – all their property: slaves, horses, camels and donkeys. In both letters the slaves are mentioned on a par with animals.[183]

It seems that the number of slaves in the Mahdist state possession was growing, especially after the conquest of Kharṭūm. There are letters in which Aḥmad Sulaymān, the person responsible for the Mahdist treasury, complains of the large sums of money necessary to care for the slaves and suggests selling them or sending them to the various regions of the country. Muḥammad Aḥmad himself issued instructions to distribute slaves to the army units and to restore slaves who were taken from his supporters to their owners.[184] On the other hand, he was unwilling to manumit slaves. A supporter of the Mahdiyya had in his possession a slave girl from Dār Fūr for eight years. Now a man came and wanted to take her from his house, claiming that she was his sister. Fearful that the case will serve as a precedent for the manumission of many women like this one, Muḥammad Aḥmad ruled against the manumission – unless the woman in question was a free woman enslaved after the emergence of the Mahdiyya.[185] There are also letters in which Muḥammad Aḥmad issues instructions to give someone a slave or a slave girl from the treasury in order to right a wrong or to alleviate a hardship afflicting one of his supporters.[186] It is also significant that when Muḥammad Aḥmad deals with the purposes for which the alms may be used (Qurʾān 9:60), he steers away from the traditional

182 For exceptions, see *Al-Āthār al-kāmila*, vol. 2, pp. 60–61; vol. 6, p. 274.

183 *Al-Āthār al-kāmila*, vol. 1, pp. 277, 281 *infra*, pp. 356–357.

184 *Al-Āthār al-kāmila*, vol. 1, pp. 277; vol. 3, pp. 155–156; vol. 4, pp. 305, 306, 336, 380.

185 *Al-Āthār al-kāmila*, vol. 4, p. 381.

186 *Al-Āthār al-kāmila*, vol. 5, pp. 393, 401, 426–427. Cf. Shuqayr, *Taʾrīkh*, vol. 3, p. 300 for a description of gathering slaves after the conquest of Kharṭūm and dispatching them to the treasury.

explanation of *fī al-riqāb* as manumission of slaves, and maintains that this expression indicates those who sacrifice themselves for the sake of God.[187]

Muḥammad Aḥmad also promulgated rules concerning land ownership. The principle guiding these pronouncements was that all land belongs to Allah and He bequeaths it to whomever He wants. This idea can easily be derived from dozens of Qur'ānic verses and appears explicitly in the tradition about the Prophet's decision to expel the Jews from Medina and take over their landed property.[188] As the *khalīfa* of Muslims and the Prophet's heir, Muḥammad Aḥmad thought that he had the right to determine matters of land ownership as he saw fit. Land ownership is not absolute: every believer has a right to his land, but if he does not need it, or cannot cultivate all of it, he must give it to one of his believing brothers. Hereditary claims for personal advantage are unacceptable: nobody has the right to claim that he inherited a piece of land in order to levy rent from it. In other words, land ownership depends on the ability of the owner to cultivate the land himself. This rule is apparently intended to limit, or impede, large land ownerships. However, if an owner of (a small plot?) is incapable of cultivating it because of physical weakness, he may rent it out.[189]

Specific rules were promulgated to deal with matters resulting from the change of regime in the Sudan. Land which was confiscated from its owners (usually because of non-payment of taxes) was to be returned to the owners on the basis of a declaration (*al-iqrār*) and reliable evidence (*al-shahāda al-amīna*), but only if the confiscation took place no more than seven years before the submission of the claim. This is in recognition of rights which ensue from lengthy use even if the taking of possession would not have been legal under the Mahdiyya. In cases when the land was not confiscated but rather sold under duress (probably because the owners were unable to pay the tax and were pursued by the collectors), the original owners can repossess their land by paying back the sum which

187 *Al-Āthār al-kāmila*, vol. 7, p. 39. See Ṭabarī, *Jāmi' al-bayān*, vol. 10, pp. 163–164 (on Qur'ān 9:60).

188 See, for instance, Qur'ān 2:284, 3:109, 189. For the tradition about the expulsion of Jews from Medina, see Bukhārī, *Ṣaḥīḥ*, *Kitāb al-jizya* 6 (vol. 2, pp. 294–295). On this occasion, the Prophet is reported to have said to the Jews: "Embrace Islam so that you are safe, and be aware that the earth belongs to God and to His Prophet and I want to expel you from this land ..." (*aslimū taslamū wa ' 'lamū anna al-arḍ li-'llāhi wa rasūlihi wa innī urīdu an ujliyakum min hādhihi al-arḍ*).

189 *Al-Āthār al-kāmila*, vol. 1, p. 277; vol. 3, p. 227; for other rulings of Muḥammad Aḥmad concerning land ownership, see Layish, *Sharī'a and the State in 19th-Century Sudan*, pp. 77–81; Abū Salīm, *Al-Arḍ fī al-Mahdiyya*, pp. 12–14.

they had received from the buyer. The buyer is not allowed to object to this transaction if the money is offered to him.[190] While the transaction which had taken place before the Mahdiyya was considered wrongful, the interests of both sides were considered in a rather balanced manner.

A loosely formulated passage speaks about the relationship between a debtor and a creditor. Someone took a loan during the Turko-Egyptian rule, gave his land as a security for the repayment of his debt and agreed that the creditor will receive the produce of his land as long as the debt was outstanding. Muḥammad Aḥmad ruled that the debtor will be responsible for the repayment of the debt only. From the establishment of the rule of the Mahdiyya in a town, the creditor will not be entitled to the produce because the transaction consisted only of incurring a debt. As Holt has observed, the produce taken by the creditor could be conceived as "hidden interest" and thus is forbidden in Islamic law. On the other hand, the creditor will not have to repay to the debtor the cost of the produce which he used before the takeover of his area by the Mahdiyya (*wa man arhana arḍahu fī daynin wa sharaṭa salba ghallatihi yu'ṭī daynahu. wa min al-ān fa-ṣā'idan bi-ḥulūl ḥukm al-mahdiyya fī balda lā ghallata lahu ḥaythu annahu dayn. wa mā sabaqa fī ḥukm al-turk lā gharāmata fīhi wa innamā lahu 'aynu daynihi faqaṭ*). In a similar vein, someone gave his slaves as security for a loan and stipulated that he would forfeit the income from the mortgaged property. This agreement is enforceable only for the period of the Turkish rule; once the Mahdiyya took over, the income will not be forfeited.[191]

Muḥammad Aḥmad issued an important ruling concerning the ownership rights of Turks and non-Muslims in June 1884. A certain Ḥabīb Allah b. Mūsā asked him for a ruling concerning a Christian named Ḥanna who purchased a plot of land from one Ibrāhīm al-Badawī. This Ibrāhīm had purchased the land from the Rifā'a and the Dāḥlāb tribes. Ḥanna entrusted Ḥabīb Allah with the cultivation of the plot six years ago. Now the Rifā'a and the Dāḥlāb demand to take the land from Ibrāhīm, arguing that he took it in contravention of the *sharī'a* (*min ghayr wajh shar'ī*). The question is whether this claim should be entertained after six years had elapsed and whether the land should be transferred to the treasury.

190 *Al-Āthār al-kāmila*, vol. 3, pp. 118, 227; vol. 4, pp. 55–56; cf. Abū Salīm, *Al-arḍ fī al-Mahdiyya*, pp. 20–22.

191 *Al-Āthār al-kāmila*, vol. 3, pp. 118–119; cf. Abū Salīm, *Al-Arḍ fī al-Mahdiyya*, pp. 22–23. Holt's observation was made in a note written on the margin of his copy of *al-Aḥkām wa al-ādāb*, vol. 3, p. 15 where this passage appears as well.

In his response, Muḥammad Aḥmad maintains that revocation of transactions contracted with the Turks and their followers would result in major disruption. Therefore, the land sale of Ibrāhīm to Ḥanna cannot be revoked in principle because it was legal according to the laws of the Turks. If Ḥanna embraced Islam, the property would be his; but if he did not, it belongs to the treasury "like the property of the Turks and the Christians who persist in their infidelity – and [like the property of] those who are in the army camps (*qaqra*)".[192] In other words, Turks and Christians are not entitled to possess land under the Mahdiyya.

VII RITUAL IN MUḤAMMAD AḤMAD'S MOVEMENT

Muḥammad Aḥmad laid considerable stress on the importance of religious ritual. He instructed his followers to build mosques and be punctilious in the observance of prayer, especially the communal prayer on Friday, even when travelling. When he spoke in a mystical mood, he viewed prayer as the believer's intimate conversation (*munājāt*) with God and even his ascension (*mi'rāj*). Those who perform the obligatory prayers with him can consider themselves as if they prayed with most of their limbs in Paradise. In common with the Ṣūfīs, he asserted that one should pray as if every prayer was his last and stressed the humility with which one should approach the performance of this ritual. During prayer, the worshipper should feel that the Ka'ba is in front of him, Paradise to his right, Hell to his left, the bridge (*ṣirāṭ*) over hell under his feet, the angel of death behind him and God above him.[193] When his main point was the necessity to ensure the correct performance of prayer in order to enhance the communal aspects of his movement, he warned his followers against being late in performing the prayer and gave them detailed instructions as to what to say when the call to prayer is sounded and what to say and do during the prayer itself. He demanded ablution with water (*wuḍū'*) before every prayer and allowed the use of sand for this purpose (*tayammum*) only when there was really no other possibility.

---

192 *Al-Āthār al-kāmila*, vol. 3, pp. 130–131; cf. Abū Salīm, *Al-Arḍ fī al-Mahdiyya*, pp. 18–19, 32.

193 *Al-Āthār al-kāmila*, vol. 7, pp. 239–242. The last sentence is on p. 242 *infra*. For a very similar description of prayer in classical Ṣūfī literature, see Ghazālī, *Iḥyā' 'ulūm al-dīn*, Cairo, n.d., vol. 1, p. 270 (on Ḥātim al-Aṣamm).

Communal prayer can be performed in three ways: the "preceding" one, in which the community members "precede" the *imām*, meaning that they move from one component of the prayer to the next before the *imām* does it; the "simultaneous", in which the *imām* and the community proceed from one stage to the next simultaneously, and the "following", in which the community moves from one stage to the next after the *imām*. "Preceding" invalidates the prayer, simultaneity makes it reprehensible and only the "following" manner makes the prayer valid (*al-ṣalāt thalāth ḥālāt: immā al-musābaqa wa immā al-musāwāt wa immā al-mutāba'a. fa-'l-musābaqa bihā tabṭulu al-ṣalāt wa al-musāwāt bihā tukrahu al-ṣalāt wa al-mutāba'a bihā taṣiḥḥu al-ṣalāt*). Accordingly, Muḥammad Aḥmad insisted that when he was leading the prayer, everyone should follow his lead rather than perform any of the prayer parts before he did: his leadership in all aspects of communal life must be clearly visible.[194] He enjoined his followers to instruct their wives, sons, daughters and slaves to observe the five obligatory prayers and beat them if they neglect this duty. Wilful abandonment of prayer is a serious transgression: some say it is tantamount to infidelity and the perpetrator is liable to execution. Even a neighbour who knows of someone who neglects prayer, does not force him to pray and does not inform on him if he fails to do so must be flogged and imprisoned. Nevertheless, Muḥammad Aḥmad himself is said to have taken considerable liberties with the timing of the prayer and its length.[195] The other four pillars of Islam are mentioned less frequently, but their neglect is also punished with great severity.[196]

Formal prayer was, however, only one part of the Mahdist ritual. Muḥammad Aḥmad instructed his followers to say the declaration of faith (*shahāda*) when they wake in the morning and to perform various supererogatory rituals, such as reading Sūra 67 (*al-Mulk*) after the evening prayer and reading Sūra 32 (*al-Sajda*) after the Friday morning prayer. Whoever heard his call to prayer and did not join him, his prayer was considered invalid. He also used to read some of the short Sūras during

---

194 *Al-Āthār al-kāmila*, vol. 7, p. 243. This is also the classical injunction: "The *imām* is there to be followed; when he says 'God is great', say 'God is great'; when he bows, bow ..." (*innamā ju'ila al-imām li-yu'tamma bihi fa-idhā kabbara fa-kabbirū wa idhā raka'a fa-'rka'ū ...*). See Bukhārī, *Ṣaḥīḥ*, vol. 1, p. 108 (*Kitāb al-ṣalāt* 18).

195 *Al-Āthār al-kāmila*, vol. 1, pp. 276, 280, 305; vol. 5, pp. 349–350; vol. 7, pp. 136, 138, 200–201, 230, 240–244. 250.

196 *Al-Āthār al-kāmila*, vol. 6, pp. 260–261.

the obligatory prayers and wipe his face with his hands when he raised them for purposes of supplication (*du'ā'*). Reading the last two Sūras of the Qur'ān (*al-mu'awwidhatān*) was considered as preventing devilish temptations (*waswās*).[197]

It is not surprising that Muḥammad Aḥmad, whose religious upbringing was steeped in the Ṣūfī tradition, would consider the repetitive utterance of a divine name (*dhikr*) as an important part of his movement's ritual. *Dhikr* should replace musical entertainment. It is mentioned twice in the "presence" (*ḥaḍra*) in which Muḥammad Aḥmad was appointed to be the *mahdī*. Two of the Ṣūfī shaykhs who participated in the visionary appointment ceremony as described by Muḥammad Aḥmad mentioned the importance of *dhikr*. Al-Shaykh al-Ṭayyib instructed Muḥammad Aḥmad to arrange *dhikr* sessions, while al-Qurashī enjoined him, in more general terms, to engage in *dhikr* and to protect those who are with him (*kun dhākiran wa li-man ma'aka sātiran*). Muḥammad Aḥmad himself considered sessions of *dhikr* as "earthly Paradise" (*janna fī al-dunyā*) which can expiate for thousands of sessions dealing with evil. It is noteworthy that Muḥammad Aḥmad used ritual as a means to enhance his standing and to instil in his followers the belief in his role as a *mahdī*. He instructed them to recite, two hundred times a day, the following:

> I accept Allah as the Lord, Islam as the religion, our master Muḥammad, may Allah bless him and grant him peace, as prophet and messenger, and the *imām mahdī* as guide and a source of knowledge. (*raḍītu bi-'llāhi rabban wa bi-'l-islāmi dīnan wa bi-sayyidinā Muḥammad ṣallā Allah 'alayhi wa sallam nabiyyan wa rasūlan wa bi-'l-imām al-mahdī 'alayhi al-salām dalīlan wa khabīran.*)[198]

Such a formulation – which is also a type of *dhikr* because it must be repeated two hundred times a day – gives Muḥammad Aḥmad a role as essential as that of the Prophet in the Muslim system of belief and should be understood in conjunction with the other ways which have been used for the same purpose.[199]

---

197 *Al-Āthār al-kāmila*, vol. 7, pp. 228–229, 252.

198 *Al-Āthār al-kāmila*, vol. 1, pp. 397–400; vol. 5, p. 208; vol. 6, pp. 37–43; vol. 7, p. 149.

199 See Section II in this chapter.

Muḥammad Aḥmad also wrote a prayer book (*rātib*).[200] The term *rātib* indicates the constancy and regularity of using the book. As is well known, the Muslim canonical prayer contains very little text; consequently, a tradition of preparing prayer books (*awrād, adhkār*) which include supplications, Qur'ānic passages and repetitive recitations of the divine name has a long history among Ṣūfī masters. The masters composed texts which became characteristic of their orders' devotional practices.[201] Muḥammad Aḥmad was part of this tradition. We have already seen that he routinely claimed to be acting according to explicit instructions of the Prophet; the writing of the prayer book and its use is no exception. The Prophet appeared to him, kissed him between his eyes, on his cheek and on his mouth and told him to instruct his followers to be assiduous in their prayers and in reciting the *rātib*. Muḥammad Aḥmad started to prepare the *rātib* immediately after the announcement of his messianic claim. He included in it Qur'ānic verses and prophetic traditions, and instructed his followers to learn it by heart and to recite it morning and evening together with a portion of the Qur'ān.[202] He considered it a means to get close to God. He was constantly adding material to the *rātib* and completed it shortly before his death. He instructed the treasury not to spare expenses and provide copies of the book to all members of the movement.[203] In contradistinction to Muḥammad Aḥmad's letters, and with the exception of two short prayers to be recited before battle,[204] the *rātib* is a text unrelated to the political and military context of his movement. There is no reference to any historical issue: the text concentrates on piety, fear of God and the repetition of His name. One would not be

---

200 The earliest edition of the *Rātib* which I have seen was published in Omdurman in 1888. Abū Salīm says that it was not printed in Muḥammad Aḥmad's lifetime, but he also says that the first edition was printed in Ramaḍān 1302 AH which corresponds to October 1884, when the *mahdī* was still alive. See *Al-Āthār al-kāmila*, vol. 6, p. 20. The *Rātib* has also been printed, with an introduction by Abū Salīm, in *Al-Āthār al-kāmila*, vol. 6.

201 See "Wird", in *EI²*, s.v. (F. M. Denny). See also Abū Salīm's introduction to the *Rātib* in *Al-Āthār al-kāmila*, vol. 6, pp. 1–35.

202 Nevertheless, Muḥammad Aḥmad's followers attribute to him a prohibition to read any book except the Qur'ān, because "[the other books] form a veil which hinders the understanding of its meaning", *Al-Āthār al-kāmila*, vol. 7, p. 82.

203 Shuqayr, *Ta'rīkh al-Sūdān*, vol. 1, p. 132; vol. 3, pp. 364–365; *Al-Āthār al-kāmila*, vol. 4, pp. 187–188, 240–241 (a question and Muḥammad Aḥmad's answer about the text of the *rātib*); vol. 5, p. 17; vol. 7, p. 248.

204 *Al-Āthār al-kāmila*, vol. 6, p. 88.

able to gauge from the text that it was written by a militant messianic leader in nineteenth-century Sudan. It could have been produced in any Ṣūfī order and is compatible with the long-standing tradition of devotional practices among the Ṣūfīs. Muḥammad Aḥmad's commentaries on several passages from the *rātib* bear the same characteristics.[205] Despite all the importance attached to the *rātib*, Muḥammad Aḥmad made it clear that the Qur'ān was more important and when someone placed the Qur'ān under the *rātib*, he immediately rectified the situation by placing the Qur'ān on top.[206] However, the *rātib* became an extremely important book in the movement. It contributed to its cohesion and became a symbol of membership in the Mahdiyya.[207]

VIII QUR'ĀN AND *ḤADĪTH* IN MUḤAMMAD AḤMAD'S WORKS

The works of Muḥammad Aḥmad are replete with quotations from the Qur'ān and the *ḥadīth*, frequently followed by an interpretation. It is noteworthy that Muḥammad Aḥmad's associates collected his utterances after his death and published them under the title *Majālis*.[208] This collection deals with Muḥammad Aḥmad's interpretations of selected Qur'ānic verses, prophetic traditions which he quoted, his own statements, his exhortations and supererogatory prayers. Many passages include disparate statements which seem to have been placed together without any regard to their content.[209] At this stage of research into the Mahdiyya, there is no way to vouch for the genuineness of this material as coming from Muḥammad Aḥmad himself; however, it is essentially compatible with views expressed in the rest of Muḥammad Aḥmad's works and may therefore be used to enrich our description and analysis of his beliefs. Some of this material has general ethical value and some of the pertinent exegetical remarks correspond to standard classical exegesis, having little bearing on the specific beliefs and activities of the Mahdiyya. A substantial

205 *Al-Āthār al-kāmila*, vol. 6, pp. 71–85.
206 *Al-Āthār al-kāmila*, vol. 7, p. 129. For various rules concerning the reading of the *rātib*, see *Al-Āthār al-kāmila*, vol. 7, pp. 248–249.
207 *Al-Āthār al-kāmila*, vol. 6, pp. 32–33.
208 Five such collections are included in vol. 7 of *Al-Āthār al-kāmila*.
209 See, for instance, *Al-Āthār al-kāmila*, vol. 7, pp. 168–169.

part of the material is, however, significant and introduces interpretations which are instructive for understanding Muḥammad Aḥmad's religious world view. Muḥammad Aḥmad has a clear tendency to choose allegorical, mystical explanations which are, at times, far removed from the standard meaning of the text. He devotes considerable attention to clarify what are the "abrogating" (*nāsikh*) and "abrogated" (*mansūkh*) verses relevant to certain issues.

Some examples of these allegorical interpretations are in order. Explaining the *Fātiḥa*, Muḥammad Aḥmad says that whoever intimately speaks to God using the *Fātiḥa*, it is as if he used the entire Qur'ān because all divine names are included in *al-ḥamdu li-'llāhi*. "Thee alone we serve; to thee alone we pray for succour" (*iyyāka na'budu wa iyyāka nasta'īn*) indicates the dismantling of the walls of hypocrisy and pride. The "straight path" (*al-ṣirāṭ al-mustaqīm*) mentioned in the next verse indicates perseverance in the face of adversity.[210] Commenting on Qur'ān 16:67 ("And of the fruits of the palms and the vines, you take from there an intoxicant and a provision fair ..."), Muḥammad Aḥmad says that this verse was revealed before the prohibition of wine and is abrogated. This is the standard interpretation. However, Muḥammad Aḥmad also suggests that "the fruits of the vines" are monotheism (*tawḥīd*), reliance on God (*tawakkul*) and certitude (*yaqīn*) – while the intoxication is with the love of God. If this is the case, there is no need to consider the verse as abrogated.[211] Qur'ān 5:7 which speaks of wiping the head and the feet as part of the ritual ablution is taken to indicate that it is necessary to wash "the head of the spirit" (*ra's al-rūḥ*) and to wipe off everything other than God and wash away everything connected to the "lower world" (*al-'ālam al-suflī*) and everything other than God.[212] "Remember God during certain days numbered" (Qur'ān 2:203), which is usually taken to mean three specific days during the pilgrimage season, is interpreted as a command to remember God throughout one's lifetime.[213] Commenting on Qur'ān 4:101 which speaks about the permissibility of shortening prayers when Muslims are in danger of being attacked by "those who

210 *Al-Āthār al-kāmila*, vol. 7, pp. 18, 225.
211 *Al-Āthār al-kāmila*, vol. 7, pp. 56–57. For the classical interpretation, see Ṭabarī, *Jāmi' al-bayān*, vol. 14, p. 134.
212 *Al-Āthār al-kāmila*, vol. 7, pp. 25, 226.
213 *Al-Āthār al-kāmila*, vol. 7, pp. 19. For the classical interpretation, see Ṭabarī, *Jāmi' al-bayān*, vol. 2, pp. 302–305.

disbelieve", Muḥammad Aḥmad explains that these disbelievers are "the (evil-bidding) soul and Satan". Such an allegorical explanation may be unexpected from the leader of a movement which conducted constant and very concrete warfare against "those who disbelieve", but it is a reflection of the decisive influence of Ṣūfī thought on Muḥammad Aḥmad. It is noteworthy that even the prominent Ṣūfī Ibn al-ʿArabī (d. 1240) did not go so far in his exegesis of the verse and only said that "those who disbelieve" are "human satans who go astray and lead others astray" (*shayāṭīn al-ins al-ḍāllīn al-muḍillīn*); this explanation allows the verse to be understood in a much more concrete sense than that of Muḥammad Aḥmad.[214] In a similar vein, the Qurʾānic prohibition of carrion is understood as prohibiting the whole world: everything mundane is as impure as carrion.[215]

A highly significant exegetical passage deals with Qurʾān 9:60.[216] This verse lists the social groups and the purposes for which the alms money (*ṣadaqāt*) can be used. The passage is significant because it deals with an important issue in the Muslim tradition and allows us to see to what extent Muḥammad Aḥmad was willing to disregard the standard interpretation in its entirety and to provide the verse with a new meaning. The poor mentioned in the verse are interpreted as "prisoners" (*asārā*). "Those who work on them" (*al-ʿāmilīna ʿalayhā*), usually understood as the tax collectors, are explained as "working in poverty and need" (*al-āmilīna ʿalā al-faqr wa al-maskana*) or "those who do good deeds" (*arbāb al-aʿmāl al-ṣāliḥa*). "Those whose hearts are to be reconciled" (*al-muʾallafa qulūbuhum*), indicating in the classical tradition those who received financial incentives in order to embrace Islam, are taken to mean those whose hearts are united by remembering God (on their way) to God (*yataʾallafu qulūbuhum bi-dhikr Allah ilā Allah*) or on poverty and need. *Ibn al-sabīl*, traditionally understood as a traveller or passer-by, is interpreted by Muḥammad Aḥmad as referring to "travellers away from the natural habitats, journeying to God in a way characteristic of the prophets (*al-musāfirūn ʿan awṭān al-ṭabīʿa wa sāʾirūn ilā Allah bi-khuluq*

214 *Al-Āthār al-kāmila*, vol. 7, p. 23. Cf. Ibn al-ʿArabī, *Tafsīr*, vol. 1, p. 282.
215 *Al-Āthār al-kāmila*, vol. 7, p. 24.
216 The verse reads: "The alms are for the poor and needy, and those who work on them, and those whose hearts are to be reconciled, the ransoming of slaves, debtors, and for the sake of Allah and the traveller; so Allah ordains; Allah is All-knowing, All-wise ..."

al-anbiyāʾ). The most significant deviation from the standard interpretation relates to the expression *fī al-riqāb,* which is usually interpreted as "ransoming of slaves". In an interpretation which bears little connection to the text, Muḥammad Aḥmad says that these are those who "sacrifice their souls in the way of God" (*bi-an yabdhulū anfusahum fī sabīl Allah*) or "manumit their hearts by abandoning everything except God" (*hum alladhīna mukātibīna* [sic] *qulūbahum bi-tarki mā siwāhu*). His adoption of these allegorical interpretations allowed Muḥammad Aḥmad to steer clear of the issue of the slave trade which was of considerable importance for the economy of the Mahdiyya.[217]

Muḥammad Aḥmad's treatment of *jihād* is significant. His Ṣūfī background is evident when he explains Qurʾān 9:60, which lists the purposes for which the money collected as alms can be used. Among these purposes is "in the way of Allah" (*fī sabīl Allah*), which is explained by most commentators as indicating the financing of *jihād*. In one place, Muḥammad Aḥmad explains it as "the greater *jihād,* which is the struggle against the (evil-bidding) soul" (*al-jihād al-akbar wa huwa jihād al-nafs*).[218] This type of *jihād* does not require much funding; nevertheless, this is Muḥammad Aḥmad's explanation. Elsewhere the references to *jihād* are much more in keeping with what is expected of a person who was engaged throughout his messianic career in military campaigns: Muḥammad Aḥmad takes pains to clarify that verses which may be interpreted as opposing *jihād* were abrogated. In a rather obscure manner, he says that Qurʾān 2:256 ("There is no compulsion in religion") was abrogated by the "*jihād* verse" (probably meaning Qurʾān 9:5) as far as its external meaning is concerned, but remains valid with regard to its internal meaning.[219] Muḥammad Aḥmad does not elaborate on the meaning of this obscure utterance.

We have frequently referred to prophetic traditions used by Muḥammad Aḥmad to substantiate his views on numerous subjects. It is noteworthy that in one case he attributes to the Prophet an utterance which is completely out of character with what can be expected in the classical *ḥadīth* collections and must have been invented by him in order to provide prophetic legitimacy for his ideas. The utterance reads: "Obeying the Turks after the *mahdī*'s appearance is tantamount to infidelity and to going astray" (*wa qawluhu ṣallā Allāh ʿalayhi wa sallama: ṭāʿat al-Turk baʿda*

217 *Al-Āthār al-kāmila,* vol. 7, pp. 39, 162.
218 *Al-Āthār al-kāmila,* vol. 7, p. 162.
219 *Al-Āthār al-kāmila,* vol. 7, pp. 20, 41, 54, 226.

ẓuhūr al-mahdī kufr wa ḍalāl)[220] and its value for Muḥammad Aḥmad's propaganda is self-evident.

IX MUḤAMMAD AḤMAD AND THE RELIGIOUS ESTABLISHMENT

The religious establishment of Sudan and Egypt has always been an anathema for Muḥammad Aḥmad. Recounting a spiritual experience which he had before declaring himself as *mahdī*, he recalls that he intended to join al-Azhar in order to strengthen Islam by studying the "external sciences" (*ʿilm al-ẓāhir*). Yet an inner voice (*hātif*) told him that if he does that, he will forfeit the Mahdiyya.[221] He never studied in al-Azhar and frequently launched scathing attacks on the *ʿulamāʾ*. In keeping with the long-standing historical tradition among Ṣūfīs and revivalists, he called them "wicked scholars" (*ʿulamāʾ al-sūʾ*) who strive for worldly positions and neglect their primary duty to fight against the blameworthy innovations (*bidaʿ*) rampant among Muslims. They refrain from giving religious advice to the rulers, agree with their satanic desires and judge the people according to man-made laws (*qawānīn*) rather than according to the *sharīʿa*. In addition, they write epistles against the *mahdī* at the behest of the rulers and behave scornfully towards him. They act like a sieve from which the flour falls out, but the dregs are retained. In recent times, the *ʿulamāʾ* stooped so low as to co-operate with the British expeditionary force, accepted General Gordon as their leader and prayed for the victory of the infidels over the believers. Consequently, "they will be killed by the sword of the Mahdiyya because they denounced us and were hypocrites" (*al-ʿulamāʾ yuqtalūna bi-sayf al-mahdiyya li-takdhībihim wa nifāqihim*).[222]

---

220 *Al-Āthār al-kāmila*, vol. 3, p. 41. A search for this *ḥadīth* in the standard concordances and search engines yielded no results. It seems that the commonly held view, according to which by the twelfth century CE "*ḥadīth* forgery had run its course" (Brown, *Ḥadīth*, pp. 71–72), is incorrect with regard to Muḥammad Aḥmad.

221 *Al-Āthār al-kāmila*, vol. 7, p. 117.

222 *Al-Āthār al-kāmila*, vol. 1, pp. 69, 78, 177–178, 434; vol. 4, p. 243; vol. 5, pp. 246–250; vol. 7, pp. 137, 232. Cf. Zahrāʾ, *al-Āyāt al-bayyināt*, p. 9: "Most of the *ʿulamāʾ* – heaven forbid – joined the infidels and preferred infidelity to belief after they had been believers" (*fa-'nḍamma ghālibuhum – wa-'l-ʿiyādh bi-'llāh – ilā al-kafara wa raḍū bi-'l-kufr baʿd al-īmān*). The last phrase is routinely used in the tradition for apostates and it reflects the attitude of Muḥammad Aḥmad's associates to the religious establishment after their leader'a death. *Al-Āyāt al-bayyināt* was published in 1887, two years after Muḥammad Aḥmad's death.

These accusations, as well as the virulent style in which they are written, enable us to appreciate the intensity of Muḥammad Aḥmad's tirade against the Sudanese religious establishment: in his eyes, there can hardly be a more serious accusation against a Muslim than collaboration with the British.

The hostility between *the mahdī* and the *ʿulamāʾ* was mutual. As could be expected, members of the religious establishment in the Sudan resented Muḥammad Aḥmad's claims to independent religious authority which threatened to undermine their own. Furthermore, they were part and parcel of the Turko-Egyptian regime against which Muḥammad Aḥmad waged his war. His success was their loss. They therefore used every opportunity to denigrate the *mahdī* and weaken his standing in the eyes of the populace.

The *mahdī*'s erstwhile mentor, Muḥammad Sharīf Nūr al-Dāʾim, had the ear of Raʾūf Pasha, the then governor of the Sudan, and notified him in the summer of 1881 of Muḥammad Aḥmad's activities. When Muḥammad Aḥmad confirmed his messianic claim to the governor in a self-confident and uncompromising letter, Raʾūf Pasha convened an assembly of *ʿulamāʾ* to discuss the issue. Some of them argued that Muḥammad Aḥmad's claims and behaviour may be the result of "heavenly attraction" (*jadhb samāwī*) caused by his excessive piety, but all agreed that he must be stopped.[223] The *ʿulamāʾ* launched a well-organized campaign in which they denounced the claims of Muḥammad Aḥmad. The campaign consisted of proclamations by groups of *ʿulamāʾ* as well as of epistles written by various individual scholars.

On 9 September 1883, a large group of Azharī *ʿulamāʾ* published a *fatwā* denouncing Muḥammad Aḥmad's messianic claim. Muḥammad Aḥmad repeatedly claimed to have seen the Prophet; the *ʿulamāʾ* countered this by asserting that seeing the Prophet after his death cannot be a basis for legal rulings. The "great *khilāfa*" claimed by Muḥammad Aḥmad cannot be recognized unless an oath of allegiance is given to him by the recognized leaders (*ahl al-ḥall wa al-ʿaqd*) of the community. Muḥammad Aḥmad's assumption of the title of *mahdī* is incompatible with the most reliable traditions concerning the *mahdī*, which predict that he will be a person who flees from Medina to Mecca and receives – unwillingly – the oath of allegiance from the people of Syria and Iraq in the sacred precinct in Mecca.[224] None of this applies to Muḥammad Aḥmad. Furthermore, a

223 Shuqayr, *Taʾrīkh*, vol. 3, pp. 127–128.

224 These details are taken from a *ḥadīth* analysed by Madelung in his "ʿAbd Allah b. al-Zubayr and the *mahdī*", cf. Chapter 1, at note 150.

claim to *khilāfa* can only be made when there is no other caliph. Asserting the existence of the Ottoman caliphate and accepting its legitimacy, the *ʿulamāʾ* maintain that the office of the caliph is not vacant. Therefore, the prophetic tradition demanding loyalty to the existing caliph (*fū li-ʾl-awwal bayʿatahu*) must be acted upon and any pretender must be opposed and even killed because he causes dissension among the Muslims.[225] Muḥammad Aḥmad's statement that the Turks are infidels and deserve to be killed is an abomination in the eyes of the *ʿulamāʾ*. They quote a prophetic *ḥadīth* according to which "whoever declares a Muslim to be an infidel is (himself) an infidel" (*man kaffara musliman fa-qad kafara*) and demand, with al-Ghazālī's *Fayṣal al-tafriqa bayna al-islām wa al-zandaqa*, extreme caution before placing any Muslim beyond the pale.[226] The thrust of the *fatwā* is twofold: first, it finds the activities of Muḥammad Aḥmad are not compatible with various details concerning the *mahdī* in the classical tradition; second, it frowns upon the rebellion instigated by Muḥammad Aḥmad against the legitimate rule of the Ottoman caliph. This is in keeping with the accepted principles of mainstream Muslim political thought which opposed rebellion almost under any circumstances.[227]

On 14 September 1884, five Sudanese *ʿulamāʾ* published a proclamation (*iʿlān*) denouncing Muḥammad Aḥmad. Among the signatories was Amīn Muḥammad al-Ḍarīr and Shākir al-Ghazzī who also wrote epistles of their own in denunciation of Muḥammad Aḥmad's messianic claims. The proclamation takes as its point of departure Qurʾān 5:4: "Today I have perfected your religion for you and I have completed my blessing upon you, and I have approved Islam for your religion." The *ʿulamāʾ* assert that this was the last Qurʾānic verse to be revealed, and contend that since the religion was made complete by God, nothing can be introduced into it afterwards. Reacting to Muḥammad Aḥmad's recurrent claims to have seen the Prophet and to have received instructions from him, the *ʿulamāʾ* affirm that seeing the Prophet in a dream cannot serve as a basis for changing the law.

---

225 The following classical tradition is quoted here: "Whoever gives allegiance to an *imām* and most sincerely clasps his hand, let him obey him if he can; if another man comes and challenges his authority, kill him" (*man bāyaʿa imāman fa-aʿṭāhu safqata yadihi wa thamrata qalbihi fa-ʾl-yuṭiʿhu in istaṭāʿa fa-in jāʾa ākhar yanāziʿuhu fa-ʾḍribū ʿunuqa al-ākhar*). Sea Muslim b. al-Ḥajjāj, *Ṣaḥīḥ*, vol. 3, p. 1473 (*Kitāb al-imāra* 46). For the special meaning of *thamrat qalbihi*, see Lane, *Lexicon*, s.v. *th-m-r*, p. 353 col. 2.
226 Muḥammad al-ʿAbbāsī al-Mahdī, *al-Fatāwā al-mahdiyya fī al-waqāʾiʿ al-miṣriyya*, vol. 2, pp, 27–32. Reproduced in Abū Salīm, *al-Khuṣūma*, pp. 501–508.
227 See Crone, *Medieval Muslim Political Thought*, pp. 135–139.

The proclamation then denounces Muḥammad Aḥmad on several grounds. As we have seen earlier, Muḥammad Aḥmad proclaimed all his opponents as infidels. The *ʿulamāʾ* accuse him of disregarding the accepted conditions of apostasy: fornication by persons who are (or have been) married, unlawful killing, renunciation of Islam or abandoning the community. All other persons who have pronounced the double declaration of faith ("There is no god except Allah and Muḥammad is the messenger of Allah") have made their lives and property inviolable. Muḥammad Aḥmad is clearly in breach of this principle: by killing Muslims, plundering their property and violating their honour, he and his followers must be considered as apostates. The *ʿulamāʾ* then quote numerous prophetic traditions supporting solidarity between Muslims and denouncing those who break it.

Other arguments relate to the traditional descriptions of the *mahdī*, to Muḥammad Aḥmad's incompatibility with them and to his personality. While the *ʿulamāʾ* assert that the traditions describing the *mahdī* are not reliable and the whole idea originated among the Shīʿa, they nevertheless point out that Muḥammad Aḥmad does not match the descriptions that exist. The wondrous events considered to be the harbingers of the *mahdī* have not taken place. Furthermore, contrary to the views of Ibn Khaldūn who maintained that a religious movement cannot succeed without enjoying the solidarity and support (*ʿaṣabiyya*) of a substantial social group, the tribe of Muḥammad Aḥmad is small; support by the riffraff (*al-ghawghāʾ wa al-dahmāʾ*) is not the required solidarity. Similarly, Muḥammad Aḥmad does not match the statements of al-Shaʿrānī whom his followers invoke: al-Shaʿrānī maintained that the *mahdī* will be a descendant of al-Ḥasan al-ʿAskarī and was born in mid-Shaʿban 255 AH. Finally, Muḥammad Aḥmad repeatedly denounces the government as being Turkish. The *ʿulamāʾ* affirm that there is not even one Turk in the Sudan any more; thus, these wars are waged for no purpose except for ruining the religion, killing Muslims, destroying mosques and houses, burning Muslim books and closing the road of the pilgrimage.[228]

During the siege of al-Kharṭūm, the *ʿulamāʾ* of the city made another proclamation. At the behest of General Gordon, they again denounced Muḥammad Aḥmad as a liar. They permitted the breaking of the fast in order to prosecute the war with greater efficiency, pointing out that the

228 The original proclamation is preserved in BL Or. 12,915–12,916, fol. 4. It has been printed in Abū Salīm, *al-Khuṣūma* ..., pp. 494–499. An English translation (to be used with care) can be found in Gordon, *The Journals* ..., pp. 287–293.

Prophet took over Mecca during the month of Ramaḍān and there is therefore no prohibition to wage war during the month of fasting.[229]

Let us now move to criticism of Muḥammad Aḥmad by individuals. One of the first documents of this type is a poem by Muḥammad Sharīf. The author gives Muḥammad Aḥmad credit for his pious behaviour, his devoted service to the community when he was a member of his Ṣūfī order and confirms that during those years he was loved by everyone. However, when he proclaimed himself to be the *mahdī* and refused to desist, Muḥammad Sharīf attributed this to satanic influence, denounced him as an infidel and recommended that the army attacks him. He calls him "the Dongolawi pretender (to be a *mahdī*), an oppressive and unjust Sudanese Khārijī" (*huwa al-mutamahdī al-Danqalāwī fa-'ʿlamū / huwa al-khārijiyyu 'l-sūdāniyyu dhī* [sic] *'l-ẓulmi wa 'l-jawri*). He refers to some of Muḥammad Aḥmad's beliefs and legal rulings. Some of the matters referred to in the poem can be located in Muḥammad Aḥmad's writings, while others seem to be pure inventions. In a sarcastic manner, Muḥammad Sharīf says that some of the *mahdī*'s falsehoods come from the Prophet, some from God and some from al-Khiḍr. He made the claim to be the *mahdī* without being ashamed of God. Muḥammad Sharīf mentions the *mahdī*'s predictions about the earth swallowing up or transforming his enemies into animals (*khasf*, *maskh*). He accuses him of allowing sexual relations without marriage or dowry with every beautiful woman, even if she was married. Muḥammad Aḥmad is said to have made rulings about the wives of absent husbands which were unheard of among Muslims and non-Muslims. He predicted that he would pray in al-Aqṣā mosque. He forbade women to wear jewellery and punished infractions by shaving their heads. He forbade smoking tobacco as if this prohibition was Qurʾānic. He forbade making a living in commerce or agriculture. He allowed things forbidden and prohibited things permissible. He forbade performing the *ḥajj*, allowed prostitution, shedding blood and selling free Muslims into slavery. He capriciously abolished divine laws and ruled to throw the *sharīʿa* into the sea. Foolishly he claimed superiority to all prophets except Muḥammad. For all this, the *mahdī* and his supporters must be fought and killed. Muḥammad Sharīf praises the Turks and their rule and predicts the victory of the Ottoman Sultan over the Mahdist army.[230]

229 Shuqayr, *Taʾrīkh*, vol. 3, pp. 231, 248.

230 I have used the part of the poem printed in Shuqayr, *Taʾrīkh*, vol. 3, pp. 116–117, 371–372, as well as the edition of Ibrāhīm Abū Salīm in *al-Khuṣūma* ..., pp. 467– 489.

In response to the demand of ʿAbd al-Qādir, the governor of the Sudan between 1882 and 1883, several scholars wrote epistles denouncing Muḥammad Aḥmad and his messianic claim. Shākir al-Ghazzī, the *muftī* of the Sudanese Appellate Council (*majlis istiʾnāf al-Sūdān*), starts his epistle by discussing the obligation of Muslims to obey their rulers. Quoting Qurʾān 4:59, which is the standard proof-text supporting obedience to the ruler, he maintains that the government (*sulṭān*) is the defender of religion which cannot exist without governmental support. This is in keeping with the mainstream idea in Muslim political thought which frowned on rebellion and discord, considering the anarchy ensuing from them as the worst of all evil. Therefore, even if someone discerns reprehensible actions being perpetrated by his ruler, let him endure rather than rebel, because whoever separates himself from the community will die as an infidel. Al-Ghazzī then surveys the various views on the future emergence of the *mahdī*. Some scholars denied his emergence, while others expected it to happen on certain dates, but none of this materialized. He affirms that Muḥammad Aḥmad cannot be the expected *mahdī* because he does not match the *mahdī*'s descriptions in the *ḥadīth*: he was not born in Mecca or in Medina, nor did he manifest himself there; his physical traits do not resemble those of the Prophet; "the complexion of the Prophet was bright with a reddish hue (*lawnuhu ṣalʿam abyaḍ mushrab bi-ḥumra*) as it is said in the *Shamāʾil Tirmidhiyya*, while the complexion of Muḥammad Aḥmad is not bright, as you can see; and whoever thinks that the complexion of our Prophet (*ṣalʿam*) is like his, denigrates the Prophet. And whoever denigrates the Prophet is judged to be an apostate (*wa ḥukm muntaqiṣihi ṣalʿam al-ridda*) ..."

Muḥammad Aḥmad's morals also do not resemble those of the Prophet: Muḥammad Aḥmad kills Muslims, plunders their property and incites them to kill each other while the Prophet was innocent of such things. Even infidels who have received a guarantee of safety or have a contract with the Muslims must not be killed or plundered, but Muḥammad Aḥmad does all these things. The *mahdī* is supposed to appear during times when Muslims are not able to find shelter from their torments; but this is clearly not such a time, due to the benevolent rule of the Khediw and of ʿAbd al-Qādir, the Governor General of the Sudan. And, asks al-Ghazzī, where is the justice with which the *mahdī* is supposed to fill the earth? There had been several messianic claimants before Muḥammad Aḥmad: Ibrāhīm al-Sūdānī claimed to be the *mahdī* in Kharṭūm and Aḥmad b. ʿUbayd made a similar claim in Upper Egypt. Both claims came to naught and Muḥammad Aḥmad's fate will be the same. His followers are uncouth Bedouins and dervishes whose only desire is to steel, plunder and kill. Al-Ghazzī uses for the Mahdists the term *khawārij*, evoking memories of the radical Muslim movement soundly defeated by the Umayyad empire in the seventh and eighth centuries. This is an effective way to deprive Muḥammad Aḥmad of any legitimacy and substantiate the idea that the Mahdists must be fought and defeated.[231]

The second *ʿālim* who wrote an epistle against Muḥammad Aḥmad was Aḥmad b. Ismāʿīl al-Azharī.[232] The epistle was completed in July 1882. Like al-Ghazzī, he quotes Qurʾān 4:59 and demands obedience to the ruler even if he is an Ethiopian slave. The only reason for which a leader may be deposed is his own apostasy or apostasy committed by another person at his behest. He then provides a long list of reasons why Muḥammad Aḥmad cannot be the expected *mahdī*: he was not born in Mecca or Medina; his physical features do not match those attributed to the *mahdī* in the classical accounts; he did not come forth in Ramaḍān as it was predicted, nor did he emerge in the Maghrib as al-Shaʿrānī expected; the Ottoman caliph is in office and is not oppressive – hence no pledge of allegiance to another caliph is possible. The main thrust of al-Azharī's arguments for the rejection of Muḥammad Aḥmad's messianic claim is the incompatibility of his biography with the classical descriptions of the *mahdī*.[233]

A third *ʿālim* who wrote against Muḥammad Aḥmad was al-Amīn b. Muḥammad al-Ḍarīr (1816–1885). He was a prolific writer on Mālikī *fiqh* (mainly inheritance law) and on prophetic genealogy. He was well connected to the government and received the title *raʾīs wa mumayyiz ʿulamāʾ al-Sūdān*, a position which, according to Abū Salīm, did not

231 Shuqayr, *Taʾrīkh*, vol. 3, pp. 375–382. A critical summary of al-Ghazzī's epistle can be found in Abū Salīm, *al-Khuṣūma* ..., pp. 270–274.

232 Al-Azharī was born in al-Ubayyiḍ in 1810 as a son of a Ṣūfī shaykh. He spent twelve years studying and teaching at al-Azhar. In 1873 he returned to the Sudan and was in al-Ubayyiḍ when the Mahdiyya started. He managed to return safely to Kharṭūm where he wrote his epistle. Late in 1882 he was appointed *qāḍī* in the newly established province of Kordofan and Darfur, but was killed by the Mahdists on his way there. His son Ismāʿīl al-Azharī was a judge and a muftī in Anglo-Egyptian Sūdān. His grandson Ismāʿīl al-Azharī was the first prime minister of independent Sūdān. See Abū Salīm, *al-Khuṣūma* ..., pp. 275–276; Hill, *Biographical Dictionary*, p. 184.

233 Shuqayr, *Taʾrīkh*, vol. 3, pp. 383–391.

demand from its incumbent any specific work, but placed him at the head of the Sudanese *ʿulamāʾ*.[234] His epistle is entitled *Hudā al-mustahdī ilā bayān al-mahdī wa al-mutamahdī*, a chronogram for 1299 AH (1882–1883) in which it was written. Al-Ḍarīr connects the spiritual ferment of the period with the end of the thirteenth century AH. He leaves no doubt as to where his sympathy lies: in his view, Muḥammad Aḥmad caused immense destruction in the Sudan and is supported only by the ignorant. He fails to fulfil the minimum requirement even for a caliph, let alone for a *mahdī*. The caliph must be a *mujtahid* or at least the best *muqallid* of his time; the *mahdī*, on the other hand, must be a *mujtahid*, as explained by Ibn al-ʿArabī and other Ṣūfīs. This, in itself, would be sufficient to reject the messianic claims of Muḥammad Aḥmad. But there are further reasons to do this. In many traditions it is said that the *mahdī* must not appear when another *khalīfa* is in office. Al-Ḍarīr therefore devotes a whole chapter in his epistle to substantiate the legitimacy of ʿAbd al-Ḥamīd's rule. Describing the deposition of Murād V and the accession of ʿAbd al-Ḥamīd II in 1876, he asserts that ʿAbd al-Ḥamīd received the support of the senior officials of the empire, as well as that of the *shaykh al-islām*. His accession was therefore legal and he is the rightful ruler. It is noteworthy that in the framework of supporting the legitimacy of ʿAbd al-Ḥamīd, al-Ḍarīr expresses his total support for the *Tanẓīmāt* reforms in the Ottoman empire.[235] Al-Ḍarīr then gives the conventional arguments forbidding rebellion against a rightful caliph. Quoting Qurʾān 4:59, referring to the *ḥadīth* which requires obedience to any ruler (even a black slave), and to numerous texts requiring the suppression of rebels, he reaches the conclusion that rebellion is not allowed even if a rightful ruler becomes oppressive. As a natural corollary of his political theory, he concludes this part of his epistle with lavishly praising the Khediw Abū al-ʿAbbās Muḥammad Tawfīq.[236]

In this way al-Ḍarīr established the legitimacy of the existing Ottoman caliph and of the Egyptian Khediw. He also attempted to expose Muḥammad Aḥmad's inadequacy for the messianic task. Now he needs to undermine

234 See Abū Salīm, *al-Khuṣūma* ..., pp. 279–282; Hill, *Dictionary*, p. 55. For full text of the epistle, see Abū Salīm, *al-Khuṣūma* ..., pp. 443–467.

235 Abū Salīm, *al-Khuṣūma* ..., pp. 449–451. Al-Ḍarīr's description of the accession of ʿAbd al-Ḥamīd is based on Muḥammad al-Jawāyib (sic) Aḥmad Fāris, *Kanz al-raghāʾib fī muntakhabāt al-jawāʾyib* (sic), vol. 5, and on *Aqwam al-masālik* by Khayr al-Dīn al-Tūnusī.

236 Abū Salīm, *al-Khuṣūma* ..., pp. 451–457.

Muḥammad Aḥmad's own basis for legitimacy: the significance of the recurrent meetings with the Prophet in which he claimed to have been appointed *mahdī* and to have received instructions on various matters. To attain this purpose, he must delve into the Muslim theory of dreams and their interpretations. More specifically, he must interpret afresh traditions according to which the Prophet said: "He who saw me, saw the truth" (*man ra'ānī fa-qad ra'ā al-ḥaqq*) or "He who saw me in a dream did indeed see me, because Satan cannot assume my form" (*man ra'ānī fī al-manām fa-qad ra'ānī li-anna al-shayṭān lā yatamaththalu bi-ṣūratī*).[237] If these traditions are taken literally, Muḥammad Aḥmad can claim absolute authority because the Prophet's appearance cannot be deceptive, and his instructions issued during such an appearance must be considered as irrevocable orders for all humanity. In al-Ḍarīr's view, this understanding is wrong. The tradition quoted means that if someone saw the Prophet in a dream after he had seen him in reality, remembers his shape and the shape in the dream is identical with that in reality, only then is it certain that he had indeed seen the Prophet. But this can only apply to the Prophet's contemporaries. In the post-prophetic period, therefore, it is not obligatory to act upon such a vision because it is not possible to ascertain the veracity of the dream (*li-'adam ḍabṭ al-manām*).[238] And, most certainly, if a Prophet orders someone in a dream to contradict the *sharī'a*, such a command must not be obeyed. Even more problematic are the claims to have seen the Prophet in a state of wakefulness. In order to undermine this claim, al-Ḍarīr musters some of the great names in the Muslim tradition: al-Qurṭubī, al-Sakhāwī and al-Sha'rānī; all these rejected the possibility of the Prophet being seen after his death and burial. He also uses two arguments from traditions about the formative period of Islam. First, the problem of the caliphate, which caused dangerous division in the community in the period immediately following the Prophet's death, could have been solved with ease if the Prophet appeared to his successors and indicated his preferences. This

237 See Wensinck, *Concordance*, s.v. *ra'ā, tamaththala*; Ibn Abī Dunyā, *Kitāb al-manām*, p. 81 (no. 134). For other dreams in which the Prophet is seen, see ibid., pp. 62ff. See Krenkow, "The Appearance of the Prophet in Dreams", and Goldziher, "The Appearance of the Prophet in Dreams".

238 This argument was used in the medieval Muslim tradition; see Krenkow, "The Appearance of the Prophet in Dreams", p. 78. For a more general survey of traditional claims to have seen the Prophet in dreams, see Goldziher, "The Appearance of the Prophet in Dreams".

is an understandable assumption in a tradition which sees history, and in particular early Muslim history, as guided by providence. Second, if anyone would have deserved to see the Prophet after his death, it would have been his daughter Fāṭima who was so sad because of her father's disappearance that she died six months later. All this notwithstanding, neither she nor anybody else in early Islam claimed to have seen the Prophet after his death. This being so, the later and less virtuous generations certainly do not deserve such a privilege.[239]

X AMBITIONS BEYOND THE SUDAN

In May 1883, Muḥammad Aḥmad wrote a rather flattering letter to Muḥammad al-Mahdī al-Sanūsī. He refers to the piety of al-Sanūsī and to his assiduous following of the prophetic *sunna*. He relates that during one of his *ḥaḍarāt*, the Prophet placed three of Muḥammad Aḥmad's associates on the chairs of Abū Bakr, ʿUmar and ʿAlī. They were ʿAbdullāhi, ʿAlī Muḥammad Ḥilw and Muḥammad Sharīf. The chair of ʿUthmān was reserved "for Ibn al-Sanūsī, until he joins you, sooner or later".[240] He continues saying that the spirituality of al-Sanūsī was with them during the encounters with the Prophet and with the other important personalities of early Islam. He instructs him to wage *jihād* in the direction of Egypt, or to perform *hijra* and join him. The latter is preferable because of the great rewards of *hijra*. The letter ends with an expression which could be interpreted as a veiled threat: "A hint is sufficient for a person like yourself" (*wa mithluka takfīhi al-ishāra*).[241] Approaching the Sanūsī seems to indicate the grand strategic plan of Muḥammad Aḥmad: he himself would attack Egypt from the south, while the Sanūsī would do the same from the west. However, the Sanūsī rejected the offer with contempt, did not answer the letter and informed the envoys who brought it that "we are not worth the soil upon which ʿUthmān trod" (*innanā lā nusāwī al-turāb alladhī kāna yaṭaʾuhu ʿUthmān*). He sent a strong denunciation of Muḥammad Aḥmad to

239 Abū Salīm, *al-Khuṣūma* ..., pp. 457–461.

240 In another description ʿUthmān's chair was given to an unnamed associate (*wāḥid min al-ikhwān*), apparently as a temporary measure, in order to enable Muḥammad Aḥmad to bestow it upon the Sanūsī if he joins the Mahdiyya. See *Al-Āthār al-kāmila*, vol. 7, p. 124.

241 *Al-Āthār al-kāmila*, vol. 1, pp. 334–339. The division of the chairs is on p. 337.

the Khediw Tawfīq.[242] Thus failed the first attempt of Muḥammad Aḥmad to spread his influence beyond the borders of the Sudan.

Muḥammad Aḥmad renewed his attempts to spread his influence abroad about one month before his death on 22 June 1885. Having become convinced that he had accomplished his mission in the Sudan, he concluded that the time hads come to move further afield. On 27 May 1885, he wrote to a certain Ḥusayn Khalīfa, appointed him as his deputy responsible for all the ʿAbābida tribes and informed him that "the affair of the infidels has come to an end in the Sudan and we have resolved, according to God's will, to apply ourselves to other countries" (*wa qad intahā amruhum bi-'l-Sūdān wa ʿazamnā bi-irādat Allāh ʿalā al-tafarrugh li-ghayrihā min al-buldān*).[243]

He also reports that the Prophet promised that he would pray in Mecca, in Medina, in Cairo, in Jerusalem, in "the mosque of Iraq" and in Kūfa.[244] Accordingly, he started writing letters to various persons beyond the borders of the Sudan. He appointed governors of various regions as if these were under his jurisdiction. On 5 May 1885 he wrote a letter to al-Ḥasan b. Muḥammad b. ʿAbd al-Raḥmān whom he describes as the governor of Fez, notifying him that certain Maghribīs in Egypt accepted his messianic claim and requested the appointment of Muḥammad al-Ghālī ʿAbd al-Salām as governor of Fez on his behalf. He sent an appointment letter to this person, but left the final decision in the hands of the people of Fez.[245] In response to a letter from the Moroccan al-Ṭayyib al-Banānī, who asked him to arrange a safe return journey to Morocco for him and his entourage, Muḥammad Aḥmad placed him in charge "of all the people of Marrakesh" and empowered him to accept the oath of allegiance on the *mahdī*'s behalf.[246] There were rumours of Muḥammad Aḥmad's emissaries reaching Tunisia and the Ḥijāz.[247] ʿAbd Allah al-Kaḥḥāl was appointed governor of Syria, but this prospective appointee set out as if for Syria,

242 Shuqayr, *Taʾrīkh*, vol. 1, p. 127; Abū Salīm, *al-Khuṣūma ...*, pp. 351–355; 521–522. See also a report in *The Times* (31 January 1884, p. 5, column d) according to which The Sanūsī "sent a circular to the religious heads of his tribe directing them to inform the Mussulmans that the Mahdi is a false prophet and an adventurer, and that they should on no account follow him".

243 *Al-Āthār al-kāmila*, vol. 5, p. 104.

244 *Al-Āthār al-kāmila*, vol. 5, p. 458. Cf. Holt, "The Sudanese Mahdia ...", p. 278.

245 *Al-Āthār al-kāmila*, vol. 5, pp. 24–25. Cf. Holt, "The Sudanese Mahdia ...", p. 282.

246 *Al-Āthār al-kāmila*, vol. 5, pp. 58–59, 108. According to Shuqayr (*Taʾrīkh*, vol. 3, pp. 353–354), al-Banānī never reached Marrakesh.

247 *The Times*, 29 November 1883, p. 5; 4 December 1883, p. 5; *The Times*, 3 January 1884, p. 3.

but stopped his journey in Egypt and resumed there his erstwhile activities as a merchant.[248] On 6 June 1885 Muḥammad Aḥmad wrote to the Khediw (*wālī Miṣr*) telling him that he is about to come to his country, with the soldiers of God, and urging him to submit or else. A letter with similar content was sent to the *ʿulamāʾ* of Egypt.[249] Muḥammad Aḥmad also anticipated that he will come to Mecca and accept there the second pledge of allegiance. He asserted that the messianic era – described in the classical traditions as characterized by justice, unprecedented wealth and peace in the animal kingdom – will begin at that time. It is noteworthy that this transformation of the human condition, which is in the classical tradition an essential element in the achievements of the eschatological *mahdī*, is not mentioned often in Muḥammad Aḥmad's pronouncements.[250] His affinity with the Prophet is much more important.

The most interesting document of this kind is the letter to the king of Ethiopia Yohannes IV (r. 1872–1889). Because of the well-known traditions concerning the connection between the early Muslims and the king of Ethiopia, known in the Muslim tradition as the Najāshī (i.e., Negus), writing a letter to Yohannes gave Muḥammad Aḥmad a golden opportunity to enhance the affinity between himself and the Prophet. Muḥammad Aḥmad calls Yohannes *ʿaẓīm al-Ḥabasha* ("the leader of the Ethiopians"), *ʿaẓīm* being the title used by the Prophet in the letters allegedly written by him to the potentates of his time. Calling upon Yohannes to convert, he uses the famous expression which appears in Muḥammad's letters to these potentates: "Embrace Islam so that you are safe, and God will give you your reward twice ..." (*aslim taslam yuʾtika Allah ajraka marratayn ...*). Since Yohannes is honoured by living in an age which became prophetic because of Muḥammad Aḥmad's appearance in it, he should be like his forebear the Najāshī who believed in the Prophet and gave shelter to his associates when they fled from Mecca to his kingdom. The letter ends with the expression "Peace be upon those who follow the straight path" (*al-salām ʿalā man ittabaʿa al-hudā*), which is, in a manner of speaking, a conditional greeting for prospective converts; it is also taken from the

248 Shuqayr, *Taʾrīkh*, vol. 3, p. 351.

249 *Al-Āthār al-kāmila*, vol. 5, pp. 245, 249–250. The letter to the Khediw is quoted in Shuqayr, *Taʾrīkh*, vol. 3, pp. 347–351. See also *The Times*, 3 January 1884, p. 3.

250 *Al-Āthār al-kāmila*, vol. 5, pp. 420–421. The Qurʾānic commentary attributed to Muḥammad Aḥmad includes some references to the coincidence of the Mahdiyya with the eschaton, but these references are few and far between. See *Al-Āthār al-kāmila*, vol. 7, p. 62 (on Qurʾān 17:58) and p. 227 (on Qurʾān 40:46).

aforementioned prophetic letters.[251] The analogy with the Prophet is evident.

The pan-Islamic overtures of Muḥammad Aḥmad ended in total failure. Those of the addressees who deemed it necessary to respond at all, treated Muḥammad Aḥmad's letters with contempt and denounced him in harsh terms. The Ottoman sultan denounced Muḥammad Aḥmad as the "false *mahdī*" and attempted to obtain an edict against him from the Sherif of Mecca.[252] Recurrent denunciations of the Ottoman rulers by Muḥammad Aḥmad caused certain anxiety among the Ottomans who were apprehensive of possible Mahdist incursions into the Arabian Peninsula. The Ottomans considered sending military reinforcements to Arabia in order to prevent such an eventuality.

XI SOME GENERAL CHARACTERISTICS OF MUḤAMMAD AḤMAD'S THOUGHT

The personality of Muḥammad Aḥmad reflects a seamless integration of the most scathing denunciations of this world with an intense desire to achieve the most spectacular successes in worldly, warlike activities. Recurrent quotations from the works of Ibn al-ʿArabī coexist with glowing descriptions of military victories, fierce cursing of defeated enemies and with burning ambition to spread the Mahdiyya across the Muslim world. Muḥammad Aḥmad's Ṣūfī association is stressed throughout his works. ʿAbd al-Qādir al-Jīlānī and thousands of unnamed *awliyāʾ* appear in his visionary appointment ceremony. Al-Khiḍr, whose importance in Ṣūfī thought is well known, is considered a constant source of inspiration. A contemporary of Muḥammad Aḥmad, who wrote a spirited defence of his messianic claims, considers him a *walī* and defends him using the *ḥadīth*

251 *Al-Āthār al-kāmila*, vol. 5, pp. 234–236.

252 ʿAbd al-Ḥamīd's proclamation has been mentioned in *The Times* (9 April 1885, p. 5). See also Abū Salīm, *al-Ṣirāʿ bayna al-mahdī* wa al-*ʿulamāʾ*, p. 23; Shuqayr, *Taʾrīkh*, vol. 3, p. 374; *The Times*, 25 December 1883, p. 3. Unfortunately, I was not able to obtain the original Ottoman proclamation and some Ottoman historians do not mention it in their studies of ʿAbd al-Ḥamīd's attitude to the Mahdiyya, though they discuss the Sultan's fear of it. See F. A. K. Yasamee, "The Ottoman Empire, the Sudan and the Red Sea Coast 1883–1889", in Selim Deringil and Sinan Kuneralp, eds, *Studies on Ottoman Diplomatic History*, vol. 5, pp. 87–102. The Moroccan sultan is also said to have denounced Muḥammad Aḥmad; see *The Times*, 7 March 1884, p. 5.

qudsī in which God says that "whoever is hostile to one of my saints, I shall wage war on him" (*man ʿādā lī waliyyan fa-qad ādhantuhu bi-'l-ḥarb*).[253] A substantial part of the book is written from a Ṣūfī perspective.

All this notwithstanding, one of the important achievements of the Mahdist movement was quite worldly: the establishment of a state with Muḥammad Aḥmad at its helm. This state waged victorious wars against the "Turko-Egyptian" regime, defeated the British in several decisive battles and managed to survive for eighteen years, fourteen of them after the death of the founder. This happened during the heyday of the British empire. The Mahdist state had a treasury; it managed considerable wealth which originated from spoils taken in battle from its vanquished enemies. This wealth included many slaves and slave girls. The state demanded total obedience to the *mahdī* as a religious and political leader, promulgated laws, determined who will succeed the founder after his death and approached foreign potentates as states are wont to do. No contradiction was felt between the recurrent declarations that Muḥammad Aḥmad has only contempt for worldly positions and these very worldly achievements.

Muḥammad Aḥmad made systematic attempts to portray himself as a successor (*khalīfa*) of the Prophet and a reviver of the early Islamic state. He evokes early Islamic times in many ways, using imagery and concepts from the classical descriptions of the prophetic period. Time and again he quotes the Prophet as saying that his own companions are like the companions of the Prophet (*aṣḥāb*); that they must treat the *mahdī* in the same way as the early *ṣaḥāba* treated the Prophet; that Muḥammad Aḥmad's successor has the standing of Abū Bakr and that the period before his emergence is equivalent to the Jāhiliyya. He claims to have constant visionary encounters with the Prophet who instructs him in many things, including military tactics. Every effort is made to create the impression that nineteenth-century Sudan is a recreation of seventh-century Arabia. The significance of this idea in comparison with the world view of other messianic claimants will be discussed in the concluding chapter of this book.

253 Al-ʿIbādī, *Al-Anwār al-saniyya*, p. 28.

5

The *mahdī* controversy in modern Muslim India

1 A BRIEF INTRODUCTION

In an epistle addressed to Queen Victoria – which was probably never delivered to the addressee – Mīrzā Ghulām Aḥmad, the founder of the Aḥmadī movement in Islam, says:

> [The Mussalmans of the old school] ... expect a *mahdī* who will be a descendant of Fatima, mother of Hussain, and a Massiha who in company with the *mahdī* will wage the destructive wars against the Kafirs. I have tried to uproot all such beliefs exposing their falsity and absurdity. Such *Mahdī* is, of course, an imaginary being and a delusion. The truth is that there shall appear no *Mahdī* from among the descendants of Fatima and the traditions speaking of such a person are all of them forged ... No doubt another person has been foretold to come under the name of ʿĪsā, but he shall neither wage wars nor shed blood; on the other hand, he, by the gentleness and humility and his strong and convincing arguments, shall turn the hearts of men to truth. It has been revealed to me that I am that promised one ... I deny the appearance of the bloody Mahdi so ardently expected by the Mussalmans ...[1]

1 Ghulām Aḥmad, *Kashf-ul-Ghiṭā'*, pp. 11–12.

This is, in a nutshell, the nature of the *mahdī* controversy which can be discerned among Indian Muslims in the second half of the nineteenth century. There were strong views on both sides of the divide. Mīrzā Ghulām Aḥmad promoted the idea of himself as a *mahdī* who will bring peace and amity to the world. Sir Sayyid Aḥmad Khān debunked the idea of the *mahdī* in its entirety. Rafīʿ al-Dīn Dihlawī (d. 1818, the son of the celebrated Shāh Walī Allah and the brother of the well-known Shāh ʿAbd al-ʿAzīz), Muḥammad Ṣiddīq Ḥasan Khān (d. 1890) and other scholars spoke about the imminent appearance of a "bloody" *mahdī* who will annihilate the infidels and conquer the world for Islam. W. W. Hunter saw this belief as a part of the "chronic conspiracy" against the British.[2] In a wider sense, the controversy was not only about the nature of the expected *mahdī*'s actions on earth. It was also about the contested image of Islam: is it a religion whose messianic aspirations include the destruction of all other faiths, or a religion promoting a peaceful message?

II THE "BLOODY" *MAHDĪ*

Let us start with an analysis of the belief in the appearance of a belligerent *mahdī*, bent on global conquest and destruction of infidels. Since the descriptions of Ṣiddīq Ḥasan Khān are much more extensive than those of the other thinkers on this side of the divide, it is appropriate to describe the "bloody" *mahdī* idea mainly on the basis of his works.

Nawwāb Ṣiddīq Ḥasan Khān (1832–1890) was a prolific writer, statesman and leader of the *ahl-ḥadīth*.[3] He wrote major works on eschatology in Persian, Urdu and Arabic.[4] Parts of these works are overlapping and it

2 Hunter, *Our Indian Musalmans*, pp. 62–64

3 Zafarul Islam Khan, "Nawwāb Sayyid Ṣiddīq Ḥasan Khān, *EI*²", s.v. This article deals mainly with his biography and political activities. In Ahmad, *Islamic Modernism* (pp. 113–119), there a brief description of his religious views. An extensive list of his works can be found in Raḥmān ʿAlī, *Tadhkira*, pp. 94–96. See also Ikrām, *Mawj-i Kawthar*, pp. 65–68, and Khān, *Taḥrīk-i ahl-i ḥadīth*, pp. 205–218. On his views on the legal status of India under the British, see Friedmann, "*Dār al-Islām* and *dār al-ḥarb* in Modern Indian Muslim Thought", pp. 359–362.

4 The Persian *Ḥujaj al-karāma fī āthār al-qiyāma*, printed in Bhopal in 1290/1873, consists of more than 500 pages in dense print in folio size. The Urdu *Iqtirāb al-sāʿa*, published in Benares in 1322/1904 consists of 226 pages. The Arabic *al-Idhāʿa* is much shorter and runs for less than 100 pages. These three books are hard to come by and have barely been mentioned in research literature.

seems that writing in the three languages reflects the author's effort to reach as wide a Muslim reading public as possible. Most of his text is based on the classical apocalyptic material from which he quotes extensively. However, in numerous places he provides his own comments on the classical tradition, sometimes introducing them by the words "I say" (*gūyam* or *qultu*). Elsewhere, his views and observations are identifiable in other ways. This material is the most significant for our purposes because it reflects the author's views, emphases and sometimes includes clear deviations from the classical approach.

It is appropriate to start the analysis of Ṣiddīq Ḥasan Khān's apocalyptics with his view of Islamic history. He belongs to a tradition which views the whole history of Islam as a long sequence of events which are understood as heralding the Day of Judgment. Because of this attitude, his works and especially the *Ḥujaj al-karāma* is much more than a work of eschatology and includes valuable material on historical matters, especially as far as Indian Islam is concerned.

Ṣiddīq Ḥasan Khān's *Iqtirāb al-sā'a* begins with a lengthy description of the various messianic pretenders in Islamic history as well as of numerous dramatic events, all of which belong, in his view, to the "distant portents" (*amārāt-i ba'īda*) of the Hour. They begin with the death of the Prophet, which was the biggest calamity in Islamic history and started to change the hearts of Muslims even before they cleaned the dust on the Prophet's grave.[5] The next is the murder of 'Uthmān b. 'Affān. The list continues with the Battle of the Camel, the Battle of Ṣiffīn, the Battle of Nahrawān between 'Alī and the Khawārij, the deposition of Ḥasan b. 'Alī from the caliphate and other misdeeds of the Umayyad caliphs.[6] Then come the developments under the 'Abbāsīs: the killing of Muḥammad *al-nafs al-zakiyya*, the imprisonment of Ja'far al-Ṣādiq, the death of Mūsā al-Kāẓim in prison, the entry of philosophy into Islam, the beating of Aḥmad b. Ḥanbal during the *miḥna* and the killing of numerous scholars who were not willing to consent to the Mu'tazilī dogma asserting the createdness of the Qur'ān. The emergence of the

---

5 The idea that the first tribulation (*fitna*) effecting the Muslim community is the Prophet's death is part and parcel of classical Muslim apocalyptics. See Abū Nu'aym, *Fitan*, pp. 25, 31 and Chapter 1, at notes 14 and 18.

6 Ṣiddīq Ḥasan Khān, *Iqtirāb al-sā'a*, pp. 12–13. A similar attitude to events in early Islamic history can be found in the works of the eighteenth-century Indian Muslim thinker Shāh Walī Allah Dihlawī; see his *Izālat al-khafā'*, vol. 1, pp. 486ff.

Shīʿa, the ascendancy of the Seljuks and the Mongol conquest are also mentioned in this context.[7]

Significantly, the situation of the Islamic world in Ṣiddīq Ḥasan Khān's days is also perceived as a "portent of the Hour".

> "Islam became a stranger while infidelity came close" (*wa al-islām qad ʿāda gharīban wa al-kufr ṣāra qarīban*).[8] This world shows signs of imminent end, The Big Hour is at hand with the appearance of the Great Portents. The infidels took over most of the Islamic lands. Tears are shed here in order to quench the fires of distress. The infidels took possession of these lands and of the abodes of Islam. The lights (of these abodes) have been replaced by darkness. Their mosques have become churches and their lions – prey to the infidel dogs. Their mosques have their doors shut and became shelter for vermin and resting place for dogs ... The Portents of Resurrection appeared ...[9]

In this way, Islamic history in its entirety becomes a long list of events heralding the apocalyptic drama. Most of them are calamitous. For an outsider, this is a very pessimistic approach to Islamic history which started according to this view at the pinnacle of glory during the lifetime of the Prophet, but immediately after his death began to deteriorate, constantly moving in the direction of the final apocalypse. Ṣiddīq Ḥasan Khān understands this to be an inexorable, pre-determined process whose direction cannot be changed; he does not make any comment on the general significance of such an approach to Islamic history.[10]

In addition to these "Portents of the Hour", numerous figures whom Ṣiddīq Ḥasan Khān calls *dajjāls* and messianic pretenders are mentioned.

7 Ṣiddīq Ḥasan Khān, *Iqtirāb al-sāʿa*, pp. 14–15.

8 This is to be understood in light of the classical *ḥadīth* which says that "Islam began as a stranger and it will return to what it was. Blessed be the strangers" (*inna al-islām badaʾa gharīban wa sa-yaʿūdu kamā badaʾ fa-ṭūbā li-'l-ghurabāʾ*). The idea is that in the beginning Islam was weak, having few believers who were like strangers in an alien environment, surrounded by infidels. This situation will recur before the Day of Judgment. See Ibn al-Athīr, *al-Nihāya fī gharīb al-ḥadīth*, in ʿAllūsh, *al-Jāmiʿ*, vol. 4, p. 242 (s. v. *gh-r-b*). For an extensive commentary on this *ḥadīth*, see Ibn Rajab al-Ḥanbalī, *Kashf al-kurba fī waṣf ʿan ḥāl ahl al-ghurba, passim*. For further references, see Wensinck, *Concordance*, s.v. *gharīb*; Friedmann, *Shaykh Aḥmad Sirhindī*, p. 16 and D. Cook, *Studies in Muslim Apocalyptic*, p. 7, note 14.

9 Ṣiddīq Ḥasan Khān, *al-Ibra*, p. 62.

10 For similar ideas in classical *ḥadīth*, see Chapter 1, Section I.

As for the *dajjāls*, the author provides an extensive list; he does this in view of the *ḥadīth* which maintains that "the Day of Judgment will not take place ... before close to thirty deceiving *dajjāls* will be sent, each claiming to be God's messenger (*lā taqūmu al-sā'a ... ḥattā yub'atha dajjālūn kadhdhābūn qarīb min thalāthīn kulluhum yaz'umu annahu rasūl Allah*).[11] Some of these *dajjāls* are rebels and heretics well known from Muslim history. Several of them belong to the Shī'a and the Ismā'īliyya: al-Mukhtār b. Abī 'Ubayd,[12] Abū Ṭāhir al-Qarmaṭī,[13] Yaḥyā b. Zikrawayhi al-Qarmaṭī[14] and Muḥammad b. Alī al-Shalmaghānī.[15] More obscure figures include Bihbūz (b. 'Abd al-Wahhāb), a warrior in the Zanj revolt,[16] a sorcerer from Malaga, an anonymous woman, who claimed prophethood for herself asserting that the prophetic *ḥadīth* saying that "there will be no prophet after me" (*lā nabiyya ba'dī*) speaks about male prophets only – and even a man who read this *ḥadīth* as meaning that "[a man called] *Lā* will be a prophet after me" (*Lā nabiyyun ba'dī*) and claimed to be that man.[17] Among the pretenders, he mentions the well-known Sayyid Muḥammad Jawnpūrī, the leader of the Indian Mahdawīs (d. 1505),[18] and Muḥammad b. 'Abd Allah, the Sudanese *mahdī* (d. 1885);[19] according to some, he says, "the leader of the *neycharī sect*" (*za'īm-i firqa-yi neychariyya*), a title normally associated with the Indian modernist Sir Sayyid Aḥmad Khān (d. 1898), also advanced a messianic claim for himself. Pretenders who were virtuous made their claim in the state of mystical intoxication (*sukr*) and repented after awakening. Those who were not virtuous made their claim for purposes of reaching

11 Bukhārī, *Ṣaḥīḥ, Kitāb al-fitan* 25 (vol. 4, p. 380). For a discussion of the significance of this *ḥadīth*, see Friedmann, *Prophecy Continuous*, pp. 64–68.

12 G. R. Hawting, "Al-Mukhtār b. Abī 'Ubayd", in *EI²*, s.v.

13 Abū Ṭāhir Sulaymān, was a leader of the Qarmaṭīs in Baḥrayn between 922 and 944. See Halm, *The Empire of the Mahdī*, pp. 251–264; Kennedy, *The Prophet and the Age of the Caliphates*, pp. 193–195.

14 A Qarmaṭī missionary and leader, nicknamed *ṣāḥib al-nāqa*, who was killed in the siege of Damascus in 903. See Kennedy, *The Prophet and the Age of the Caliphates*, p. 288.

15 Al-Shalmaghānī was a prominent Imāmī scholar who claimed to be the "agent" (*wakīl*) of the hidden *imām* and even the *imām* himself. He was executed in 933–934. See Pellat, "Muḥammad b. 'Ali al-Shalmaghānī", in *EI²*, s.v.; Sachedina, *Islamic Messianism*, pp. 95–96, 98.

16 Bihbūz died in 882. See Popovic, *The Revolt of African Slaves in Iraq*, pp. 104–105 and index.

17 Ṣiddīq Ḥasan Khān, *Iqtirāb al-sā'a*, pp. 18–19.

18 See Chapter 3 above.

19 See Chapter 4 above.

power (*mulk gīrī*). The people of knowledge did not recognize any of these claims.[20]

The description of the *mahdī* in *Ḥujaj al-karāma* is based on classical apocalyptic material, but the choice of the traditions and their arrangement and augmentation is significant. From the outset, the description creates an affinity between the *mahdī* and the Prophet. The *mahdī* will come with the Prophet's shirt, sword and flag in his possession. This flag has not been unfurled since the Prophet's death and will remain in this condition until the *mahdī* manifests himself. On the flag, made of black fabric, will be an inscription saying: "Allegiance to God" (*al-bayʿa li-'llāh*). A cloud will spread shade over the *mahdī*'s head and announce: "This is the *mahdī*, the *khalīfa* of God; follow him." A hand will point in the direction of the *mahdī*, symbolizing allegiance.[21]

In Ṣiddīq Ḥasan Khān's description, the *mahdī* will transform society and will be engaged in wide-ranging military exploits. The military activities of the *mahdī* should be understood against the background of the great importance which the author ascribes to *jihād*. He wrote an extensive treatise devoted to military expeditions, martyrdom and *hijra*, in the sense of migration from non-Muslim to Muslim territory. Following the pertinent classical traditions, he maintains that the "*jihād* will not cease as long as there is Islam or Muslims in any country on the face of the earth ... until the appearance of the *dajjāl* at the end of times".[22] The *mahdī* will bring *jihād* to its completion: he will move from Mecca to Medina and visit the Prophet's tomb. From there he will march to Syria and reach Damascus. He will conquer al-Andalus, reach Rome (*Rūmiyya*)[23] and conquer it as well. From there he will return to the east and conquer Constantinople. Like Dhū al-Qarnayn and Sulaymān, he will become ruler over the (entire) world (*yaṣīru lahu mulk al-arḍ*). He will revive Islam and make it strong

20 Ṣiddīq Ḥasan Khān, *Iqtirāb al-sāʿa*, pp. 2–4 *supra*.

21 Ṣiddīq Ḥasan Khān, *Ḥujaj al-karāma*, pp. 365 *infra* – 366 *supra*; 367 line 22.

22 Ṣiddīq Ḥasan Khān, *al-ʿIbra*, p. 16.

23 Translating into Persian a passage from Sulamī, *ʿIqd al-durar* (p. 173), Ṣiddīq Ḥasan Khān describes Rome in the following words: "Rūmiyya is the mother of the land of Rūm. The title of the king of that place is *al-bāb*, whoever he may be. The ruler of that place has the same status in Christianity as the *khalīfa* has among Muslims. There is no city that resembles (Rūmiyya) in the lands of Islam" (*Rūmiyya umm bilād-i Rūm ast wa bādshāh-i ān jā-rā al-bāb laqab ast har kih bāshad. wa ḥākim-i ān-jā bar dīn-i naṣrāniyyat bi-manzila-yi khalīfa dar musalmānān bāshad wa mānand-i ān kudām balda dar bilād-i ahl-i islām nīst*). See *Ḥujaj al-karāma*, p. 379 lines 8–9. Sulamī's text has *wa laysa fī bilād al-Rūm mithluhā*.

and exalted.[24] He will call people to God with the sword; whoever disputes (his authority) will be killed and whoever refuses to answer his call will be defeated (*bi-khwānad mardum-rā bi-sū-yi khudā ba-shamshīr pas har kih abā kunad kushta shawad wa har kih nizā' kunad makhdhūl gardad*).[25] He is the "bloody *mahdī*" whom Ghulām Aḥmad mentioned in his (apparently undelivered) message to Queen Victoria.

The *mahdī's* victories will not be accomplished easily. The Christians will make a great effort to thwart him. They will gather a huge army from their own people and from the people of Rūm to fight him. Their army will consist of 960,000 men, holding 80 banners. Under each banner there will be 12,000 men.[26] The army of the *mahdī* will consist of three units. One will escape out of fear of the Franks and will separate itself from the army of the *mahdī*. God will not accept their repentance. Another group, which will be with the *mahdī*, will be martyred and reach the (spiritual) rank of those who fell in the Battles of Badr and Uḥud. Some of them will be victorious with divine help, without being enmeshed in *fitna* and without going astray. Then the *mahdī* will arraign a new army to fight the Christians. A large number of Muslims will take an oath that they will not return without victory. These will be martyred. The *mahdī* will return with a small number to the camp. On the second morning, a great multitude will again take an oath that they will not return without achieving victory. They will come with the *mahdī*, will show their valour (*dād-i jawān-mardī dihand*), but will also be martyred. In the evening, the *mahdī* returns with a small number to his camp. The same happens on the third day. On the fourth day, a small group who remained to guard the camp (on the previous day) will set out with the *mahdī* in order to fight; this time God will grant them a resounding victory. So many Christians will be killed that "the smell of sovereignty will not remain in the noses of those who will survive" (*bū-yi riyāsat dar dimāgh-i bāqī māndagān na-mānad*). The tiny number of Christian survivors will run away in humiliation, disperse and go to Hell.[27] Killing myriads of infidels is mentioned also with regard to

24 Ṣiddīq Ḥasan Khān, *Ḥujaj al-karāma*, p. 366, lines 24–25; p. 367 line 15; 379 lines 23–24; 381 lines 6–9.

25 Ṣiddīq Ḥasan Khān, *Ḥujaj al-karāma*, p. 382, lines 15–16. This is translated into Persian from Ibn al-'Arabī, *Futūḥāt*, vol. 3, p. 327, line 27: *wa yad'ū ilā Allāh bi-'l-sayf fa-man abā qutila wa man nāza'ahu khudhila*.

26 For these numbers in classical apocalyptics, see Nu'aym, *Fitan*, p. 31 *infra*. Rafī al-Dīn (*Alāmāt-i qiyāmat*, p. 6) speaks about 840,000 only.

27 Ṣiddīq Ḥasan Khān, *Ḥujaj al-karāma*, p. 373 lines 14–27; cf. ibid, p. 378 *supra*.

the conquest of Constantinople[28] as well as in the mythical city of Qāṭiʿ, on the shores of the Atlantic Ocean.[29] After the apocalyptic drama is over, there will not remain even one infidel in the lands of Islam.[30]

A lesson is to be learned from this description: huge armies are not able to achieve victory without divine help, while a small number can achieve it if God is on their side. We are not told why God allowed the *mahdī*'s army to be defeated for three consecutive days, but the description of the initial defeats followed by a final triumph certainly intensifies the dramatic atmosphere pervading the story.

After this victory, the *mahdī* will bestow innumerable gifts on the valiant warriors who brought it about. Yet because of the great number of the fallen, the people will not rejoice in this bounty. The apocalyptic victory was achieved at an unbearable price: in many households and tribes there was only one survivor out of a hundred. The *mahdī* will now engage in the organization of the Muslim countries and in giving the people their rights. He will dispatch his victorious armies in all directions and distribute treasures with his two hands in an unlimited manner.[31] Having accomplished these tasks, he will set out for Constantinople in order to conquer it. Following this conquest, "the whole face of the earth will come under the *mahdī*'s power" (*sipas tamām-i rū-yi zamīn bi-qabẓa-yi iqtidār-i mahdī āyad*).[32]

Classical Muslim apocalyptics include wars against Byzantines,[33] Jews,[34] Turks[35] and Indians.[36] Naturally enough, traditions related to India find their proper place in the apocalyptic vision of Ṣiddīq Ḥasan Khān. Like everything else in *ḥadīth* literature, the tradition concerning India is an early one: it is the Prophet's companion Abū Hurayra, who responds to this tradition by expressing his wish to participate in it. The tradition speaks

28 Ṣiddīq Ḥasan Khān, *Ḥujaj al-karāma*, pp. 378 lines 26–27; 379 line 11.

29 Ṣiddīq Ḥasan Khān, *Ḥujaj al-karāma*, p. 379 lines 19–20. For the city of Qāṭiʿ, see Cook, *Studies in Muslim Apocalyptic*, pp. 171–172.

30 Rafiʿ al-Dīn, *ʿAlāmāt-i qiyāmat*, p. 11, line 14.

31 For the boundless generosity of the *mahdī* in the classical traditions, see Chapter 1, Section IV.

32 Ṣiddīq Ḥasan Khān, *Ḥujaj al-karāma*, p. 374 *supra* (quotation in lines 6–7). Essentially the same story, in a slightly shorter version, can be found in Rafiʿ al-Dīn, *ʿAlāmāt-i qiyāmat*, pp. 6–7.

33 D. Cook, *Studies in Muslim Apocalyptic*, index, s.v. Byzantium and Byzantines.

34 See Bukhārī, *Ṣaḥīḥ*, vol. 2, pp. 229–230 (*Kitāb al-jihād*, 94).

35 See Bukhārī, *Ṣaḥīḥ*, vol. 2, p. 230 (*Kitāb al-jihād*, 95–96).

36 Nuʿaym b. Ḥammād, *Kitāb al-fitan*, pp. 252–253.

about a "king in Jerusalem" – probably identical with the *mahdī*[37] – who will send an army to India. The army will conquer the country, take hold of its treasures and bring back the captive Indian kings in chains. Except for this victorious result, we do not hear any details about the battles in which the army is expected to be engaged in India; nevertheless, it is clear that the *mahdī* initiates a military expedition to a distant land. When the warriors return, they find Jesus in Syria. This means that the Indian expedition is expected to take place in apocalyptic times.[38] Ṣiddīq Ḥasan Khān notes that some scholars from the eastern part of the Muslim world (*ba'ẓī 'ulamā'-i bilād-i mashriqiyya*) interpreted these traditions as relating to the *jihād* of Sayyid Aḥmad Barēlwī or some early Muslim incursions into India, but he rejects these attempts and asserts that they must be understood as apocalyptic ones.[39]

III THE "PEACEFUL" *MAHDĪ*

The chief protagonist of the idea that the *mahdī* will be a peaceful figure was Mīrzā Ghulām Aḥmad, the founder of the Aḥmadī movement in Islam. His biography, an analysis of his ideas and the significance of the movement which he established have been dealt with elsewhere.[40] Ghulām Aḥmad made numerous religious claims: he saw himself as the "renewer" (*mujaddid*) of the fourteenth Islamic century, "a person to whom Allah (or an angel) spoke" (*muḥaddath*), a *mahdī* and a prophet.[41] These religious claims created a storm of controversy as soon as they were made. The claim to prophethood led to the most serious rift with mainstream Islam and eventually caused the State of Pakistan – and many Muslim organizations – to declare the Aḥmadīs non-Muslims.

Ghulām Aḥmad's ideas about the *mahdī* are part and parcel of his reformulation of several central beliefs in Islam. His transformation of the *mahdī* into a peaceful figure is intimately related to his reformulation

37 D. Cook, *Studies in Muslim Apocalyptic*, pp. 172–182.

38 Nu'aym b. Ḥammād, *Fitan*, pp. 252–253; Nasā'ī, *Sunan*, vol. 6, p. 42; Ibn al-Athīr, *al-Nihāya fī gharīb al-ḥadīth wa al-athar*, s.v. *ḥ-r-r*. On the historical significance of these traditions, see Friedmann, "A Contribution to the Early History of Islam in India", pp. 318–319.

39 Ṣiddīq Ḥasan Khān, *Ḥujaj al-karāma*, p. 343 lines 17–26.

40 Friedmann, *Prophecy Continuous*, *passim*.

41 Friedmann, *Prophecy Continuous*, pp. 105–146.

of the idea of *jihād*. This reformulation should be understood against the background of a wide-ranging debate between Muslims, Christian missionaries and leaders of the Ārya Samāj concerning the nature of Islam. The debate began in the mid-nineteenth century when the Christian missionary C. G. Pfander published a number of polemical treatises in which he criticized various aspects of Islam. He saw in it a "system of falsehood", a "mire of error and superstition", and a religion the adherents of which "do not know of such a thing as prayer in the scriptural sense of the word".[42] He argued that Islam, with the help of the sword, was propagated by division of spoils, legalizing polygamy and promises of sensual paradise, and he asserted that such a religion cannot be divine.[43] Leaders of the Ārya Samāj argued in a similar vein and also took Islam to task for being a belligerent faith.[44] Pandit Lēkh Rām, a member of the Ārya Samāj, published in 1892 a book on *jihād*. He maintains that his times are a period in which science and intellect (*ʿilm o ʿaql*) make progress, when the wheel of freedom starts turning freely and educated people despise religious coercion. At this time, some modernist (*naycharī*) Muslims make the futile effort to say that Islam never waged *jihād*, no people were ever forced to embrace Islam, Muslims never destroyed any temple and never sacrificed cows in a temple. They say this in total disregard of dozens of Qurʾānic verses, prophetic traditions and historical facts.[45] Lekh Rām then adduces a long list of Qurʾānic verses which call for *jihād*[46] and gives extensive descriptions of the violent ways in which various geographical areas came under the sway of Islam.[47]

The best-known Muslim response to these attacks in English was written by Cheragh Ali, whose *A critical exposition of the popular jihād* asserted that "all the wars of Mohammad were defensive and that aggressive war or compulsory conversion is not allowed in the Koran".[48] The book was first published in 1885. Ghulām Aḥmad argued along similar lines and devoted a significant part of his activity to the refutation of the attacks on Islam and to the reformulation of the idea of *jihād*. As is well known, the Qurʾān includes numerous verses pertinent to this issue. Some verses speak

42 Pfander, *Remarks on the Nature of Muhammadanism*, pp. 3, 7 and *passim*.

43 Pfander, *Mizan-ul-Huqq* [sic], pp. 352–367; cf. Arabic version, pp. 232–233; Persian version, pp. 279–282; Urdu version, pp. 223–230.

44 Jones, *Arya Dharm*, pp. 148–153; Friedmann, *Prophecy Continuous*, pp. 8–9.

45 Lēkh Rām, *Risāla-yi jihād*, pp. 1–2.

46 Lēkh Rām, *Risāla-yi jihād*, pp. 3–15.

47 Lēkh Rām, *Risāla-yi jihād*, pp. 24–58.

48 Cheragh Ali, *A Critical Exposition of Popular Jihad*, title page.

about explicitly defensive war, while others speak about a war initiated by Muslims. Classical commentators of the Qur'ān and scholars of *fiqh* interpreted the diverse Qur'ānic ideas about *jihād* by using the exegetical principle of abrogation (*naskh*), according to which verses revealed or composed in the later years of the Prophet's career may abrogate rulings included in verses revealed or composed earlier. The "circumstances of revelation" (*asbāb al-nuzūl*) literature maintains, in general, that the "defensive" verses are earlier than the "offensive" ones and the "defensive" verses are therefore abrogated. A convenient summary of this development can be found in al-Qasṭallānī's commentary on al-Bukhārī's *Ṣaḥīḥ*:

> [The *jihad*] was forbidden before the *hijra*; after it the Prophet was ordered to fight those who fought him; then it was allowed to initiate fighting except during the sacred months; then the Prophet was ordered to engage in *jihād* without restriction. (*wa kāna qabla 'l-hijra muḥharraman thumma umira ba'dahā bi-qitāli man qātalahu thumma ubīḥa al-ibtidā' bihi fī ghayr al-ashhur al-ḥurum thumma umira bihi muṭlaqan.*)[49]

The unconditional order to fight prevailed in Muslim jurisprudential discourse. Having surveyed the meanings of *jihād* in the Qur'ān, Ella Landau-Tasseron maintains that "very little of the peaceful sense of *j-h-d* remained in Muslim culture and the understanding of *jihād as* war became predominant".[50] The same idea is expressed by the eleventh-century Ḥanafī scholar Abū Bakr al-Sarakhsī who surveys the development of the commandment of *jihād* in the Qur'ān and concludes by saying: "The matter settled on the obligation of *jihād* against the polytheists. This is an obligation which will be valid until the Day of Judgment" (*fa-'staqarra al-amr 'alā faraḍiyyat al-jihād ma'a al-mushrikīn wa huwa farḍun qā'imun ilā qiyām al-sā'a*).[51]

In reformulating the concept of *jihād*, Ghulām Aḥmad abandoned the idea of internal abrogation of Qur'ānic verses and restricted the meaning of abrogation to the abrogation of former religions by Islam. This is not an unknown approach in classical exegesis: in the same way as Christianity maintained that it abrogated Judaism, some Muslim thinkers believed that

49 Qasṭallānī, *Irshād al-sārī*, vol. 6, p. 275.
50 Landau-Tasseron, "Jihād", in the *Encyclopaedia of the Qur'ān*, s.v.
51 Sarakhsī, *al-Mabsūṭ*, vol. 10, pp. 2–3.

Islam replaced both Judaism and Christianity.[52] This approach is integral to the Aḥmadī emphasis on the unquestionable validity and unsurpassable beauty of the Qur'ān in its entirety, and Ghulām Aḥmad transformed it into a central tool in his reinterpretation of *jihād*. By abandoning the idea that a ruling included in one verse can be abrogated by a ruling included in a verse revealed later, he created a situation in which all Qur'ānic verses carry the same authority. Naturally enough, this does not remove the contradictions from the Qur'ānic text, but it allows Ghulām Aḥmad to provide an interpretation without resorting to the abrogation (*naskh*) principle. The period in which a verse was composed or revealed is now devoid of any importance. What is important are the circumstances in which the revelatory process took place. In Ghulām Aḥmad's view, if there are in the Qur'ān contradictions on a certain issue, one should act according to verses which were revealed in circumstances similar to his own. The verses enjoining unrestricted *jihād* were revealed when Islam was facing military attack and was in danger of physical extinction; therefore, military *jihād* was called for. In nineteenth-century India, the situation is different: Islam is not in physical danger because the British government has granted religious freedom to its Muslim subjects. However, Islam is facing the polemical attacks of the Christian missionaries who systematically defame Islam and its founder. These attacks can be repelled only by arguments, not by the sword. Thus, the appropriate way to fight for Islam in nineteenth-century India is by preaching and refuting the slanderous attacks of the Christian missionaries.[53]

Ghulām Aḥmad's reformulation of the idea of *jihād* is designed to promote the image of Islam as a peaceful religion. The same purpose is served by transforming the pugnacious *mahdī*, described in the classical *ḥadīth* and adopted by Ṣiddīq Ḥasan Khān, into a peaceful figure in order to prove that Islam's vision for the Last Day is not bellicose and does not strive for the eschatological destruction of all religions other than Islam. Ghulām Aḥmad also needs to contend with the Muslim traditions referring to the second coming of Jesus and with the violent actions – both symbolic and concrete – which Jesus is expected to perform. We shall

52 See J. Burton, "Abrogation", and C. P. Adang, "Torah", in the *Encyclopaedia of the Qur'ān*, s.v.

53 For a more extensive discussion of the transformation of *jihād* in Aḥmadī thinking, see Friedmann, *Prophecy Continuous*, pp. 165–180. See also Ghulām Aḥmad, *I'jāz al-masīḥ*, pp. 156–157.

now analyse the nature of the whole eschatological drama as presented by Ghulām Aḥmad, looking at the anticipated activities of the *mahdī*, of the *dajjāl* and of Jesus – all of whom are active participants in the drama preceding the Last Day.

As we have shown elsewhere,[54] Ghulām Aḥmad made several religious claims during the twenty-eight years of his career. He claimed to be the "renewer" (*mujaddid*) of the fourteenth Islamic century, "a person spoken to (by God or an angel)" (*muḥaddath*), a *mahdī* and *masīḥ* and, finally, a prophet. The titles *mahdī* and *masīḥ* will be treated here. Ghulām Aḥmad's standard appellation in the Aḥmadī movement is "the Promised Messiah" (*al-masīḥ al-maw'ūd*) or "the Promised Messiah and *mahdī*" (*al-masīḥ al-maw'ūd wa al-mahdī al-ma'hūd*).[55] His successors in the leadership of the movement bear the title "successor of the Messiah" (*khalīfat al-masīḥ*). Ghulām Aḥmad's understanding of these titles has to be analysed against the background of his polemical activities against the Christian missionaries and against Christianity in general.

In Chapter 1 we surveyed the eschatological drama as described in the classical Muslim literature. A cardinal element in this drama is the appearance of the *mahdī*. Ghulām Aḥmad considered the expectation of such a reformer to be common to many nations,[56] but thought that the decadence of Islam in his times makes the appearance of such a figure in Islam an absolute necessity. He was convinced that Allah entrusted him with this task not only with regard to Muslims in India, but also with regard to Muslims everywhere. This is clear from the fact that Ghulām Aḥmad wrote on this topic in Urdu, Persian and Arabic and some of his books are bi-lingual.[57] The multilingual nature of his literary production indicates his desire to reach out to the Islamic world in its entirety.

In his capacity as *masīḥ* and *mahdī*, Ghulām Aḥmad will "call to God with gentleness, abolish war, place the destructive sword in its sheath and muster the people by signs from the Merciful rather than by sword and spear" (*yad'ū ilā Allāh bi-'l-ḥilm yaḍa'u al-ḥarb wa yuqarrib al-sayf al-mujīḥ – dar ghilāf kunad shamshīr-i halāk kunandah-rā, pas ḥashr-i*

54 Friedmann, *Prophecy Continuous*, pp. 105–146.
55 At times Ghulām Aḥmad himself uses these terms; see Ghulām Aḥmad, *I'jāz al-masīḥ*, pp. 8, 71 (in *Rūḥānī Khazā'in*, vol. 18).
56 Ghulām Aḥmad, *Rūḥānī Khazā'in*, second series, vol. 10 (*Malfūẓāt*), p. 445.
57 Such as *I'jāz al-masīḥ* (Arabic and Persian).

mardum bar nishān-hā-yi khudā shawad, na bi nēza o sinān).[58] The task of the *mahdī* is to put an end to wars and elevate the word of Islam by prayer and pen. The traditions about the "bloody *mahdī*" (*khūnī mahdī*) are all false, not only according to Ghulām Aḥmad, but also according to thinkers such as Nadhīr Ḥusayn and Muḥammad Ḥusayn Baṭālwī.[59] "Do not forget the tradition about the abolition of war" (*wa lā tansaw ḥadītha yaḍa ʿu al-ḥarb*), says Ghulām Aḥmad.[60]

In order to substantiate his messianic claim on the basis of the Muslim tradition, Ghulām Aḥmad draws inspiration from the theological discussions relating to the "beautiful names" (*al-asmāʾ al-ḥusnā*) of Allāh. He gives an extensive analysis of the divine names *al-raḥmān* and *al-raḥīm*, of the prophetic names Muḥammad and Aḥmad and of the two aspects of divinity: the divine awe (*jalāl*) and the divine beauty (*jamāl*). These distinctions give him the opportunity to describe two ways in which God operates in the world and two characteristics which He bestowed on the Muslim community. He sees great importance in the analogy between God who has two aspects and Muḥammad who was given two names, while prophets such as Moses and Jesus were given one name only.[61]

In Ghulām Aḥmad's analysis, the divine epithet *al-raḥmān* conveys that aspect of divine mercy which has existed since all eternity, even before creation, and does not depend on man's obedience or disobedience; it is bestowed on believers, infidels and animals alike. It also represents God's awe and coercive force (*qahr*) which subdues all creatures to humans and allows killing inferior beings for the sake of superior ones (*qatl alladhī huwa adnā li-'lladhī huwa aʿlā*): worms are killed to protect camels, and camels are killed to provide food and clothing for humans. This use of coercive force enables God to be merciful to mankind. In the Muslim community, this type of divine mercy is reflected in the Prophet's name Muḥammad and in his companions who killed some people in order to save others from going astray. They extirpated polytheists by the sword and fulfilled

58 Ghulām Aḥmad, *Iʿjāz al-masīḥ*, p. 144; *idem*, *Āʾina-yi kamālāt-i islām*, p. 456. For the "abolition of war" in the classical *ḥadīth* collections, see Chapter 1, at notes 30, 61, 63, 65.

59 Ghulām Aḥmad, *Lecture Ludhyāna*, p. 279. Both were members of the *ahl-i ḥadīth*. For a description of this movement, see Ahmad, *Islamic Modernism*, pp. 113–122 and Khān, *Taḥrīk-i ahl-i ḥadīth*.

60 Ghulām Aḥmad, *al-Hudā wa al-tabṣira li-man yarā*, in *Rūḥānī Khazāʾin*, vol. 18, p. 319. See Bukhārī, *Ṣaḥīḥ*, vol. 2, p. 370 (*Kitāb al-anbiyāʾ*, 49).

61 Ghulām Aḥmad, *Iʿjāz al-masīḥ*, p. 107.

the duties of the "Muḥammadī attribute" (*ṣifat al-muḥammadiyya*). From this point of view, Muḥammad was a prophet of the same kind as Moses who also reflected divine awe.[62]

God planned to bestow both *raḥmāniyya* and *raḥīmiyya* on the Muslim community. *Raḥmāniyya* was bestowed on Muḥammad and his companions who resemble from this viewpoint Moses and his companions. *Raḥīmiyya*, which is a different type of mercy and is bestowed as recompense for performing good deeds and abandoning base desires, represents the other aspect of divine activity in the world. It represents the prophetic name Aḥmad, God's beauty (*jamāl*) and kindness as well as the prophetic characteristics of Jesus. Jesus and Aḥmad are identical in their essence, compatible in their nature and indicate beauty and abandonment of warlike characteristics (*fa-inna 'sma 'Īsā wa 'sma Aḥmad muttaḥidāni fī al-huwiyya wa mutawāfiqāni fī al-ṭabī'a yadullāni 'alā al-jamāl wa tark al-qitāl min ḥaythu al-kayfiyya*). Ghulām Aḥmad identifies himself with the divine name Aḥmad, says that God made his heart full of mercy and gentleness and that he is the promised *mahdī* and *masīḥ*.[63]

The duality of Muḥammad and Aḥmad is explained also in a different manner. Discussing the expression *rabb al- 'ālamīn*, Ghulām Aḥmad asserts that in the *'ālamīn* there was a time in which the Prophet Muḥammad was sent. At another time, God will send "Aḥmad of the end of time" (*Aḥmad ākhir al-zamān*) who is called *masīḥ* and *mahdī*. These are the two Aḥmads who were granted divine revelation (*awḥā fīhi ilā Aḥmadayn*).[64] In the latter's time, God will show a "model" (*namūdhaj*) of the resurrection; it will be "a Day of Judgment before the Day of Judgment" (*yawm al-dīn qabla yawm al-dīn*) and will occur during the lifetime of Ghulām Aḥmad.[65]

One of the most important themes in Aḥmadī world view and in Aḥmadī polemics is the denial of the crucifixion of Jesus and of his second coming. On these issues Ghulām Aḥmad came into conflict both with the Christian missionaries and with his Sunnī adversaries. The missionaries believed both in the crucifixion and in the second coming, while the Sunnī mainstream denied the crucifixion (on the basis of Qur'ān 4:157)[66] but believed in

62 Ghulām Aḥmad, *I'jāz al-masīḥ*, pp. 112–114, 117, 126, 151 and *passim*.
63 Ghulām Aḥmad, *I'jāz al-masīḥ*, pp. 110–111.
64 Ghulām Aḥmad, *I'jāz al-masīḥ*, pp. 138–139.
65 Ghulām Aḥmad, *I'jāz al-masīḥ*, pp. 144, 153–154.
66 "We (i.e., the People of the Book) slew the Messiah, Jesus the son of Mary, the Messenger of God" – yet they did not slay him, neither crucified him, only a likeness of that was shown to them."

the second coming. The fact that mainstream Sunnī *ʿulamāʾ* supported the idea of the second coming placed Ghulām Aḥmad in an advantageous position in his polemics: he could castigate his Sunnī adversaries for supporting the beliefs of Christians and for helping them in their proselytizing activities among Muslims.

Ghulām Aḥmad devoted much attention to propagate the idea that Jesus died a natural death and will never return to earth again. The second coming of a prophet like Jesus would contradict the status of Muḥammad as the "seal of the prophets".[67] The assertion that Jesus died is a boost for the denial of his second coming. In one of his early works, Ghulām Aḥmad mentions the death of Jesus in Galilee,[68] but later he developed the idea for which he became famous: after the attempt to crucify Jesus was foiled by God, he was taken down from the cross, recuperated from his wounds, travelled to Kashmir, died a natural death in Srinagar at the age of 120 years and was laid to rest there.[69]

Jesus is thus dead and will never come to earth again. His burial in Srinagar is supported by an interpretation of Qurʾān 23:50 where it is said that God gave Jesus and Mary refuge upon "a height where was a hollow and a spring" (*rabwa dhāt qarār wa maʿīn*).[70]

The question whether Jesus is alive or dead has been important in Christian-Muslim polemics since medieval times: Christian polemicists relished in comparing Jesus who is alive in heaven, sitting at the right hand of God, with Muḥammad who died and is buried in Medina with decayed

---

67 Ghulām Aḥmad, *Tuḥfa Gōlaŕwiyya*, p. 174; Friedmann, *Prophecy Continuous*, pp. 116–117.

68 Ghulām Aḥmad, *Izāla-yi awhām*, p. 473.

69 Ghulām Aḥmad devoted a distinct book to the substantiation of this notion: *Masīḥ Hindustān mēñ*. This was translated into English as *Jesus in India*. See also Ghulām Aḥmad, *Barāhīn-i Aḥmadiyya*, vol. 5, pp. 262 (margin) - 263, 351; *idem*, *al-Hudā wa al-tabṣira li-man yarā*, pp. 319–320, 361–362, 371–373. The incompatibility of the view that Jesus died in Galilee and that he wandered to Kashmir and died there is denounced in Siyālkōtī's polemics against the Aḥmadīs in *al-Khabar al-ṣaḥīḥ ʿan qabr al-masīḥ*, p. 5. The idea that Jesus spent some of his years in India was propagated by the Russian author Nicolas Notovitch in his *The Unknown Life of Jesus Christ, from Buddhist Records*. Ghulām Aḥmad mentioned this book in an appendix to *Jesus in India*, though the Notovitch story is not identical with his own. For the controversy aroused by the book of Notovitch and his admission that he fabricated the evidence, see McGetchin, *Indology, Indomania and Orientalism*, p. 133.

70 For a more extensive discussion of the Aḥmadī view of the crucifixion and ascension of Jesus, see Friedmann. *Prophecy Continuous*, pp. 110–115 and the sources quoted there. See also Muhmammad Ali, *The Holy Qurʾān*, pp. 231–232, notes 645–650.

bones: from this comparison they drew the conclusion that Christianity is superior to Islam. While engaging in this kind of polemics with mainstream Muslims, the Christians were in an exceedingly advantageous position: they could use the sacred literature of their Muslim adversaries in order to prove their belief that Jesus is alive. On the other hand, the mainstream Muslims found themselves in a precarious situation: their Christian opponents could find support for their stance in the Muslim sources.

Ghulām Aḥmad resolved to extricate Islam from this predicament. He was convinced that if a religion's founder is deemed to be alive, his religion is bound to prosper and increase in numbers and strength. He considered the belief in the life of Jesus as the principal reason for the substantial increase in the number of Indian Christians during his lifetime and thought that this belief serves as a weapon for converting Muslims to Christianity. He quotes a conversation with Christian priests who told him that Christianity would not survive if it is proven that Jesus is dead. If he is dead, neither his vicarious suffering (*kaffāra*), nor his divinity (*ulūhiyyat*), nor his sonship (*ibniyyat*) can be sustained and this would result in the demise of Christianity. On the other hand, he asserts, if the Prophet Muḥammad was believed to be alive, not even one infidel would remain on the face of the earth.[71] Ghulām Aḥmad therefore devoted tremendous efforts to "prove" that Jesus was dead. He asserted: "By God, there is life for Islam in the death of the son of Mary" (*wa 'llāhi, innī arā ḥayāt al-islām fī mawt Ibn Maryam*).[72]

To prove that Jesus is indeed dead and will never appear on earth again required a reinterpretation of several Qur'ānic verses. The most important is Qur'ān 3:55 which we have already discussed in Chapter 1.[73] Ghulām Aḥmad argues that the sequence of the verbs in *innī mutawaffīka wa rāfi'uka ilayya* means: "I cause you to die and raise you to myself" and indicates that the ascension of Jesus took place after his death. Those who reverse the sequence of events as described in the Qur'ān and claim that Jesus was raised alive are guilty of corrupting the Qur'ānic text (*taḥrīf*). In other Aḥmadī writings, the raising of Jesus is not to be understood literally but rather in a metaphorical way: God raised Jesus in rank, elevating his

71 Ghulām Aḥmad, *Lecture Ludhyāna*, in *Rūḥānī Khazā'in*, vol. 20, p. 264; cf. *idem*, *Lecture Lahore*, in *Rūḥānī Khazā'in*, vol. 20, p. 196.

72 Ghulām Aḥmad, *al-Hudā wa al-tabṣira li-man yarā*, p. 320; *idem*, *Barāhīn-i Aḥmadiyya*, vol. 5, p. 406; cf. Friedmann, *Prophecy Continuous*, p. 115.

73 See Chapter 1, Section IV.

stature, honouring him and bringing him close to Himself in the spiritual, rather than corporal, sense (*fa-'l-raf'u hunā rif'at al-maqām wa al-darajāt wa al-tashrīf wa al-taqrīb rūḥiyyan lā jasadiyyan*).[74] Qur'ān 5:121[75] is also interpreted as proving the death of Jesus. The verse says that when Jesus was alive, he was a "witness" over his community, but when God took him to Himself – which is understood by the Aḥmadīs as death – God took over as a "watcher" (*raqīb*) over them.[76] Another verse which serves the same Aḥmadī purpose is Qur'ān 4:158: "There is not one of the People of the Book but will assuredly believe in him before his death (*qabla mawtihi*) and on the Day of Resurrection he will be a witness against them." As we have shown in Chapter 1, this has been interpreted as saying that when Jesus descends to earth before the Day of Judgment, all People of the Book will believe in him before he dies after the completion of his apocalyptic role.[77] This understanding is not compatible with the Aḥmadī denial of the second coming. The Aḥmadīs therefore prefer to relate the pronoun in "before his death" to a scriptuary, one of the People of the Book. From their point of view, it is even better to accept the Qur'ānic reading (*qirā'a*) of Ubayy b. Ka'b, "before their death" (*qabla mawtihim*): in this case it is clear that the verse does not refer to the death of Jesus in the apocalyptic period, but rather to the death of the People of the Book.[78]

Ghulām Aḥmad needed also to reinterpret numerous prophetic traditions. In the classical descriptions of the Prophet's ascension to heaven (*mi'rāj*), we read that Muḥammad saw Jesus and other prophets on his way to meet God in the seventh heaven. He greeted them all and they returned his greetings. This seems to indicate that all the prophets, including Jesus, are alive in heaven.[79] The Aḥmadī interpretation is different: Muḥammad met in heaven only spirits of dead prophets – none of them was alive.[80]

74 Friedmann, *Prophecy Continuous*, p. 114 and the sources quoted there; Aḥmad, *al-Qawl al-ṣarīḥ fī ẓuhūr al-mahdī wa al-masīḥ*, pp. 6–7.
75 Jesus says in this verse: "And I was a witness over them, while I remained among them; but when You took me (*tawaffaytanī*) to Yourself, You were Yourself the watcher over them."
76 Ghulām Aḥmad, *Barāhīn-i Aḥmadiyya*, vol. 5, in *Rūḥānī Khazā'in*, vol. 21, p. 51; Aḥmad, *Masīḥ awr mahdī ḥaźrat Muḥammad kī naźar mēñ*, pp. 3–4.
77 See Chapter 1 at note 79.
78 Aḥmad, *al-Qawl al-ṣarīḥ fī ẓuhūr al-mahdī wa al-masīḥ*, p. 24.
79 Bukhārī, *Ṣaḥīḥ*, vol. 3, pp. 31–33 (*Kitāb manāqib al-anṣār, bāb al-mi'rāj* (42)).
80 Ghulām Aḥmad, *Tadhkirat al-shahādatayn*, in *Rūḥānī Khazā'in*, vol. 20, p. 22; *idem*, *Lecture Ludhyāna*, in *Rūḥānī Khazā'in*, vol. 20, pp. 266–267; cf. Aḥmad, *Masīḥ awr mahdī ḥazrat Muḥammad kī naẓar mayñ*, p. 2.

It was even more important to reinterpret the numerous traditions in which the second coming of Jesus is explicitly mentioned. Ghulām Aḥmad asserts that whenever the second coming is mentioned in the Muslim tradition, it means not the second coming of Jesus himself, but of a Muslim who is similar to him (*mathīl-i* ʿĪsā). This person is Ghulām Aḥmad who is the manifestation of Jesus and who is to be considered not only the Promised Messiah (*masīḥ mawʿūd*) of the Muslims, but also of the Christians. He bears absolute affinity with Jesus: "We became like one thing, bearing the same name" (*wa ṣirnā ka-shayʾ wāḥid yaqaʿ ʿalayhi ism wāḥid*).[81] It is important to observe that in denying that Jesus is alive and in asserting that he will never come again, Ghulām Aḥmad is struggling – at the same time – against the perception of Christians and of mainstream Muslims: both believe in the second coming of Jesus. From the vantage point of his polemics against mainstream Muslims, he was in an advantageous position: he could accuse his Muslim adversaries of supporting the Christian viewpoint.[82]

In contradistinction to all the other *mahdī*s discussed in the present work, Ghulām Aḥmad's spiritual claim went beyond the boundaries of the Muslim community. He believed that God sent him to reform not only Muslims, but Christians and Hindūs as well. This is the reason why Ghulām Aḥmad bears affinity also with Raja Krishna: "From the point of view of spiritual reality, I am he" (*rūḥāni ḥaqīqat kē rū sē mayñ wuhī hūñ*). Raja Krishna was a "perfect man", an *avatār* of the Hindūs. In Ghulām Aḥmad's understanding, this means that Krishna was a prophet of his times. The spirit of God descended upon him. He was victorious (*fatḥmand*) and fortunate (*bā iqbāl*) and cleansed Aryavarta from evil. He was full with the love of God and God promised that he will create an avatar of his at the end of times. This promise was fulfilled by the appearance of Ghulām Aḥmad who received a revelation (*ilhām*) saying: "Oh Krishna, the formidable protector of cows, your greatness is written in the Gītā" (*hay Krishna rawdra gōpāl tērī mahmā Gītā mēñ likhī gaʾī hay*). He continues saying: "I love Krishna because I am his manifestation" (*sō mayñ Krishna sē maḥabbat kartā hūñ kyūn kih mayñ us kā maẓhar hūñ*). Qualities attributed to Krishna such as eradication of vice, sympathy for the poor and their protection are also the qualities

81 Friedmann, *Prophecy Continuous*, p. 117.
82 Ghulām Aḥmad, *al-Hudā wa al-tabṣira li-man yarā*, p. 317.

of the Promised Messiah. It is thus possible to say that Krishna and the Promised Messiah are one and the same in the spiritual sense. They differ only in popular parlance (*qawmī iṣṭilāḥ*). Ghulām Aḥmad is keenly aware of the danger that assuming the identity of an infidel will result in being himself considered an infidel by "ignorant" Muslims, but in his view, this is a recurring divine revelation (*waḥy*) which cannot be kept secret.[83]

Describing the religious history of the world from creation to the seventh millennium, Ghulām Aḥmad comes to the conclusion that his lifetime is the messianic period. Without quoting a specific source, he maintains that God determined the age of the world to be seven thousand years;[84] in his view, this is clear from the books of all the prophets as well as from the Qur'ān. Each millennium has its peculiar characteristics. Millennia of divine guidance alternate with millennia of error (*khudā nē ... hidāyat awr gumrāhī kē li'ē hazār hazār sāl kē dawr muqarrar ki'ē hayñ*). The first millennium after creation was one of guidance – there was no sign of polytheism in it. In the second millennium the situation was reversed and this millennium saw the ascendancy of polytheism. Probably referring to the activities of Abraham, the foundations of monotheism were laid in the third millennium. In the fourth millennium there was again ascendancy of polytheism. In that millennium, the religiosity of the Children of Israel changed for the worse. The Christian religion came into being, but immediately became dry and moribund. The fifth millennium was again one of guidance. It is the millennium in which Muḥammad was sent and established monotheism for the second time. This was a millennium which was determined since all eternity (*rōz-i azal sē*) for Muḥammad's appearance. The sixth millennium is again one of error. It started after the third century AH – which ended on 17 August 912 CE – and continued until the beginning of the fourteenth – which started on 12 November 1882, this is to say very close to the beginning of Ghulām Aḥmad's activity in 1880. The Prophet called the people of this millennium "the crooked

83 Ghulām Aḥmad, *Islām* [*Lecture Siyālkōt*] in *Rūḥānī Khazā'in*, vol. 20, pp. 228–229. For different versions of the revelation concerning Krishna, see Ghulām Aḥmad, *Tadhkira*, pp. 380–381; English translation: Zafrullah Khan, *Tadhkira*, pp. 220–221. Cf. Friedmann, *Prophecy continuous*, pp. 123–124.

84 For a convenient summary of Muslim traditions on the seven millennia of the world's existence, see al-Suyūṭī, *al-Kashf*, pp. 249–251. These traditions maintain that the Prophet Muḥammad was sent at the end of the sixth millennium and paint a picture different from that of Ghulām Aḥmad.

crowd" (*fayj-i a'waj*). Similarly, to Adam, who was created at the end of the sixth day of creation, Ghulām Aḥmad was born at the end of the sixth millennium "with the rank of Adam" (*Ādam kē rang par*), and manifested himself at the beginning of the seventh which is destined to be the last one. It is hence inescapable that the "*imām* of the last days" (*imām-i ākhir al-zamān*) be born in this period. This *imām* is both the *mujaddid* of the (fourteenth) century and the *mujaddid* of the last millennium.[85] After him there will be no *imām* nor *masīḥ*; in this millennium the world will come to an end.[86]

In another description of human history, Ghulām Aḥmad reviews the developing relationships between the nations of the world. In the earliest period, immediately following creation, there was only one human being with his small family. In the second period, the duration of which is not specified, people split into numerous nations and religions and spread all over the world without knowing much about each other. In the third one, nations gained more mutual awareness, some difficulties in travel were removed and new ways of meeting between nations became feasible. Some nations reached out to their counterparts and certain nations adopted religions of other nations, though to a limited extent. The description of these three periods is designed to show that the fourth period, in which Ghulām Aḥmad appeared, is substantially different from the previous ones and its characteristics have been predicted in the Qur'ān. Providing radically new interpretations of a few Qur'ānic verses and prophetic traditions, Ghulām Aḥmad concludes that his period is close to the Day of Resurrection and is the period in which the Promised Messiah is to appear. Several verses in Qur'ān 81, which classical exegesis understood as listing the signs of the approaching Hour, are given new meanings. The abandonment of pregnant camels in Qur'ān 81:4, which classical commentators understood to mean that even the most precious possessions will be of no value when the Hour strikes, is taken to mean the development of new means of travel, such as steamships and railways which replace the camels and bring the various parts of the world close to each other. The prophetic *ḥadīth* which says that "the young camels will be abandoned and will not be ridden (*yutraku*

85 For a discussion of the idea of a "millennial renewer" in the Islamic tradition, see Friedmann, *Shaykh Aḥmad Sirhindī*, pp. 13–21.
86 *Islām* [*Lecture Siyālkōt*] in *Rūḥānī Khazā'in*, vol. 20, pp. 207–209.

al-qilāṣu fa-lā yusʿā ʿalayhā) is given the same meaning.[87] The "coupling of souls",[88] which was understood in classical exegesis as joining people with similar records in their lifetimes in order to send them together to Paradise or Hell, or as a reference to the reuniting of the souls with their bodies after resurrection,[89] is interpreted as the coming together of various nations, the improvement of communication between people and the emergence of a changed world – "a worldwide revolution" (*ēk ʿālamgīr inqilāb ẓuhūr mēñ āyā gūyā dunyā badal gaʾī*).[90] This will not happen before nations engage in religious quarrels and wars which will spread hatred and divisions between people.

> When these things come to a completion, God will blow His trumpet from heaven; by means of the Promised Messiah, who is His trumpet, God will call out to the world. Those who are fortunate to hear this call, will unite in one religion, divisions will be removed and the various nations of the world will become one.

Those who refuse this call, will be punished in Hell.[91] All this has been predicted in Qurʾān 18:100.[92]

In order to complete the transformation of the eschatological drama into a peaceful one, Ghulām Aḥmad also needs to reinterpret the classical material about the *dajjāl*. As we have seen in Chapter 1,[93] the classical *ḥadīth* describes the *dajjāl* as a concrete, appalling and frightful figure, intent on fighting Jesus with the help of the Jews, and destined to be killed by him at the gates of Lydda before the end of days. Since Ghulām Aḥmad has identified himself with Jesus and Jesus plays a violent role in the classical perception of the eschatological drama, he needs to

87 Ghulām Aḥmad, *Chashma-yi maʿrifat*, in *Rūḥānī Khazāʾin*, vol. 23, p. 81, note. For the same motif in later Aḥmadī literature, see Aḥmad, *al-Qawl al-ṣarīḥ fī ẓuhūr al-mahdī wa al-masīḥ*, pp. 111–112.

88 Qurʾān 81:7

89 Ṭabarī, *Jāmiʿ al-bayān*, vol. 30, pp. 70–71 (on Qurʾān 81:6).

90 Ghulām Aḥmad, *Chashma-yi maʿrifat*, in *Rūḥānī Khazāʾin*, vol. 23, pp. 81–83 (quotation on p. 82); Aḥmad, *al-Qawl al-ṣarīḥ fī ẓuhūr al-mahdī wa al-masīḥ*, pp. 112–113.

91 Ghulām Aḥmad, *Chashma-yi maʿrifat*, pp. 83–85.

92 "Upon that day, we shall leave them surging on one another and the Trumpet shall be blown, and We shall gather them and upon that day, we shall present Hell to the unbelievers ..."

93 See Chapter 1, Section III.

give a new interpretation to the apocalyptic struggle between Jesus and the *dajjāl*. This is done in several ways which are not always compatible with each other. Noting that the *dajjāl* is not mentioned in the Qur'ān, Ghulām Aḥmad concludes that the personified *dajjāl* is only a figment of people's imagination (*laysa dajjālukum illā fī ru'ūsikum ka-'l-takhayyulāt*).[94] He attempts to undermine the common perception of this apocalyptic figure in several ways. Identifying the *dajjāl* with Satan (*shayṭān*) or *Iblīs*[95] serves his purpose well because both are Qur'ānic figures who take no part in the apocalyptic drama. Throughout history, Satan used to send his offspring in order to destroy religion and lead people astray. At the end of the seventh millennium – in which the world will come to an end – he will be killed. But in contradistinction to the classical *ḥadīth*

> he will be killed by a heavenly lance which means the grace of God, not by human force. There will be neither war no beating, only a command coming down from the Presence of the One God (*wa lā yuqtalu al-dajjāl illā bi-'l-ḥirba al-samāwiyya ay bi-faḍlin min Allāh lā bi-'l-ṭāqa al-bashariyya fa-lā ḥarb wa lā ḍarb wa lākin amr nāzil min al-ḥaḍra al-aḥadiyya*).[96]

Thus, the times of the *dajjāl* are coming to a close. He will still meet a violent death, but he will not be killed by Jesus or by any other human agency, but rather by divine intervention. In some places Ghulām Aḥmad goes even further and says that the killing of the *dajjāl* only means that he will be overpowered by force of arguments. Defeating enemies by force of arguments is a recurring motif in Ghulām Aḥmad's thought, and is frequently used in the Aḥmadī perception of *jihād*.[97]

Ghulām Aḥmad supports his reinterpretation of the apocalyptic drama and the transformation of the *dajjāl* by asserting that when God speaks about things transcendental, He uses varied ways of expression (*inna*

94 Ghulām Aḥmad, *al-Hudā wa al-tabṣira li-man yarā*, in *Rūḥānī Khazā'in*, vol. 18, p. 339 *infra*.

95 Ghulām Aḥmad, *I'jāz al-masīḥ*, p. 88; *idem*, *Malfūẓāt*, vol. 10, p. 60.

96 Ghulām Aḥmad, *I'jāz al-masīḥ*, pp. 85–87; *idem*, *Tuḥfa Gōlaŕwiyya*, pp. 268–269. Cf. *idem*, *Malfūẓāt*, vol. 10, p. 180 where Ghulām Aḥmad says that in his time the *dajjāl* will disappear.

97 Ghulām Aḥmad, *Tuḥfa Gōlaŕwiyya*, p. 240 note; *idem*, *Malfūẓāt*, in *Rūḥānī Khazā'in*, vol. 10, p. 180; cf. Friedmann, *Prophecy Continuous*, pp. 177–178.

li-'llāhi 'inda dhikr anbā' al-ghayb alsina shattā). Sometimes he uses explicit words which clearly describe the intended realities; at other times he uses exaggerated or metaphorical language (*lisān al-tajawwuz wa 'l-isti'āra*). For instance, Abraham's dream in which he was instructed to sacrifice his son was only a metaphor for sacrificing the ram. The divine promise to aid the Muslims in the Battle of Badr with five thousand angels[98] is not to be understood literally. God wanted to allay the worries of the Muslims and spoke about five thousand angels though even one of them would have been sufficient to defeat the enemy.[99]

The assumption that metaphorical language is used in the sacred literature of Islam enables Ghulām Aḥmad to move the *dajjāl* from the mythical realm to modern history and to maintain that he is not an individual, but a metaphor for certain human groups. He mentions first the philosophers, by whom he means the atheists. They deny the existence of God, and lean toward this world to such an extent that they consider religion unnecessary and totally concentrate on their worldly advancement.[100] More important is Ghulām Aḥmad's identification of the *dajjāl* with Christians in general and with Christian missionaries in particular. In contradistinction to the classical *ḥadīth* which routinely associated the *dajjāl* with Jews,[101] Ghulām Aḥmad exempts the Jews of this association, arguing that they are in a state of humiliation, are not masters of their destiny and it is therefore impossible that the *dajjāl* would emerge in their midst.[102] He replaces Jews with the Christians who now play the role of the villain in his description of the apocalypse. Focusing on the Christians in this matter can be easily understood if we keep in mind that Ghulām Aḥmad devoted a substantial amount of his time to polemical encounters with Christian missionaries, and to the refutation of the Christian belief in the second coming of Jesus.[103] Time and again he asserts that he appeared in a period when Christianity is in power, or, in his words, during "the dominance of the cross" (*ṣalīb kā ghalaba*). The religion of the cross spreads oppression and deceit. It is the most severe and dangerous affliction that Islam has ever suffered. Christian men and women defame Islam and try to convert people to Christianity.

98 Qur'ān 3:125.
99 Ghulām Aḥmad, *Ā'ina-yi kamālāt-i islām*, pp. 446–449; *idem*, *Malfūẓāt*, in *Rūḥānī Khazā'in*, vol. 4, pp. 23–25.
100 Ghulām Aḥmad, *Malfūẓāt*, in *Rūḥānī Khazā'in*, vol. 9, p. 304.
101 See Chapter 1, at notes 41–44.
102 Ghulām Aḥmad, *Ā'ina-yi kamālāt-i Islām*, p. 452.
103 Friedmann, *Prophecy Continuous*, pp. 6–7, 111–118.

They do this even in hospitals and engage in preaching Christianity while administering medicine to their Muslim patients. The missionaries translate the Bible (into Indian languages) from other translations rather than from the original. Inspired by the classical theory according to which the People of the Book are guilty of corrupting the scripture (*taḥrīf*), he accuses the missionaries of constantly introducing changes into the biblical text. In his view, this is tantamount to a claim of prophethood.[104] Or, in the language of a later Aḥmadī thinker, "they covered the face of monotheism with the trinity veil" (*ghaṭṭaw wajh al-tawḥīd bi-ḥijāb al-tathlīth*).[105]

Ghulām Aḥmad was sent by God in order to redress these iniquities. Since these were caused by Christians and Christianity is "the worship of the cross" (*ṣalīb parastī*), Ghulām Aḥmad's endeavour is "breaking the cross" (*kasr-i ṣalīb*) and he is the "breaker of the cross" (*kāsir al-ṣalīb*). But, again, this is to be understood metaphorically. This is necessary because *jihād* is now forbidden. Ghulām Aḥmad is not going to break some wooden crosses which can easily be replaced. He has a grand scheme: breaking the cross is no less than the "total elimination of the Christian religion" (*ʿĪsawī dīn kā ibṭāl-i kullī*) by arguments and divine support.[106] The confutation of Christianity by denying the crucifixion and the second coming of Jesus as well as declaring himself the manifestation of Jesus was, in Ghulām Aḥmad's eyes, his central achievement as the *mahdī*.

The identification of the *dajjāl* with the Christians is also proven by referring to the classical *ḥadīth* in which the Prophet instructed the believers to read the first verses of *Sūrat al-Kahf* (Qurʾān 18) in the *dajjāl*'s face when they meet him.[107] Since these verses contain an attack on Christian beliefs, the *dajjāl* necessarily represents the Christians or the Russians and the British (*qawm al-Rūs wa qawm al-Barāṭina*).[108] They have a record of deception. They spread polytheism, atheism and licentiousness (*shirk, dahriyya, ibāḥa*) and "slide down out of every slope" (*min kulli ḥadbin yansallūn*), like the mythical Gog and Magog who are expected to arrive

---

104 Ghulām Aḥmad, *Malfūẓāt*, in *Rūḥānī Khazāʾin*, series 2, vol. 4, pp. 19–20; *idem*, *Malfūẓāt*, in *Rūḥānī Khazāʾin*, series 2, vol. 9, p. 304.

105 Aḥmad, *al-Qawl al-ṣarīḥ fī ẓuhūr al-mahdī wa al-masīḥ*, p. 160.

106 Ghulām Aḥmad, *Malfūẓāt*, in *Rūḥānī Khazāʾin*, vol. 4, pp. 17–19.

107 Qurʾān 18:4–5: "... and to warn those who say: 'God has taken to Himself a son'". I regret having misplaced Ghulām Aḥmad's reference to the connection between these verses and the *dajjāl*.

108 Ghulām Aḥmad, *Āʾina-yi kamālāt-i islām*, p. 460.

before the Day of Judgment.[109] In a rather far-fetched interpretation, he also maintains that if the *dajjāl* had any separate existence, he would have been mentioned in the *Fātiḥa* together with "those against whom you are wrathful" and "those who are astray".[110] According to standard exegesis, "those who are astray" are the Christians. Since the *dajjāl* is not mentioned separately, he is to be identified with Christians.[111]

In the passage quoted at the beginning of this chapter, Ghulām Aḥmad dissociated himself from the idea that the "bloody" *mahdī* will destroy all religions except Islam. This does not mean, however, that he also abandoned the idea that at the end of days Islam will be transformed into the sole religion. But instead of having Jesus fighting for the sake of Islam and annihilating all religions except it, religions other than Islam will somehow disappear on their own:

> Time has come when falsehood will vanish, corruption and darkness will not remain and all religions except Islam will fade out. The earth will be filled with equity, justice and light as it was replete with iniquity, infidelity, oppression and corruption (*wa qad atā zamānun tahliku fīhi al-abāṭīl wa lā tabqā* [sic] *al-zūr wa al-ẓalām wa tafnī* [sic] *al-milal kulluhā illā al-islām. wa tumlaʾu al-arḍ qisṭan wa ʿadlan wa nūran kamā muliʾat ẓulman wa kufran wa jawran wa zūran*).[112]

In other words, the messianic ideal which was achieved in classical *ḥadīth* by the violent actions of Jesus, will now be realized on its own, without his intervention. The way in which this will be done is obscure and the violence which is a central element in the classical *ḥadīth* is no longer part of the apocalyptic drama.

When discussing the three *mahdīs* in the previous chapters, we said that each one of them considered those who did not acknowledge their messianic claims and did not join their movements as infidels. The idea that Muslims who do not acknowledge Ghulām Aḥmad's messianic status

---

109 Ghulām Aḥmad, *Āʾina-yi kamālāt-i islām*, pp. 451–452; Qurʾān 21:96.

110 Qurʾān 1:7.

111 Ghulām Aḥmad, *Tuḥfa Gōlaṛwiyya*, pp. 211, 231, 234–236; *idem*, *Chashma-yi maʿrifat*, p. 87 note; *idem*, *Malfūẓāt*, vol. 9, p. 59. Cf. Aḥmad, *al-Qawl al-ṣarīḥ fī ẓuhūr al-mahdī wa al-masīḥ*, pp. 103–104.

112 Ghulām Aḥmad, *Iʿjāz al-masīḥ*, p. 85.

are unbelievers does exist in his works, but not in his early ones. Then he maintained that nobody can become an infidel by rejecting his messianic claim. This was his view despite the fact that Sunnī Muslims issued *fatāwā* declaring him an infidel soon after he made his claim to spiritual eminence in 1889. However, in his later years Ghulām Aḥmad's views developed in an exclusionary direction. In the last years before his death in 1908, he stated that anybody who rejected his claim to spiritual eminence was an infidel. The most unequivocal statement of this attitude is found in the fifth volume of the *Barāhīn-i Aḥmadiyya*, written in 1905. It reads: "He who denies this mission, will be declared infidel" (*jō shakhṣ is da'wē sē munkir hay wuh bi-har ḥāl kāfir ṫherā'ēgā*).[113] It is thus clear that all four messianic claimants discussed in this work eventually developed an exclusionary attitude to Muslims who did not join their movements. It is, however, noteworthy that in recent decades the Aḥmadī movement seems to have distanced itself from the stringent views of its founder in the last years of his life.[114]

IV INDIAN MUSLIM OPPONENTS OF THE AḤMADIYYA

Ghulām Aḥmad's radical reinterpretation of the Muslim apocalypse was not left unanswered. The issue of the life of Jesus and his second coming has exercised the minds of Indian Muslims for decades, and numerous book-length works were written in order to refute the views of Ghulām Aḥmad who maintained that Jesus died like any other mortal. The Deobandī scholar Anwar Shāh Kashmīrī (1875–1933), a student of *shaykh al-Hind* Maḥmūd al-Ḥasan (1851–1920) and a scholar famous for his proficiency in *ḥadīth*,[115] devoted to it his "Clear announcement on the authentic traditions concerning the descent of Jesus" (*al-Taṣrīḥ bi-mā tawātara fī nuzūl*

113 *Barāhīn-i Aḥmadiyya*, vol. 5, p. 82, note. For the date of this book, see Qayyūm, *Ta'āruf-i Kutub*, p. 45.

114 For more details on Ghulām Aḥmad's attitudes to non-Aḥmadīs, see Friedmann, *Prophecy Continuous*, pp. 154–156.

115 The only edition of this work which I was able to locate was published in 1965, 32 years after Kashmīrī's death. For essential details about the author, see Metcalf, *Islamic Revival in British India*, index; Riżwī, *Ta'rīkh-i Deoband*, pp. 460–468; Kashmīrī. *Fayḍ al-bārī*, vol. 1, pp. 17–20. For a laudatory and anecdotal description of Kashmīrī's personality, see 'Uthmānī, *Akābir-i Deoband kyā thē?*, pp. 41–53.

al-masīḥ). After a scathing attack on the "ignorance" of the Aḥmadīs,[116] the book is essentially a collection of the classical traditions on the appearance of the *dajjāl* and on the second coming of Jesus. Kashmīrī also includes in the book a list of dozens of treatises written against Ghulām Aḥmad.[117] Kashmīrī's student Muḥammad Shafīʿ (1897–1976)[118] provided the book with an extensive preface in which he gives a summary of Ghulām Aḥmad's claims and tries to refute them by contrasting them with the classical traditions.[119]

Another scholar who opposed the Aḥmadī perception was Nāẓir Shāh, whose "The accepted view asserting the life of the *masīḥ* and [his] descent" (*al-Qawl al-maqbūl fī ithbāt ḥayāt al-masīh wa al-nuzūl*)[120] was published in 1914. He starts his attempt to undermine the Aḥmadī view by tackling Qurʾān 3:55, the most difficult Qurʾānic verse for the supporters of the idea that Jesus is alive in heaven.[121] He takes the phrase *innī mutawaffīka* to mean "I am making you perfect" (*mayñ tujhē pūrā karnē-wālā hūñ*) rather than "I cause you to die." From the point of view of Arabic, this is not easy; in order to reach this understanding, he resorts to a rather far-fetched etymological exercise, basing his interpretation not on the fifth form of *w-f-y* as it appears in Qurʾān 3:55, but on its second form as it appears in Qurʾān 53:38 where Abraham is described as someone who *waffā*; Nāẓir Shāh glosses this by saying: "(Abraham) completed what he was commanded to do in truth; this is to say, Abraham was a person who fulfilled God's command (*ay tammama mā umira bihi bi-ḥaqq yaʿnī Ibrāhīm ʿalayhi al-salām wuh thē jinhōñ-nē khudā kē ḥukm kō pūrā kiyā*). He also asserts – rather problematically – that various forms of one root carry the same meaning.[122] Additionally, he suggests understanding *mutawaffīka* and *rāfiʿuka ilayya* in reverse order and arguing that God raised Jesus to himself after his first mission on earth came to a close, and will cause him to die only after his second coming in the apocalyptic period. The Arab

116 Kashmīrī, *Taṣrīḥ*, p. 99.
117 Kashmīrī, *Taṣrīḥ*, pp. 49–56.
118 Among other positions, Muḥammad Shafīʿ served as the chief *muftī* of Pakistan. For a short biography, see https://en.wikipedia.org/wiki/Muhammad_Shafi%27_Deobandi (accessed on 25 November 2020).
119 Much of this book is repeated in English in Muḥammad Shafīʿ, *Signs of Qiyāma*.
120 This work is hard to come by. There is a copy in the British Library. The minuscule and sometimes fading print is in many places illegible.
121 For the classical exegesis of this verse, see Chapter 1, Section IV.
122 For another attempt to prove this meaning of *tawaffā*, see Muhr al-Dīn, *Ḥayāt-i ʿĪsā*, p. 54 and Kāndhlawī, *Ḥayāt-i ʿĪsā*, pp. 71–72.

grammatical rule, according to which the conjunction *wāw* between two verbs does not indicate a fixed sequence of the two actions (*tartīb*) but rather their "togetherness" (*jam'*), is used to support the idea that the "raising" of Jesus precedes his death. Even if the reversal of this sequence is not accepted, and one does want to understand *mutawaffīka* as "I am causing you to die" – according to the interpretation of Ibn 'Abbās – there is still a question how can it mean that the death of Jesus has already occurred. Active participles (such as *mutawaffīka*) normally relate to the present and the future. It is true that it sometimes includes the sense of the past, but this is rare and must be in a special context. Without such a context, a participle does not indicate the past.[123] Nāẓir Shāh also quotes several classical commentators who interpreted *mutawaffīka* as unrelated to death.[124] Qur'ān 2:281, 3:161 and 16:111 which read *tuwaffā kullu nafsin mā kasabat* or *'amilat* are explained by saying that "each soul will be given its full reward" (*har ēk nafs kō pūrā pūrā ajr diyā jā'ēgā*). Other verses in which *w-f-y* appears are used for the same purpose. Verses in which the root appears in the sense of death (such as Qur'ān 2:234 and 4:14) are described as "odd and rare" (*shādhdh o nādir*). Other scholars go even further and say that *tawaffā* carries the meaning of death only "metaphorically and by necessity" (*kināyatan awr luzūman*) "because the completion of lifetime (*istīfā'-i 'umr awr itmām-i 'umr*) necessarily results in death".[125]

The famous denial of crucifixion in Qur'ān 4:156 and Qur'ān 43:61 ("He is the knowledge of the Hour") which is understood as predicting the apocalyptic descent of Jesus, as well as the numerous prophetic traditions about his second coming, also serve to strengthen the claim that Jesus is alive.[126] Furthermore, according to the classical *ḥadīth*, during his return to earth Jesus will fight for the sake of Islam and annihilate all religions other than Islam. This has not yet happened and the Aḥmadīs, who assert

123 Nāẓir Shāh, *al-Qawl al-maqbūl*, pp. 3–5.
124 Nāẓir Shāh, *al-Qawl al-maqbūl*, p. 6 *infra*.
125 Kāndhlawī, *Ḥayāt-i 'Īsā*, p. 71. This author also mentions Qur'ān 39:42: "God takes souls at the time of their death" (*Allah yatawaffā al-anfusa ḥīna mawtihā*) and asserts that the separate reference to death (*mawt*) in this verse is a proof that *tawaffā* in itself does not mean "death". See ibid., p. 74. The author quotes also Ibn Manẓūr, *Lisān al-arab*, s.v. *w-f-y* (ed. Beirut 1956, vol. 15, p. 400): *tawaffī al-mayyit istīfā' muddatihi allatī wufiyat lahu wa 'adadi ayyāmihi wa shuhūrihi wa a'wāmihi fī al-dunyā*.
126 Nāẓir Shāh, *al-Qawl al-maqbūl*, p. 7. For similar arguments, see Muhr al-Dīn, *Ḥayāt-i 'Īsā*, pp. 52–53 and *passim*.

that Jesus is dead and deny his second coming, need to answer the question why this *ḥadīth* did not materialize. The clear conclusion from this argumentation is that Jesus must come again in order to fulfil the predictions included in the *ḥadīth*. Additionally, the Aḥmadī claim that Jesus is buried in Srinagar contradicts a tradition according to which Jesus will be buried in the grave of the Prophet in Medina when he dies after his second coming and will be resurrected together with him.[127] The Aḥmadī interpretation of "a height where was a hollow and a spring" (*rabwa dhāt qarār wa ma ʿīn*) as a reference to Kashmīr is far-fetched, unsupported by evidence and not specific to Kashmīr. Numerous places in the world could be meant by this description.[128]

The passage in Qur ʾān 3:144 according to which "Muḥammad is naught but a Messenger. Messengers have passed away before him" (*wa mā Muḥammadun illā rasūlun qad khalat min qablihi al-rusulu*) is one of the more difficult passages for the supporters of the idea that Jesus is alive. It can easily be interpreted as indicating the death of all prophets, Jesus included.[129] Having summarized first the interpretations following this line, Muḥammad Muhr al-Dīn devoted several pages in his *Ḥayāt-i ʿĪsā* to their refutation. Quoting several classical dictionaries of Arabic, he points out that the basic meaning of *khalā* is not to die, but rather to move from one place to another or from one time to another.[130] Furthermore, the definite article in *al-rusul* does not mean "all messengers" and therefore includes Jesus; in many Qur ʾānic passages the definite article refers in such cases only to one or at most several individuals in the relevant group. For instance, when the Qur ʾān says in Sūra 3:45 "When the angels said: Mary, God gives you the glad tidings of a Word from him ...", only

127 Nāẓir Shāh, *al-Qawl al-maqbūl*, pp. 11–12. Cf. Siyālkōtī, *al-Khabar al-ṣaḥīḥ*, pp. 1, 4. For the classical *ḥadīth* about Jesus annihilating all religions except Islam, see Chapter 1, at note 48. For the idea of his death and burial in the Prophet's grave, see Chapter 1, at note 87.

Naturally enough, Aḥmadī thinkers denied the authenticity of this *ḥadīth*. Their reasoning is based on principles of the traditional *ḥadīth* criticism: the *ḥadīth* was related on the authority of ʿAbd Allah b. Salām and ʿAbd Allah b. ʿAmr b. al-ʿĀṣ who transmitted traditions from the People of the Book (*isrā ʾīliyyāt*), as well as of Salmān al-Fārisī whose credibility is low. See Aḥmad, *al-Qawl al-ṣarīḥ fī ẓuhūr al-mahdī wa al-masīḥ*, pp. 22–23.

128 Siyālkōtī, *al-Khabar al-ṣaḥīḥ*, pp. 8–9.

129 For the use of this verse in Aḥmadī writings, see Aḥmad, *al-Qawl al-ṣarīḥ fī ẓuhūr al-mahdī wa al-masīḥ*, p. 8.

130 Muhr al-Dīn, *Ḥayāt-i ʿĪsā*, pp. 60–62.

Gabriel was meant, not all the angels. Many similar cases can be found in classical Arabic.[131]

Muḥammad Manẓūr Nuʿmānī (1905–1997), a Deobandī scholar and prolific writer on Islamic subjects, devoted a monograph to a critique of the Aḥmadī view of Jesus. The date of this book is not certain, but it was written after the partition of the subcontinent. The book starts with the assertion that Muslims believe in the finality of Muḥammad's prophethood and anybody who disputes this, including Ghulām Aḥmad, is beyond the pale of Islam. The Aḥmadīs developed their view of Jesus because they are westernized (*maghribiyyat zada*) to such an extent that they are willing to deny any religious belief which is incompatible with the intellectual bases of British education, still in effect in India and in Pakistan. Their intellect has been transmogrified (*maskh shuda ʿaqlēñ*) and they are therefore willing to deny the existence of God, Paradise or the angels because their existence does not stand up to arguments of western rationalism.[132] The idea that Jesus is alive and will descend to earth again is of this type: is it rational to assume that a person would live for two thousand years? What arrangements are there in heaven for eating, drinking and answering the call of nature?[133] Nuʿmānī does not respond to these questions directly; instead, he dismisses them with the argument that materials from the Qurʾān and the *ḥadīth* prevail and should not be subjected to rational questioning of this kind. Noah lived 950 years,[134] the People of the Cave 300 years.[135] Asserting that there is not even a single verse in the Qurʾān which refutes the belief that Jesus is alive in heaven and will return to earth again, he launches a spirited defence of this initially Christian idea. In Nuʿmānī's view, the absence of such a refutation is even more telling in view of the fact that the Qurʾān does include refutations of cardinal Christian ideas – such as the divinity of Jesus, his being the son of God and his crucifixion.[136] As far as the *ḥadīth* is concerned, the number of

131 Muhr al-Dīn, *Ḥayāt-i ʿĪsā*, pp. 63–64.

132 Nuʿmānī, *Masʾala-yi nuzūl-i masīḥ*, pp. 77–78. A discussion of the "westernization" of the Aḥmadīs is beyond the scope of this work. But to say that they do not believe in God or renounce other basic principles of Islam is preposterous.

133 Nuʿmānī, *Masʾala-yi nuzūl-i masīḥ*, pp. 83–84.

134 Cf. Qurʾān 29:14. This is also the life span of Noah in the genre of the "Tales of the prophets" (*qiṣaṣ al-anbiyāʾ*). See for, instance, Naysābūrī, *Qiṣaṣ al-anbiyāʾ (Dāstānhā-yi payghāmbarān)*, p. 33.

135 Cf. Qurʾān 18:24.

136 Nuʿmānī, *Masʾala-yi nuzūl-i masīḥ*, pp. 94–98.

the Prophet's companions who related these traditions is so great that it is not possible to perceive them as a conspiracy. The great number of these traditions and their ubiquity create irreproachable reliability (*rasūl Allah ... kī kathīr al-ta'dād aḥādīth jō majmū'ī awr ma'nawī ḥaythiyyat sē yaqīnan ḥadd-i tawātur pohonchī hu'ī hayñ*).[137]

This is essentially an *argumentum ex silentio*: since there is no Qur'ānic refutation of the idea that Jesus is alive, the idea is correct. Additionally, Nu'mānī follows the classical exegetical tradition and makes wide use of the commentaries on Qur'ān 4:157 and 43:61 which were interpreted as hinting at the apocalyptic descent of Jesus. He also finds support for his ideas in the works of al-Ash'arī, Ibn Taymiyya, 'Abd al-Wahhāb al-Sha'rānī and several other medieval commentators.[138]

v THE *MAHDĪ* DEMYSTIFIED

Muslim messianic thought in modern India was not restricted to the question of the "bloody" versus the "peaceful" *mahdī* and we need to analyse also the thought of scholars who approached the issue from a different vantage point. Prominent among them is Shāh Ismā'īl Shahīd (d. 1831, in the Battle of Bālākōt), who is best known for his activities as a warrior against the Sikhs in the Panjab, but who also left a vast literary legacy in which he struggled against various kinds of "innovations" (*bida'*) rampant among Indian Muslims.[139] Marc Gaborieau is the first scholar who recognized the importance of the messianic element in the thought of Shāh Ismā'īl Shahīd and devoted his monograph, *Un mahdī incompris*, to this issue.[140] Shāh Ismā'īl Shahīd promoted the idea that Sayyid Aḥmad Shahīd (Barēlwī) ought to be considered a *mahdī*.[141] There are references to messianic claims made on behalf of Sayyid Aḥmad also in the works

137 Nu'mānī, *Mas'ala-yi nuzūl-i masīḥ*, p. 88.
138 Nu'mānī, *Mas'ala-yi nuzūl-i masīḥ*, pp. 112–131.
139 For general information about Shāh Ismā'īl Shahīd, see Bazmee Ansari, "Ismā'īl Shahīd" in *EI²*, s.v.
140 Our discussion expands the analysis of Ismā'īl Shahīd's thought in a different direction and would not have been possible without the highly original contribution of Gaborieau.
141 Like Ismā'īl Shahīd, Sayyid Aḥmad is primarily known for his activities as a warrior against the Sikhs. See Gaborieau, "Barēlwī, Sayyid Aḥmad", in *EI³*, s.v. For the most recent analysis of Sayyid Aḥmad Shahīd's thought, based on hitherto untapped sources, see Tareen, *Defending Muḥammad in Modernity*, especially pp. 66–73.

of contemporary British observers,[142] as well as in the works of ʿUbayd Allah Sindhī (d. 1944).[143]

It is also noteworthy that Shāh Ismāʿīl Shahīd prepared a compilation entitled *Kitāb arbaʿīn fī aḥwāl al-mahdiyyīn* ("A book of forty traditions about the *mahdīs*") which seems to have been written in order to support this claim. On the other hand, Ṣiddīq Ḥasan Khān asserts that Sayyid Aḥmad Shahīd never made the claim himself and the claims made on his behalf by his followers were based on error and emanated from a desire to rule.[144] Whatever the truth of this matter may be, the relevant theory of Shāh Ismāʿīl Shahīd merits detailed investigation.

The thrust of Shāh Ismāʿīl Shahīd's thinking is to transform the *mahdī* from an eschatological figure into an ideal leader of the Muslim community in historical times. In order to achieve this goal, Ismāʿīl Shahīd integrated the *mahdī* idea into his perception of the various types of government which existed in Islamic history. His *Manṣab-i imāmat* is a major work in Muslim political theory; it is not possible to analyse here all its contents and we will restrict our discussion to those chapters which are essential for Shāh Ismāʿīl Shahīd's perception of the *mahdī*.

Shāh Ismāʿīl Shahīd asserted that the *mahdī* will establish the ideal type of "righteous caliphate". In order to understand his contribution to Muslim messianic thought, we need to analyse his understanding of the various types of Muslim governance.

At the beginning of Islam, the system of government was a "perfect caliphate" (*khilāfat-i tāmma*), also called "righteous caliphate" (*khilāfat-i rāshida*), "caliphate on the prophetic model" (*khilāfa ʿalā minhāj al-nubuwwa*) or the "caliphate of mercy" (*khilāfat-i raḥmat*). With this caliphate, divine grace brought its activity for the sake of mankind to perfection. The well-being of the people of the time required that they accept it,

142 Anon, "A Sketch of the Wahhabis in India", pp. 95–99, 102; Hughes, *A Dictionary of Islam*, pp. 305a, 861a. On the other hand, James Russel Colvin is not aware of any messianic claim of Sayyid Aḥmad and describes him only as an opponent of religious "innovations". See Colvin, "Notice of the Peculiar Tenets ...", *passim*. Cf. Gaborieau, Le *mahdī incompris*, pp. 219–225.

143 Ubayd Allah Sindhī describes Sayyid Aḥmad as "the Indian *mahdī*" (*al-mahdī al-hindī*) in his *Tamhīd*, p. 3. He also mentions that some of his contemporaries considered him a *mahdī* and believed that he did not die in battle but went into hiding and will eventually return. On this idea he quotes the *ʿAwn al-maʿbūd* (a commentary on the *Sunan* of Abū Dāwūd) of ʿAẓīmābādī (d. 1911); see ibid., vol. 11, pp. 367–368. See also his *Tamhīd*, p. 136.

144 Ṣiddīq Ḥasan Khān, *Ḥujaj al-karāma*, p. 392 lines 8–15.

because it is "a prerequisite for faith-based policy" (*muqaddima-yi siyāsat-i īmānī*). When there is a righteous caliph who receives the support of the people, his caliphate is known as "well-ordered" (*khilāfa muntaẓama*). In early Islamic history, the caliphates of Abū Bakr, ʿUmar and ʿUtmān were "well-ordered", while that of ʿAlī was "in disorder" (*ghayr muntaẓama*), presumably because of the Khārijī rebellion. According to an additional classification, the "well-ordered caliphate" is also of two types: it can be "protected" (*maḥfūẓa*) or "challenged" (*maftūna*). In early Islamic history, the caliphates of Abū Bakr and ʿUmar were "protected", while that of ʿUthmān – in which there was opposition which did not reach the stage of rebellion or cancellation of the oath of allegiance (*bayʿa*) – was "challenged". This is a somewhat benevolent classification with regard to ʿUmar and ʿUthmān, both of whom were assassinated. Because of the disparity between the four "righteous caliphs", and the orderliness (*intiẓām*) or dissolution (*intishār*) of their rule, there are differences of opinion on the question for how long the early ideal caliphate existed. Some traditions may be interpreted as indicating that the ideal era ended with ʿUmar b. al-Khaṭṭāb or ʿUthmān b. ʿAffān, apparently because of the problems which plagued the reigns of ʿUthmān b. ʿAffān and ʿAlī b. Abī Ṭālib.[145]

Shāh Ismāʿīl Shahīd is willing to countenance the possibility that the ideal period of early Islam lasted only until the death of ʿUmar b. al-Khaṭṭāb. However, this does not mean that Islam will not rise and live up to its ideals again at some point in the future. The tradition about the righteous caliphate that will last for thirty years[146] only means that the righteous caliphate which followed the emergence of Islam will last for that period. After these thirty years are over, a new righteous caliph can rise to power at any time. Whoever holds the position of an *imām* and conducts a faith-based policy is a righteous caliph, whether he acted at the beginning of Islamic history or later, whether he is Qurashī, a Fāṭimī or a Hāshimī. This is not only a theoretical possibility: the Umayyad ʿUmar b. ʿAbd al-ʿAzīz (r. 717–720) was so considered by his contemporaries.[147]

145 Ismāʿīl Shahīd, *Manṣab-i imāmat*, pp. 58–60.

146 See Tirmidhī, *Ṣaḥīḥ*, vol. 9, p. 71: "The caliphate (will last) in my community for thirty years; thereafter will be kingdom" (*al-khilāfa fī unnatī thalāthūna sana thumma mulk baʿda dhālika*). This is a commonly quoted *ḥadīth*; thirty years is the combined reign of the four "righteous" caliphs.

147 Ismāʿīl Shahīd, *Manṣab-i imāmat*, p. 62 lines 8–9.

In addition to the idea that a righteous caliph may arise after the classical righteous caliphate came to an end in the seventh century CE, Shāh Ismā'īl Shahīd also speaks about *mahdīs* whose emergence is not related to the end of days. As we have seen in Chapter 1, the classical *mahdī* traditions describe the emergence of the *mahdī* in various ways. Some provide an explicitly eschatological context for his coming, while others leave the period of his coming unspecified but include thinly veiled references to real historical figures. These latter traditions, such as those which speak about a *mahdī* coming from Khurāsān or Transoxania, enable Shāh Ismā'īl Shahīd to argue that the *mahdī* is not only an eschatological figure and to assert that there could also be a *mahdī* in historical times.[148] The same purpose is served by his *Aḥwāl al-mahdiyyīn*. The first chapter of this work is entitled "all-inclusive traditions about the *mahdī*s" (*fī aḥādīth jāmi'a fī al-mahdiyyīn*). While most of the book recounts the classical material about the eschatological *mahdī*, it is significant to observe that it starts with the *ḥadīth* about the centennial *mujaddidūn* which maintains that at the beginning of each century God will send to the Muslim community a person who will renew its religion.[149] These "renewers" are non-eschatological figures; placing this tradition at the beginning of a book about the *mahdī*s serves Shāh Ismā'īl Shahīd's purpose to dissociate the *mahdī* from its eschatological background and to transform him into a historical figure whose task is to lead the Muslim community here and now, not in a distant eschatological future.[150] The same purpose is served by a prophetic tradition which asserts that "a community of which I am the first, Jesus is at its end and the *mahdī* is in its middle cannot perish" (*kayfa tahliku ummatun anā awwaluhā wa 'Īsā fī ākhirihā wa al-mahdī fī wasaṭihā*).[151] This *ḥadīth* is considered "weak" by classical scholars, but it seems to have been widely circulated by the supporters of Sayyid Aḥmad

148 Ismā'īl Shahīd, *Manṣab-i imāmat*, p. 62 *infra*.

149 See Ismā'īl Shahīd, *Fī aḥwāl al-mahdiyyīn*, p. 1. The *ḥadīth* reads: "God will send to this community on the eve of every century a man who will renew its religion" (*inna Allah yab'athu li-hādhihi al-umma 'alā ra'si kulli mi'a sana man yujaddidu lahā dīnahā*). See Abū Dāwūd, *Sunan*, vol. 2, p. 518. For different interpretations of this *ḥadīth*, see Friedmann, *Shaykh Aḥmad Sirhindī*, pp. 13–21 and Landau-Tasseron, "The 'cyclical reform'".

150 See later, at notes 223–231 of this chapter, for a similar attitude of Abū al-A'lā Mawdūdī.

151 Ismā'īl Shahīd, *Fī aḥwāl al-mahdiyyīn*, p. 6. For this tradition in the classical *ḥadīth*, see Chapter 1, at notes 92–93, and cf. Gaborieau, *Le mahdī incompris*, pp. 222–226.

Shahīd and even gained the attention of British observers.[152] It strengthens Shāh Ismā'īl Shahīd's argument about a *mahdī* who is disconnected from eschatological times. Indeed, Shāh Ismā'īl Shahīd's *mahdī* is nothing but a new "righteous caliph" in the mould of Abū Bakr or 'Umar b. al-Khaṭṭāb.

VI MODERN CRITIQUE AND DEBUNKING

We cannot complete the discussion of the *mahdī* idea in nineteenth-century India without mentioning Sir Sayyid Aḥmad Khān (1817–1898), leader of India's Muslim modernist movement. Sir Sayyid devoted a short booklet to this issue[153] which includes an unequivocal debunking of the *mahdī* idea. In his view, the predictions (*bashārāt*) of the *mahdī*'s emergence are not genuine. He attacks the *mahdī* traditions in two ways. Following the classical method of "impugning the veracity [of *ḥadīth* transmitters] and declaring [them] trustworthy" (*al-jarḥ wa al-ta'dīl*), as employed by the scholars of *ḥadīth*, he quotes negative statements from biographical literature and in this way finds fault with numerous scholars who have transmitted the *mahdī* traditions. Furthermore, in the manner of modern scholarly criticism of *ḥadīth*, he shows that many of the *mahdī* traditions serve particular interests of Muslim groups such as the Shī'īs and the 'Abbāsīs. Anticipating the conclusions of Attema and Madelung, he asserts that a famous *ḥadīth* which appears in Abū Dāwūd's *Sunan* was created in order to promote the interests of the "anti-caliph" 'Abd Allah b. al-Zubayr who rebelled against the Umayyad caliphate and took over Mecca in 683.[154] His argument is that traditions which clearly deal with political issues in a certain period cannot be considered as apocalyptic in nature and could not have been intended to predict eschatological events. It is also noteworthy that in several places Sir Sayyid approvingly quotes the critical analysis of the *mahdī* idea by Ibn Khaldūn, mentioned in Chapter 1.[155] It is fascinating to observe the direct connection between Ibn Khaldūn, perhaps the most original thinker in medieval Islam, and a prominent Muslim modernist.

152 See Anon, "A sketch of the Wahhabis in India", p. 96 note.
153 Sir Sayyid Aḥmad Khān, *Mahdī-yi ākhir al-zamān*.
154 See Sir Sayyid Aḥmad Khān, *Mahdī-yi ākhir al-zamān*, pp. 5–7; Madelung, "'Abd Allah b. al-Zubayr and the *mahdī*", *passim*. Cf. Chapter 1, at note 150.
155 Sir Sayyid Aḥmad Khān, *Mahdī-yi ākhir al-zamān*, pp. 16, 34, 35. See Chapter 1, at notes 136–139.

Another scholar who set out to debunk the eschatological drama is Ubayd Allah Sindhī (1872–1944). His thought has been briefly surveyed by several scholars who gave details of his conversion from Sikhism to Islam at the age of sixteen,[156] described his social views, surveyed the revolutionary aspects of his thought, his journeys to Afghanistan and Turkey, his socialist ideas, his support of Indian nationalism, and his support of *jihād* as well as of Ṣūfism as a tool for resolving the conflict between Hindūism and Islam.[157] These ideas are seemingly incompatible with each other and a comprehensive synthesis of Sindhī's religious and political thought which would elucidate these complexities has yet to be written.

Sindhī's short monograph on Islamic eschatology, entitled "The dogma concerning the expectation of the *masīḥ* and the *mahdī*" (*ʿAqīda-yi intiẓār-i masīḥ o mahdī*), which is devoted to the second coming of Jesus and to the coming of the *mahdī*, is highly critical in its approach to the classical tradition and should be understood against the background of Sindhī's revolutionary world view. In his criticism of the *ḥadīth*, Sindhī is willing to reject even traditions which he himself considers sound according to the traditional criteria. The monograph starts with a humorous, light-hearted passage referring to the eschatological descent of Jesus: "Our view concerning the second coming of Jesus, peace be upon him, is as follows: if he comes – well and good; if he does not – no disaster will result from it" (*ḥaźrat ʿĪsā ʿalayhi al-salām kē dō bāra ānē kā masʾalē mēñ hamārī raʾy yih hay kih ā gayā tō – achhā; nahīñ tō – us sē kōʾī muṣībat nahīñ āʾēgī*). The second coming of Jesus should certainly not be made into an article of faith. Muḥammad's being the last prophet who was sent to all people, the Qurʾānic verse according to which Allah made the religion of the Muslims perfect – all these preclude the necessity to expect another prophet or a *mahdī*.[158]

As we have seen in Chapter 1, the second coming of Jesus is not explicitly mentioned in the Qurʾān and Sindhī can easily use this absence to substantiate his rejection of it. In the prophetic tradition, on the other

156 For Sindhī's own description of his conversion, see *Tamhīd*, pp. 8–9.

157 W. C. Smith, *Modern Islam in India*, pp. 235–236; A. Ahmad, *Islamic modernism*, pp. 195–201 and index; Anjum, "Bridging tradition and modernism"; for a biography, see Ikrām, *Mawj-i kawthar*, pp. 345–350. For a monograph dedicated to Sindhi's life and activities, see Shaikh, *Maulana Ubaid Allah Sindhi*. None of these scholars had Sindhī's book on the expectation of the *mahdī* at his disposal.

158 Sindhī, *ʿAqīda-yi intiẓār-i masīḥ o mahdī*, p. 11. Sindhī refers here to Qurʾān 33:40, 34:28 and 5:4.

hand, the second coming is an integral part of the apocalyptic drama and Sindhī needs to grapple with numerous traditions in order to substantiate his negative stance towards it. In some cases, he interprets these traditions in a way which seems to be his own; in others he uses the traditional method of "impugning and declaring trustworthy" (*al-jarḥ wa al-ta ʿdīl*), but sometimes he is willing to discredit even tradition which he considers trustworthy according to the criteria of traditional *ḥadīth* criticism. The tradition in which both Jesus and the *dajjāl* are performing *ṭawāf* of the Ka ʿba is considered by Sindhī a dream which is in need of interpretation. His rather far-fetched interpretation considers the story to be a metaphor for the bifurcation of the Muslim community into pious people on the one hand and world-seeking ones on the other.[159] Another radical departure from the mainstream interpretation is related to the *ḥadīth* about the future descent of Jesus and his deeds.[160] This *ḥadīth* is attributed to the Prophet on the authority of Abū Hurayra, but Sindhī asserts that these are the words of Abū Hurayra himself and he heard them from the People of the Book rather than from the Prophet. The fact that they appear in the *Ṣaḥīḥ* of al-Bukhārī does not make them any more credible in Sindhī's eyes: he argues that more than one hundred traditions included in that collection were declared "faulty" (*mu ʿallal*) by later scholars of *ḥadīth*. If we have proof, we can declare even a seemingly sound *ḥadīth* with a good chain of transmission to be weak (*jab hamēñ thubūt milēgā, tō ham is ṣaḥīḥ musnad ḥadīth kō (jinhēñ imām Bukhārī ṣaḥīḥ qarār dē kar apnī kitāb Ṣaḥīḥ-i Bukhārī mēñ lātē hayñ) źa ʿīf thābit kar saktē hayñ*).[161] Sindhī became firm in

159 Ubayd Allah Sindhī, *ʿAqīda yi intiẓār-i masīḥ o mahdī*, pp. 12–13. For a description of this *ḥadīth* as a Prophet's dream, see Muslim b. Ḥajjāj, *Ṣaḥīḥ*, vol. 1, p. 155 (*Kitāb al-īmān, bāb 75*). For a version in which this is not defined as a dream, see Mālik b. Anas, *Muwaṭṭa ʾ*, vol. 2, p. 920 (*Kitāb ṣifat al-nabī, bāb* 2).

160 See Chapter 1, at notes 48–49, and my *Prophecy Continuous*, pp. 167–168. The reference to Tirmidhī, *Ṣaḥīḥ*, on p. 167, note 8 is erroneous; the passage is in vol. 10, pp. 76–77, not in vol. 9.

161 Ubayd Allah Sindhī, *ʿAqīda-yi intiẓār-i masīḥ o mahdī*, pp. 13–15, 28. The quotation is on p. 28 *supra*. Sindhi quotes in support for his view the introduction of al-ʿAsqalānī (d. 1449) to *Fatḥ al-bārī*, his voluminous commentary on al-Bukhārī's *Ṣaḥīḥ*. In this introduction, al-ʿAsqalānī mentions classical scholars of *ḥadīth*, such as Abū al-Ḥasan al-Dārquṭnī (d. 995) and Ibn Ṣalāḥ (d. 1245), who accepted the authenticity of most traditions included in al-Bukhārī's *Ṣaḥīḥ*, but maintained that in some cases both al-Bukhārī and Muslim b. al-Ḥajjāj violated their own conditions of authenticity (*akhallā bi-sharṭihimā*) and these traditions are therefore "disputable" (*mutanāza ʿ ʿalayhā*). Al-ʿAsqalānī maintains that in some cases there are good counter arguments to these criticisms. See al-ʿAsqalānī, *Hudā al-sārī*, pp. 347ff.

his denial of the second coming of Jesus when he started reading the New Testament and found the belief in the second coming of Jesus originates in the Christian tradition. Only people who do not understand the Qur'ān, disregard the *ḥadīth* according to which the Prophet Muḥammad appeared simultaneously with the Hour, do not understand that the Kingdom of God mentioned in the New Testament has already been established by the Prophet Muḥammad and that no saviour will appear after him – only such people can believe in the Christian idea of the second coming, mix it with the idea of the *mahdī* and assert that both Jesus and the *mahdī* will appear at the end of days.[162] The idea of the second coming is also rooted in the Shīʿī belief in the return of a descendant of ʿAlī b. Abī Ṭālib. Sindhī does not disregard the necessity to interpret the traditions about the *mahdī*: he believes that they speak about an ʿAbbāsī caliph rather than about a messianic figure who will come at the end of time. He supports his view by referring to Shāh Walī Allāh who interpreted the *mahdī* traditions in an identical manner.[163]

It is legitimate to ask what was the reason for Sindhī's radical approach to the eschatological material, for his willingness to reject even traditions which were included in the canonical collections and considered sound for centuries. He was convinced that the passive expectation of a mythical saviour who will come at the end of time and change the situation of Muslims for the better had a debilitating effect on the Muslim psyche. Even if the *mahdī* traditions are sound, it is wrong to entrust the *mahdī* with the well-being of Muslims.[164] Sindhī was deeply impressed by the fact that contemporary non-Muslim nations were full of activity and exertion, while the Muslims had the mentality of a defeated nation, and were in a state of idleness and lethargy[165] and perhaps will never have a chance of waking up.[166] As a thinker who opined that revolutionary activity is the key for human betterment, he

162 Ubayd Allah Sindhī, *ʿAqīda-yi intiẓār-i masīḥ o mahdī*, pp. 20–24.

163 Ubayd Allah Sindhī, *ʿAqīda-yi intiẓār-i masīḥ o mahdī*, pp. 29–31; *idem, Shāh Walī Allāh*, p. 145. For the view of Shāh Walī Allah, see his *Izālat al-khafāʾ*, vol. 1, p. 593 *infra*.

164 Sindhī, *Shāh Walī Allāh*, p. 146. For a similar criticism of passivity in the Arab cultural area, see Natshah, *al-Mahdī masbūq bi-dawla islāmiyya*, pp. 7–9, 53, and McCants analysis of the absence of the *mahdī* from ISIS propaganda; see McCants, *The ISIS Apocalypse*, pp. 142–144. See also Muqaddam, *al-Mahdī wa fiqh ashrāṭ al-sāʿa*, pp. 598–599.

165 Literally in "a slumber of a hare" (*khwāb-i khar-gōsh*).

166 Ubayd Allah Sindhī, *ʿAqīda-yi intiẓār-i masīḥ o mahdī*, pp. 30–31, 34.

was convinced that it was his duty to undermine an idea which sapped the vitality of Muslims and propagate an opposite one: Muslims should not wait for a mythical saviour but rather take their destiny in their own hands – here and now.

A similar approach was taken up by Akhtar Kāshmīrī, who wrote a major book on this topic: *The theory of expecting the mahdī* (*Naẓariyya-yi intiẓār-i mahdī*).[167] In his argument, the author follows in the footsteps of Ibn Khaldūn and Sir Sayyid Aḥmad Khān, using the methods of classical *ḥadīth* criticism in order to debunk the belief in the *mahdī's* appearance. He asserts that the idea is not mentioned in the Qur'ān and has neither logical nor traditional proof. Al-Bukhārī – whose *Ṣaḥīḥ* does not include a reference to the *mahdī* – is praised for the extreme care with which he selected the traditions to be included in his compilation. On the other hand, Kāshmīrī impugns the reliability of several *ḥadīth* compilations which do include traditions about the *mahdī*. Some of these books are traditionally included in the six canonical books of *ḥadīth* (*al-kutub al-sitta*), but this does not deter Kāshmīrī from questioning their reliability. He asserts that the reliability of al-Tirmidhī, Abū Dāwūd, Ibn Māja and al-Ḥākim al-Naysabūrī is "debatable" (*mutakallam fīhi*) and that they included many weak traditions in their compilations. Such traditions cannot justify transforming an idea or a belief into an article of faith. Furthermore, the *mahdī* idea is not mentioned in the books of the founders of the four schools of law (*madhāhib*) and in the works of the early Ḥanafī scholars Abū Yūsuf (d. 798) and al-Shaybānī (d. 805). Kāshmīrī considers this absence as additional support for his view. Is it possible that these four Muslim grandees were not aware of an important Islamic dogma? The inescapable conclusion from this situation is that the *mahdī* idea is outside the consensus (*ijmā'*) of the Muslim community.[168]

Kāshmīrī has also to contend with the existence of a substantial number of late medieval books dedicated to the description of the *mahdī* idea. Some of their authors, such as Jalāl al-Dīn al-Suyūṭī, Ibn Ḥajar al-'Asqalānī and 'Alī al-Muttaqī, have unassailable credentials as Islamic scholars.

167 The title page of the book does not carry its publication date, but the introduction of the author is dated 1984 (see p. 22). I was not able to find much information about the author, but the book carries an introduction by Asrār Aḥmad (d. 2010), the founder and long-time leader of the *Tanẓīm-i Islāmī*, an offshoot of the *Jamā'at-i Islāmī*. The author may have been associated in some way with that organization.

168 Kāshmīrī, *Naẓariyya-yi intiẓār-i mahdī*, pp. 112–118, 163–164.

In Kāshmīrī's view, these scholars did not write their books in order to impose the belief in the coming of the *mahdī* on Muslims, but only to preserve the historical record of ideas which were widespread among them. The authors of these books do not say that Muslims must believe in the coming of the *mahdī* or that someone who denies his coming becomes an infidel. The books in question contain many weak or forged traditions and no scholar has ever claimed that they create the "absolute certainty" (*ḥaqq al-yaqīn*) which is indispensable for including an idea in the Islamic articles of faith.[169]

Kāshmīrī includes in his work a substantial list of messianic pretenders who appeared both in the Shīʿī and Sunnī traditions. The Shiʿī list includes pretenders usually associated with the "extremist" (*ghulāt*) Shīʿīs, such as Mughīra b. Saʿīd, Bayān b. Samʿān and Abū Manṣūr ʿIjlī.[170] They are accused of claiming to be not only *mahdī*s but also prophets; some are said to be guilty also of believing in the transmigration of souls and in the dwelling of the divine in the human (*tanāsukh o ḥulūl*) and even of being influenced by Hindū beliefs.[171] The person most harmful to Islam and Muslims in this group was Abū Ṭāhir Qarmaṭī.[172]

Kāshmīrī says that it would be possible to present the names and lives of hundreds of messianic pretenders (*muddaʿiyān-i mahdawiyyat*) who caused internal struggles in the Muslim community. Such a survey would enable us to answer the question from where the messianic idea came, what were its reasons and what were the objectives of its initiators. He chose to present briefly the biographies and activities of thirty-eight such pretenders and leaves no doubt that in his view they led people astray and caused harm to the Muslim community. The only significant exception to this negative assessment of the *mahdī*s is the Sudanese Muḥammad Aḥmad. Kāshmīrī belittles his claim to be the *mahdī*, but he greatly appreciates his endeavours because of his anti-British struggle.[173]

169 Kāshmīrī, *Naẓariyya-yi intiẓār-i mahdī*, pp. 114–116.
170 Kāshmīrī, *Naẓariyya-yi intiẓār-i mahdī*, pp. 141–142.
171 Kāshmīrī, *Naẓariyya-yi intiẓār-i mahdī*, pp. 141–142.
172 Kāshmīrī, *Naẓariyya-yi intiẓār-i mahdī*, pp. 155–159.
173 Kāshmīrī, *Naẓariyya-yi intiẓār-i mahdī*, pp. 141–159. For the appreciation of the Sudanese *mahdī*, see ibid., pp. 153–154. See also Chapter 6.

VII MAWDŪDĪ'S "POTENTIAL" *MAHDĪ*S AND THEIR FAILURES

Abū al-Aʿlā Mawdūdī (1903–1979), one of the most influential thinkers in modern Islam,[174] discusses the *mahdī* issue in his extensive biography of the Prophet (*Sīrat-i sarwar-i ʿālam*), in his work on religious renewal and revival in Islam (*Tajdīd o iḥyāʾ-i dīn*) and in his commentary on the Qurʾān (*Tafhīm al-Qurʾān*).[175] He observes that certain scholars criticized the traditions about the *mahdī* very severely and some even concluded that he would never appear. He also notes that most transmitters of the *mahdī* traditions were Shīʿīs and that some groups, such as the ʿAbbāsīs and certain Shīʿīs, used them for their own political purposes, trying to attach the "signs" (ʿ*alāmāt*) of the *mahdī*'s appearance to their own protagonists. A good example is the famous tradition about the black flags which is designed to prove that the ʿAbbāsī caliph al-Mahdī (r. 775–785) was the expected *mahdī*.[176] Nevertheless, Mawdūdī concludes that the traditions are basically sound as far as the appearance of the *mahdī* itself is concerned, but the particular "signs" are in most cases forged (*waḍʿī*) and deserve little credence; it is possible that people with vested interest (*ahl-i gharaḍ*) added this material to the basically authentic prophetic traditions. The Prophet spoke about the *mahdī* in general terms; he did not give particulars.[177]

Mawdūdī's substantiated his own ideas on the *mahdī* in two ways. The first one is almost completely detached from the traditional material on the apocalypse and reflects Mawdūdī's perception of Islamic history as a

174 Scholarly literature dealing with Mawdūdī is enormous. For the most recent major evaluation and analysis of Mawdūdī's thought system, see Hartung, *A System of Life. Mawdūdī and the Ideologisation of Islam.* On the influence which Mawdūdī wielded on the radical Arab Muslim thinkers such as Sayyid Quṭb, see Lav, *Radical Muslim Theonomy, passim,* especially pp. 252–253. On Mawdūdī's political activities, see Nasr, *The Vanguard of the Islamic Revolution.*

175 Some passages dealing with these issues are repeated in these three works. *Tajdīd o iḥyā-ʾi dīn* has been translated into English by Al-Ashaʿri, *A Short History of the Revivalist Movement in Islam,* Lahore: Islamic Publications Limited, 1963. It is very difficult to do justice to Mawdūdī's complex ideas, steeped in Islamic tradition, in a translation without annotations. There are also two printings of an Arabic translation: *Mūjaz taʾrīkh tajdīd al-dīn wa iḥyāʾihi wa Wāqiʿ al-muslimīn wa sabīl al-nuhūḍ bihim.* Beirut: Dār al-fikr al-ḥadīth 1967 and Beirut: Muʾassasat al-risāla 1975. The translator is Muḥammad Kāẓim Sibāq.

176 See Chapter 1, at notes 151–152.

177 Mawdūdī, *Sīrat-i sarwar-i ʿālam,* vol. 1, pp. 405–406; *idem, Tajdīd o iḥyāʾ-i dīn,* pp. 162–163; *Rasāʾil o masāʾil,* vol. 1, p. 39.

perennial struggle between Islam and its historical antithesis, the *jāhiliyya*. The *jāhiliyya* is represented not only by the non-Muslims, but also by the nominally Muslim rulers who adopt un-Islamic policies. The cause of Islam in this struggle is taken up by "renewers (of religion)" (*mujaddidūn*). In contrast to the classical view, the expected *mahdī* belongs to the category of these "renewers"; yet in contradistinction to his predecessors who were only "partial" (*juzwī*) renewers, he will be a "perfect" one (*mujaddid-i kāmil*) and will perform a crucial and decisive role in this historical struggle. In order to do justice to Mawdūdī's messianic thought, it is therefore necessary to analyse his views on the enmity between Islam and the *jāhiliyya*, on the idea of renewal (*tajdīd*), on the contributions of the various *mujaddidūn* to it and on the expected appearance of the *mahdī*. As for Mawdūdī's other approach to the *mahdī* idea, it is substantially different and uses the classical apocalypse enacted by the *mahdī*, the *dajjāl* and Jesus in order to describe a radical change in the world order, here and now.[178]

Let us start with the analysis of the first approach. Mawdūdī maintains that any system of human life on earth must relate to metaphysical and divine considerations. The cardinal question is what should be the human way of life on earth and what should be its characteristics. The answer to this question is important because it determines the moral character of society. Mawdūdī asserts that there are four possible ways. Three of them are various types of the *jāhiliyya* discussed below. These three types substantially differ from each other, but all are named *jāhiliyya* which denotes any social structure or belief system which is not identical with Mawdūdī's perception of Islam and is perceived as trying to undermine it. The fourth answer is Islam which is, naturally enough, Mawdūdī's natural choice. In his perception, Islam means that the whole universe is the kingdom of one king who created it and is its only possessor and ruler. All are His subjects and all the powers are vested in His hands. Human beings are His subjects by birth (*paydā'ishī ra'iyyat*). Therefore, their status as subjects does not depend on their consent: they have no other option. There is no place for independence or disobedience (*khwud mukhtārī o ghayr dhimma dārī*) and subjects do not have the right to determine their way of life. Their only task is to follow the guidance of their divine ruler which is brought to them by prophets.[179]

178 For the analysis of this approach, see Section VII.
179 Mawdūdī, *Tajdīd o iḥyā'-i dīn*, p. 27.

The struggle between Islam and the *jāhiliyya* began very soon after the emergence of Islam. The Prophet Muḥammad was able to establish the Islamic way of life and perfect it during the twenty-three years of his prophetic activities. His work was preserved and advanced by Abū Bakr and ʿUmar b. al-Khaṭṭāb as well as by ʿUthmān b. ʿAffān in the first years of his caliphate. In ʿUthmān's later years, however, the situation changed for the worse. Uthmān did not have the qualities of his two illustrious predecessors, and in the late years of his rule the *jāhiliyya* had an opportunity to force its way back into the Islamic social order.[180] He tried to stop the *jāhilī* resurgence but failed – and the same happened to ʿAlī b. Abī Ṭālib who also could not stand up to the "counter revolution" (*inqilāb-i maʿkūsī*) staged by the *jāhiliyya*. In this way "the caliphate based on the prophetic model" (*al-khilāfa alā minhāj al-nubuwwa*) as established by Abū Bakr and ʿUmar came to an end and was replaced by a "tyrannical kingdom" (*mulk ʿaḍūḍ*).[181]

This transition of power enabled the *jāhiliyya* to assail the Islamic way of life and the beliefs behind it. Originally the name for the pre-Islamic period in Arab history, *jāhiliyya* became in Mawdūdī's thought a term describing any value system or mental attitude opposed to the Islamic one and bent on the destruction of Islam. The *jāhiliyya* takes on different shapes and sometimes operates in insidious ways in order to undermine the Islamic principles.

Its clearest variety is the "pure *jāhiliyya*" (*jāhiliyya khāliṣa*). This "pure *jāhiliyya*" is atheistic. It denies the existence of God and maintains that the universe came into being for no particular reason. There is no wisdom, interest or purpose behind its existence and it will end without any consequence. Humans also came into being accidentally. There is no discussion of the question who created them and for what purpose. They have no supernatural source of knowledge or guidance on the basis of which they could formulate their laws. They must therefore take them from the conditions in their environment and from their historical experience.[182] There

180 Criticism of ʿUthmān b. ʿAffān's policies – especially appointments of his relatives to lucrative offices and erecting sumptuous buildings in the last six years of his reign – is standard in classical Muslim historiography. By way of example, see Ibn Qutayba, *al-Imāma wa al-siyāsa*, vol. 1, pp. 50–52.

181 Mawdūdī, *Tajdīd o iḥyāʾ-i dīn*, pp. 35–36.

182 These are the man-made laws which Mawdūdī systematically denounced in his writings. Cf. Hartung, *A System of Life*, pp. 64–66; Lav, *Radical Muslim Theonomy ...*, pp. 229–232.

is no afterlife and this "purely *jāhilī*" (*jāhiliyyat-i khāliṣa*) world view is utterly materialistic (*mādda parastāna*).[183] Furthermore, this *jāhilī* assault brought about the emergence of sects such as the Muʿtazila, encouraged various types of heresies and brought into Islam un-Islamic forms of art such as dancing, painting and music.[184]

The second type of *jāhiliyya* is the "associationist" one (*jāhiliyyat-i mushrikāna*) and is a reflection of what we know about Arab beliefs in the pre-Islamic period. This type is as dangerous as the "pure" one and co-operated with it throughout the ages. It attacked mainly the common people and led them astray in many ways. It differs from its "pure" counterpart by maintaining that the universe is not godless (*bē khudā*), but rather subject to numerous gods one of whom is superior to the others and has ministers, courtiers and associates at his service. In this type of *jāhiliyya* there was no outright polytheism, but other forms of *shirk* did take their place among the Muslims. The lesser gods were dispensed with, but were replaced with various Ṣūfī figures such as *awliyāʾ*, *mashāyikh*, and *aqṭāb*. Polytheistic prayers are replaced with ceremonies such as visitations to the tombs of saints (*ziyārat*), celebrations of their death anniversary (*ʿurs*), commemorating the martyrdom of Ḥusayn b. ʿAlī (*taʿziya*), carrying various standards during this commemoration (*nishān*, *ʿalam*), offerings made to the tombs of saints (*chaṙhāwā*) and rubbing the grave of the saint with pieces of sandalwood dipped in water; all these are tantamount to a new *sharīʿa*.[185]

The third variety is the "monastic *jāhiliyya*" (*jāhiliyyat-i rāhibāna*) which assailed the *ʿulamāʾ*, the Ṣūfī shaykhs, the ascetics and other honest people. It introduced into Islam the Neoplatonic philosophy and monastic morals. It influenced the literature and the sciences; it introduced despondency into Muslim society, caused stagnation and narrow-minded attitudes in Islamic sciences. It had an effect of a "morphine injection" (*mārfiyā kā injection*), causing idleness and inactivity. It reduced the whole religiosity to a limited number of religious commandments.[186] It spread the idea that this world is a place of punishment for man and his spirit is a prisoner in his material body. His pleasures and desires are

183 Mawdūdī, *Tajdīd o iḥyāʾ-i dīn*, pp. 14–16.
184 Mawdūdī, *Tajdīd o iḥyāʾ-i dīn*, p. 39.
185 Mawdūdī, *Tajdīd o iḥyāʾ-i dīn*, pp. 18–20, 39–40. I am grateful to Professor Muzaffar Alam of Chicago University for explaining to me some of these customs.
186 Mawdūdī, *Tajdīd o iḥyāʾ-i dīn*, p. 40.

nothing but shackles in this mundane prison. The more he is attached to worldly things, the greater will be his punishment. This type of *jāhiliyya* maintains that in order to extricate himself from this predicament, man must cut his connection to worldly affairs, suppress his desires, refrain from pleasures and refuse to fulfil the desires of his body and soul (*nafs*) to prevent them from taking over his spirit. Only in this way will his spirit attain salvation.[187]

Monastic philosophy is in Mawdūdī's view an "anti-social"[188] theory. It is the mainstay of Buddhism, Vedantism, Manichaeism, Neoplatonism, Yoga, Ṣūfism and Christian monasticism. It is "anti-social" because it debilitates the people's determination to resist evil. It creates among them misguided theories supporting passive endurance, spreads despondency and makes them meek and docile vis-à-vis their oppressors. History knows no example in which monastic philosophy fought against imperialism, capitalism or the power of the Pope (*pāpā'iyyat*). It is a negative way of thinking which has the effect of opium and cocaine wherever it is found. It bars good people from social engagement, imposes on them seclusion and austerity (*tapasyā*), and clears the way for villains to take power and spread corruption at will. Therefore, the rulers and the leaders of religion happily spread this philosophy.[189]

One of the factors which made the struggle against the *jāhiliyya* extremely difficult was that it did not appear in its naked form, "without a veil", but rather posed as Islam, appeared under "Islamic" guise (*jāhiliyyat bē niqāb hō kar sāmnē na ā'ī thī bal kih "musalmān" ban kar ā'ī thī*). Had it appeared in its manifest, "naked" form (*jāhiliyyat-i ṣarīḥa, 'uryān jāhiliyyat*), thousands of warriors would have taken to the field and no Muslim would have openly supported it. But this was not the case. The *jāhiliyya* affirmed the existence of one God, the belief in Muḥammad, performed the prayers, observed the fast of Ramaḍān, quoted from the Qur'ān and the *ḥadīth* – and insidiously did its work behind the scenes.[190]

How did Islam cope with these recurrent assaults of the *jāhiliyya*?

187 Mawdūdī, *Tajdīd o iḥyā'-i dīn*, p. 23.

188 This is Mawdūdī's translation of *ghayr tamaddunī*. See Mawdūdī, *Tajdīd o iḥyā'-i dīn*, p. 23 *infra*.

189 Mawdūdī, *Tajdīd o iḥyā'-i dīn*, pp. 23–25.

190 Mawdūdī, *Tajdīd o iḥyā'-i dīn*, p. 37. For a different, more extensive and more philosophical analysis of Mawdūdī's understanding of the *jāhiliyya*, see Hartung, *A System of Life*, pp. 61–72.

In nations which were influenced by Islam, the *jāhiliyya* was not able to eliminate Islam totally and vestiges of Islamic influence always remained. Some tyrannical rulers even adopted the right way because of their fear of God. But the task to counter the *jāhiliyya* assaults fell mainly upon the "centennial renewers" (*mujaddidūn*). In order to enhance the importance of these renewers, Mawdūdī takes pains to explain that the famous *ḥadīth* according to which "God will send to this community on the eve of every century a man who will renew its religion" (*inna Allah yabʿathu li-hādhihi al-umma ʿalā raʾsi kulli miʾa sana man yujaddidu lahā dīnahā*) was misinterpreted. The *ḥadīth* was not meant to indicate that there was only one renewer in every century. Since the particle *man* in Arabic can be used for both the singular and the plural, Mawdūdī asserts that there could be numerous renewers in every century and there could be different renewers, even whole groups and political administrations, in different regions of the Muslim world.[191] This interpretation allows him to argue that the contribution of these personalities to the renewal of Islam is much greater than one renewer in each century could accomplish.

Mawdūdī starts his discussion of the renewal idea with a clarification of what he deems to be the widespread conceptual confusion between "becoming modern" (*tajaddud*) and "renewal" (*tajdīd*). People usually do not distinguish between these two concepts and call every *mutajaddid* a *mujaddid*. Yet the two concepts are not identical. A *mutajaddid* is someone who invents a new way (of doing things) and vigorously brings it into use, or attempts to protect the worldly interests of a declining Muslim community. At times he tries to forge some compromise with the *jāhiliyya* in which his community is steeped, or to produce a "new composite" (*nayā makhlūṭa*) between *jāhiliyya* and Islam. In other words, a *mutajaddid* is someone who invents ideas or ways of life which are unrelated to Islam or even harmful to it, someone whom we may call in modern parlance a "modernist". Such people do not deserve the title of renewer (*mujaddid*). A real renewer does not forge compromises with the *jāhiliyya*; his task is to cleanse Islam from all *jāhilī* elements and restore its original splendour. In his confrontation with the *jāhiliyya*, the *mujaddid* is a most uncompromising person (*sakht ghayr muṣālaḥat pasand ādmī*).[192]

191 Mawdūdī, *Tajdīd o iḥyāʾ-i dīn*, pp. 42–43.
192 Mawdūdī, *Tajdīd o iḥyāʾ-i dīn*, pp. 44–45.

A renewer is not a prophet – because no prophet can be sent after Muḥammad – but he is very close to him in character (*mujaddid nabī nahīñ hōtā magar apnē mizāj mēñ mizāj-i nubuwwat sē bohot qarīb hōtā hay*). He does not bring a new set of laws, nor does he receive divine revelation (*waḥy*) and belief in him is not a condition of being a Muslim. Still, the nature of his work is identical with that of prophets. He has an absolutely pure mind, is able to penetrate reality, is free from any crookedness or excess and has a special ability to adopt the straight path of moderation (*i ʿtidāl, tawassuṭ*). He is free from centuries-old superstitions, has an inborn leadership ability and is able to distinguish between Islam and *jāhiliyya* in the smallest details. Nobody can be a renewer without possessing all these qualities.[193]

The renewers are not equal in stature. A renewer who performs a part of the tasks mentioned previously is a "partial renewer" (*mujaddid-i juzwī*). Mawdūdī provides an interpretation of the thought and activities of several personalities of this kind in order to explain why all of them failed to reach the rank of a "perfect renewer" (*mujaddid-i kāmil*).[194] In other words, he sets out to explain why none of the "partial renewers" succeeded in fulfilling his potential and becoming a "perfect renewer" who is identical with the *mahdī.*

The first of these "partial renewers" – or "potential *mahdī*s" – was the Umayyad caliph ʿUmar b. ʿAbd al-ʿAzīz (680?–720).[195] He belonged to a wealthy family and his father was the governor of Egypt. He received a good education and became a prominent *muḥaddith* and *mujtahid.* At the same time, he had a huge income and lived a princely life. Though he must have been aware of the principles of frugality and morality which guided Muslim society during the time of the Prophet and the first four "righteous" caliphs, he felt constrained to give preference to the economic interests of his family. His ancestors were instrumental in the "*jāhilī* revolution" (*jāhilī inqilāb*) which transformed the pious

193 Mawdūdī, *Tajdīd o iḥyā ʾ-i dīn*, pp. 45–46.

194 Hartung (*A System of Life*, pp. 80–81) sees a connection between this "perfect *mujaddid*" and the "perfect man" (*al-insān al-kāmil*) of Ibn al-ʿArabī and the "believing man" (*mard-i mu ʾmin*) of Muḥammad Iqbāl.

195 It is well known that ʿUmar b. ʿAbd al-ʿAzīz is highly appreciated in Muslim historiography. The following passage is relevant to Mawdūdī's discussion: "Wahb b. Munabbih said: 'If there is a *mahdī* in this community, it is ʿUmar b. ʿAbd al-ʿAzīz.'" See Suyūṭī, *Ta ʾrīkh al-khulafā ʾ*, p. 205.

caliphate into the Umayyad monarchy; his solidarity (*ʿaṣabiyyat*) with them prevented him from taking the straight path and he continued to live in luxury, "like a Pharaoh".[196] However, when he became caliph by sheer accident in 717, he changed his lifestyle abruptly, without any deliberation, as if he had planned it before. His income was drastically reduced. He dispensed with the pomp and luxury which characterized his predecessors' rule and adopted a style which should be followed by a Muslim caliph, increasing equality between Muslims and removing unjust practices. He started purging the people's lives of the evil effects of *jāhilī* rule which lasted for half a century before his assumption of power and revived the Islamic system of government (*islāmī niẓām-i ḥukūmat do bāra zinda huʾa*).[197] The Umayyads could not tolerate this: they were convinced that "the life of Islam is tantamount to their death" (*islām kī zindagī mēñ un-kī mawt thī*) and poisoned him at the young age of thirty-nine. Thus ended the first struggle between *jāhiliyya* and Islam after the death of the Prophet. The reins of political power were permanently seized by *jāhilī* forces (*ḥukūmat kī bāgēñ mustaqill ṭawr par jāhiliyyat kē hāthōñ mēñ chalī gaʾīñ*), among which Mawdūdī lists the Umayyads, the ʿAbbāsīs and various later dynasties of Turkish origin. These dynasties slavishly spread the *jāhilī* philosophies of Greece, Rome and Iran, adding to them all the errors of the "first *jāhiliyya*" (*jāhiliyyat-i ūlā*) – by which term Mawdūdī probably means the belief system and social customs of the pre-Islamic Arabs.[198]

Yet the endeavours of ʿUmar b. ʿAbd al-ʿAzīz were not in vain: they paved the way for the intellectual resurgence initiated by Abū Ḥanīfa, al-Shāfiʿī, Mālik b. Anas and Aḥmad b. Ḥanbal, the eponymous founders of the four schools of law in Islam.[199] As a result of their efforts and despite the strong opposition of the ruling dynasties, Islamic laws were deduced from the principles of religion, they were recorded in books and a whole civilizational infrastructure based on Islam was established

---

196 Mawdūdī goes far beyond the traditional description of ʿUmar's lifestyle before assuming the caliphate. The traditional biographies of ʿUmar speak about his proud gait, elegant clothing and lavish use of perfume, but there is no reference to nepotism mentioned by Mawdūdī. See Ibn ʿAbd al-Ḥakam, *Sīrat ʿUmar b. ʿAbd al-ʿAzīz*, pp. 20–21; Ibn al-Jawzī, *Manāqib ʿUmar b. ʿAbd al-ʿAzīz*, p. 17, *supra*.

197 Mawdūdī, *Tajdīd o iḥyāʾ-i dīn*, pp. 55–59.

198 Mawdūdī, *Tajdīd o iḥyāʾ-i dīn*, pp. 60–61, 63–64. For the term *al-jāhiliyya al-ūlā*, see Qurʾān 33:33.

199 Mawdūdī, *Tajdīd o iḥyāʾ-i dīn*, p. 59.

between the second and fourth centuries AH. Mawdūdī takes pains to emphasize that all this work was done in defiance of the political authorities and the four scholars suffered persecution, imprisonment and torture. This description fully fits only the biography of Ibn Ḥanbal, but Mawdūdī sees all the four scholars in the same light. Because of their endeavours – which inspired scholars in later centuries – they are entitled to the rank of *mujaddid*.[200]

The same goes for the major Muslim thinker Abū Ḥāmid al-Ghazālī (d. 1111). His period was characterized by the prevalence of Greek philosophy which shook the very foundations of Islam, but no qualified Muslim scholars of stature were available to confront it. This caused the common people to consider Islam as a religion which cannot withstand the test of reason. Since the ignorant rulers turned a blind eye to religion, there was no material support for the dissemination of religious sciences and there was no *ijtihād*. The rulers were not able even to appoint qualified people to positions of judges and *muftīs*. Rigid adherence to schools of law (*taqlīd*) took over and new sects emerged because of differences of opinion on insignificant details. The Qur'ān and the prophetic *sunna* fell into disuse. Moral degeneration set in across the Muslim world.

Al-Ghazālī rose to the challenge and made valiant efforts to improve the situation. Basing himself on al-Ghazālī's spiritual autobiography, "The deliverer from error" (*al-Munqidh min al-ḍalāl*), Mawdūdī describes al-Ghazālī's personal crisis, his abandonment of the lucrative position as the rector of the Niẓāmiyya *madrasa* in Baghdad, and the years he spent in travel, study and meditation. In Mawdūdī's view, his main achievement was that after mastering the principles of Greek philosophy, he was able to loosen the grip of this philosophy on Muslims, defend Islam using rational arguments and, so to speak, beat the philosophers at their own game. This is a reference to al-Ghazālī's work "Incoherence of the philosophers" (*Tahāfut al-falāsifa*).[201]

Despite all these efforts, al-Ghazālī failed to improve the situation. In Mawdūdī's opinion, he failed mainly because he did not initiate any organized movement to effect a political revolution and could not exercise even the slightest influence on the governmental system which continued to

200 Mawdūdī, *Tajdīd o iḥyā'-i dīn*, pp. 62–63.
201 Mawdūdī, *Tajdīd o iḥyā'-i dīn*, pp. 63–72.

deteriorate despite his efforts. Ibn Khaldūn said that al-Ghazālī wanted to establish a state built on pure Islamic principles and the state of the Almohads (*al-muwaḥḥidūn*) in the Maghrib was established by a student of his, but this was only a marginal part of al-Ghazālī's activity.[202] As far as the content of al-Ghazālī's thought is concerned, Mawdūdī considered it deficient because of his weakness in *ḥadīth,* his excessive inclination to Ṣūfism and the prevalence of the "rational" sciences (*ʿaqliyyāt*) in his mentality.[203]

Thus, Mawdūdī opines that al-Ghazālī's mastery of the "rational" sciences, praised by him as a very important achievement, took him too far. This is understandable against the background of Mawdūdī's general view on the task of rationality in Islam. In his view, Islam is "a rational religion" (*ēk ʿilmī awr ʿaqlī madhhab*) and, therefore, people who use their intellect will necessarily reach the conclusion that it is also the true one. Hence rationalism is a strategy for converting people to Islam or fighting deviations from "correct" belief rather than a guide for human life in general. Therefore al-Ghazālī was on the right path when he used rational arguments to undermine the views of the *falāsifa*. But he should not have given rationality a permanent place in the Islamic world view. Once a person embraces Islam on the basis of

---

202 Mawdūdī hints here at the famous – but historically impossible – story according to which al-Ghazālī met Ibn Tūmart, the founder of the Almohad empire, in Baghdad and asked him to overthrow the Almoravid empire because it ordered the burning of his book, "The revival of religious sciences" (*Iḥyāʾ ʿulūm al-dīn*). To call Ibn Tūmart a student of al-Ghazālī because of this meeting seems highly exaggerated. See Ibn Qaṭṭān, *Naẓm al-jumān*, pp. 14–18 (extensive bibliography on the story can be found on p. 16, note 5) and Ibn Qunfudh, *al-Fārisiyya*, p. 100. Ibn Khaldūn himself mentions this meeting in a hesitant way ("... according to what they say, he met Abū Ḥāmid al-Ghazālī ...") and says that they discussed the disintegration of Islam in the Maghrib. See Ibn Khaldūn, *Kitāb al-ʿibar*, vol. 6, pp. 465–466. The meeting between Ibn Tūmart and al-Ghazālī is mentioned also in Marrākushī, *al-Muʿjib*, pp. 155–156. Ibn Kathīr (*Kitāb al-bidāya wa al-nihāya*, vol. 12, p. 230) mentions Ibn Tūmart's studies with Ghazālī, but does not mention the episode related here. Griffel has cogent arguments to deny the historicity of the story: when Ibn Tūmart reached Baghdad, al-Ghazālī was no longer there and Ibn Tūmart's political heirs spread the story after his death. See Griffel, *Al-Ghazālī's Philosophical Theology*, p. 77.

203 Mawdūdī, *Tajdīd o iḥyāʾ-i dīn*, pp. 63–73. Mawdūdī mentions Subkī's *Ṭabaqāt al-Shāfiʿiyya al-kubrā* as his sources for al-Ghazālī's thinking. And, indeed, this source includes critical remarks by medieval scholars which resemble Mawdūdī's views. See ibid., vol. 6, pp. 240ff.

"rational" analysis and arguments, rationalism has done its duty and must go. It is no longer needed and is even dangerous because it could make obedience to Islamic commandments contingent upon rational deliberations. This is an undesirable result of rationalism and should be avoided.[204]

The next *mujaddid* who had the right ideas but failed in his efforts to revive Islam was Ibn Taymiyya (d. 1328)[205] who lived in the catastrophic period which followed the Mongol invasion of the Muslim world. Though the Mongols were in the process of embracing Islam, their influence on all parts of Muslim society was even worse than that of their Turkish predecessors. The worst reflection of this influence was the acquiescence of the Muslim leadership in non-Muslim rule. To his great consternation, Mawdūdī notes that the Baghdad *ʿulamāʾ* ruled – in response to Hulagu's question – that a just infidel ruler is preferable to an oppressive Muslim one. For a thinker like Mawdūdī, who has always maintained that implementation of Islamic law by a Muslim ruler is a religious imperative, such a statement is tantamount to sacrilege.[206] No less outrageous in Mawdūdī's eyes is the fact that even in areas which did not succumb to the Mongol onslaught, such as Syria and Egypt, Mongol laws were widely used.[207]

In these adverse conditions, Ibn Taymiyya continued al-Ghazālī's criticism of Greek philosophy and did it in a way which was more effective and closer to the spirit of Islam. Al-Ghazālī used the technical vocabulary of rational sciences, while Ibn Taymiyya placed more emphasis on common sense arguments. He also vehemently criticized numerous un-Islamic customs which spread among Muslims. In contradistinction to al-Ghazālī, he was also a recognized expert on *ḥadīth*. However, like al-Ghazālī before

204 For a more extensive discussion of rationalism in Mawdūdī's thought, see Friedmann, "Quasi-Rational and Anti-Rational Elements in Radical Muslim Thought: The Case of Abū al-Aʿlā Mawdūdī".

205 The bibliography on Ibn Taymiyya is enormous. The last major collection of articles on him is Rapoport and Ahmad, eds, *Ibn Taymiyya and his Times*. The book includes an extensive bibliography on pp. 367–388.

206 Mawdūdī, *Tajdīd o iḥyāʾ-i dīn*, p. 74, note. This idea has been broached in Arabic literature much before the Mongol conquest. For a profound analysis of the idea and extensive bibliography, see Sadan, "'Community' and 'Extra-Community' as a Legal and Literary Problem".

207 On the question to what extent the Yāsa of Chinggis Khān was known or implemented in the Mamlūk state, see Ayalon, "The Great Yāsa of Jingis Khān", pp. 105, 115 and *passim*.

him, he did not initiate a political movement which could result in the transfer of power to Islam.[208]

The next person discussed as a *mujaddid* is Shaykh Aḥmad Sirhindī (d. 1624) who is known as "the renewer of the second millennium" (*mujaddid-i alf-i thānī*). His description by Mawdūdī follows the well-known interpretation of Pakistani historians in whose view the "un-Islamic" policies of Emperor Akbar (r. 1556–1605) would have caused the disintegration of Islam in India if Aḥmad Sirhindī had not stepped into the breach, had not fearlessly fought against Akbar's "innovations" and had not paved the way for the orthodox reforms of Awrangzēb.[209] Seemingly because of this perceived achievement, Mawdūdī refrains from criticizing Sirhindī for failing to launch a political movement in the way he criticized al-Ghazālī and Ibn Taymiyya, but his failure to do so may be due to oversight.

Mawdūdī described the achievements of Aḥmad Sirhindī (d. 1624) in glowing terms. Yet these achievements seem to have been short-lived: when Mawdūdī comes to describe the renewal efforts of Shāh Walī Allāh (d. 1762) a century later, he again finds the situation of Islam extremely bad and marvels how it is possible that a man of such insight and mentality as Shāh Walī Allah could have been born in such a decadent age. Mawdūdī has good reason to include Walī Allah in the category of renewers, because Walī Allah made this claim for himself.[210] In Mawdūdī's view, he was one of those leaders who are able to disentangle the jungle of convoluted ideas and create out of it a clear and straight path. Mawdūdī divides the work of Walī Allah into two parts: his criticism of the situation of Islam (*tanqīdī kām*) in his age and his suggestions for reconstruction (*taʿmīrī kām*). He adduces lengthy passages from Shāh Walī Allah's works and credits him with important intellectual achievements.[211] He feels close spiritual affinity with Walī Allah because he perceives in the latter's works a clear distinction between Islamic rule and its *jāhilī* counterpart – a distinction

208 Mawdūdī, *Tajdīd o iḥyā'-i dīn*, pp. 76–80.

209 See, for instance, Qureshi, *The Muslim Community of the Indo-Pakistan Subcontinent*, pp. 149–153. For a critique of this interpretation, see Friedmann, *Shaykh Aḥmad Sirhindī*, pp. 77–111.

210 See Walī Allah, *Tafhīmāt*, vol. 1, p. 40: "When I reached the stage of wisdom, God bestowed upon me the robe of being a renewer" (*lammā tammat bī dawrat al-ḥikma, albasanī Allāh khilʿat al-mujaddidiyya*).

211 Mawdūdī, *Tajdīd o iḥyā'-i dīn*, pp. 89–113.

which is the mainstay of Mawdūdī's thought.[212] However, he also criticizes Shāh Walī Allah for being totally absorbed in his intellectual pursuits of criticism and reconstruction of religious thought rather than in taking concrete steps of reform.[213]

The last figures in Mawdūdī's list of (partial) *mujaddidūn* are Sayyid Aḥmad Barēlwī and Shāh Ismāʿīl Shahīd, the leaders of the famous movement of the *mujāhidīn*.[214] Mawdūdī considers their work to be complementary to that of Shāh Walī Allāh. Again, Mawdūdī describes their personalities and efforts in glowing terms. In the regions where they were active, life was revolutionized to such an extent that people were reminded of the period of the Prophet's companions. In the difficult conditions of India in the beginning of the nineteenth century, they made preparations for *jihād*. They chose the North Western Province area as their base and this was an appropriate choice. Their fighting was guided by the high moral principles characteristic of those who fight for the sake of Allah rather than for worldly gain. When they had a chance to establish their rule in an area, they established "caliphate on the model of prophecy" (*khilāfa ʿalā minhāj al-nubuwwa*).[215]

This last movement of renewal was successful in the moral sense, because its members worked sincerely to win the favour of Allah. However, in the worldly sense they failed, because they were unable to put an end to the *jāhilī* rule and replace it with the Islamic one. One needs to understand

---

212 Mawdūdī, *Tajdīd o iḥyā'-i dīn*, p. 113.

213 According to Mawdūdī, Walī Allah indicated that "if the circumstances of the place required it, I would truly have the aptitude to make reform by means of war" (*agar mawqiʿ o maḥall kā iqtiżā hōtā, tō mayñ jang kar kē ʿamalan iṣlāḥ karnē kī qābiliyyat rakhtā thā*) ((Mawdūdī, *Tajdīd o iḥyā'-i dīn*, pp. 90–91). But the passage which he mentions does not refer to Walī Allah. It rather says that "the universal soul does not descend on the day it descends in the speaking souls except in the form of the greatest man ... If it is assumed that this man will exist at a time when the circumstances require reforming the people by waging war and he would be inspired to reform them, he would wage war in a perfect manner ... " (... *inna al-nufūs al-nāṭiqa lā tanzilu fīhā al-nafs al-kulliyya illā bi-ṣūrat al-shakhṣ al-akbar yawma tanazzulihā ... wa ka-dhālika law furiḍa an yakūna hādhā al-rajul fī zamān wa 'qtaḍat al-asbāb an yakūna iṣlāḥ al-nās bi-iqāmat al-ḥurūb wa nufitha fī qalbihi iṣlāḥuhum la-qāma hādhā al-rajul bi-amr al-ḥarb atamma qiyām*). The passage then speaks about other possibilities of reform by this "greatest man" such as science or building activities. See Walī Allah, *Tafhīmāt*, vol. 1, pp. 100–101. "The greatest man" is part of Walī Allah's cosmic philosophy and Mawdūdī did not correctly understand Walī Allāh's Neoplatonic text. See Jalbani, *Teachings of Shāh Walī Allah of Delhi*, pp. 169–170.

214 See Gaborieau, "Barēlwī, Sayyid Aḥmad", *EI*³, s.v.

215 Mawdūdī, *Tajdīd o iḥyā'-i dīn*, pp. 114–117.

why the British succeeded in establishing their purely *jāhilī* rule (*khāliṣ jāhilī ḥukūmat*) though they came to India from a great distance, while the dedicated and enthusiastic *mujāhidīn* failed to achieve their objective. This understanding is necessary so that Muslims do not get despondent and do not get the impression that the world cannot be reformed by means of *jihād*.[216] The first reason for their failure was Ṣūfism. Mawdūdī is careful not to criticize Ṣūfism in general. In his view, thinkers such as Aḥmad Sirhindī and Shāh Walī Allah represented "authentic Ṣūfism" (*aṣlī taṣawwuf*) which is not different from benevolence (*iḥsān*).[217] However, other components of Ṣūfism and mainly the absolute, blind obedience of the Ṣūfī novice to his *pīr* is subject to Mawdūdī's criticism. This obedience paralyses the Ṣūfī's mind, prevents him from using his intelligence and makes him servile to the *pīr* as if the *pīr* were his God. There is no difference between the *pīrī–murīdī* relationship and between "taking others than God as Lords" which was condemned in the Qur'ān. The debilitating influence of this "*jāhilī* Ṣūfism" (*jāhilī taṣawwuf*) explains also the failure of some previous "partial renewers".[218]

Mawdūdī has also an insight which is specific to the movement of Sayyid Aḥmad Barēlwī and Ismā'īl Shahīd. Though the members of this movement were highly motivated and pious Muslims, they came to the North Western Province from all parts of India and were considered "immigrants" (*muhājirūn*) who were not integrated into the local population. It is a little surprising that Mawdūdī sees this as a problem; after all, *hijra* has been part and parcel of the Islamic ethos since the very beginning. Another reason relates to the religious standards of the North Western Province Muslims. The *mujāhidūn* expected the local Muslims to react to the establishment of their caliphate as "real" Muslims (*aṣlī musalmān*) should. But the local Muslims were only "nominal" Muslims (*nām kē musalmān*), did not live up to the expectations of the *mujāhidīn* and were not able to sustain the

216 Mawdūdī, *Tajdīd o iḥyā'-i dīn*, pp. 118–119.

217 In classical *ḥadīth*, *iḥsān* is sometimes described as the highest degree of religiosity, above *islām* and *īmān*. In a famous tradition included in al-Bukhārī's *Ṣaḥīḥ* (vol. 1, p. 21, *Kitāb al-īmān* 37), *islām* is defined as the performance of the five principal commandments (*arkān al-islām*); *īmān* as believing in God, in His angels, books and messengers, and in the divine decree, both good and bad; *iḥsān* is defined as worshipping God as if you see Him, and if you do not see Him – as if He sees you (*an ta'bud Allah ka-annaka tarāhu wa in lam takun tarāhu fa-innahu yarāka*).

218 Mawdūdī, *Tajdīd o iḥyā'-i dīn*, pp. 119–122. Cf. Qur'ān 3:64 and 9:31. For another analysis of Mawdūdī's view of Ṣūfism, see Hartung, *A System of Life*, pp. 68–69.

caliphate.[219] A further reason for their failure was the *mujāhidīn*'s ignorance of contemporary developments in Europe. Mawdūdī mentions names of numerous modern European philosophers and scientists and takes the leaders of the movement to task for disregarding the momentous changes which took place in Europe in the eighteenth and nineteenth centuries, such as the industrial, economic, scientific and philosophical revolution which created a new civilization and completely changed the balance of power between the world of Islam and the West. These developments which enabled the British to establish their *jāhilī* rule in India went totally unnoticed by the leaders of the *mujāhidīn*.[220] It should have been clear to them that the real enemy in nineteenth-century India were the British rather than the Sikhs. They made a serious blunder when they directed their *jihād* against the wrong enemy.[221]

In Mawdūdī's view, these were the reasons for the failure of renewal efforts throughout Muslim history. In other words, this explains why none of the "partial" *mujaddid*s was able to rise to the rank of the "perfect" one and thus become the *mahdī*. All these *mujaddidūn* were persons who possessed a potential to become *mahdī*s, but failed to realize it. All of them had the right ideas on the necessary reforms, but were not able to implement them. The main reason for their failure was their inability – or misguided unwillingness – to initiate political movements which would have implemented their worthy ideas and replaced the *jāhilī* rule with an Islamic one.

In classical Islamic thought, religious renewal is not discussed in conjunction with the idea of the *mahdī*. As Ella Landau-Tasseron has called it, *tajdīd* is "cyclical reform".[222] It needs to be repeated periodically and is not expected to effect a long-lasting or permanent transformation in the condition of Islam. Mawdūdī's *mujaddidūn*, on the other hand, are partial, potential *mahdī*s. Mawdūdī's idea that such *mahdī*s existed throughout Islamic history, but failed to realize their potential because they concentrated on moral and intellectual reforms while neglecting to take concrete, political action – seems to be novel in Islamic thought.

219 Mawdūdī, *Tajdīd o iḥyā'-i dīn*, pp. 120–123.
220 Mawdūdī, *Tajdīd o iḥyā'-i dīn*, pp. 124–129.
221 Mawdūdī, *Tajdīd o iḥyā'-i dīn*, p. 128. Mawdūdī refers here to the well-known fact that the *mujāhidīn* directed their *jihād* against the Sikhs rather than against the British. See Qureshi, *The Muslim Community of the Indo-Pakistan Subcontinent*, pp. 199–201 and other studies of Indian Muslim history in the nineteenth century.
222 Landau-Tasseron, "The 'Cyclical Reform': A Study of the *Mujaddid* Tradition".

VIII MAWDŪDĪ'S TRADITIONAL JESUS, MODERN *MAHDĪ* AND MODERN *DAJJĀL*

In addition to the historical survey of the renewal movements in Islam and their failure, Mawdūdī elaborates his own ideas on the *mahdī*, who is "the perfect renewer" (*mujaddid-i kāmil*) in his parlance. This elaboration entails a major reinterpretation of the classical material and is included in his extensive biography of the Prophet, in his commentary on the Qur'ān and in his *Rasā'il o masā'il*. He includes his views on the *mahdī* in a chapter dealing with "predictions" (*pēshīn gū'īyāñ*) in the *ḥadīth*. Like in the classical tradition, the *mahdī* envisaged by Mawdūdī will achieve world domination. He will accomplish this by his intellectual leadership, as well as by political and military prowess. Mawdūdī has no use for the fantastic stories about cataclysmic eschatological battles in which the Muslim supporters of the *mahdī* kill myriads of infidels in order to take over the world or about the unlimited amount of money supplied by the *mahdī* during the apocalyptic period. In contradistinction to what Mawdūdī sees as the perception of common Muslims, his *mahdī* will not be of the Ṣūfī or Mawlwī type who suddenly emerges from some *khāngāh* or *madrasa* with a rosary (*tasbīḥ*) in hand and declares himself a *mahdī*. Mawdūdī also mocks the common belief that the *'ulamā'* will compare his bodily features to the classical descriptions of the *mahdī*, and if they find them compatible, will swear allegiance to him and *jihād* will be declared.[223]

Mawdūdī's *mahdī* will be different. He will have an independent understanding (*mujtahidāna baṣīrat*) of all the new sciences of his time. He will understand all the important problems of life. Though he will establish "a caliphate following the prophetic model" (*al-khilāfa 'alā minhāj al-nubuwwa*), he will be an absolutely new type of leader (*jadīd-tarīn ṭarz kā līdar*). He will profoundly understand all problems of life. This does not mean that he will be a clean-shaven, beardless person, wearing jacket and trousers according to the latest (Western) fashion; it rather means that "he will surpass all new things of his times and a new 'novelty' will be established" (*apnē 'ahd kē tamām jadīdōñ sē baṙh kar jadīd thābit hōgā*). If the Prophet Muḥammad used the mote (*khandaq*), the catapult (*manjanīq*) and the battering ram (*dabbāba*), there is no reason why his

223 Mawdūdī, *Sīrat-i sarwar-i 'ālam*, vol. 1, pp. 405–406; cf. Mawdūdī, *Tajdīd o iḥyā'-i dīn*, p. 52. Parts of these texts are identical in the two sources.

successor (*jā-nishīn*) – the *mahdī* – should not use the latest technology, such as tanks and planes.[224]

The Mawlwīs and the Ṣūfīs will at first oppose the *mahdī*'s innovations. He will not be the person they expected: he will not have a body different from that of a regular person, so that it will not be possible to recognize him by the signs (*ʿalāmāt*) mentioned in the classical literature. Mawdūdī does not expect that he will even declare himself a *mahdī*. Possibly he will not even know that he was one – and the world will become aware of his standing only after his death, in view of his accomplishments.[225] Despite the clearly Islamic nature of the state which he will establish – a caliphate following the prophetic model – he will not be a religious leader in whom one must believe as one must believe in prophets. Essentials of belief and disbelief have all been made clear in the Qurʾān. The Qurʾānic verse which says that "Surely upon Us rests the guidance" (*inna ʿalaynā 'l-hudā*)[226] is taken to mean that it is God's duty to clarify these essentials and He does not leave such things to the decision of humans. Prophetic traditions in themselves cannot decide such issues. Had God wanted to make the belief in the *mahdī* obligatory, He would have included a commandment to this effect in the Qurʾān.[227]

Mawdūdī's *mahdī* will have no place for miracles, supernatural inspiration (*kushūf o ilhāmāt*), prolonged fasting (*chillā*) or ascetic exercises (*mujāhadāt*). Like other revolutionary leaders, the *mahdī* will have to endure trials, tribulations and struggles. He will establish a new school of thought on a purely Islamic basis. He will transform ways of thinking and establish a powerful movement, both civilizational and political. Against the determined opposition of the un-Islamic political order (*jāhiliyya*), he will establish a powerful Islamic state where the Islamic spirit will reign supreme, and at the same time it will reach the pinnacle of scientific development.[228]

Furthermore, the *mahdī* will not be infallible as the Shīʿīs would have it. He will be a leader who is "on the straight path" (*rāh-i rāst par*). He is a *mahdī*, "a guided one" rather than a *hādī*, "a guiding one". By stressing

224 This passage has already been noted by Hartung, *A System of Life*, p. 82.

225 Mawdūdī, *Sīrat-i sarwar-i ʿālam*, vol. 1, pp. 406–408; *idem*, *Tajdīd o iḥyāʾ-i dīn*, pp. 52–53; *idem*, *Rasāʾil o masāʾil*, vol. 1, p. 44.

226 Qurʾān 92:12.

227 Mawdūdī, *Tajdīd o iḥyāʾ-i dīn*, p. 165. See also ibid., p. 146.

228 Mawdūdī, *Sīrat-i sarwar-i ʿālam*, vol. 1, pp. 407–408; *idem*, *Tajdīd o iḥyāʾ-i dīn*, p. 54.

that the word *mahdī* is grammatically a passive participle, Mawdūdī is substantially changing the nature of this office.[229] He achieves the same purpose by blurring the distinction between the *mahdī* and the "centennial renewers" (*mujaddidūn*). These religious reformers, whose emergence is predicted in a famous prophetic *ḥadīth*,[230] were numerous and none of them had any apocalyptic significance. True to his general world view, Mawdūdī describes them as revolutionary reformers whose task is to diagnose the situation of Islam in their time and place, to determine the extent to which un-Islamic beliefs and practices (*jāhiliyya*) seeped into Muslim life, to bring about an intellectual revolution (*dhihnī inqilāb*) which will bring Muslim thinking into an Islamic mould and restore the hold of Islam on social life. The crowning achievement of their activity is initiating a global revolution (*ʿālamgīr inqilāb*) which will place the moral, intellectual and political leadership of the whole world into the hands of Islam and transform Islam into a civilization ruling the universe.[231] The *mahdī* is thus identical with a "perfect renewer", has a revolutionary task, and is definitely not a participant in the eschatological drama expected by the classical sources to take place before the Day of Judgment.

Like the classical apocalypse, Mawdūdī also includes Jesus in his reformulated apocalyptic drama. Mawdūdī's main purpose here is to undermine the beliefs of the Aḥmadīs. Following mainstream Muslim traditions, Mawdūdī accepts the idea of the second coming, and tries to make sure that it will not diminish the stature of Islam in any way. Jesus will not come as a prophet and will not receive divine revelation. He will not bring any new message or new laws from God and will not add or remove anything from the *sharīʿa*. Also, he will not establish a new religious community. He will integrate into the Muslim community, will pray behind the *imām* of the time and give precedence to the incumbent Muslim leader. His behaviour will leave no doubt that he is not coming in order to perform prophetic duties again. The second coming of Jesus is like the visit of a former ruler who performs some services for the state under the authority of the incumbent. His coming does not make any change in the "constitutional" situation: Islam will remain the sole legitimate religion despite the

229 Mawdūdī, *Sīrat-i sarwar-i ʿālam*, vol. 1, p. 405 note; Mawdūdī, *Tajdīd o iḥyāʾ-i dīn*, pp. 164–165.

230 For this *ḥadīth* and its interpretation by Mawdūdī, see earlier, at note 191 in this chapter.

231 Mawdūdī, *Tajdīd o iḥyāʾ-i dīn*, pp. 47–48.

appearance of Jesus. This should not be surprising: after all, Jesus himself will be a Muslim when he descends to earth again.

After quoting a substantial number of classical traditions which speak about the descent of Jesus before the end of time, Mawdūdī launches a scathing attack on the Aḥmadī beliefs, summarily asserting that

> whoever reads these traditions will see for himself that from the very beginning there is no reference in them to the "Promised Messiah" or someone "similar to the Messiah" or "the manifestation of the Messiah". Neither do they leave room for anybody who is born at this time from the womb of a mother and a sperm of a father to claim that he is the *mahdī* whose coming our leader Muḥammad, may God bless him and grant him peace, predicted. All these traditions indicate in clear and explicit words the descent of Jesus who was born two thousand years ago, without a father, from the womb of Mary (*jō shakhṣ bhī in aḥādīth kō parhēgā wuh khwud dēkh lēgā kih in mēñ "masīḥ-i maw ʿūd" yā "mathīl-i masīḥ" yā "burūz-i masīḥ" kā sarē sē ko ʾī dhikr hī nahīñ hay. na in mēñ is amr kī gunjā ʾish hay kih kō ʾī shakhṣ is zamānē mēñ kisī māñ kē pīt awr kisī bāp kē nutfē sē paydā hō kar yih da ʿwa kar dē kih 'mayñ hī wuh masīḥ hūñ jis kē ānē kī sayyidunā Muḥammad ṣallā Allah ʿalayhi wa sallam nē pēshīn gū ʾī farmā ʾī thī. yih tamām ḥadīthēñ ṣāf awr ṣarīḥ alfāẓ mēñ un Īsā ʿalayhi al-salām kē nāzil hōnē kī khabar dē rahī hayñ jō ab sē dō hazār sāl pahlē bāp kē ba-ghayr ḥaźrat Maryam kē baṭn sē paydā hu ʾē thē*).[232]

The three terms which Mawdūdī denounces in the preceding passage are characteristically Aḥmadī parlance. He asserts that the person who will descend at the end of days is the same Jesus who was born two thousand years ago, not someone who is "similar" to him or his "manifestation". It is useless to revisit here the question whether Jesus died or not; even if he did die, the omnipotent God would be capable to bring him back to life and raise him to Himself.[233]

---

232 Mawdūdī, *Sīrat-i sarwar-i ʿālam*, vol. 1, pp. 415–416; *idem, Tafhīm al-Qur ʾān*, vol. 4, p. 163.

233 Mawdūdī, *Sirat-i sarwar-i ʿālam*, vol. 1, pp. 190–191; *idem, Tafhīm al-Qur ʾān*, vol. 4, p. 163, on Qur ʾān 2:259. The relevant part of this long verse reads: "... Or such as he who passed by a city that was fallen down upon its turrets; he said: 'How shall God give life to this now it is dead?' So God made him die a hundred years, then he raised him up ..."

Mawdūdī speaks also about the reliability of the traditions about the *dajjāl*. Following again the mainstream Muslim beliefs, he maintains that the belief in the *dajjāl*'s coming is valid. From the relevant prophetic traditions one can understand that God informed the Prophet that "a big *dajjāl*" (*baŕā dajjāl*) would appear at some point in time and will bear certain characteristics. However, when the Prophet spoke about the appearance of the *dajjāl* in more specific terms, he described it in different ways: once he said that the *dajjāl* will emerge in Khurāsān, while at other times he mentioned Iṣfahān or the area between ʿIrāq and Syria as the places of his expected appearance. He also expressed doubts on other relevant details. It is clear that on these matters the Prophet did not speak on the basis of divine revelation (*waḥy*), but only on the basis of conjecture (*ẓann o qiyās*). The traditions about a meeting between Tamīm al-Dārī and the *dajjāl* on an uninhabited island and about Ibn Ṣayyād are incoherent. Ibn Ṣayyād lived in Mecca and Medina, embraced Islam and Muslims prayed at his funeral. How could a convert to Islam possibly be the *dajjāl*? Such ideas are not part of Islamic beliefs and the *sharīʿa* does not make them obligatory. It is thus clear that Mawdūdī accepts the appearance of the *dajjāl* in principle, but denies the details of the classical tradition and interprets the belief in the *dajjāl* in a new way.[234] Reviving the classical motif of the *dajjāl* being allied with the Jews, he connects his coming to contemporary times and specifically to the establishment of the State of Israel. In order to give substance to this theory, Mawdūdī ventures into an interpretation of Jewish history. His historical survey begins with the death of King Solomon. He asserts that after his death the situation of the Children of Israel deteriorated to such an extent that Babylonia and Assyria enslaved them and dispersed them all over the world. By way of consolation for their people, the prophets of the Children of Israel started spreading good news about the coming of a messiah who will save them from their humiliation. As a result of these predictions, the Jews began to expect a messiah who will be a king, will conquer their country, gather them in Palestine and establish a powerful state. Yet, contrary to their expectations, when Jesus was sent by God as a messiah, he did not bring an army. The Jews therefore rejected him and tried to bring about his demise. Jews of the entire world still expect the

234 Mawdūdī, *Sīrat-i sarwar-i ʿālam*, vol. 1, pp. 416–417; *idem*, *Rasāʾil o masāʾil*, vol. 1, pp. 33–35. In another place in the *Rasāʾil o masāʾil* (vol. 3, pp. 117–121), Mawdūdī responds to a questioner who took issue with the idea that some of the Prophet's words were not based on revelation.

messiah about whose coming they had been informed. Their literature is replete with pleasing dreams about his coming. They hope that he will be a strong military and political leader who will give them back the area between the Nile and the Euphrates which Jews consider their patrimony, and gather them again from all corners of the globe.[235]

According to Mawdūdī, if anyone looks at the contemporary situation in the Middle East and sees it against the background of the Prophet's predictions, he will perceive immediately that the stage is set for the appearance of the big *dajjāl*. At this point in his rather incoherent argumentation, Mawdūdī mentions the prophetic prediction about the appearance of the Jewish "promised messiah" (*yahūdiyyōñ kā masīḥ-i maw'ūd*[236]) – apparently meaning the *dajjāl* – and jumps straight to the establishment of Israel as a result of which Muslims were expelled from a great part of Palestine. In their place a state called Israel was established. Jews from the entire world crowded into this state. The US, England and France transformed it into a great military power. Limitless contributions of Jewish capital caused Jewish scientists and professionals to make it advance day by day. Its power became a danger to the neighbouring Muslim countries. The leaders of this state have not concealed their dream to expand over the whole Middle East. Looking at this situation, one can expect that they will take advantage of some future world war and attempt to take hold of all these territories. The implication seems to be that Israel is the *dajjāl* whom the Prophet mentioned, also describing the calamities inflicted by him on the Muslims. The *dajjāl* is thus in the Middle East. Therefore Jesus, whose main task will be to eliminate the *dajjāl*, must also descend in the Middle East, not in India as the Aḥmadīs opined. He will descend next to the white minaret east of Damascus, barely fifty or sixty miles from the Israeli border. The *dajjāl* will rush to that city with an army of 70,000 Jews. In this critical situation, Jesus will rally the Muslims after the morning prayer to confront the *dajjāl*. As a result of the Muslim attack, the *dajjāl* will retreat and run away from the Afīq ravine[237] in the direction of Israel. Jesus will pursue him and kill him near Lydda Airport.

---

235 Mawdūdī, *Sirat-i sarwar-i 'ālam*, vol. 1, p. 193.

236 The term *masīḥ-i maw'ūd* is characteristically Aḥmadī – rather than Jewish – parlance.

237 This is one of the venues in which the *dajjāl* is active in the classical traditions. See Cook, *Studies in Muslim Apocalyptics*, p. 105 and index, s.v. Afīq.

> Then the Jews will be gathered and killed and Judaism will come to an end. After Jesus reveals the truth, Christianity will also come to an end and all religions will join together in one Muslim religion (*us kē ba'd yahūdī chun-chun kar qatl ki'ē jā'ēñgē awr millat-i yahūd kā khātima hō jā'ēgā. 'Īsā'iyyat bhī ḥaẓrat 'Īsā kī ṭaraf sē iẓhār-i ḥaqīqat hō jānē kē ba'd khatm hō jā'ēgī awr tamām millatēñ ēk hī millat-i muslima mēñ ẓamm hō jā'ēñgē*).[238]

Mawdūdī's use of the apocalyptic elements in the Islamic tradition is complex. On the one hand, the *mahdī* will establish his authority all over the world and his state will be "a caliphate following the prophetic model" (*khilāfa 'alā minhāj al-nubuwwa*). All religions except Islam will be destroyed. These are ideas present in traditional Muslim thinking. On the other hand, Mawdūdī's *mahdī* is clearly not an eschatological figure: there is no anticipation of the Day of Judgment in the wake of his coming. The *dajjāl* is identified with contemporary Jews and the establishment of the State of Israel.[239] Neither the *mahdī* nor the *dajjāl* belong to the Portents of the Hour any more. They have their traditional roles transposed from the end of times to the contemporary period. Jesus, however, keeps some of his classical, supernatural features. He descends from heaven next to the white minaret in Damascus – as the *ḥadīth* predicted – but is recruited to accomplish a contemporary goal: killing the Jews and killing the *dajjāl* who is now identical with the State of Israel. The military exploits of Jesus are made "modern" by replacing the classical "gates of Lydda" with Lydda Airport.

All this is well in line with Mawdūdī's thinking: Islam is in his perception a revolutionary movement striving for changing the existing world order, not a messianic one preparing the believers for the hereafter. His *mahdī* is a demystified, human leadership figure, intent on transforming the situation of the world here and now. The classical belief in the appearance of an apocalyptic saviour is transformed into the expectation of a modern, determined and effective political leader. This idea caused some of Mawdūdī's critics to accuse him of claiming to be the *mahdī*, but he vigorously rejected this accusation.[240]

---

238 Mawdūdī, *Sirat-i sarwar-i 'ālam*, vol. 1, pp. 193–194 (the quoted passage is on p. 194); *idem*, *Tafhīm al-Qur'ān*, vol. 4, pp. 165–166. Cf. D. Cook, *Studies in Muslim Apocalyptic*, p. 104.

239 For the same motif in contemporary Arab apocalypticism, see D. Cook, *Contemporary Muslim Apocalyptic Literature*, pp. 184–200.

240 Mawdūdī, *Tajdīd o iḥyā'-i dīn*, pp. 156–161.

The *dajjāl* is also demystified and understood as a metaphor for the State of Israel. The apocalyptic destruction of Judaism and Christianity is moved to historical times, though the chief actor in this drama is Jesus whose appearance and military exploits retain their supernatural character. Though the *mahdī* is expected to achieve world domination and all religions other than Islam are expected to disappear, Mawdūdī does not mention in his apocalyptic vision any changes in the religious situation of areas not prominent in the classical Muslim literature, such as China or Japan. Even India goes unmentioned in our context. It is noteworthy that Mawdūdī does not feel any contradiction between the vision in which Judaism and Christianity are destroyed and the rules about the rights of the non-Muslims in the Islamic state which he formulated in numerous places in his writings.[241] The situation after the apocalypse takes place will be completely different.

Mawdūdī disconnected the *mahdī* from the end of times and transformed him into a leader in historical times. This reinterpretation of the Muslim messianic idea could be seen as a modernist element in his thinking, but this "modernism" is only partial: it did not prevent Mawdūdī from preserving at the same time the supernatural intervention of Jesus in the now non-eschatological drama.

IX THE DIVERSITY OF MESSIANIC THOUGHT AMONG INDIAN MUSLIMS

Muslims of the Indo-Pakistan subcontinent have produced in the modern period messianic thought of fascinating diversity. This diversity must have been caused by the momentous developments in the history of the Indian Muslims since the nineteenth century. The demise of the Muslim Mughal empire, the gradual British takeover, the transformation of the Muslims from a ruling minority into a subjected one, the necessity to defend the faith against the onslaught of the Christian mission and the Hindū revivalist movements, the awareness of the Western incursions into the Muslim world – all these served as a fertile ground for the emergence of messianic ideas of different types. The thinkers who developed these ideas used the

241 See mainly Mawdūdī's *Islāmī riyāsat mēñ dhimmiyyōñ kē ḥuqūq* ("The rights of the *dhimmī*s in the Islamic state"). Arabic version: *Ḥuqūq ahl al-dhimma fī al-dawla al-islāmiyya.*

relevant classical material, but reached diametrically opposed conclusions. We have, on the one hand, major works of Ṣiddīq Ḥasan Khān who developed the classical theme of the apocalypse in which huge armies of the *mahdī* defeat the Christians and make Islam reign supreme in the world. On the other hand, we have the enormous literary output of Ghulām Aḥmad who claimed to have confounded Christianity by mere force of argument, by proving to his own satisfaction that Jesus died a natural death like any other mortal, will never return to earth and that Ghulām Aḥmad himself came in his stead. We also have Ismāʿīl Shahīd and Abū al-Aʿlā Mawdūdī who strove to transform the *mahdī* from an apocalyptic figure into an effective political leader who is expected to change the situation of the world here and now, without waiting for the eschaton. At the other end of the spectrum we have Sir Sayyid Aḥmad Khān, ʿUbayd Allāh Sindhī and Akhtar Kāshmīrī who are willing to dispense with the *mahdī* idea altogether. Sir Sayyid and Akhtar Kāshmīrī do it mainly on the basis of the traditional *ḥadīth* criticism, while Sindhī is willing to reject even traditions which are traditionally considered authentic, because of the debilitating effect of the belief in a mythical saviour on the Muslim psyche. Like in many other fields, Muslim India has been a veritable laboratory which produced new ideas on numerous important issues in Muslim messianic thought.

6

Concluding observations

I ESCHATOLOGICAL VERSUS NON-ESCHATOLOGICAL *MAHDĪS*

It is now appropriate to make some concluding observations, to characterize the *mahdī* movements included in our analysis, to compare them to each other, to evaluate their achievements, their failures and their place in Islamic history.

Perhaps the most conspicuous characteristic of the *mahdī* movements is their endeavour to allow for a non-eschatological *mahdī*. This tendency began in the classical literature: the idea of the eschatological *mahdī* existed side by side with historical leaders whose followers awarded them the title of *mahdī*. It is even possible to envisage that an *isnād-cum-matn* analysis of the relevant traditions would reveal that the traditions about "historical" *mahdīs* came into being earlier than their "eschatological" counterparts. Yet theoretically explicit acknowledgments of non-eschatological *mahdīs* as legitimate Muslim leaders came to fruition only in the thought of the Indian Mahdawīs, of the supporters of Sayyid Aḥmad Shahīd and in the works of Abū al-Aʿlā Mawdūdī. The Mahdawīs used to say that their leader Sayyid Muḥammad Jawnpūrī "came and departed" (*āmad o gudhasht*), and did not expect the Day of Judgment to come in his wake. Ismāʿīl Shahīd used the classical traditions about *mahdīs* who are not described as attached to the end of days in order to indicate that a non-eschatological *mahdī* is a possibility sanctioned in the classical tradition. Mawdūdī is not a messianic claimant: he is rather a theoretician of the *mahdī* idea. He is particularly important here: his *mahdī* will establish a powerful Islamic state while being a thoroughly modern leader, totally stripped of the characteristics attributed to the *mahdī* in the classical tradition. While the *mahdī*s discussed in this work appeared in history but paid lip service to the eschatological traditions, Mawdūdī provided a theoretical – and unapologetical – underpinning for the idea that the *mahdī* is nothing but an effective Muslim political leader, operating here and now. This is comparable with the ISIS replacement of the *mahdī* with a caliph, who is an effective political leader. McCants aptly described this development when he said that the "messiah gave way to management".[1]

The dissociation of the *mahdī* from the eschaton can also be illustrated by the fact that the four *mahdī*s described in this book had successors, each of whom carried the title of *khalīfa*. Ibn Tūmart established a dynasty which lasted for almost 150 years. Sayyid Muḥammad Jawnpūrī was politically not as successful, but he also had successors and his son Sayyid Maḥmūd came to be known as the "second *mahdī*" (*thānī mahdī*). The Sudanese Muḥammad Aḥmad had one successor who ruled the Mahdist state for fourteen years, until its destruction in 1899. And Masrūr Aḥmad, the present leader of the Aḥmadī movement, is the fifth *khalīfa* of Ghulām Aḥmad. These *mahdī*s used occasionally to mention the end of days, but it was not a central or very significant element in their or in their followers' thought. All of them anticipated that their movements would continue to exist after they passed away.

Muslim sources relevant to the *mahdī* idea can be divided into two major groups. The first one, which is preponderant in the classical period, deals with the prophetic traditions (*aḥādīth*) which mention the *mahdī* in connection to the end of days. Only occasionally we find references to personalities such as the Umayyad caliphs Sulaymān b. ʿAbd al-Malik (r. 715–717) or ʿUmar b. ʿAbd al-ʿAzīz (r. 717–720) for whom messianic claims were normally made by others. Though there were certain messianic elements in the ʿAbbāsī movement, no explicitly messianic movements in Sunnī Islam were established in this period. It is noteworthy that the discussions on the reliability or otherwise of the eschatological predictions, which abound in *ḥadīth* literature, were adapted by Ibn Khaldūn in order to debunk the messianic idea and were revived in the modern period by thinkers such as Shāh Ismāʿīl Shahīd and Abū al-Aʿlā Mawdūdī. In the post-classical and modern periods, the theoretical discussions continue,

1 McCants, *The ISIS Apocalypse*, p. 147.

but the emphasis moves to works authored by the messianic claimants themselves and by their followers. Ibn Tūmart, Muḥammad Aḥmad and Mīrzā Ghulām Aḥmad were themselves authors of books and epistles, while the views of Sayyid Muḥammad Jawnpūrī are found in books penned by his immediate followers.

The *mahdī* movements described in the present work operated in diverse areas and strove for different objectives. They also produced ideologies with different emphases. The medieval movements operated in areas under Muslim rule and involved denunciations of and revolts against existing Muslim governments. This is also a prominent characteristic of the ʿAbbāsī revolution some of whose legitimizing efforts included messianic elements. Ibn Tūmart was similar in this respect: he rebelled against the dynasty of the Almoravids, found fault with its belief systems and customs, toppled it and established the new Almohad dynasty which existed for almost 150 years, between 1121 and 1269 CE. His struggle was directed first and foremost against his Muslim rivals; only his successors directed their activities also against the non-Muslims rulers of Spain. The Mahdawīs of Sayyid Muḥammad Jawnpūrī rebelled against the Muslim rulers of Gujarāt, but unlike the movement of Ibn Tūmart failed to establish a political entity of their own because they were weak and few, and their military endeavours ended in failure. On the other hand, they produced an elaborate and sophisticated belief system. Three nineteenth-century movements emerged in areas under British rule. The movement of Sayyid Aḥmad Shahīd – for whom Shāh Ismāʿīl Shahīd claimed the title of *mahdī* – rose in early nineteenth-century India, but its military struggle was directed against the Sikhs rather than the British. The Sudanese *mahdī* Muḥammad Aḥmad (1844–1885) rose when the Sudan was under the so-called Turko-Egyptian regime which was allied with the British and therefore had no ideological difficulty when he denounced his enemies as infidels and declared *jihād* against them. Mīrzā Ghulām Aḥmad (183?-1908), the founder of the Aḥmadī movement, emerged in British India, but his messianic movement was devoid of any military or political aspirations. It devoted its main efforts to the polemical confutation of Christianity, to the denial of the second coming of Jesus and to the reinterpretation of Islamic beliefs on issues such as *jihād*, prophecy and the nature of the apocalyptic drama.

It is thus clear that we cannot discern any unifying "model" in the Sunnī messianic movements. The denominator common to all of them is only the fact that their leaders claimed the title of *mahdī* or a variation on it. In some cases, the claim was not made by the leader himself, but rather by his followers. Furthermore, all the claimants discussed previously convinced a substantial number of people of their time and place to accept the veracity of their claim and caused them to join their movements. On the other hand, none of them succeeded in commanding acceptance or support in the worldwide Muslim community.

In the cases of Ibn Tūmart, Muḥammad Jawnpūrī and Muḥammad Aḥmad, joining the *mahdī* movements involved dramatic changes in the lifestyle of those who joined. These changes included leaving the place of domicile, abandonment of family life, abandonment of gainful work or employment and extreme asceticism. There was no requirement of celibacy. Among the four *mahdī*s, only Ibn Tūmart was a celibate; it is not clear whether by choice or because of a sexual dysfunction. The success of these *mahdī* claimants in mobilizing local support is an example of how ascetic behaviour, piety, personal charisma, ability to use appropriate aspects of the Islamic tradition with impressive eloquence, and social discontent among the people of the area in question – all these can transform a previously obscure individual into a leader of thousands.

In what follows, I shall compare a few central features in each of the movements analysed in this work.

II MOTIVATION AND "APPOINTMENT"

The motivation of the messianic claimants is closely related to their fervent belief that Islam and Muslims of their time and place fail to live up to the Islamic ideal as envisaged by the Prophet Muḥammad. This is, in turn, related to the commonly held traditional perception that Islam started its history at the pinnacle of glory, but quickly deteriorated and therefore needs to be revived and restored to its pristine ideal. This is the basic ideological underpinning of the messianic ideologies described in the previous chapters of this book. In this respect, the messianic movements bear partial affinity to contemporary radical Muslim groups which support the ideal of reviving the pristine purity of Islam, but do not necessarily envisage that it is the *mahdī* who will accomplish this goal.

Perhaps the first question which we should pose at this juncture is how does one become a *mahdī*. In a more academic formulation, we should ask how did each of these religious personalities attempt to establish his legitimacy and what arguments did he use in order to convince a substantial number of people of his crucial importance in the religious history of Islam. It is surprising how easy it was to make a successful messianic claim. The most elaborate appointment ceremony is undoubtedly that of the Sudanese *mahdī* Muḥammad Aḥmad. In a series of visionary encounters with the Prophet who is said to have come to meet him on numerous occasions – together with numerous grandees from Islamic history – he was appointed to the messianic task by the Prophet himself. The presence of numerous "friends of God" (*awliyā'*) in these encounters is understandable because of the Ṣūfī affiliation of Muḥammad Aḥmad before his manifestation as a *mahdī*. These visionary ceremonies of appointment are described time and again in the Sudanese *mahdī*'s epistles. Their repetition is designed to provide legitimacy and increase the awareness of the appointment among as many Sudanese and in as many regions as possible. The thousands of personalities from Islamic history who are said to have witnessed these events increase the credibility of Muḥammad Aḥmad's claim in the same way as the credibility of a *ḥadīth* is increased by the number of transmitters relating it. The involvement of the Prophet Muḥammad in his appointment is crucial because his authority is undisputed and there is no way to challenge it.

Nothing as elaborate is claimed for Sayyid Muḥammad Jawnpūrī. He was described as *mahdī* by a Ṣūfī leader in Jawnpūr who heard about the miraculous circumstances of the boy's birth from his father. A Qur'ānic verse (17:81) about the coming of the truth and the vanishing of falsehood reverberated in the city at the time of his birth. It is noteworthy that the mythical figure of al-Khiḍr is said to have been present when Jawnpūrī started his religious studies and greeted him as "the *imām* of latter days". It seems safe to assume that these traditions came into being when Jawnpūrī made his claim to be the *mahdī* when he reached the age of forty years. The involvement of Shaykh Dāniyāl and al-Khiḍr in Jawnpūrī's hagiography creates a certain connection between him and the Ṣūfīs, but beyond that – and in contradistinction to Muḥammad Aḥmad who transformed himself from a practising Ṣūfī into a militant *mahdī* – we do not know of any substantial connection between Jawnpūrī and any Ṣūfī fraternity.

The appointment of Ibn Tūmart is said to have been very simple. In 1121–1122 CE, after returning to his native place from the journey to the Mashriq, he delivered a speech in which he quoted classical traditions about the *mahdī*. A relatively small number of listeners asserted that the classical characteristics of the *mahdī* exist only in Ibn Tūmart and therefore he is the *mahdī*. These followers pledged allegiance to him in emulation of the pledge which was given to the Prophet by his Companions. In another description, he made the claim himself: he collected classical traditions about the *mahdī* and convinced the people that he was the infallible *mahdī* (*al-mahdī al-maʿṣūm*). In contrast to the two *mahdī*s discussed previously, here we have neither divine nor prophetic intervention; we have only a declaration of the claimant and an agreement of a rather small number of supporters.

Ghulām Aḥmad's claim to religious eminence was legitimized in a very different way. He asserted that since his youth he had visions and revelations granted him by God. These revelations enabled Ghulām Aḥmad to claim the titles of *mujaddid*, *muḥaddath*, *mahdī*, *masīḥ* and, finally, prophet. They were initially published in his books or printed in newspapers issued by the Aḥmadī movement. The messianic title preferred in this literature is *al-masīḥ* because of Ghulām Aḥmad's perceived affinity with Jesus, whose common name in the Muslim tradition is *al-masīḥ*. Nevertheless, the title *mahdī* is also used, especially in the expression *al-masīḥ al-mawʿūd wa al-mahdī al-maʿhūd*.[2] Ghulām Aḥmad extensively quoted these revelations in his writings and they served as the main source of his legitimacy.[3] Only in 1889, nine years after Ghulām Aḥmad published his first book in 1880, there was also a *bayʿa* ceremony in which several persons pledged allegiance to him and the Aḥmadī movement came formally into being.[4] There is no noticeable Ṣūfī element in Ghulām Aḥmad's writings and activities.

III SOURCES OF INSPIRATION

What are the aspects of Islamic thought which were most prominent in the works of the various *mahdī*s? Sayyid Muḥammad Jawnpūrī drew

2 Ghulām Aḥmad's revelations were later collected by members of the movement and published in a bulky volume of more than 800 pages. The first edition was printed in 1935 and the book has seen several editions since then. See Ghulām Aḥmad, *Tadhkira* and the English translation by Muhammad Zafrullah Khan.

3 For an analysis of some of the revelations, see Friedmann, *Prophecy Continuous*, pp. 134–142. A full analysis of Ghulām Aḥmad's revelations is still a scholarly desideratum.

4 Friedmann, *Prophecy Continuous*, p. 5.

his inspiration mainly from Ṣūfī thought. The works of his immediate followers, which abound in quotations of his sayings, include extensive discussions of such time-honoured Ṣūfī topics as the relative worth of prophethood (*nubuwwa*) and sainthood (*wilāya*), extreme asceticism, stringent objection to gainful employment and reticence to accept even unsolicited donations. Strict disengagement from family and social relationships with non-Mahdawīs, even if they are first degree relatives, were also prominent, though these are not necessarily Ṣūfī. The same can be said about the Sudanese Muḥammad Aḥmad who was a Sammānī Ṣūfī before he made his claim to spiritual eminence, and his epistles are replete with denunciations of wealth and with laudatory statements about poverty.

The inspirational sources of Ibn Tūmart were varied, but his works deal mainly with theology and the "principles of religion" (*uṣūl al-dīn*). According to al-Marrākushī, the first books which he wrote dealt with articles of faith (*uṣūl al-dīn, ʿaqīda*). He is said to have supported the Ashʿarī school of theology, except on the issue of divine attributes in which he followed the Muʿtazila.[5] Theological issues abound in his major work *Aʿazzu mā yuṭlab*, though it includes some legal matters as well. His *ʿAqīda* includes topics such as the intellectually unavoidable knowledge of God, His unity (*tawḥīd*), and His being incomparable with any of His creation.[6] The *Murshida* starts with support for "the way in which there is no crookedness, the way between the two ways, neither anthropomorphism nor denial of divine attributes" (*al-ṭarīq alladhī lā ʿiwaja fīhi wa huwa ṭarīq bayna ṭarīqayn lā tajsīm wa lā taʿṭīl*).[7] It is also significant that he castigated his principal opponents on a theological issue, accusing them of anthropomorphism (*tajsīm*).

In matters of *sharʿī* relevance, the *mahdī*s tended to disregard the rulings of the legal schools (*madhāhib*) and issued, in some cases, legal rulings of their own. This tendency is compatible with the idea that legal rulings should be based on the Qurʾān and the *ḥadīth* rather than on the books of law. This phenomenon is most conspicuous in the epistles of Muḥammad Aḥmad who issued numerous rulings, mostly relevant to women and morals, which have no basis in the *sharīʿa*. The same was done on a smaller scale by Ibn Tūmart and Sayyid Muḥammad Jawnpūrī. We do not have much material of this sort in the works of Ghulām Aḥmad,

5 Marrākushī, *al-Muʿjib*, pp. 161–162.
6 Ibn Tūmart, *ʿAqīda, passim.*
7 Ishbīlī, *Sharḥ Murshidat Muḥammad b. Tūmart*, p. 9.

though further research is required in order to make a full evaluation of this issue in Aḥmadī thought.

IV EXCLUSIVITY

A major characteristic of the four messianic claimants is their claim to religious exclusivity. The early prophetic *ḥadīth* frowns upon declaring Muslims to be infidels, but side by side with this ecumenical attitude there was also a different one: in the eyes of most Khawārij, anybody who does not join their cause is an infidel.[8] The *mahdī*s discussed previously fall within this exclusionary category. All of them asserted in various ways that whoever denied their claim to messianic status was an infidel. In the case of Ibn Tūmart, this was directed – in addition to a statement of principle – against the dynasty of the Almoravids (*al-Murābiṭūn*) whom he considered infidels because of their alleged anthropomorphism and un-Islamic attire: their men veil their faces while their women have their faces uncovered. If we move to Sayyid Muḥammad Jawnpūrī, we find a similar attitude. Non-acceptance of Sayyid Muḥammad Jawnpūrī's messianic claim is tantamount to the non-acceptance of the Prophet Muḥammad which necessarily means that deniers of Jawnpūrī's claims must be considered non-Muslims. From the point of view of mainstream Islam, this is a totally unacceptable assertion because it makes the belief in the Prophet somehow contingent on the belief in Sayyid Muḥammad Jawnpūrī, as if the belief in Muḥammad's prophethood does not stand on its own. It is also noteworthy that Ṣūfī concepts are used in order to dissociate the Mahdawīs from all other Muslims and declare all non-Mahdawī Muslims as infidels. This stringent attitude had serious ritual and social consequences. Mahdawīs were not permitted to pray behind non-Mahdawī *imām*s and enter into matrimony with non-Mahdawīs.

We find similar attitudes in the thought of Muḥammad Aḥmad, the Sudanese *mahdī*. As is well known, the four years of Muḥammad Aḥmad's activity as a *mahdī* was characterized by constant war against the British and the so-called Turko-Egyptian regime. This war was routinely described as *jihād*; since *jihād* is a war against non-Muslims, it was essential for

8 For the various views on excommunication in the Islamic tradition, see Friedmann, "Conversion, Apostasy and Excommunication", pp. 146–167.

Muḥammad Aḥmad to declare his opponents as infidels. Time and again he declares that whoever denies his claim to be the *mahdī* belongs to this category. He routinely asserts that the Prophet himself had affirmed that whoever rejects the *mahdī* is an infidel (*man ankara al-mahdī fa-qad kafara*).

The case of Ghulām Aḥmad is more complex. He is the only *mahdī* discussed in this book whose attitudes to his opponents changed during his lifetime. As we have seen in Chapter 5, he started with a rather ecumenical stance, refusing to anathemize anyone who utters the Muslim declaration of faith (*kalima-gū*). Only later he declared those who rejected his claim to be a *mahdī* as infidels. But since he did not advocate military *jihād* and did not establish a polity, his attitude had only social consequences. The excommunication of the Aḥmadiyya by mainstream Islam was much more important. It caused extensive persecution of the Aḥmadīs in Pakistan and elsewhere.[9]

V *HIJRA*

The exclusionary attitude to the "others" and the struggle against them by military action or by other means are common to the four messianic claimants discussed in this work. Three of these claimants, Ibn Tūmart, Sayyid Muḥammad Jawnpūrī and the Sudanese Muḥammad Aḥmad also advocated migration (*hijra*), which was intended to bring about a substantial transformation of the existing social order. *Hijra* was essential because it enabled the three leaders to gather a military force and engage in *jihād* without being encumbered by non-combatant family members.

The most extensive theory of *hijra* was elaborated by Sayyid Muḥammad Jawnpūrī. In his view, *hijra* is not only physical: it involves complete dissociation from the biological family and severance of all social, even emotional, ties with non-Mahdawīs. Nobody could be a fully-fledged member of the movement without performing *hijra*. Those who accepted Jawnpūrī's messianic claims but did not perform it were called "hypocrites" or "nominal" Mahdawīs. Severance of all family relationships was necessary in order to transform the movement's members into a group of single-minded devotees, unencumbered by family responsibilities; Jawnpūrī must have

9 See Friedmann, *Prophecy Continuous*, pp. 38–46.

thought that this was a reasonable price to pay in order to strengthen the loyalty of the Mahdawīs to their movement.

The *hijra* was of major importance also in the thought of Muḥammad Aḥmad. Its importance in the Sudanese movement can be easily understood if we take into account the fact that the short career of this *mahdī* was replete with military operations which needed large numbers of warriors. Therefore, nothing could serve as a reason for refraining from *hijra*: neither family obligations, nor economic considerations. Refraining from *hijra* and staying at home was tantamount to infidelity. It is interesting to note that the classical notion according to which Muslims should not live in an area dominated by non-Muslims is not prominent in the exhortations of the three *mahdī*s to perform *hijra*.[10]

Again, Ghulām Aḥmad is completely different. Since the Aḥmadī movement advocated neither military *jihād* nor the establishment of a political entity, no *hijra* was required. A small number of Aḥmadīs travelled to countries outside the Indian subcontinent in order to propagate the Aḥmadī version of Islam, but this is a case of *da ʿwa* and there is no similarity between this and *hijra* for the purpose of amassing a military force.

VI *JIHĀD*

One conclusion from the exclusionary world view was the obligation to wage *jihād* against the opponents, though the *jihād* is not of the same type in all cases. Ibn Tūmart fought against the dynasty of the Almoravides (*al-Murābiṭūn*) whom he accused of anthropomorphistic attitudes, which in his view are tantamount to infidelity. A secondary accusation related to the Almoravid customs, and especially their attire: their men veil themselves while their women do not cover their faces as they should. Hostile statements about "the veiled infidels" (*al-kafara al-mulaththamūn*) or "the veiled anthropomorphists" (*ahl al-tajsīm al-mulaththamūn*) are frequently found in his works.[11]

The *jihād* of the Mahdawī movement in India had several distinctive characteristics. In contradistinction to Ibn Tūmart and Muḥammad Aḥmad who initiated military operations themselves, the Mahdawī movement

10 For a discussion of this idea, see Friedmann, "Muslim Minorities ...", pp. 9–19.
11 Muḥammad b. Tūmart, *A ʿazzu mā yuṭlab*, ed. Ṭālibī, pp. 260, 262.

acquired military characteristics only under Jawnpūrī's successors. The Mahdawīs also debated some issues of principle related to *jihād*. The most important of them was the question whether it was legitimate to wage *jihād* against Muslims who refused to acknowledge the messianic status of Jawnpūrī but were, of course, people who pronounce the Muslim declaration of faith (*kalima-gūyān*), and were Muslims according to the standard definition of the term. Both sides in the controversy found support for their attitudes in the classical Muslim sources. Those who doubted the legitimacy of fighting Muslims found support in the traditions against declaring Muslim as infidels, while their opponents stressed the tradition according to which anyone who rejects the *mahdī* is, indeed, an infidel. The Mahdawīs also attempted to make a synthesis between *jihād* against the "evil-bidding" soul and military *jihād*. The former – called in Ṣūfī parlance "the greater *jihād*" (*al-jihād al-akbar*) – should be waged before the fighting begins, but when the battle is joined the Mahdawīs should fight with the sword, while remembering God frequently.

The dilemma of the Sudanese *mahdī* Muḥammad Aḥmad in declaring *jihād* against his enemies was easier because the so-called Turko-Egyptian regime against which he fought was in manifest alliance with the British and the army included British units. In contradistinction to the Indian Mahdawīs, Muḥammad Aḥmad never had any scruples when he waged *jihād* against the Muslim allies of the British and *jihād* is undoubtedly the prevalent motif in his thinking. Naturally enough, most of the exhortations to join the *jihād* are taken from the classical material, but there are specific emphases which are characteristic of Muḥammad Aḥmad and reflect the peculiar circumstances of his struggle. The necessity to recruit a strong army seems to be the background to the repeated assertions saying that livelihood is God's responsibility, criticizing agricultural work which interferes with *jihād* and brings humiliation to those who till the land. The same necessity is also the reason for debunking the value of family life. The numerous victories of the Mahdist army explain the great attention given to the division of spoils and to threatening those who plunder.

The thinking of Mīrzā Ghulām Aḥmad, the founder of the Aḥmadī movement, was completely different in this respect. As is well known, the Aḥmadī movement never advocated military *jihād*, but this does not mean that it refrained from other types of struggle against its opponents. The Aḥmadīs held that military struggle was justified in the early days of Islam when the religion had to resist military assault and faced physical extinction. By the time of Ghulām Aḥmad the situation had changed. The threat facing Islam in his time was not military but ideological; therefore the appropriate defence must also be ideological. Ghulām Aḥmad did his best to refute the views of the Christian missionaries and of those Muslims who propagated ideas which he considered wrong. Regarding the Christians missionaries, he rejected their description of Islam as a violent religion spread by the sword, as well as their belief that Jesus was alive in heaven and will descend to earth for the second time. As for the mainstream Muslim *ʿulamāʾ*, he rejected their support for the second coming of Jesus and their descriptions of the expected *mahdī* as a bloody figure who will destroy all religions except Islam. He thought that both these views provided the missionaries with weapons which they effectively used in anti-Muslim polemics and in their attempts to defame Islam. Aḥmadī *jihād*, waged by means of polemical encounters, preaching and writing, was designed to undermine these ideas and deprive the missionaries of their advantage in polemics.

VII *MAHDĪ*S AND PROPHETS

As we have seen, the idea of the *mahdī* originated in classical Muslim literature dealing with the wondrous events expected to precede the Day of Judgment. However, in the works of the messianic claimants whom we surveyed in the preceding chapters, this motif has receded into the background and we barely hear them saying that Judgment Day is imminent. Instead, some of them developed the idea that in their times the period of the Prophet has been recreated and they themselves have been given some prophetic qualities. Except for the case of Ghulām Aḥmad, who explicitly claimed to be a prophet in the last part of his career, the *mahdī*s stop short of such an explicit prophetic claim, though they come rather close to it.

In the thought of Sayyid Muḥammad Jawnpūrī, affinity with the Prophet is most conspicuous. His followers did their best to endow their leader with characteristics well known from classical descriptions of the Prophet. They hinted that he was born circumcised and saw to it that the names of his parents were changed to ʿAbd Allah and Āmina. Though Jawnpūrī is said to have been a gifted boy who completed the standard Islamic curriculum by the age of twelve, he was transformed into an illiterate once he made his claim to be the *mahdī* at the age of forty. This makes him similar to the

Prophet in the latter's alleged illiteracy. The most striking – and to the best of my knowledge unprecedented – attempt to create affinity with the Prophet is the audacious use of the formula *ṣallā Allah ʿalayhi wa sallam* in the dual form (*ṣallā Allah ʿalayhimā wa sallam*), so that it includes both the Prophet Muḥammad and Sayyid Muḥammad Jawnpūrī. And, like the Prophet himself, Jawnpūrī will destroy whatever exists in his times and "will launch Islam afresh".[12]

A similar affinity between a messianic claimant and the Prophet is maintained for Muḥammad Aḥmad, the Sudanese *mahdī*. The period of the *mahdī* is equated with the period of the Prophet. The associates of Muḥammad Aḥmad and his family are routinely equated with the companions of the Prophet. He claims to have had direct communication with God, and his supporters did not hesitate to characterize it as *waḥy*, a term used exclusively for divine revelation to prophets. The pledge of allegiance to the *mahdī* is inspired – and partly identical – with the pledges of ʿAqaba in the Prophet's time. To make the similarity even more convincing, he appoints four *khulafāʾ* who are meant to replicate the four "righteous" caliphs, though one of them spurned the appointment with unmitigated scorn. Being the only *mahdī* with pan-Islamic aspirations, Muḥammad Aḥmad writes a letter to the Ethiopian king using the expressions which the Prophet Muḥammad is said to have used in his letter to the *najāshī*, the Ethiopian potentate of the seventh century.

VIII ACHIEVEMENTS

We may now ask ourselves what were the achievements of these four movements and what impact did they have in the regions in which they operated. Though the Gujarātī Mahdawīs produced a very sophisticated system of ascetic and messianic thought, they accomplished little in practical terms. The community continues to exist; it has a centre in Chicago, some community centres in India and a website from which information about community activities may be gleaned,[13] but it seems to be rather small. Its activities in the fifteenth century and beyond did not bring about very impressive practical results.

12 See Chapter 4, at notes 61–66.
13 http://www.miccusa.org (accessed on 18 October 2021).

The achievements of the Almohads, of the Sudanese Mahdists and of the Aḥmadīs were much more substantial. The Almohads established an empire which ruled over parts of north Africa and Spain between roughly 1130 and 1270. The doctrine of Ibn Tūmart was abandoned by his successors in the early 1230s, but was restored as state ideology a few years later. The Sudanese Muḥammad Aḥmad acted as a *mahdī* for only four years, but had spectacular military successes against the British, and the state which he established lasted for fourteen years after his death, until the British reconquest of the Sudan in 1899. Ghulām Aḥmad had no political aspirations, but he established a movement which has successfully remained active for 130 years despite the incessant attacks by mainstream Islam, has maintained durable leadership and institutions, elected leaders who replaced Ghulām Aḥmad, engaged in constant missionary activity and boasts of approximately seventeen million adherents across the world.

It is quite clear that all these achievements are in no way near the classical image of the *mahdī* who was expected to bring about a sea-change in the Muslim and human condition. It is therefore interesting to pose the following question: how did these messianic claimants themselves evaluate their achievements? We cannot answer this question for all of them, because not all of them related to it. We can say, however, that in the thought of all of them, the eschatological expectations of messianic justice and prosperity have only a minimal importance and are mentioned only rarely. In the works of the Sudanese Muḥammad Aḥmad and in the writings of Mīrza Ghulām Aḥmad it is possible to discern their own evaluation of their achievements and prospects. As for Muḥammad Aḥmad, it is clear that he considered the elimination of Turko-Egyptian rule in the Sudan as an enormous achievement. Encouraged by this military and political success, culminating in the takeover of the Sudan and the killing of General Gordon, he developed pan-Islamic aspirations and became convinced that the conquest of Egypt would follow, that he would rule Syria and the Maghrib, and anticipated a triumphant entry and an allegiance ceremony in Mecca. His early death in 1885 – at the age of forty-one – prevented any attempt to attain these ambitious goals.

Ghulām Aḥmad, on the other hand, saw his achievements in a completely different light. A substantial part of his activities was in the field of inter-religious polemics and so was his perceived achievement. He was convinced that he had successfully confuted Christianity and hit Christians at the most sensitive Christological point: he had proved to his own satisfaction that Jesus died a natural death, like any other mortal, and refuted the belief that he would ever descend to earth again. This was also a success in the internal Muslim polemics because the mainstream *ʿulamāʾ* embraced the Christian belief in the second coming of Jesus.

IX SUNNĪ AND SHĪʿĪ *MAHDĪ*

The idea of the *mahdī* as a redeemer exists in both branches of Islam, but it has distinct characteristics in each one of them. In the Twelver Shīʿa it is a central, generally accepted article of faith and the constant expectation of the *mahdī*'s reappearance is an essential part of the Shīʿī religious experience. There were some isolated cases of Twelver Shīʿīs who claimed to be *mahdī*s, but since the identity of the Shīʿī *mahdī* – as well as his name – are well known, there were no full-fledged *mahdī* movements in the Twelver Shīʿa. It was not possible for a Shīʿī leader to rise and assert that he was Muḥammad b. al-Ḥasan al-ʿAskarī. The Shīʿī belief in the *mahdī* has always been extremely powerful, but it had to remain in the eschatological realm. On the Sunnī side, the traditional descriptions of the Sunnī *mahdī* were less exact and could be easily attributed to the various claimants. They were also much more amenable to interpretations which allowed for the transfer of the figure of the *mahdī* to historical times. There was no rigour in this procedure. Even the most exact requirement for the *mahdī* status – the name Muḥammad b. ʿAbd Allah – was taken lightly and none of the *mahdī*s discussed in this work bore exactly this name. It was very easy for prospective Sunnī leaders to stake their claims to messianic status and Sunnī history has seen many such pretenders. In the Sunnī tradition there was more debate about the authenticity of the *mahdī* idea in Islam, but the numerous *mahdī* movements prove that the idea has been an integral part of Sunnī Islam and a powerful tool for initiating social and political movements. Messianic claims were made for several figures in early Islam and this early phenomenon provided legitimacy for *mahdī* claimants in later periods.

The idea of the *mahdī* is absolutely essential in the Shīʿī system of belief and one cannot envisage the Shīʿa without it. No Shīʿī leader or thinker would countenance the debunking of the *mahdī* idea as was done by the Almohad caliph al-Maʾmūn who in 1230 CE stripped Ibn Tūmart of his messianic title and debunked the *mahdī* idea by asserting that "there is no *mahdī* except Jesus" and that Jesus was called *mahdī* only because "he spoke in the cradle (*mahd*)" and not because of any messianic task.[14] This could not have happened in a Shīʿī context.

At this point we need to return to Goldziher's statement that "in Sunnī Islam the pious awaiting of the *mahdī* never took the fixed form of dogma", despite the fact that it was treated and documented in the *ḥadīth*.[15] This should not be understood to mean that the idea has had little importance in Sunnī Islam. As we have seen in Chapter 1, Goldziher's statement is true only for the early Muslim creeds. As for creeds produced in the late medieval period, they did include the *mahdī* in the Sunnī articles of faith. While some Sunnī scholars took pains to undermine the *mahdī* traditions and even considered them unreliable, numerous Sunnīs made messianic claims throughout Islamic history and Sunnī literature is replete with traditions supportive of the *mahdī* idea. None of the Sunnī *mahdī*s commanded universal acceptance, but they made considerable impact in the regions in which they emerged. In two cases they managed to establish significant political units. Though these were not destined to last, during the relatively short periods of their existence they produced a variety of Muslim regimes which are highly significant for understanding the historical background of the radical Muslim movements and their objectives in modern times. One would therefore hesitate to agree with Lazarus-Yafeh who categorically stated that "the idea of redemption is certainly not a central one in Islam".[16]

Summing up, we should mention again one of the common features of the four movements which are discussed in this book: their exclusivity and denunciation of all Muslims who did not join the fold. It stands to reason that this radical approach to the question of community boundaries was the main reason for the failure of the *mahdī* movements to gain wider acceptance and to make a more lasting impact on Muslim history and society. From this point of view, the Almohads, the Gujarātī Mahdawīs and the followers of the Sudanese *mahdī* belong to the same tradition as the radical Islamic movements which gained prominence in recent decades and should be viewed as their precursors. It is also reasonable to say that the *mahdī* idea is absolutely central in the Shīʿī system of belief, but its historical impact has been greater in the Sunnī branch of Islam.

---

14 See Chapter 2, at notes 69–72.

15 Goldziher, *Introduction*, pp. 200–202. See a critique of this view in D. Cook, *Studies in Muslim Apocalyptic*, p. 30.

16 Lazarus-Yafeh, "Is There a Concept of Redemption in Islam?", p. 168.

It is perhaps advisable to conclude this work by stressing again the special case of the Aḥmadiyya which is substantially different from the other three movements discussed in the present work. As we have seen, the Aḥmadiyya shares with the other movements the messianic claim of its founder and – to a certain extent – its exclusivity, but is different from them in all other aspects of thought and action. It is also a good example of the wide range of interpretive options available to Muslim thinkers when they come to develop a system of belief for a religious and political movement which they intend to launch.

Bibliography

ʿAbbādī, Aḥmad Mukhtār, *Fī taʾrīkh al-Maghrib wa al-Andalus*, Beirut: Dār al-nahḍa al-ʿarabiyya, 1978.

ʿAbd Allāh ʿAlī Ibrāhīm, *al-Ṣirāʿ bayn al-mahdī wa al-ʿulamāʾ*, Kharṭūm: Jāmiʿat al-Kharṭūm, 1968.

ʿAbd Allāh Muḥammad b. ʿUmar al-Makkī, *Ẓafar al-wālih bi-Muẓaffar wa ālih*, ed., E. Denison Ross, Indian Texts Series, London: John Murray, 1910.

Abrahamov, Binjamin, *Islamic Theology: Traditionalism and Rationalism*, Edinburgh: Edinburgh University Press, 1998.

Abū Dāwūd, Sulaymān b. al-Ashʿath al-Sijistānī al-Azdī, *Sunan*, ed., Muḥammad Muḥyī al-Dīn ʿAbd al-Ḥamīd, Cairo: Maṭbaʿat Muṣṭafā Muḥammad, n.d.

Abū Dāwūd, Sulaymān b. Ashʿath b. Isḥāq al-Azdī al-Sijistānī, *Sunan*, Cairo: Muṣṭafā al-Bābī al-Ḥalabī, 1983.

Abū Ḥanīfa, *al-Fiqh al-Akbar*, n.p. (India), 1874(?).

Abū Maʿāsh, Saʿīd, *al-Imām al-mahdī fī al-Qurʾan wa al-sunna*, Mashhad: Muʾassasat al-ṭabʿ al-tābiʿa li-'l-āstana al-riźawiyya al-muqaddasa, 1422 AH.

Abū Rajā, Muḥammad, *Hadiyya Mahdawiyya*, Kānpūr: Maṭbaʿ-i Niẓāmī, 1293 AH/1877 CE another edition: 1287 AH/1869 CE.

Abū Salīm, Muḥammad Ibrāhīm, *al-Āthār al-kāmila li-'l-imām al-mahdī*, Al-Kharṭūm: Dār Jāmiʿat al-Kharṭūm li-'l-nashr, 1990–1993.

_______, *Fihris āthār al-imām al-mahdī*, Beirut: Dār al-jīl, 1995.

_______, *Al-khuṣūma fī mahdiyyat al-Sūdān*, Al-Kharṭūm: Markaz Abū Salīm li-'l-dirāsāt, 2004.

_______, *Manshūrāt al-Mahdiyya*, n.p., 1969.

Abu Sway, "Jesus Christ: A Prophet of Islam", in Rafiq Khoury and Mustafa Abu Sway, *Jesus in the Christian and Muslim Faiths*, Jerusalem:

Palestinian Academic Society for the study of international affairs, 2007, pp. 25–58.

Abū Zuhra, Muḥammad, "al-Imām al-Kawtharī", in *Muqaddimāt al-imām al-Kawtharī*, pp. 11–17.

Ādam ʿAlī, ʿAbd al-Raḥmān, *al-Imām al-Shāṭibī, ʿaqīdatuhu wa mawqifuhu min al-bidaʿ wa ahlihā*, Riyāḍ: Maktabat al-rushd, 1998.

Ahmad, Aziz, *Islamic Modernism in India and Pakistan*, London: Oxford University Press, 1967.

Aḥmad, Ḥāfiẓ Muẓaffar, *Masīḥ awr mahdī ḥaẓrat Muḥammad rasūl Allah kī naẓar mēñ*, Islamabad (Tilford): Raqeem Press, 2011.

Aḥmad, Muḥammad, *Rātib al-imām al-mahdī*, Omdurman: 1307 AH.

Aḥmad, Nadhīr, *al-Qawl al-ṣarīḥ fī ẓuhūr al-mahdī wa al-masīḥ*, Tilford: al-Shirkatul Islāmiyyah, 1410 AH.

Aḥmad, Ẓuhūr al-Dīn Akmal, *Karāmāt al-mahdī*, Qādiyān: Muḥammad Yamīn, 1911.

Aḥmad Khān, Sir Sayyid, *Mahdī-yi ākhir al-zamān*, Lahore: Nawal Kishōr Steam Press, n.d.

Ājurrī, Abū Bakr Muḥammad b. al-Ḥusayn, *Kitāb al-ghurabāʾ min al-muʾminīn*, ed., Ayyūb Ramaḍān, Beirut: Dār al-bashāʾir, 1992.

Akmal, Muḥammad Ẓahūr al-Dīn, *Ẓuhūr al-masīḥ*, Siyālkōt: Mufīd-i ʿāmm Press, 1908.

Āl Muḥsin, ʿAlī, *al-Radd al-qāṣim li-daʿwat al-muftarī ʿalā al-imām al-qāʾim*, Beirut: 2013.

Albānī, Muḥammad Nāṣir al-Dīn, *Silsilat al-aḥādīth al-ḍaʿīfa wa al-mawḍūʿa wa atharuhā al-sayyiʾ fī al-umma*, Riyāḍ: Maktabat al-maʿārif li-'l-nashr wa al-tawzīʿ, 2000.

Alexander, Paul J., "Medieval apocalypses as historical sources", *American Historical Review* 73 (1968), pp. 997–1018.

Ali, Moulvi Cherágh, *A Critical Exposition of the Popular "Jihád" Showing that all the Wars of Mohammad Were Defensive; and that Aggressive War, or Compulsory Conversion is Not Allowed in the Koran*, Karachi: Karimsons, 1977 (first published in Calcutta: Thacker, Spink and Co., 1885).

Ali, Muhammad, *The Ahmadiyya Movement*, Lahore: Coloured Printing Press, 1918.

______, *The Holy Qurʾān. Arabic text, Translation and Commentary*, Lahore: Anjuman-i Ishāʿat-i Islam, 1951.

ʿAlī, Muḥammad ʿAlī, *al-Qaḍāʾ fī dawlat al-mahdiyya*, Cairo: Markaz al-dirāsāt al-sūdāniyya, 2002.

ʿAlī al-Qāriʾ, *Kitāb al-fiqh al-akbar li-ʾl-imām ... Abī Ḥanīfa al-Nuʿmān b. Thābit al-Kūfī wa sharḥuhu li-ʾl-imām ... ʿAlī al-Qāriʾ al-Ḥanafī*, Cairo: Maṭbaʿat al-taqaddum, 1323 AH.

______, *Kitāb sharḥ al-Fiqh al-akbar li-Abī Ḥanīfa*, Cairo: Maṭbaʿat al-taqaddum, 1333 AH.

ʿAlī, Sayyid Ashraf (known as Achchhā Miyāñ), *Siyar-i Masʿūd, Wāqiʿāt-i Mahdī-yi Mawʿūd*, Murādābād: Bidyā Bhūshan, 1315 AH.

Ali, Shawkat, *Millenarian and Messianic Tendencies in Islamic History*, Lahore: Publishers United, 1993.

Ali, Sher, "The *mahdī*", *The Review of Religions* 7 (1908), pp. 26–33.

ʿAllūsh, Abū ʿAbd Allah ʿAbd al-Salām b. Muḥammad b. ʿUmar, *al-Jāmiʿ fī gharīb al-ḥadīth* wa *yashtamil al-matn ʿalā al-Nihāya li-Ibn al-Athīr*, Riyāḍ: Maktabat al-rushd, 2001.

Amanat, Abbas, "The Resurgence of Apocalyptic in Modern Islam", in Stephen J. Stein, ed., *The Encyclopedia of Apocalypticism*, vol. 3: *Apocalypticism in the Modern Period and the Contemporary Age*, New York: Continuum, 1999, pp. 230–64.

ʿĀmilī, Ibn Sammāk, *al-Ḥulal al-mawshiyya fī al-akhbār al-Marrākushiyya*, ed. ʿAbd al-Qādir Bū Bāya, Beirut: Dār al-kutub al-ʿilmiyya, 1971; also: Tūnis: Maṭbaʿat al-taqaddum al-islāmiyya, n.d. (*c.*1909?), attributed to Lisān al-Dīn Ibn al-Khaṭīb; also: ed., I. S. Allouche, Ribāṭ al-Fath: al-Maktaba al-iqtiṣādiyya, 1936 (considered anonymous).

Amīn, Aḥmad, *Al-Mahdī wa al-mahdawiyya. Iqraʾ 103*, Cairo: Dār al-maʿārif, 1951.

Amīn, ʿIzz al-Dīn, *Turāth al-shiʿr al-Sūdānī*, Cairo: Maʿhad al-buḥūth wa al-dirāsāt al-ʿarabiyya, 1969.

Amīn Muḥammad, Muḥammad Khawjalī, Shākir Efendī. Ḥusayn al-Muḥammadī, Mūsā Muḥammad, *Iʿlān fatwā ʿulamāʾ al-islām al-manqūla min ʿulamāʾ al-Kharṭūm al-aʿlām fī al-radd ʿalā Muḥammad Aḥmad al-muddaʿī annahu al-mahdī fī hādhihi al-ayyām*, BL MS OR. 12915.

Anjum, Tanvir, "Bridging Tradition and Modernism: An Analysis of ʿUbaid-Allah Sindhī's Religious Thought", *Journal of the Pakistan Historical Society* 61 (2013/3), pp. 7–35.

Anonymous, *Aḥādīth al-mahdī min Musnad Aḥmad b. Ḥanbal*, Qum: Muʾassasat al-nashr al-islāmī, 1409 AH.

Anonymous, *Kitāb al-istibṣār fī ʿajāʾib al-amṣār*, ed. Saʿd Zaghlūl ʿAbd al-Ḥamīd, Al-Dār al-Bayḍāʾ: Dār al-nashr al-maghribiyya, 1985.

Anonymous, *Mafākhir al-Barbar*, in *Thalāthat nuṣūṣ ʿarabiyya ʿan al-Barbar fī al-gharb al-islāmī*, Madrid: Consejo Superior de Investigaciones Científicas, 1996.

Anonymous, "A Sketch of the Wahhabis in India Down to the Death of Sayyid Ahmad in 1831", *Calcutta Review* 100 (1870), pp. 73–104.

Ansari, Bazmee A. S., "Ismāʿīl Shahīd", in *EI²*, s.v.

_______, "Sayyid Muḥammad Jawnpūrī and His Movement (A Historico-Heresiological Study of the Mahdiyya in the Indo-Pakistan Subcontinent)", *Islamic Studies* 2 (1963), pp. 41–74.

ʿAqūn, Malīka, *Ishkāliyyat al-imāma fī al-fikr al-ʿarabī al-siyāsī al-islāmī. Al-mahdī Ibn Tūmart namūdhajan*, Tlemçen: al-Nashr al-jāmiʿī al-jadīd, 2018.

ʿArab, Amīr, *al-Mahdī al-muntaẓar: ḥaqīqa am khurāfa?* Beirut: Dār al-rasūl al-akram wa Dār al-maḥajja al-bayḍāʾ, 1998.

Arazi, Albert, "Noms de vêtements et vêtements d'aprés *al-Aḥādīth al-ḥisān fī faḍl al-ṭaylasān* d'al-Suyūṭī", *Arabica* 23 (1976), pp. 109–155.

Arberry, Arthur J., *The Koran Interpreted*, London: George Allen & Unwin Ltd, 1955.

Arjomand, S. A., "Islam in Iran. vi. The Concept of Mahdī in Sunnī Islam", *Encyclopaedia Iranica*, s.v.

_______, "Islamic Apocalypticism in the Classic Period", in Bernard McGinn, ed., *Encyclopaedia of Apocalypticism, vol. 2: Apocalypticism in Western History and Culture*, New York: Continuum, 1999, pp. 238–283.

_______, "Messianism, Millennialism and Revolution in Early Islamic History", in Abbas Amanat and Magnus Thorkell Bernhardsson, eds, *Imagining the End: Visions of Apocalypse from the Ancient Middle East to Modern America*, London and New York: I. B. Tauris, 2002, pp. 106–125, 355–359.

Arnold, T. W. and B. Lawrence, "Mahdawīs", *EI²*, s.v.

ʿAskarī, Najm al-Dīn b. Jaʿfar b. Muḥammad, *al-Mahdī al-mawʿūd al-muntaẓar ʿinda ʿulamāʾ ahl al-sunna wa al-imāmiyya*, Tehran: 1406 AH.

ʿAsqalānī, Ibn Ḥajar, *Fatḥ al-bārī li-sharḥ Ṣaḥīḥ al-Bukhārī*, ed. Muḥammad Fuʾād ʿAbd al-Bāqī, Beirut: Dār al-fikr, n.d.

_______, *Hudā al-sārī, muqaddimat Fatḥ al-bārī bi-sharḥ Ṣaḥīḥ al-Bukhārī*, Beirut: Dār al-fikr, n.d.

Ayalon, David, "The Great Yāsa of Jingis Khān", *Studia Islamica* 33 (1971), pp. 97–140.

ʿAynī, Badr al-Dīn Abū Muḥammad Maḥmūd b. Aḥmad, *ʿUmdat al-qārī sharḥ Ṣaḥīḥ al-Bukhārī*, Beirut: Dār iḥyāʾ al-turāth al-ʿarabī, n.d.

Ayoub, Mahmoud M., "Towards an Islamic Christology, II: The Death of Jesus, Reality or Delusion: A Study of the Death of Jesus in *Tafsīr* Literature", *The Muslim World* 70 (1980), pp. 91–121.

ʿAyyāshī, Abū Naṣr Muḥammad b. Masʿūd b. ʿAyyāsh al-Sulamī al-Samarqandī, *Tafsīr al-ʿAyyāshī*, Beirut: Muʾassasat al-Aʿlamī li-'l-maṭbūʿāt, 1991.

Azāykū, ʿAlī Ṣidqī, *Namādhij min asmāʾ al-aʿlām al-jughrāfiyya al-bashariyya al-maghribiyya*, Rabāṭ: 2004.

ʿAẓīmābādī, Shams al-Ḥaqq, *ʿAwn al-maʿbūd sharḥ Sunan Abī Dāwūd*, Medina: al-Maktaba al-salafiyya, 1969.

ʿAzzāwī, Aḥmad, ed., *Rasāʾil muwaḥḥidiyya, majmūʿa jadīda*, ʿAl-Qunayṭira: Jāmiʿat Ibn Ṭufayl, 1995.

Badāʾūnī, ʿAbd al-Qādir b. Mulūk Shāh, *Muntakhab al-tawārīkh*, vol. 1 eds Aḥmad ʿAlī and Kabīr al-Dīn Aḥmad, vol. 2 eds, W. N. Lees and Aḥmad ʿAlī, vol. 3 eds, Aḥmad ʿAlī and Kabīr al-Dīn Aḥmad, Bibliotheca Indica, Calcutta: College Press, vol. 1, 1868; vol. 2, 1865; vol. 3, 1869.

_______, *Muntakhabu-t-tawārīkh*, vol. 1, translated by George S. A. Ranking, Baptist Mission Press, 1898.

Badāʾūnī, ʿAbd al-Qādir, *Najāt Al-Rashīd*, ed. Sayyid Muʿīn al-Ḥaqq; Idāra-yi taḥqīqāt-i Pākistān, Dānishgāh-i Panjāb, Lahore: Ẓafar Sons Printers, n.d.

Baḥrānī, Hāshim al-Ḥusaynī, *al-Burhān fī tafsīr al-Qurʾān*, Qum: Muʾassasat al-baʿtha, 1415 AH.

Bakrī, Abū ʿUbayd, *al-Masalık wa al-mamālik: al-juzʾ al-khāṣṣ bi-bilād al-Maghrib*, ed. Zaynab al-Hakkārī, Rabāṭ: n.d. (2012?).

Balkhī, Abū Zayd Aḥmad b. Sahl, *Kitāb al-badʾ wa al-taʾrīkh*, Paris: 1901.

Barrāk, Mubārak, *Al-ḍaʿīf wa al-mawḍūʿ min akhbār al-fitan wa al-malāḥim wa ashrāṭ al-sāʿa*, Cairo: Dār al-salām, 1996.

Barzanjī, Muḥammad b. ʿAbd al-Rasūl, *al-Ishāʿa li-ashrāṭ al-sāʿa*, Damascus(?): Dār Qutayba, 1989; also, ed., Ḥusayn Muḥammad ʿAlī Shukrī, with commentary, Muḥammad Zakariyāʾ al-Kāndhlawī, Jidda: Dār al-minhāj li-'l-nashr wa al-tawzīʿ, 1997.

Bashear, Suliman, "Early Muslim Apocalyptic Materials", *Journal of the Royal Asiatic Society* 1991, pp. 173–207.

_______, "Muslim Apocalypses and the Hour: A Case-Study in Traditional Interpretation", *Israel Oriental Studies* 13 (1993), pp. 75–99.

_______, "*Qibla musharriqa* and Early Muslim Prayer in Churches", *The Muslim World* 86 (1991), pp. 267–282 (reprinted in Bashear, *Studies in Early Islamic Tradition*, Jerusalem: The Max Schloessinger Memorial Foundation, 2004, VI).

Bastawī, ʿAbd al-ʿAlīm ʿAbd al-ʿAẓīm, *al-Mahdī al-muntaẓar fī ḍawʾ al-aḥādīth wa al-āthār al-ṣaḥīḥa wa aqwāl al-ʿulamāʾ wa al-firaq al-mukhtalifa*, Mecca and Beirut: Al-Maktaba al-Makkiyya wa Dār Ibn Ḥazm, 1999.

Baude de Maurceley, Charles, *L'armée du mahdī à vol d'oiseau*, Paris: Librairie coloniale, 1884.

Bawwiz, Fāris, *Dirāsa fī fikr al-mahdī Muḥammad b. Tūmart al-zaʿīm al-rūḥī wa al-siyāsī li-ḥarakat al-muwaḥḥidīn*, Damascus: Dār Ḥāzim li-'ṭibāʿa wa al-nashr wa al-tawzīʿ, 2001.

Bayḍāwī, ʿAbd Allah b. ʿUmar, *Anwār al-tanzīl wa asrār al-taʾwīl*, ed. H. O. Fleischer, Leipzig: 1846.

al-Baydhaq, Abū Bakr al-Ṣinhājī, *Kitāb akhbār al-mahdī Ibn Tūmart wa ibtidāʾ dawlat al-muwaḥḥidīn*, ed., E. Lévi-Provençal, Paris: 1928.

_______, *Kitāb akhbār al-mahdī Ibn Tūmart*, ed. ʿAbd al-Ḥamīd Ḥājiyyāt, Algiers: Al-Muʾassasa al-waṭaniyya li-'l-kitāb, 1986.

Bayhaqī, Abū Bakr Aḥmad b. al-Ḥusayn, *Bayān Khaṭaʾ Man Akhṭaʾa ʿalā Al-Shāfiʿī*, Nāyif al-Daʿīs (Duʿʿayyis?), Beirut: Muʾassasat al-Risāla, 1983.

Bayley, Edward Clive (translator), *The Local Muhammadan Dynasties. Gujarat. The History of India as Told by its Own Historians*, London: W. H. Allen, 1886.

Bel, Alfred, *La religion musulmane en Berbérie. Esquisse d'histoire et de sociologie religieuses*, Tome I, Paris: Librairie Orientaliste Paul Geuthner, 1938.

Bennison, Amira K., *The Almoravid and Almohad Empires*, Edinburgh: Edinburgh University Press, 2016.

Bermann, Richard Arnold, *The Mahdī of Allah*, London and New York: Putnam, 1931.

Bijlefeld, Willem A., "Eschatology: Some Muslim and Christian Data", *Islam and Christian-Muslim Relations* 15 (2004), pp. 35–54.

Blichfeldt, Jan-Olaf, *Early Mahdism*, Studia Orientalia Lundensia, Leiden: E. J. Brill, 1985.

Blochet, E., *Le messianisme dans l'hétérodoxie musulmane*, Paris: Maisonneuve, 1903.

Brockelmann, Carl, *Geschichte der arabischen Litteratur,* Leiden: Brill 1937–1942.
Brown, Jonathan A. C., *Hadith. Muhammad's Legacy in the Medieval and Modern World,* Oxford: Oneworld Publications, 2011.
Brunschwig, R., "Sur la doctrine du Mahdī Ibn Tūmart", *Arabica* 2 (1955), pp. 137–49.
Bukhārī, Muḥammad b. Ismāʿīl, *Ṣaḥīḥ*, ed., Krehl, Leiden: E. J. Brill, 1908.
Casanova, Paul, *Mohammed et la fin du monde: étude critique sur l'Islam primitive*, Paris: Librairie Orientaliste Paul Geuthner, 1911.
Cherif, Mohamed, "Encore sur le statut des ḏimmī-s sous les Almohades", in Maribel Fierro and John Tolan, eds, *The legal status of ḏimmī-s in the Islamic West (second/eighth–ninth/fifteenth centuries),* Turnhout: Brepols, 2013.
Chodkiewicz, Michel, *Seal of the Saints: Prophethood and Sainthood in the Doctrine of Ibn ʿArabī*, Cambridge: The Islamic Texts Society, 1993.
Colvin, James Russel (J. R. C.), "Notice of the Peculiar Tenets Held by the Followers of Syed Ahmed, Taken chiefly from the 'Sirát-ul-Mustaqím', a Principal Treatise of that sect, written by Moulaví Mahommed Ismaíl", *Journal of the Royal Asiatic Society of Bengal* 1 (1832), pp. 479–498.
Cook, David, "Apocalypse", *Encyclopaedia of Islam Three*, s.v.
______, "Apocalyptic Events during the Mongol Invasions", in Wolfram Brandes and Felicitas Schmieder, eds, *Endzeiten. Eschatologie in den monotheistischen Weltreligionen*, Berlin and New York: Walter de Gruyter, 2008, pp. 293–312.
______, *"The Book of Tribulations": The Syrian Muslim Apocalyptic Tradition. An annotated translation by* [sic] *Nuʿaym b. Ḥammād al-Marwazī*, Edinburgh: Edinburgh University Press, 2017.
______, *Contemporary Muslim Apocalyptic Literature*, Syracuse: Syracuse University Press, 2005.
______, "Early Islamic and Classical Sunnī and Shiʿite Apocalyptic Movements", in Catherine Wessinger, ed., *The Oxford Handbook of Millennialism*, Oxford: Oxford University Press, 2011, pp. 267–283.
______, "The Image of the Turk in Classical and Modern Muslim Apocalyptic Literature", in Brandes Wolfram, Felicitas Schmieder and Rebekka Voss, eds, *Peoples of the Apocalypse*, Berlin: De Gruyter, 2016, pp. 225–235.

_______, "The Mahdi's Arrival and the Messianic Future State according to Sunni and Shiʿite Apocalyptic Scenarios", The Seventh Annual Levtzion Lecture, Jerusalem: The Hebrew University, 2014.

_______, "Messianism and Astronomical Events in the First Four Centuries of Islam", in Mercedes García-Arenal, ed., *Revue des mondes musulmans et de la Méditerranée* 91–94, *Mahdisme et Millénarisme en Islam*, Aix-en-Provence: Édisud, 2000, pp. 29–51.

_______, *Studies in Muslim Apocalyptic*, Princeton: The Darwin Press, 2002.

Cook, Michael, "An Early Islamic Apocalyptic Chronicle" *Journal of Near Eastern Studies* 52 (1993), pp. 25–29.

_______, "Eschatology and the Dating of Traditions", *Princeton Papers in Near Eastern Studies* 1 (1992), pp. 23–47.

_______, "The Heraclian Dynasty in Muslim Eschatology", *al-Qanṭara* 13 (1992), pp. 3–23.

Crone, Patricia, "The First-Century Concept of the *Hiǧra*", *Arabica* 41 (1994), pp. 352–387.

_______, *Medieval Islamic Political Thought*, Edinburgh: Edinburgh University Press, 2012.

Crone, Patricia and Martin Hinds, *God's Caliph. Religious Authority in the First Centuries of Islam*, Cambridge: Cambridge University Press, 1986.

Daḥlān, Aḥmad b. Zaynī, *al-Futūḥāt al-islāmiyya baʿd muḍiyy al-futūḥāt al-nabawiyya*, Cairo: Muʾassasat al-Ḥalabī, 1968.

Dandash, ʿIṣmat ʿAbd al-Laṭīf, *Aḍwāʾ jadīda ʿalā al-murābiṭīn*, Beirut: Dār al-gharb al-islāmī, 1991.

Dānī, Abū ʿUmar ʿUthmān b. Saʿīd, *al-Sunan al-wārida fī al-fitan wa ghawāʾilihā wa al-sāʿa wa ashrāṭihā*, Beirut: Dār al-kutub al-ʿilmiyya, 1997.

Dārimī, Abū Muḥammad ʿAbd Allah, *Sunan*, Riyāḍ: Dār al-mughnī, 2000.

Darmesteter, James, *Le Mahdī: depuis les origines de l'Islam jusqu'a nos jours*, Paris: 1885.

Dāwūd, Muḥammad ʿĪsā, *Mā qabl al-damār: marratan ukhrā, iḥdharū wa 'ntahū, al-masīkh* [sic] *al-dajjāl ʿalā al-abwāb*, Cairo: Dār al-bashīr, 1999.

Dekmejian, R. H. and M. J. Wyszomirski, "Charismatic Leadership in Islam: The *mahdī* of the Sudan", *Comparative studies in society and history* 14 (1972), pp. 193–214.

Dhahabī, Shams al-Dīn Muḥammad b. ʿUthmān, *Siyar aʿlām al-nubalāʾ*, Beirut: Muʾassasat al-risāla, 1986.

______, *Talkhīṣ kitāb al-ʿIlal al-mutanāhiya fī al-aḥādīth al-wāhiya*, Riyāḍ: Maktabat al-rushd, 1998.

Dihlawī, Rafīʿ al-Dīn, *ʿAlāmāt-i qiyāmat*, Urdu translation by Nūr Muḥammad, Delhi: Thakur Das, 1920.

Dimashqī, Shams al-Dīn Abū ʿAbd Allah Muḥammad b. Abī Ṭālib al-Anṣārī, *Nukhat al-dahr fī ʿajāʾib al-barr wa al-baḥr*, Beirut: Dār iḥyāʾ al-turāth al-ʿarabī, 1988.

Djebbar, Ahmed, "Ibn Qunfudh", in *EI*², s.v.

Donner, Fred M., "La question du messianisme dans l'Islam primitif", in Mercedes García-Arenal, ed., *Revue des mondes musulmans et de la Méditerranée* 91–94, *Mahdisme et Millénarisme en Islam*, Aix-en-Provence: Édisud, 2000, pp. 17–27.

Dray, Maurice, *Dictionnaire Berbère-Français. Dialecte des Ntifa*, Paris: L'Harmattan, 2001.

Dujarric, Gaston, *L'état Mahdiste du Soudan*, Paris: Librairie Orientale et Américaine, 1901.

Dūrī, ʿAbd al-ʿAzīz, "al-Fikra al-mahdiyya bayna al-daʿwa al-ʿAbbāsiyya wa al-ʿaṣr al-ʿAbbāsī al-awwal", in Wadād al-Qāḍī, ed., *Studia Arabica and Islamica: Festschrift for Iḥsān ʿAbbās on his sixtieth birthday*, Beirut: American University of Beirut, 1981, pp. 123–132.

During, J., "Samāʿ", in *EI*², s.v.

El Hour, Rachid, "The Andalusian *qāḍī* in the Almoravid Period: Political and Judicial Authority", *Studia Islamica* 90 (2000), pp. 67–83.

Elad, Amikam, *The Rebellion of Muḥammad al-nafs al-zakiyya in 145/762. Ṭālibīs and Early ʿAbbāsīs in Conflict*, Leiden and Boston: E. J. Brill, 2016.

______, "The Struggle for Legitimacy of Authority as reflected in the *ḥadīth* al-*mahdī*", in John Nawas, ed., *ʿAbbasid Studies II*, Leuven–Paris–Walpole: 2010, pp. 39–96.

Elder, Earl Edgar, *A Commentary on the Creed of Islam. Saʿd al-Dīn al-Taftāzānī on the Creed of Najm al-Dīn al-Nasafī*, New York: Columbia University Press, 1950.

Ende, Werner, "Shaltūt, Maḥmūd", *EI*², s.v.

Erskine, William, *A History of India Under the Two First Sovereigns of the House of Timur, Bāber and Humāyūn*, Shannon: Irish University Press, 1972.

Fāsī, Abū al-Ḥasan ʿAlī b. Maymūn al-Ghumārī, *Bayān ghurbat al-islām bi-wāsiṭat al-ṣinfayn min al-mutafaqqiha wa al-mutafaqqira min ahl*

Miṣr wa al-Shām wa mā yalīhā min bilād al-aʿjām, Beirut: Dār al-kutub al-ʿilmiyya, 2007.

Fatlāwī, Mahdī, *Maʿa al-mahdī al-muntaẓar fī dirāsa manhajiyya bayn al-fikr al-islāmī al-shīʿī wa al-sunnī*, Beirut: Dār al-kirām, 1995.

Ferhat, Halima and Hamid Triki, "Faux prophètes et Mahdīs dans le Maroc mediéval", *Hesperis-Tamuda* 26–27 (1988–1989), pp. 5–24.

Fierro, Maribel, "The Islamic West in the Time of Maimonides: The Almohad Revolution", in Lukas Muehlethaler, ed., *"Höre die Wahrheit wer sie auch spricht." Stationen von Moses Maimonides vom islamischen Spanien bis ins moderne Berlin*, Schriften des Jüdischen Museums Berlin, Band 2, 2014, pp. 21–31.

______, "A Land Without Jews or Christians. Almohad Policies regarding the 'Protected People'", in Mathias M. Tischler and Alexander Fidora, eds, *Christlicher Norden – Muslimischer Süden*, Münster: Aschendorf, 2011, pp. 231–247.

______, "The Legal Policies of the Almohad Caliphs and Ibn Rushd's *Bidāyat Al-mujtahid*", *Journal of Islamic Studies* 10 (1999), pp. 226–48.

______, "The *mahdī* Ibn Tūmart and al-Andalus: The Construction of Almohad Legitimacy", in *idem*, *The Almohad Revolution. Politics and Religion in the Islamic West During the Twelfth–Thirteenth Centuries*, Farnham: Ashgate Publishing Company, 2012.

______, "Mahdism et eschatologie en al-Andalus", in Abdelmajid Kaddouri, ed., *Mahdisme. Crise et changement dans l'histoire du Maroc*, Rabāṭ, 1994.

Filiu, Jean Pierre, *Apocalypse in Islam*, Berkeley, Los Angeles and London: University of California Press, 2011.

Fletcher, Madeleine, "The Almohad *tawḥīd*: Theology which Relies on Logic", *Numen* 38 (1991), pp. 110–127.

______, "Ibn Tūmart's Teachers: The Relationship with al-Ghazālī", *Al-Qantara* 18 (1997), pp. 305–330.

Friedländer, Israel, *Die Messiasidee im Islam*, Berlin: H. Itskowski, 1903; English translation in *idem*, *Past and Present. A Collection of Jewish Essays*, Cincinnati: Ark Publishing, 1919, pp. 139–158.

Friedmann, Yohanan, "A Contribution to the Early History of Islam in India", in Rosen-Ayalon, Myriam, ed., *Studies in Memory of Gaston Wiet*, Jerusalem: Institute of Asian and African Studies, 1977, pp. 309–333.

______, "Conversion, Apostasy and Excommunication in the Islamic tradition", in Friedmann, Yohanan, ed., *Religious Movements and*

Transformations in Judaism, Christianity and Islam, Jerusalem: The Israel Academy of Sciences and Humanities, 2018, pp. 109–177.

_______, "Dār al-Islām and *dār al-ḥarb* in modern Indian Muslim thought", in G. Lancioni and V. Calasso, *Dār al-islām/dār al-ḥarb: Territories, People, Identities*, Leiden: E. J. Brill, 2017, pp. 341–380.

_______, "Finality of Prophethood in Sunnī Islam", *Jerusalem Studies in Arabic and Islam* 7 (1986): 177–215.

_______, "The Messianic Claim of Ghulām Aḥmad", in Peter Schäfer and Mark R. Cohen, eds, *Toward the Millennium. Messianic Expectations from the Bible to Waco*, Leiden: E. J. Brill, 1998.

_______, "Muslim Minorities: An Introductory Essay", in Yohanan Friedmann, ed., *Muslim Minorities in Modern Times*, Jerusalem: The Israel Academy of Sciences and Humanities, 2019.

_______, *Prophecy Continuous. Aspects of Aḥmadī Religious Thought and its Medieval Background*, Los Angeles: University of California Press, 1989; rep. New Delhi: Oxford University Press, 2003.

_______, "Quasi-Rational and Anti-Rational Elements in Radical Muslim Thought: The Case of Abū al-Aʿlā Mawdūdī", in Yohanan Friedmann and Christoph Markschies, eds, *Rationalization in Religions*, Berlin: De Gruyter, 2019, pp. 289–300.

_______. *Shaykh Aḥmad Sirhindī. An Outline of His Thought and a Study of His Image in the Eyes of Posterity*, Montreal and London: McGill University Press, 1971.

Fromherz, Allen J., *The Almohads. The Rise of an Islamic Empire*, London and New York: I. B. Tauris, 2010.

Furnish, T. R., "Appearance or Reappearance? Sunni Mahdism in History and in Theory and its Differences from Shiʿi Mahdism", International conference on Imam Mahdi, justice and globalisation, London: Institute of Islamic Studies, 2004, pp. 113–132.

Gaborieau, Marc, *Le mahdī incompris*, Paris: CNRS Éditions, 2010.

Ganjī, Abū ʿAbd Allāh Muḥammad b. Yūsuf b. Muḥammad, *Kifāyat al-ṭālib fī manāqib ʿAlī b. Abī Ṭālib wa yalīhi al-Bayān fī Akhbār ṣāḥib al-zamān*, Beirut: Sharikat al-Kutubī, 1993.

Gannūn (Guennoun), ʿAbd Allah, "ʿAqīdat al-Murshida li-'l-mahdī Ibn Tūmart", in ʿUthmān Amīn, ed., *Nuṣūs falsafiyya muhdāt ilā Ibrāhīm Madkūr*, Cairo: Al-Hayʾa al-miṣriyya al-ʿāmma li-'l-kitāb, 1976.

García-Arenal, Mercedes, ed., *Mahdisme et Millénarisme en Islam. Revue des mondes musulmans et de la Méditerranée*. Aix-en-Provence: Édisud, 2000.

______, *Messianism and Puritanical Reform. Mahdīs of the Muslim West*, Leiden and Boston: E. J. Brill, 2006.

Garçon, Augustin, *Guerre de Soudan (le mahdī)*, Paris: Henri Charles-Lavazuelle, 1884.

Ghazālī, Muḥammad Abū Ḥāmid, *Iḥyā' 'ulūm al-dīn*, Damascus: Dār al-khayr, 1994.

Ghulām Aḥmad, *Ā'ina-yi kamālāt-i Islām*, in *Rūḥānī Khazā'in*, vol. 5.

______, *Chashma-yi ma'rifat*, in *Rūḥānī Khazā'in*, vol. 23, pp. 1–436.

______, *Ḥamāmat al-bushrā ilā ahl Makka wa ṣulahā' umm al-qurā*, Haifa: n.d; also, Qādiyān: al-Maṭba'a al-Yūsufiyya, 1341 AH.

______, *al-Hudā wa al-tabṣira li-man yarā*, in *Rūḥānī Khazā'in*, vol. 18, pp. 1–204.

______, *I'jāz al-masīḥ*, in *Rūḥanī Khazā'in*, vol. 18.

______, *Islām. Lecture Siyālkōt*, in *Rūḥanī Khazā'in*, vol. 20, pp. 203–247.

______, *Izāla-yi awhām*, Amritsar: 1891.

______, *Kashf al-ghiṭā'*, Lahore: 1898.

______, *Lecture Ludhyāna*, in *Rūḥanī Khazā'in*, vol. 20, pp. 249–298.

______, *Malfūẓāt*, in *Rūḥānī Khazā'in*, series 2, vol. 4.

______, *Malfūẓāt*, in *Rūḥānī Khazā'in*, series 2, vol. 7.

______, *Malfūẓāt*, in *Rūḥānī Khazā'in*, series 2, vol. 9.

______, *Malfūẓāt*, in *Rūḥānī Khazā'in*, series 2, vol. 10.

______, *Masīḥ Hindustān mēñ*; English translation *Jesus in India*, Lagos: 1962.

______, *Rūḥānī Khazā'in*, 23 volumes, Rabwa: 1957–1968.

______, *Shinākht-i masīḥ-i maw'ūd*, ed. Muḥammad Yāmīn, Lahore: Karīmī Press, 1920.

______, *Tadhkira. Majmū'a-yi ilhāmāt kushūf o ru'yā* [sic] *Ḥaẑrat-i masīḥ-i maw'ūd 'alayhi al-salām*, Rabwa: al-Sharika al-islāmiyya, 1977; translation by Muḥammad Zafrullah Khan, *Tadhkirah. English translation of the dreams, visions and verbal revelations vouchsafed to the Promised Messiah on whom be peace*, London: The London Mosque, 1976.

______, *Tuḥfa Gōlaṙwiyya*, in *Rūḥānī Khazā'in*, vol. 17.

Goldziher, Ignáz, "The Appearance of the Prophet in Dreams", *Journal of the Royal Asiatic Society* 27 (1912), pp. 503–506.

______, "Ghair Mahdī", *Encyclopaedia of Religion and Ethics*, New York: Scribner, 1955, s.v.

______, *Le livre de Mohammed Ibn Toumert, Mahdī des Almohades*, Alger: Imprimerie Orientale Pierre Fontana, 1903.

______, "Materialien zur Kentniss der Almohadenbewegung in Nordafrica", in *Zeitschrift der Deutschen Morgenländischen Gesellschaft* 41 (1887), pp. 30–140.

Graham, H. R., *Three Months on the Nile. Defying the Mahdī*, London: R. J. Hammond, 1884.

Griffel, Frank, *Al-Ghazālī's Philosophical Theology*, Oxford: Oxford University Press, 2009.

______, "Ibn Tūmart's Rational Proof for God's Existence and Unity and His Connection to the Niẓāmiyya *madrasa* in Baghdad", in Patrick Cressier, Maribel Fierro and Louis Molina, eds, *Los Almohades: problemas y perspectivas*, Madrid: Consejo Superior de Investigaciones Científicas, 2005, pp. 753–813

Guillaume, Alfred, *The Life of Muḥammad. A translation of Isḥāq's Sīrat Rasūl Allah*, Lahore, Karachi and Dhaka: Oxford University Press, 1967.

Gujarātī, Shaykh Muṣṭafā, *Jawāhir al-taṣdīq*, Ḥaydarābād: Mu'īn Press, 1367 AH.

______, *Majālis, mutarjam bi-ihtimām Sayyid Sharīf*, Mushīrābād(?) (Deccan): Maktaba-yi Ibrāhīmiyya, 1367 AH.

Haddad, Yvonne and Jane I. Smith, "The Anti-Christ and the End of Time in Christian and Muslim Eschatological Literature", *The Muslim World* 100 (2010), pp. 505–529.

Hake, A. Egmont, *The Journals of Major-General C. G. Gordon, C. B., at Kartoum*. London: Kegan Paul, Trench and Co., 1885.

Ḥakīm al-Tirmidhī, *Kitāb Khatm al-awliyā'*, ed., 'Uthmān Yaḥyā, Beirut: Al-Maṭba'a Al-Kāthūlikiyya, 1965.

Ḥakīmī, Muḥammad Riḍā, *al-Imām al-mahdı fı kutub al-umam al-sābiqa wa 'inda 'l-muslimīn*, translated by Ḥaydar Āl Ḥaydar, Beirut: al-Dār al-islāmiyya li-'l-ṭibā'a wa al-nashr wa al-tawzī', 2003.

Halperin, David J., "The Ibn Ṣayyād Traditions and the Legend of Al-Dajjāl", *Journal of the American Oriental Society* 96 (1976), pp. 213–25.

Ḥamzāwī, Ḥasan al-'Adawī, *Mashāriq al-anwār fī fawz ahl al-i'tibār*, Cairo: al-Maṭba'a al-Kāstaliyya, 1280 AH.

Ḥanbalī, Ibn Rajab, *Kalimat al-ikhlāṣ wa taḥqīq ma'nāhā*, ed., 'Imād Ṭāhā Firra, Ṭanṭā: Maktabat al-ṣaḥāba, 1408 AH.

______, *Kashf al-kurba fī waṣf 'an ḥāl ahl al-ghurba*, Cairo: Maṭba'at al-manār, 1340 AH.

Harawī, 'Alī al-Qāri', *al-Maṣnū' fī ma'rifat al-ḥadīth al-mawḍū'*, Ḥalab: Maktab al-Maṭbū'āt al-Islāmiyya, 1969.

Hartmann, Richard, "Der Sufyānī", *Studia Orientalia Ioanni Pedersen septuagenario ... a collegis discipulis amicis dicata*, Hauniae (Copenhagen): Einar Munsgaard, 1953.

Hartung, Jan-Peter, *A System of Life. Mawdūdī and the Ideologisation of Islam*, New York: Oxford University Press, 2014.

Ḥasan, Saʿd Muḥammad, *al-Mahdiyya fī al-Islām mundhu aqdam al-ʿuṣūr ḥattā al-yawm: dirāsa wāfiya li-taʾrīkhihā al-ʿaqadī wa al-siyāsī wa al-adabī*, Cairo: Dār al-kitāb al-ʿarabī, 1953.

Ḥasanī, ʿAbd al-Ḥayy b. Fakhr al-Dīn, *al-Iʿlām bi-man fī taʾrīkh al-Hind min al-aʿlām al-musammā bi-Nuzhat al-khawāṭir wa bahjat al-masāmiʿ wa al-nawāẓir*, Beirut: Dār Ibn Ḥazm, 1999.

Ḥassān b. Thābit, *Dīwān*, ed., Walid N. Arafat, London: Luzac and Company Ltd., 1971.

Haytamī, Aḥmad Shihāb al-Dīn b. Ḥajar al-Makkī, *Kitāb al-fatāwā al-ḥadīthiyya*, Cairo: Maḥmūd Tawfīq, 1934.

Haytamī, Ibn Ḥajar Abū al-ʿAbbās, *al-Qawl al-mukhtaṣar fī ʿalāmāt al-mahdī al-muntaẓar*, Cairo: al-Zahrāʾ li-'l-iʿlām al-ʿarabī, 1994.

Heghammer, T. and S. Lacroix, "Rejectionist Islamism in Saudi Arabia: The Story of Juhayman al-ʿUtaybī Revisited", *International Journal of Middle Eastern Studies* 39 (2007), pp. 103–122.

Hennebert, Eugène, *The English in Egypt. England and the Mahdi. Arabi and the Suez Canal*, translated by B. Pauncefote, London W. H. Allen and Co., 1884.

Hermansen, Marcia, "Eschatology", in Tim Winter, ed., *The Cambridge Companion to Classical Islamic Theology*, Cambridge: Cambridge University Press, 2008, pp. 308–324.

Hill, Richard, *A Biographical Dictionary of the Sudan*, London: Frank Cass 1967.

Hodgkin, Thomas, "Mahdism, Messianism and Marxism in the African setting", *Sudan in Africa. Studies presented to the First International conference sponsored by the Sudan Research Unit, 7–12 February, 1968*, Kharṭūm: Kharṭūm University Press, 1971, pp. 109–141.

Hofmann, I. and A. Vorbichler, *Das Islam-Bild bei Karl May und der Islamo-christliche Dialog. Veröffentlichungen der Institute für Afrikanistik und Ägyptologie der Universität Wien. Beiträge zur Afrikanistik, Band 4. Wien 1979.*

Holt, P. M., "The Archives of the Mahdia", *Sudan Notes and Records* 36 (1955), pp. 1–10.

______, "Islamic Millenarianism and the Fulfilment of Prophecy: A Case Study", in Ann Williams, ed., *Prophecy and Millenarianism: Essays in Honour of Marjorie Reeves*, Burnt Hill: Longman, 1980.

______, *The Mahdist State in the Sudan, 1881–1898. A Study of Its Origins, Development and Overthrow*, Oxford: Clarendon Press, 1970.

______, *A Modern History of the Sudan. From the Funj Sultanate to the Present Day,* London: Weidenfeld and Nicholson, 1973.

______, "The Sudanese Mahdia and the Outside World: 1881–9", *BSOAS* 21 (1958), pp. 276–290.

Holtzman, Livnat, *Anthropomorphism in Islam*, Edinburgh: Edinburgh University Press, 2018.

Hoover, Jon, "Creed", *EI*^{3}, s.v.

Hopkins, J. F. P., "The Almohade Hierarchy", *Bulletin of the School of Oriental and African Studies* 16 (1954), pp. 93–112.

______, *Medieval Muslim Government in Barbary*, London: Luzac, 1958.

Hunter, W. W., *Our Indian Musalmans: Are They Bound in Conscience to Rebel Against the Queen?* London: Trübner and Company, 1871.

Hurgronje, C. Snouck, *Der Mahdī*, Leiden: E. J. Brill, 1883.

ʿIbādī, al-Ḥasan b. Saʿd, *al-Anwār al-saniyya al-māḥiya li-ẓalām al-munkirīn ʿalā ḥadrat al-mahdiyya*, Omdurman(?): 1305 AH.

Ibn ʿAbd al-Ḥakam, Abū Muḥammad ʿAbd Allah, *Sīrat ʿUmar b. ʿAbd al-ʿAzīz ʿalā mā rawāhu al-imām Mālik b. Anas*, ed. Aḥmad ʿUbayd, Cairo: al-Maṭbaʿa al-Raḥmāniyya, 1927.

Ibn ʿAbd al-Ḥalīm, *Kitāb al-ansāb*, in *Thalāth nuṣūṣ ʿarabiyya ʿan al-Barbar fī al-gharb al-islāmī*, Madrid: Consejo Superior de Investigaciones Científicas, 1996.

Ibn Abī Shayba, ʿAbd Allah b. Muḥammad, *al-Muṣannaf fī al-aḥādīth wa al-āthār*, Beirut: Dār al-fikr, 1989.

Ibn Abī Yaʿlā, Abū al-Ḥusayn, *Ṭabaqāt al-Ḥanābila*, ed. Muḥammad Ḥāmid al-Fīqī. Cairo(?): Maṭbaʿat al-sunna al-muḥammadiyya, 1952.

Ibn Abī Zarʿ, ʿAlī al-Fāsī, *al-Anīs al-muṭrib bi-rawḍ al-qirṭās fī akhbār mulūk al-Maghrib wa taʾrīkh madīnat Fās*, al-Rabāṭ: al-Maṭbaʿa al-malakiyya, 1993.

Ibn ʿAsākir, Abū al-Qāsim ʿAlī b. Al-Ḥasan, *Sīrat al-sayyid al-masīḥ*, ed. Sulaymān ʿAlī Murād, ʿAmmān: Dār al-shurūq li-'l-nashr wa al-tawzīʿ, 1996.

________, *Taʾrīkh madīnat Dimashq*, Beirut: Dār al-fikr, 1997.

Ibn al-Athīr, *al-Kāmil fī al-taʾrīkh*, Beirut: Dār Ṣādir, 1966.

Ibn Bābūya al-Qummī, *Kamāl al-dīn wa tamām al-niʿma*, Tehran: Dār al-kutub al-islāmiyya, 1395 AH.

Ibn Bashkuwāl, Khalaf b. ʿAbd al-Malik, *Kitāb al-ṣila*, Cairo: al-Dār al-Miṣriyya li-'l-taʾlīf wa al-nashr, 1966.

Ibn al-Ḥājj, *al-Madkhal*, Beirut: Dār al-gharb al-islāmī, 1972.

Ibn Ḥanbal, Aḥmad, *al-ʿAqīda li-Aḥmad b. Ḥanbal bi-riwāyat Abī Bakr al-Khallāl*, Damascus: Dār Qutayba, 1988.

______, *Musnad*, Beirut: al-Maktab al-Islāmī, 1978.

Ibn Ḥazm, *ʿUqūd al-dhahab fī jamharat ansāb al-ʿarab*, ed. Kāmil Salmān al-Jabūrī, Beirut: Dār wa Maktabat al-Hilāl, 2009.

Ibn ʿIdhārī al-Marrākushī, *al-Bayān al-mughrib fī akhbār al-Andalus wa al-Maghrib. Qism al-Muwaḥḥidīn*, Beirut: Dār al-gharb al-islāmī, 1985.

______, *al-Bayān al-mughrib fī akhbār al-Maghrib*, vol. 1, ed., R. Dozy, Leiden: E. J. Brill, 1848; translated as *Histoire de l'Afrique et de l'Espagne* intitulée *al-Bayanol-Mogrib* by E. Fagnan, Leiden: E. J. Brill, 1901.

Ibn al-Jawzī, Abū al-Faraj ʿAbd al-Raḥmān b. ʿAlī. *al-ʿIlal al-mutanāhiya fī al-aḥādīth al-wāhiya*, ed. Khalīl al-Mays, Beirut: Dār al-kutub al-ʿilmiyya, 1983.

______, *Manāqib ʿUmar b. ʿAbd al-ʿAzīz*, ed. Carl Heinrich Becker, Leipzig: Drugulin, 1899.

Ibn Kathīr, Abū al-Fidāʾ Ismāʿīl, *al-Bidāya wa al-nihāya*, Beirut: 1993.

______, *al-Fitan wa al-malāḥim al-wāqiʿa fī ākhir al-zamān*, ed. Yūsuf ʿAlī Badīwī, Damascus and Beirut: Dār Ibn Kathīr, 1993.

______, *Al-Muntaẓam fī taʾrīkh al-mulūk wa al-umam*, Beirut: Dār al-kutub al-ʿilmiyya, 1992.

______, *Tafsīr al-Qurʾān al-ʿaẓīm*, Cairo: al-Fārūq al-ḥadītha, 2000.

Ibn Khaldūn, ʿAbd al-Raḥmān b. Muḥammad, *Muqaddima*, Beirut: Dār al-Kitāb al-ʿArabī, 2006.

______, ʿAbd al-Raḥmān b. Muḥammad, *The Muqaddima. An Introduction to History*, translated from the Arabic by Franz Rosenthal, Princeton: Princeton University Press, 1967.

Ibn Khallikān, *Wafayāt al-aʿyān wa anbāʾ abnāʾ al-zamān*, ed. Iḥsān ʿAbbās, Beirut: Dār al-thaqāfa, n.d.

Ibn al-Khaṭīb, Abū ʿAbd Allāh al-Salmānī Dhū al-wizāratayn, *Raqm al-ḥulal fī naẓm al-duwal*, Tūnus: al-Maṭbaʿa al-ʿumūmiyya, 1316 AH.

Ibn al-Khaṭīb, Lisān al-Dīn, *Aʿmāl al-aʿlām*, ed., Aḥmad Mukhtār al-ʿAbbādī and Muḥammad Ibrāhīm al-Kattānī, Al-Dār al-Bayḍāʾ: 1964.

______, *Sharḥ raqm al-ḥulal fī naẓm al-duwal*, ed. ʿAdnān Darwīsh. Damascus: 1993.

Ibn Māja, Abū ʿAbd Allāh Muḥammad b. Yazīd al-Qazwīnī, *Sunan*, ed., Muḥammad Fuʾād ʿAbd al-Bāqī, 1953.

Ibn al-Qaṭṭān, *Naẓm al-jumān*, ed., Maḥmūd ʿAlī Makkī, Tetwan: n.d. (196?); second edition: *Naẓm al-jumān li-tartīb mā salafa min akhbār al-zamān*, ed. Maḥmūd ʿAlī Makkī, Beirut: Dār al-gharb al-islāmī, 1990.

Ibn Qayyim al-Jawziyya, *al-Manār al-munīf fī al-ṣaḥīḥ wa al-ḍaʿīf*, ed., ʿAbd al-Raḥmān b. Yaḥyā al-Muʿallimī, Riyāḍ: Dār al-ʿāṣima li-ʾl-nashr wa al-tawzīʿ, 1996.

______, *Tahdhīb madārij al-sālikīn*, Beirut: Muʾassasat al-risāla, 1989.

Ibn Qudāma al-Maqdisī, Muwaffaq al-Dīn Abū Muḥammad ʿAbd Allāh, *ʿAqīda*, in Faraj Allah Zakī al-Kurdī, ed., *al-Majmūʿ*, Cairo: Maṭbaʿat Kurdistān al-ʿilmiyya, 1329 AH, pp. 551–560.

Ibn Qunfudh, Aḥmad b. al-Ḥusayn Abū al-ʿAbbās, *al-Fārisiyya fī mabādiʾ al-dawla al-Ḥafsiyya*, Tūnus: al-Dār al-Tūnusiyya li-ʾl-nashr, 1968.

Ibn Qutayba, *al-Imāma wa al-siyāsa al-maʿrūf bi-taʾrīkh al-khulafāʾ*, Beirut: Dār al-aḍwāʾ, 1990.

Ibn Ṣāḥib al-Ṣalāt, ʿAbd al-Malik, *Kitāb al-mann bi-ʾl-imāma*, ed., ʿAbd al-Hādī Tāzī, Beirut: Dār al-Andalus, 1964.

Ibn al-Ṣiddīq, Aḥmad b. Muḥammad, *Ibrāz al-wahm al-maknūn min kalām Ibn Khaldūn aw al-Murshid al-mubdī li-fasād ṭaʿn Ibn Khaldūn fī aḥādīth al-mahdī*, Damascus: Maṭbaʿat al-taraqqī, 1347.

Ibn Taymiyya, *Ghurbat al-islām*, ed., Abū Muḥammad Mukhtār al-Djibālī, Beirut: Dār al-Bayāriq, 1995.

______, *Minhāj al-sunna al-nabawiyya fı naqḍ kulūm al-shīʿa wa al-qadariyya*. Cairo: Muʾassasat Qurṭuba, 1986.

Ibn Tūmart, Muḥammad, *Aʿazzu mā yuṭlab*, Al-Jazāʾir: Al-Muʾassasa al-waṭaniyya li-ʻl-kitāb, 1985.

______, *Aʿazzu mā yuṭlab*, ed., ʿAbd al-Ghanī Abū al-ʿAzm, Muʾassasat al-ghinā li-ʾl-nashr, Rabāṭ: 1997.

______, *Aʿazzu mā yuṭlab*, ed., J. D. Luciani, Algiers: Imprimerie Orientale Pierre Fontana, 1903.

______, *Aʿazzu mā yuṭlab*, ed., ʿAmmār Ṭālibī, Algiers: Al-Muʾassasa Al-waṭaniyya li-ʾl-kitāb, 1985. (All references are to this edition unless noted otherwise.)

______, *ʿAqīda*, in *Majmūʿat al-rasāʾil*, Cairo: Maṭbaʿat Kurdistān al-ʿilmiyya, 1327 AH, pp. 45–61.

Ibrāhīm, ʿAbd Allāh ʿAlī, *al-Ṣirāʿ bayna al-mahdī wa al-ʿulamāʾ*, Al-Kharṭūm: 1966.

Idlibī, Muḥammad Munīr, *Intabihū! al-dajjāl yajtāḥ al-ʿālam*, Haifa: al-Jamāʿa al-Islāmiyya al-Aḥmadiyya, 2008.

Idrīsī, al-Sharīf, *Nuzhat al-mushtāq fī ikhtirāq al-āfāq*, Beirut: Dār al-kutub, 1989.

Ikrām, Muḥammad, *Mawj-i kawthar. Musalmānōñ kī madhhabī awr ʿilmī taʾrīkh kā dawr-i jadīd*, Lahore: Firooz Sons, 1968 (eighth edition).

Iṣfahānī, Abū Nuʿam Aḥmad b. ʿAbd Allah, *Ḥilyat al-awliyāʾ wa ṭabaqāt al-aṣfiyāʾ*, Beirut: Dār al-kutub al-ʿilmiyya, 1997.

Al-Ishbīlī, ʿAbd Allah Muḥammad b. Khalīl al-Sakūnī, *Sharḥ Murshidat Muḥammad b. Tūmart*, ed., Yūsuf Aḥnānā, Beirut: Dār al-gharb al-islāmī, 1993.

Jackson, Alice F., *With Mahdi and Khalifa*, London: The Sheldon Press, 1930(?).

Jalbani, G. N., *The Teachings of Shāh Walīullāh of Delhi*, Lahore: Muhammad Ashraf, 1967.

Jok, Madut Jok, *War and Slavery in Sudan*, Philadelphia: University of Pennsylvania Press, 2001.

Jones, Kenneth W., *Arya Dharm. Hindu Consciousness in 19th-Century Punjab*, New Delhi: Manohar, 1976.

Juday', ʿAbd Allah b. Yūsuf, *Kashf al-lithām ʿan ṭuruq ḥadīth ghurbat al-islām*, Al-Riyāḍ: Maktabat al-rushd, 1989.

Kaḥḥāla, ʿUmar Riḍā, *Muʿjam al-muʾallifīn*, Beirut: Muʾassasat al-risāla, 1993.

Kāndhlawī, Muḥammad Idrīs, *Kalimat Allah fī ḥayāt rūḥ Allah yaʿnī ḥayāt-i ʿĪsā*, Lahore: Idāra-yi Islāmiyyāt, 1977.

Karrar, Ali Salih, *The Sufi Brotherhoods in the Sudan*, Evanston: Northwestern University Press, 1992.

Kāshmīrī, Akhtar, *Naẓariyya-yi intiẓār-i mahdī*, Lahore: Nadīm Book House, 1984(?).

Kashmīrī, Muḥammad Anwar Shāh, *Fayḍ al-bārī ʿalā Ṣaḥīḥ al-Bukhārī maʿa ḥāshiyat al-Badr al-sārī ilā Fayḍ al-Bukhārī min ṣāḥib al-faḍīla al-ustādh Muḥammad Badr-i ʿĀlam al-Mērathī*, Deoband: Ḥiẓr Rāh Book Depot, 1980.

______, *al-Taṣrīḥ bi-mā tawātara fī nuzūl al-masīḥ*, Ḥalab: Dār al-salām, 1965.

Kattānī, Jaʿfar al-Ḥasanī al-Idrīsī, *Naẓm al-mutanāthir min al-ḥadīth al-mutawātir*, Beirut: Dār al-kutub al-ʿilmiyya, 1983.

Kawtharī, Muḥammad Zāhir, *Maqālāt al-Kawtharī*, Cairo: Dār al-Salām, 1998.

_______, *Muqaddimāt al-imām al-Kawtharī*, Damascus and Beirut: 1997.

_______, *Naẓra ʿābira fī mazāʿim man yunkiru nuzūl ʿĪsā ʿalayhi al-salām qabl al-ākhira*. In *idem*, *al-ʿAqīda wa ʿilm al-kalām*, Beirut: Dār al-kutub al-ʿilmiyya, 2009, pp. 37–87.

Keenan, Jeremy H., "The Tuareg Veil", *Middle Eastern Studies* 13 (1977), pp. 3–13.

Kennedy, Hugh, *The Prophet and the Age of the Caliphates*, London and New York: Longman, 1986.

Khalidi, Tarif, ed., *The Muslim Jesus. Sayings and Stories in Islamic Literature*, Cambridge: Harvard University Press, 2001.

_______, "The Role of Jesus in Intra-Muslim Polemics in the First Two Islamic Centuries", in Khalil Samir and Jorgen S. Nielsen, eds, *Christian Arabic Apologetics During the Abbasid Period (750–1258)*, Leiden: E. J. Brill, 1994, pp. 146–156.

Khān, Muḥammad Khālid, *Taḥrīk-i ahl-i ḥadīth. Āghāz, muḥarrikāt awr khidmāt*, New Delhi: 2011.

Khaṭṭābī, Abū Sulaymān Ḥamd b. Muḥammad, *Aʿlām al-ḥadīth fī sharḥ Ṣaḥīḥ al-Bukhārī*, ed., Muḥammad b. Saʿd b. ʿAbd al-Raḥmān Āl Saʿūd, Mecca: Jāmiʿat Umm al-Qurā, 1988.

Kinberg, Leah, "*Muḥkamāt* and *mutashābihāt* (Koran 3/7): implication of a Koranic pair of terms in medieval exegesis", *Arabica* 35 (1988), pp. 143–172.

Kister, M. J., "'And He Was Born Circumcised ...' Some Notes on Circumcision in Ḥadīth", *Oriens* 34 (1994), pp. 10–30.

_______, "'Do Not Assimilate Yourselves ...': *Lā Tushabbahū*", with an appendix by Menahem Kister, *Jerusalem Studies in Arabic and Islam* 12 (1989), pp. 321–371 (reprinted in Kister, M. J., *Concepts and Ideas at the Dawn of Islam*, Aldershot: Variorum, 1997, no. VI; also, online at Kister.huji.ac.il).

_______, "Exert Yourselves, O Banū Arfida! Some Notes on Entertainment in the Islamic Tradition", *Jerusalem Studies in Arabic and Islam* 23 (1999), pp. 53–78 (also online at Kister.huji.ac.il).

_______, "'God Will Never Disgrace Thee' (The Interpretation of an Early *ḥadīth*)", *Journal of the Royal Asiatic Society* ½ (1956), pp. 27–32 (also online at Kister.huji.ac.il).

_______, "'... *ʿillā bi-ḥaqqihi* ...': A Study of an Early *Ḥadīth*", *Jerusalem Studies in Arabic and Islam* 5 (1984), pp. 33–52 (reprinted in M. J. Kister,

Society and Religion from Jāhiliyya to Islam, Aldershot: Variorum, 1990; also online at Kister.huji.ac.il).

______, "Land Property and *jihād*: A Discussion of Some Early Traditions", *Journal of the Economic and Social History of the Orient* 14 (1991), pp. 270–311 (reprinted in Kister, M. J., *Concepts and Ideas at the Dawn of Islam*, Aldershot: Variorum, 1997, no. IV; also online at Kister.huji.ac.il).

______, "The Struggle Against Musaylima and the Conquest of Yamāma", *Jerusalem Studies in Arabic and Islam* 27 (2002), pp. 1–56 (also online at Kister.huji.ac.il).

Kohlberg, Etan and Mohammad Ali Amir-Moezzi, *Revelation and Falsification. The Kitāb al-qirāʾāt of Aḥmad b. Muḥammad al-Sayyārī*, Leiden and Boston: E. J. Brill, 2009.

Krenkow, Fritz, "The Appearance of the Prophet in Dreams", *Journal of the Royal Asiatic Society* 27 (1912), pp. 77–79.

Kūrānī, ʿAlī, *ʿAṣr al-ẓuhūr*, Beirut: Muʾassasat al-shahīd, 1314 AH.

Kurdufānī, Ismāʿīl b. ʿAbd al-Qādir, *al-Ṭirāz al-manqūsh bi-bushrā qatl Yūḥannā malik al-Ḥubūsh*, eds, Muḥammad Ibrāhīm Abū Salīm and Muḥammad Saʿīd al-Qaddāl, Jāmiʿat al-Kharṭūm: Shuʿbat abḥāth al-Sūdān maʿhad al-dirāsāt al-Ifrīqiyya wa al-Asyawiyya, al-Kharṭūm, 1972.

Lakhnawī, Murtaźā Ḥusayn, *Ākhirī tājdār-i imāmat imām mahdī*, Karachi: 2007

Lālakāʾī, Abū al-Qāsim Hibat Allah b. Manṣūr al-Ṭabarī, *Sharḥ uṣūl al-iʿtiqād li-ahl al-sunna wa al-jamāʿa min al-kitāb wa al-sunna wa ijmāʿ al-ṣaḥāba wa al-tābiʿīn min baʿdihim*, ed., Aḥmad Saʿd Ḥamdān, Mecca: 1402 AH.

Landau-Tasseron, Ella, "The 'Cyclical Reform': A Study of the *mujaddid* Tradition", *Studia Islamica* 70 (1989), pp. 79–117.

______, "Zaydī Imāms as Restorers of Religion: *Iḥyāʾ* and *tajdīd* in Zaydī Literature", *Journal of Near Eastern Studies* 49 (1990), pp. 247–263.

Landolt, Hermann, "Walāya", in Mircea Eliade, ed., *The Encyclopaedia of Religion*, New York: Macmillan Publishing Company, 1987.

Lane, Edward William, *An Account of the Manners and the Customs of the Modern Egyptians*, London: John Murray, 1860.

Laoust, Henri, "Une *fetwā* d'Ibn Taymiyya sur Ibn Tūmart", *Bulletin de l'Institut français d'archéologie orientale* 59 (1960), pp. 157–184.

______, *La profession de foi d'Ibn Baṭṭa*, Damas: Institut français de Damas, 1958.

Laroui, Abdallah, "Sur le Mahdisme d'Ibn Tūmart", in Abdelmajid Kaddourie, ed., *Mahdisme: Crise et Changement dans l'histoire du Maroc*, 9–13, Casablanca: Najah El Jadida, 1994.

Layish, Aharon, "The Legal Methodology of the *mahdī* in the Sudan, 1881–1885: Issues in Marriage and Divorce", *Sudanic Africa* 8 (1997): 37–66.

_______, *Sharī'a and the Islamic State in 19th-Century Sudan. The Mahdī's Legal Methodology and Doctrine*, Leiden: E. J. Brill, 2016.

_______, "The Sudanese *mahdī*'s Legal Methodology and its Ṣūfī Inspiration", *Jerusalem Studies in Arabic and Islam* 33 (2007), pp. 279–308.

Lav, Daniel, *Radical Muslim Theonomy: A Study in the Evolution of Salafī Thought*, unpublished PhD thesis, The Hebrew University of Jerusalem, 2016.

Lazarus-Yafeh, Hava, "Is There a Concept of Redemption in Islam?" in Bleeker C. Jouco and R. J. Z. Werblowsky, eds, *Types of Redemption. Contributions to the Theme of the Study-Conference Held at Jerusalem 1968*, Numen Book Series, vol. 18, pp. 168–180.

Lēkh Rām, *Risāla-yi jihād*, Jallandhar: 1898.

Le Tourneau, Roger, "Sur la disparition de la doctrine almohade", *Studia Islamica* 32 (1970), pp. 193–201.

Lévi-Provençal, M. E., "Ibn Tūmart et 'Abd Al-Mu'min. 'Le Faqīh du Sus' et le 'flambeau des Almohades'", in *Mémorial Henri Basset. Nouvelles études Nord-africaines et Orientales*, Paris: Librairie Orientaliste Paul Geuthner, 1928, pp. 21–37.

Livne-Kafri, O., "Some Notes on the Muslim Apocalyptic Tradition", *Quaderni di Studi Arabi* 17 (1999), pp. 71–94.

Lyle, S., *The Mahdi and other poems*. London: George Allen & Sons, 1910.

MacLean, Derryl N., "Real Men and False Men at the Court of Akbar. *The Majālis of Shaykh Muṣṭafā Gujarātī*", in David Gilmartin and Bruce B. Lawrence, eds, *Beyond Turk and Hindu: Rethinking Religious Identities in Islamicate South Asia*, Gainsville: University Press of Florida, 2000, pp. 199–215.

Madelung, Wilferd, "'Abd Allāh b. al-Zubayr and the Mahdī", *Journal of Near Eastern Studies* 40 (1981), pp. 291–305.

_______, "Apocalyptic Prophecies in Ḥimṣ", *Journal of Semitic Studies* 31 (1986), pp. 141–185.

_______, "'Iṣma", in *EI*², s.v.

______, "Mahdī", in *EI²*, s.v.

______, "The Sufyānī Between Tradition and History", *Studia Islamica* 63 (1986), pp. 5–48.

Maghnīsāwī, Abū al-Muntahā Aḥmad b. Muḥammad, *Kitāb sharḥ al-fiqh al-akbar*, Ḥaydarābād: Dā'irat al-ma'ārif al-niẓāmiyya, 1321 AH.

Mahamid, Hatim and Chaim Nissim, "Ṣūfīs and Coffee Consumption: Religio-Legal and Historical Aspects of a Controversy in the Late Mamlūk and Early Ottoman Periods", *Journal of Sūfī Studies* 7 (2018), pp. 140–164.

Mahdī, al-Ṣādiq, *Yas'alūnaka 'an al-mahdiyya*, Cairo: al-Ahrām al-tijāriyya, 1975.

Maḥmūd, Ḥasan Aḥmad, *Qiyām dawlat al-murābiṭīn*, Cairo: Maktabat al-nahḍa al-Miṣriyya, 1957.

Makkī, Abū Ṭālib, *Qūt al-qulūb fī mu'āmalat al-maḥbūb*, Cairo: Muṣṭafā al-Bābī al-Ḥalabī, 1961.

Mālik b. Anas, *al-Mudawwana al-kubrā*, Cairo: Maṭba'at al-sa'āda, 1323 AH.

______, *al-Muwaṭṭa'*, ed., Muḥammad Fu'ād 'Abd al-Bāqī, Cairo: Dār Iḥyā' al-kutub al-'arabiyya, 1951.

Maqqarī, Aḥmad b. Muḥammad, *Nafḥ al-ṭīb min ghuṣn al-Andalus al-raṭīb*, Beirut: Dār al-kutub al-'ilmiyya, 1995.

Margoliouth, D. S., *On Mahdis and Mahdiism*, Oxford: Oxford University Press, n.d. (*c.* 1916).

Markaz al-risāla, *al-Mahdī al-muntaẓar fī al-fikr al-islāmī*, Qum: Mihr, 1417 AH.

Markaz al-risāla (no author mentioned), *al-Imām al-mahdī al-muntaẓar. Silsilat al-ma'ārif al-islāmiyya*, Qum: Mihr, 1996.

Marrākushī, 'Abd al-Wāḥid, *al-Mu'jib fī talkhīṣ akhbār al-Maghrib. Muḥammad Zaynuhum Muḥammad 'Azb*, Cairo: Dār al-Farjānī li-'l-nashr wa al-tawzī', 1994.

Massé, Henri M., "La profession de la foi (*'aqīda*) et les guides spirituels (*morchida*) du *mahdī* Ibn Toumart", in *Mémorial Henri Basset. Nouvelles Études Nord-Africaines et Orientales, 21–37. Publications de l'Institute des Hautes-Études Marocains*, vol. 17, Paris: Libraire Orientaliste Paul Geuthner, 1928, pp. 105–121.

Matar, Nabil, "The English Merchant and the Moroccan Sufi: Messianism and Mahdism in the Early Seventeenth Century", in *Journal of Ecclesiastical History* 65 (2014), pp. 47–65.

Mawdūdī, Abū al-A'lā, *Islāmī riyāsat mēñ dhimmiyyōñ kē ḥuqūq*, Lahore: Islamic Publications Limited, 1970 (first publication in 1954); Arabic translation: *Ḥuqūq ahl al-dhimma fī al-dawla al-islāmiyya*, n.p.: Dār al-fikr, n.d.

______, *A Short History of the Revivalist Movement in Islam*, translated by Al-Ash'arī, Lahore: Islamic Publications Limited, 1963.

______, *Sīrat-i Sarwar-i 'ālam*, eds, Na'īm Ṣiddīqī and 'Abd al-Wakīl 'Alawī, New Delhi: Markazī Maktaba-yi Islāmī Publishers, 2013.

______, *Tafhīm al-Qur'ān*, Delhi: Islāmī Publishers, 2011.

______, *Tajdīd o iḥyā'-i dīn*, Lahore: Islamic Publications Limited, 1977.

May, Karl, *Karl May's Gesammelte Werke: Menschenjäger, Der Mahdi, Im Sudan*, Bamberg: Karl-May Verlag, 1952.

McCants, William, *The ISIS Apocalypse. The History, Strategy, and Doomsday Vision of the Islamic State*, New York: St. Martin's Press, 2015.

McGetchin, Douglas T., *Indology, Indomania and Orientalism: Ancient India's Rebirth in Modern Germany*, Madison, N. J.: Farleigh Dickinson University Press, 2009.

Metcalf, Barbara, *Islamic Revival in British India: Deoband, 1860–1900*, Princeton: Princeton University Press, 1982.

Mīkha'il, Sa'd, *Shu'arā' al-Sūdān*, al-Kharṭūm: Maktabat al-Sharīf al-Akadīmiyya, 2009.

Mīlānī, 'Alī al-Ḥusaynī, *al-Imām al-mahdī*, Qum: Markaz al-abḥāth al-'aqā'idiyya, 1420 AH.

Miller, Kathryn A., "Muslim Minorities and the Obligation to Emigrate to Islamic Territory: Two Fatwās from Fifteenth-Century Granada", *Islamic Law and Society* 7 (2000), pp. 256–288.

Molénat, J. P., "Sur le rôle des Almohades dans la fin du Christianisme local au Maghreb et en al-Andalus", *Al-Qanṭara* 18 (1997), pp. 389–413.

Möller, H., "Wie die SS sich einmal mit den Koran beschäftigte und dabei auf Iran sties", *Orient* 45 (2004), 329–332.

Motadel, David, *Islam and Nazi Germany's War*, Cambridge: Harvard University Press, 2014.

Mowafi, Reda, *Slavery, Slave Trade and Abolition Attempts in Egypt and the Sudan*, Stockholm: Esselte Studium, 1981.

Mubārak, Badr al-Dīn, *Ẓuhūr al-Ḥaqq*, Siyālkōt: 1894.

Muḥammad, 'Abd al-Mu'ṭī 'Abd al-Maqṣūd, *al-Mahdī al-muntaẓar fī al-mīzān*, Cairo(?): 1980.

Muḥammad Aḥmad, *al-Āthār al-kāmila li-'l-imām al-mahdī*, ed., Muḥammad Ibrāhīm Abū Salīm, Al-Kharṭūm: Dār Jāmiʿat al-Kharṭūm li-'l-nashr, 1990–1993.

Muḥammad ʿAta'ur-Rahim and Ahmad Thomson, *Jesus the Prophet of Islam*, London: Ta-Ha Publishers, 1996.

Muḥammad Kāẓim, *Mawsūʿat al-mahdī*, Beirut: Manshūrāt al-fajr, 2005.

Muhr al-Dīn, Muḥammad, *Ḥayāt-i ʿĪsā*, Lahore: Dār al-tablīgh-i ahl-i sunnat, n.d. (*c.* 1970).

Mujeeb, Muḥammad, *The Indian Muslims*, London: George Allen & Unwin, 1967.

Mulayk, Ṣalāḥ al-Dīn, *Shuʿarāʾ al-waṭaniyya fī al-Sūdān min ʿahd al-Fūnj ilā ʿām 1970*, al-Kharṭūm: Dār al-taʾlīf wa al-tarjama wa al-nashr, 1975.

Munāwī, ʿAbd al-Raʾūf, *Fayḍ al-qadīr sharḥ al-jāmiʿ al-ṣaghīr min aḥādīth al-bashīr al-nadhīr*, Beirut: Dār al-kutub al-ʿilmiyya, 2001.

Muqaddam, Muḥammad Aḥmad Ismāʿīl, *al-Mahdī wa fiqh ashrāṭ al-sāʿa*, Alexandria: al-Dār al-ʿālamiyya, 2002.

Muqātil b. Sulaymān, *Tafsīr*, Cairo: Al-Hayʾa al-miṣriyya al-ʿāmma li-'l-kitāb, 1979.

Murād, Sulaymān ʿAlī, *Sīrat al-sayyid al-masīḥ li-Ibn ʿAsākir*, ʿAmmān: Dār al-shurūq li-'l-nashr wa al-tawzīʿ, 1996.

Muslim b. al-Ḥajjāj, *Ṣaḥīḥ*, ed., Muḥammad Fuʾād ʿAbd al-Bāqī, Cairo: 1955.

Muttaqī, ʿAlī b. Ḥusām al-shahīr bi-'l-Muttaqī al-Hindī, *al-Burhān fī ʿalāmāt mahdī ākhir al-zamān*, ed., Jāsim b. Muḥammad b. Muhalhil al-Yāsīn, Kuwayt(?): Dhāt al-Salāsil, 1988.

Najjār, ʿAbd al-Majīd, *Al-Mahdī Ibn Tūmart. Ḥayātuhu wa ārāʾuhu wa thawratuhu al-fikriyya wa al-ijtimāʿiyya wa atharuhu bi-'l-maghrib*, Beirut: Dār al-gharb al-islāmī, 1983.

______, *Tajribat al-iṣlāḥ fī ḥarakat al-mahdī Ibn Tūmart*, Al-ḥaraka al-muwaḥḥidiyya bi-'l-Mahgrib awāʾil al-qarn al-sādis al-hijrī, Hendon: The International Institute of Islamic Thought, 1994.

Nāṣirī, Muḥammad Amīr, *al-Imām al-mahdī fī al-aḥādīth al-mushtaraka bayna al-sunna wa al-shīʿa*, Tehran: al-Majmaʿ al-ʿālamī li-'taqrīb bayna al-madhāhib al-islāmiyya, 2007.

Nasr, Seyyed Wali Reza, *The Vanguard of the Islamic Revolution: The Jamāʿat-i Islāmī of Pakistan*, Berkeley and Los Angeles: University of California Press, 1994.

Natsha, Jawād Baḥr, *al-Mahdī masbūq bi-dawla islāmiyya*, Hebron: Markaz Dirāsāt al-Mustaqbal, 2009.

Nawawī, Muḥyi al-Dīn Abū Zakariyā b. Sharaf, *Sharḥ Ṣaḥīḥ Muslim*, ed., Khalīl al-Mays, Beirut: Dār al-Qalam, n.d.

Naysābūrī, Abū ʿAbd Allah Muḥammad b. ʿAbd Allah al-Ḥākim, *al-Mustadrak ʿalā al-Ṣaḥīḥayn*, Beirut: Dār al-Maʿrifa, 1998.

Naysābūrī, Abū Isḥāq Ibrāhī b. Manṣūr b. Khalaf, *Qiṣas al-anbiyāʾ (dāstānhā-yi payghāmbarān)*, Tehran: 1961.

Nāẓir Shāh, Abū Nūr, *al-Qawl al-maqbūl fī ithbāt ḥayāt al-masīḥ wa al-nuzūl al-maʿrūf bi-radd-i Qādiyānī*, Lahore: 1914.

Norris, H. T., *The Berbers in Arabic Literature*, Harlow: Longman and Librairie du Liban, 1982.

______, "New Evidence on the Life of ʿAbd Allah b. Yāsīn and the Origins of the Almoravid Movement", *The Journal of African History* 2 (1971), pp. 255–268.

Notovitch, Nicolas, *The Unknown Life of Jesus Christ*, Joshua Tree (California): Tree of Life Publications, 1980 (first published in 1894).

Nuʿaym b. Ḥammād, Abū ʿAbd Allah, *Kitāb al-fitan*, ed., Suhayl Zakkār, Mecca: Muṣṭafā Aḥmad al-Bāz, n.d.

Nuʿmānī, Muḥammad Manẓūr, *Qādiyānī kyūñ musalmān nahīñ? awr masʾala-yi nuzūl-i masīḥ o ḥayāt-i masīḥ*, Lahore: ʿImrān Academy, n.d.

Nūrsī, Badīʿ al-Zamān, *Mirqāt al-sunna wa tiryāq maraḍ al-bidʿa*, translated by Iḥsān Qāsim al-Ṣāliḥī, Baghdad: 1988.

Nuṣrat, Sayyid Mahdawī, *Kuḥl al-jawāhir*, British Library Or. 6653, 337 folios (incomplete).

______, *Urdū adab mēñ mahdawiyyōñ kā ḥiṣṣa, 1496 tā 1800*, Ḥaydarābād (Deccan): Iʿjāz Printing Press, 1984.

Nuwayrī, Shihāb al-Dīn Aḥmad b. ʿAbd al-Wahhāb, *Nihāyat al-arab fī funūn al-adab*, Cairo: Maktabat al-kutub al-miṣriyya, 1923–1985.

O'Fahey, S., "Islamic Hegemonies in the Sudan. Sufism, Mahdism and Islamism", in L. Brenner, ed., *Muslim identity and social change in sub-Saharan Africa*, London: Hurst & Company, 1993, pp. 21–35.

______, "Sufism in Suspense: The Sudanese *mahdī and the Ṣūfīs*", in Bernd Radtke and Frederick De Jong, eds, *Islamic mysticism contested. Thirteen centuries of controversy and polemics*, Islamic history and civilization, Studies and texts 29, Leiden: E. J. Brill, 1999, pp. 266–82.

Ohtsuka, Kazuo, "Salafī Orientation in Sudanese Mahdism", *The Muslim World* 87 (1999), pp. 17–33.

Pahlūwārwī, Tamannā ʿImādī Mujībī, *Intiẓār-i mahdī o masīḥ fann-i rijāl kī rawshnī mēñ*, Karachi: Qurʾānic Center, 1992.

Patrick, Thomas, *A Dictionary of Islam*, London: W. H. Allen, 1895.

Patterson, H. Sheridan, *The Imām Mahdi; or the Moslem Millennium from the Koran and Authentic Traditions*, London: Hamilton, Adans & Co., 1884.

Pfander, Carl Gottlieb, *Kitāb Mīzān al-Ḥaqq*, Akbarābād: 1849 (in Persian).

______, *Kitāb Mīzān al-Ḥaqq*, Akbarābād: 1850.

______, *Mizan-ul-Huq* (sc. Mīzān al-Ḥaqq). *A Treatise on the Controversy Between Christians and Muhammadans*, Agra: 1849; Arabic version: *Kitāb mīzān al-ḥaqq*, Leipzig: Brockhaus, 1874.

______, *Remarks on the Nature of Muhammadanism*, Calcutta: Baptist Mission Press, 1840.

Poston, Larry, "The Second Coming of ʿĪsā: An Exploration of Islamic Premillennialism", *The Muslim World* 100 (2010), pp. 100–116.

Powell, Eve Troutt, "Brothers Along The Nile: Egyptian Concepts of Race and Ethnicity, 1895–1910", in Erlich, Haggai and Israel Gershoni, eds, *The Nile: Histories, Cultures, Myths*, Boulder: Lynne Reiner Publishers, 2000, pp. 171–181.

Qaddāl, Muḥammad Saʿīd, *al-Imām al-mahdī Muḥammad Aḥmad b. ʿAbd Allāh (1844–1885)*, Beirut: Dār al-Jīl, 1992.

______, *al-Mahdiyya wa al-Ḥabasha: dirāsa fī al-siyāsa al-dākhiliyya wa al-khārijiyya li-dawlat al-mahdiyya (1881–1898)*, Beirut: Dār al-Jīl, 1992.

______. *al-Siyāsa al-iqtiṣādiyya li-ʾl-dawla al-mahdiyya*, Kharṭūm: Dār Jāmiʿat al-Kharṭūm li-ʾl-nashr, 1986.

al-Qāḍī ʿIyāḍ, *Tartīb al-madārik wa taqrīr al-masālik li-maʿrifat aʿlām madhhab Mālik*, Beirut: Dār Maktabat al-Ḥayāt, 1968(?).

Qamaruddin, Dr, *The Mahdawī Movement in India*, New Delhi: Idara-i Adabiyat-i Delli (sc. Delhi), 1985.

Qandūzī, Sulaymān b. Ibrāhīm, *Yanābiʿ al-mawadda*, Najaf: al-Maktaba al-Ḥaydariyya, 1965.

Qasmi, Matloob Ahmed, *The Emergence of Dajjāl, the Jewish King*, New Delhi: Adam Publishers, 2005.

Qasṭallānī, Shihāb al-Dīn Abū al-ʿAbbās Aḥmad b. Muḥammad, *Irshād al-sārī sharḥ Ṣaḥīḥ al-Bukhārī*, Beirut: Dār al-kutub al-ʿilmiyya, 1996.

Qayyūm, ʿAbd al-Bārī, *Taʿāruf-i kutub-i bāni-yi sislila-yi Aḥmadiyya*, Rabwa: 1977.

Qureshi, Ishtiaq Husain, *The Muslim Community of the Indo-Pakistan Subcontinent (610–1947). A Brief Historical Analysis*, The Hague: Mouton & Co., 1962.

Qurṭubī, Abū ʿAbd Allah Muḥammad b. Aḥmad, *Kitāb al-tadhkira fī aḥwāl al-mawtā wa umūr al-ākhira*, ed., Ṣādiq b. Muḥammad b. Ibrāhīm, al-Riyāḍ: Maktabat al-Minhāj, 1425 AH.

Raḥmān, ʿAlī, *Tadhkira-yi ʿulamā-yi Hind*, Lucknow: Nawal Kishōr, 1894.

Raven, Wim, "Ibn Ṣayyād as an Islamic 'Antichrist'. A Reappraisal of the Texts", in Wolfram Brandes and Felicitas Schmieder, eds, *Endzeiten. Eschatologie in den monotheistischen Weltreligionen*, Berlin and New York: Walter de Gruyter, 2008, pp. 261–291.

Rāzī, Fakhr al-Dīn, *ʿIsmat al-anbiyāʾ*, Qumm: Maṭbaʿat al-shahīd, 1406 AH.

Reynolds, Gabriel Said, "The Muslim Jesus: Alive or Dead?" *Bulletin of the School of Oriental and African Studies* 72 (2009), pp. 237–258.

Riẓwī, Muḥammad Ḥusayn, *Al-mahdī al-mawʿūd fī al-Qurʾān al-karīm*, Beirut: Dār al-hādī li-'l-ṭibāʿa wa al-nashr wa al-tawzīʿ, 2001.

Rodd, Francis Rennel, *People of the Veil*, London: Macmillan, 1926.

Sachedina, Abdulaziz Abdulhussein, *Islamic Messianism. The Idea of the Mahdī in Twelver Shiism*, Albany State University of New York Press, 1981.

Sadan, Joseph, "'Community' and 'Extra-Community' as a Legal and Literary Problem", *Israel Oriental Studies* 10 (1980), pp. 102–115.

Saeedullah, *The Life and Works of Muḥammad Ṣiddīq Hasan Khan, Nawab of Bhopal (1248–1307/1832–1890)*, Lahore: Sh. Muhammd Ashraf, 1973

Saffārīni, Muḥammad b. Aḥmad al-Atharī al-Ḥanbalī, *Ahwāl yawm al-qiyāma wa ʿalāmātuhā al-kubrā*, Cairo(?): Dār al-Fatḥ li-'l-iʿlām al-arabī, 2002.

______, *al-Buḥūr al-zākhira fī ʿulūm al-ākhira*, ed. Muḥammad Ibrāhīm Shalabī Shūmān, Kuwayt: 2007.

______, *Lawāʾiḥ al-anwār al-bahiyya wa sawāṭiʿ al-asrār al-athariyya li-sharḥ al-durra al-muḍiyya fī ʿaqd(?) al-firqa al-marḍiyya*, Cairo: Maṭbaʿat Majallat al-Manār, 1323 AH.

Al-Sammānī, ʿAbd al-Maḥmūd, *Azāhīr al-riyāḍ*, Cairo: Maktabat al-Qāhira, 1997.

Searcy, Kim, *The Formation of the Sudanese Mahdist state: Ceremony, Symbols and Authority, 1882–1898*, Leiden and Boston: E. J. Brill, 2011.

Serrano Ruano, Delfina, "Why Did the Scholars of al-Andalus Distrust al-Ghazālī? Ibn Rushd al-Jadd's *fatwā* on *awliyāʾ Allāh*", *Der Islam* 83 (2006), pp. 137–156.

Shaddel, Mehdy, "ʿAbd Allāh ibn al-Zubayr and the Mahdī: Between Propaganda and Historical Memory in the Second Civil War", *Bulletin of the School of Oriental and African Studies* 80 (2017), pp. 1–19.

Shafīʿ, Mufti Mohammad, *Signs of Qiyāmah and the Arrival of the Maseeḥ*, Karachi: Dār al-Ishāʿat, 1973(?).

Shāh Dilāwar, Bandagī Miyāñ, *Khaṣāʾiṣ al-imām mahdī mawʿūd khalīfat Allāh*, Ḥaydarābād: 1368 AH.

Shāh Ismāʿīl Shahīd, *Khuṭab majmūʿah*, Lucknow: 1926.

______, *Kitāb arbaʿīn fī aḥwāl al-mahdiyyīn*, Calcutta: 1268 AH.

______, *Manṣab-i imāmat*, Delhi: Maṭbaʿ-i Fārūqī, n.d.

______, *Manṣab-i imāmat*, Urdu translation by Muḥammad Ḥusayn ʿAlawī, Lahore: Āʾina-yi Adab, n.d. (*c.* 1980).

Shāh Qāsim, Bandagī Miyāñ, *al-Ḥujja*, n.p.: Aʿẓam Steam Press, 1364 AH.

Shaikh, Muḥammad Hajjan, *Maulana Ubaid Allah Sindhi: A Revolutionary Scholar*, Islamabad: National Institute of Historical and Cultural Research, 1986.

Shaked, H., *The Life of the Sudanese Mahdī. A Historical Study of Kitāb Saʿādat Al-mustahdī Bi-sīrat Al-imām Al-Mahdī (The Book of the Bliss of Him Who Seeks Guidance by the Life of the Imam the Mahdi)*, by Ismāʿīl b. ʿAbd Al-Qādir, New Brunswick: Transaction Books, 1978.

Shalabī, ʿAbd al-Wadūd Ibrāhīm, *al-Uṣūl al-fikriyya li-ḥarakat al-mahdiyya*, Cairo: Dār al-maʿārif, n.d.

Shaltūt, Maḥmūd, "Āyatāni", in *al-Risāla* 11 (1943), pp. 424–426.

______, *al-Fatāwā*, Cairo: Dār al-Qalam, n.d. (ca. 1964).

______, "al-Ijmāʿ wa thubūt al-ʿaqīda", *al-Risāla* 11 (1943), pp. 464–466.

______, "Nuzūl ʿĪsā", *al-Risāla* 11 (1943), pp. 363–366.

______, "Rafʿ ʿĪsā", *al-Risāla* 10 (1943), pp. 515–517.

______, "al-Sunna wa thubūt al-ʿaqīda", *al-Risāla* 11 (1943), pp. 443–446.

Sharkey, Heather J., "Aḥmad Zaynī Daḥlān's Al-Futūḥāt Al-islāmiyya: A Contemporary View of the Sudanese Mahdī", *Sudanic Africa* 5 (1994), pp. 67–75.

Sharon, Moshe, *Black Banners from the East, II. Revolt: The Social and Military Aspects of the ʿAbbāsid Revolution*, Jerusalem: The Hebrew University, 1990.

Shāṭibī, Abū Isḥāq Ibrāhīm b. Mūsā b. Muḥammad al-Lakhmī al-Gharnāṭī, *Fatāwā*, ed., Muḥammad Abū al-Ajfān, Tunis: 1985.

______, *Kitāb al-iʿtiṣām*, Beirut: Dār al-Fikr, 1996.

Shawkānī, Muḥammad b. ʿAlī, *al-Fawāʾid al-majmūʿa fī al-aḥādīth al-mawḍūʿa*, Beirut: al-Maktab al-Islāmī, 1986.

Shīrāzī, Ṣādiq al-Ḥusaynī, *Al-Mahdī fī al-Qurʾān*, Beirut: Dār Ṣādiq, 1978.

Shoufani, Elias, *Al-Riddah and the Muslim Conquest of Arabia*, Toronto: The Arab Institute for Research, 1973.

Shuqayr, Naʿūm, *Taʾrīkh al-Sūdān al-qadīm wa al-ḥadīth wa jughrāfiyyatuhu*, Cairo: 1903.

Shurreef, Jaffur (Sharīf, Jaʿfar), *Qanoon-e Islam, or the Customs of the Moosulmans of India*, composed under the direction of and translated by G. A. Herklots, London: Parbury, Allen and Co., 1832.

Ṣiddīq Ḥasan Khān, Muḥammad, *Ḥadīth al-ghāshiya ʿan al-fitan al-khāliya wa al-fāshiya*, Benares: 1309 AH.

______, *Ḥujaj al-karāma fī āthār al-qiyāma*, Bhopal: Shāhjahānī, 1875.

______, *al-ʿIbra mimmā jāʾa fī al-ghazw wa al-shahāda wa al-hijra*, Beirut: Dār al-kutub al-ʿilmiyya, 1988.

______, *al-Idhāʿa li-mā kāna wa mā yakūnu bayna yaday al-sāʿa*, Bhopal: Maṭbaʿ-i Ṣiddīqī, 1294 AH.

______, *Iqtirāb al-sāʿa*, Varanasi (Benares): Saʿīd al-Maṭābiʿ, 1322 AH.

Sienkiewicz, Henryk, *In Desert and Wilderness*, translated by Max A. Drezmal, Edinburgh: Polish Book Depot, 1945.

Sikand, Yoginder, *Pseudo-Messianic Movements in Contemporary Muslim South Asia*, New Delhi: Global Media Publications, 2008.

Sikandar b. Muḥammad, *Mirʾāt-i Sikandarī*, n.p., 1831.

________, *Mirʾāt-i Sikandarī*, Bombay: Fatḥ Al-Karīm, 1308 AH (1891?).

________, *Mirʾāt-i Sikandarī*, translated by Fazlullah Lutfullah Faridi, Bombay: 1891.

Sikandarābādī, Sayyid Walī, *Sawāniḥ-i Mahdī-yi mawʿūd*, Agra: Maṭbaʿ-i Mufīd-i ʿĀmm, 1321 AH/1903 CE.

Sindhī, ʿUbayd Allah, *ʿAqīda-yi intiẓār-i masīḥ o mahdı*, Karachi: Al-Raḥmān Publishing Trust, 1998.

_______, *Shāh Walī Allah awr unkī siyāsī taḥrīk*, Lahore: al-Maḥmūd Academy, 1944(?).

______, *al-Tamhīd li-taʿrīf aʾimmat al-tajdīd*, Jām Shōrō: Lajnat Iḥyāʾ al-Adab al-Sindī, 1976.

Siyālkōtī, Ibrāhīm, *al-Khabar al-ṣaḥīḥ ʿan qabr al-masīḥ*, Siyālkōt: 1910.

Slatin, Rudolf C., *Fire and Sword in the Sudan*, London and New York: Edward Arnold, 1898.

Smith, Wilfred Cantwell, *Modern Islam in India. A Social Analysis*, Lahore: Shaykh Muḥammad Ashraf, 1963.

Storey, C. A., *Persian literature: a bio-bibliographical survey*, London: Luzac and Co., 1953.

Subkī, Tāj al-Dīn, *Ṭabaqāt al-Shāfiʿiyya al-kubrā*, Cairo: ʿĪsā al-Bābī al-Ḥalabī, 1968.

Sudhoff, Dieter and Voller Hartmut, eds, *Karl Mays "Im Lande Des Mahdi". Literatur- und Medienwissenschaft, 92*, Oldenburg: IGEL Verlag, 2003.

Suhaylī, ʿAbd al-Raḥmān, *al-Rawḍ al-unuf fī sharḥ al-sīra al-nabawiyya li-Ibn Hishām*, ed. ʿAbd al-Raḥmān al-Wakīl, Cairo: Dār al-Naṣr li-'l-Ṭibāʿa, 1967.

Sulamī, Abū ʿAbd al-Rạmān, *Jawāmiʿ ādāb al-ṣūfiyya wa ʿuyūb al-nafs wa mudāwātuhā*, ed., E. Kohlberg, Jerusalem: The Hebrew University, 1976.

Sulamī, Yūsuf b. Yaḥyā b. ʿAlī b. ʿAbd al-ʿAzīz al-Maqdisī al-Shāfiʿī, *ʿIqd al-durar fī akhbār al-mahdī al-muntaẓar*, ed., ʿAbd al-Fattāḥ Muḥammad al-Ḥilw, Cairo: Maktabat ʿĀlam al-Fikr, 1979.

Suyūṭī, Jalāl al-Dīn, *al-Aḥādīth al-ḥisān fī faḍl al-ṭaylasān*, ed., A. Arazi, Jerusalem: Magnes Press, 1983.

______, *al-ʿArf al-wardī fī akhbār al-mahdī*, in *al-Ḥāwī li-'l-fatāwī*, vol. 2, pp. 213–47. Cairo 1351 AH.

______, *al-Jāmiʿ al-ṣaghīr*, Beirut: Dār al-kutub al-ʿilmiyya, 2002.

______, *al-Kashf ʿan mujāwazat hādhihi al-umma al-alf*, in *al-Ḥāwī li-'l-fatāwī*, vol. 2, pp. 248–256.

______, *Kitāb al-iʿlām bi-ḥukm ʿĪsā ʿalayhi al-salām*, in al-Ḥāwī li-'l-fatāwī, vol. 2, pp. 338–355.

______, *Taʾrīkh al-khulafāʾ*, Beirut: Dār al-maʿrifa, 2004.

Sviri, Sara, *Perspectives on Early Islamic Mysticism. The World of al-Ḥakīm al-Tirmidhī and His Contemporaries*, London and New York: Routledge, 2020.

Szilágyi, Krisztina, "A Prophet like Jesus? Christians and Muslims Debating Muḥammad's Death", *Jerusalem Studies in Arabic and Islam* 36 (2009), pp. 131–171.

Ṭabarānī, Abū al-Qāsim Sulaymān b. Ayyūb al-Lakhmī, *Musnad al-Shāmiyyīn*, Beirut: Muʾassasat al-Risāla, 1989.

Ṭabarī, Muḥammad b. Jarīr, *Jāmiʿ al-bayān ʿan taʾwīl āy al-Qurʾān*, Cairo: 1954.

Ṭabrisī, Abū ʿAlī al-Faḍl b. al-Ḥusayn, *Majmaʿ al-bayān fī tafsīr al-Qurʾān*, Beirut: Dār al-Fikr, 1957.

Taftāzānī, Saʿd al-Dīn Masʿūd b. ʿUmar, *Sharḥ al-ʿaqāʾid al-nasafiyya fī uṣūl al-dīn wa ʿilm al-kalām*, ed., Claude Salāma, Damascus: Wizārat al-thaqāfa wa al-irshād al-qawmī, 1974.

Ṭaḥāwī, Abu Ja'far Aḥmad b. Muḥammad b. Salāma, *'Aqīdat al-Ṭaḥāwī*, Kazan: Maktabat al-Shirka, 1902.

Ṭā'ī, Ṣāliḥ, *'Awālim al-ḥukūma al-mahdawiyya: ghazw al-faḍā' wa fatḥ al-majarrāt fī 'aṣr al-ẓuhūr*, Beirut: Sharikat al-'ārif li-'a'māl, 2012.

Tareen, Sherali, *Defending Muḥammad in Modernity*, Notre Dame: Notre Dame University Press, 2020.

Ṭarīqī, 'Abd Allah b. Ibrāhīm b. 'Alī, *al-Isti'āna bi-ghayr al-muslimīn fī al-fiqh al-islāmī*, (Riyāḍ?): n.p., 1414 AH.

Tha'labī, Abū Isḥāq Aḥmad b. Muḥammad b. Ibrāhīm, *Qiṣaṣ al-anbiyā' al-musammā bi-'l-'Arā'is*, Cairo: Muṣṭafā al-Bābī al-Ḥalabī, 1340 AH.

Theobald, A. B., *The Mahdīya: A History of the Anglo-Egyptian Sudan, 1881–1889*, London: Longmans, Green and Co., 1951.

Tirmidhī, Abū 'Īsā Muḥammad b. Sawra, *Ṣaḥīḥ al-Tirmidhī bi-sharḥ Abī Bakr b. al-'Arabī al-Mālikī*, Cairo: Maṭba'at al-Sādī, 1934.

Tissot, Victor and G. Maldague, *La prisonnière du mahdī*, Paris: Librairie Blériot, *c.* 1897.

Ṭurṭūshī, Abu Bakr b. Al-Walīd, *Kitāb al-ḥawādith wa al-bida'*, ed., Muḥammad al-Ṭālibī, Tūnus: al-Maṭba'a al-rasmiyya li-'l-jumhūriyya al-Tūnusiyya, 1959.

______, *Kitāb al-ḥawādithh wa al-bida'*, Traducción y estudio – Maribel Fierro, Madrid: Consejo Superior de Investigaciones Científicas, 1993.

Ṭūsī, Abū Ja'far Muḥammad b. al-Ḥasan, *Kitāb al-ghayba*, Qum: Mu'assasat al-ma'ārif al-islāmiyya, 1411 AH.

Tyan, Emile, *Histoire de l'organisation judiciaire en pays d'Islam*, Leiden: E. J. Brill, 1960.

Urvoy, Dominique, "La pensée d'Ibn Tūmart", *Bulletin d'Études Orientales* 27 (1974), pp. 19–44.

'Uthaymīn, Muḥammad b. Ṣāliḥ, *Sharḥ al-'aqīda al-Saffārīniyya*, Cairo: Dār al-'aqīda, 2006.

'Uthmānī, Muḥammad Taqī, *Akābir-i Deoband kyā thē?* Deoband: Zamzam Book Depot, 1995.

Viguera Molins, Maria Jésus, "'Abd al-Wāḥid al-Marrākushī", in *EI*[3], s.v.

Voll, J. O., "The Mahdī's Concept and Use of *Hijra*", *Islamic Studies* 26 (1987), pp. 31–42.

______, "Wahhabism and Mahdism: Alternative Styles of Islamic Leadership", *Arab Studies Quarterly* 4 (1982), pp. 110–126.

Walī Allah, Shāh, *Izālat al-khafā' 'an khilāfat al-khulafā'*, Damascus: Dār al-qalam, 2013.

_______, *al-Tafhīmāt al-ilāhiyya*, Bijnore: Barqi Press, 1936.

Walī b. Yūsuf, *Inṣāf Nāma: al-ma ʿrūf bi-matn-i sharīf*, Jamʿiyya Mahdawiyya dāʾira-yi Zamistānpūr, Mushīrābād, Ḥaydarābād (Deccan): 1368 AH.

Wansharīsī, Aḥmad b. Yaḥyā, *al-Miʿyār al-muʿrib wa al-jāmiʿ al-mughrib ʿan fatāwā ʿulamāʾ Ifrīqiya wa al-Andalus wa al-Maghrib*, Beirut: Dār al-gharb al-islāmī, 1981.

Wasserstein, David J., "A Jonah Theme in the Biography of Ibn Tūmart", in Farhad Daftary and Josef W. Meri, eds, *Culture and Memory in Medieval Islam. Essays in Honour of Wilferd Madelung*, London and New York: I. B. Tauris, 2003, pp. 232–249.

Watt, M. Montgomery, *The Formative Period of Islamic Thought*, Oxford: Oneworld, 1973.

_______, *Islamic Creeds. A Selection*, Edinburgh: Edinburgh University Press, 1994.

Wensinck, A. J., *The Muslim Creed. Its Genesis and Historical Development*, Cambridge: Cambridge University Press, 1932.

Yarbrough, Luke, "'I'll Not Accept Aid from a *mushrik*'. Rural Space, Persuasive Authority, and Religious Difference in Three Prophetic *ḥadīths*", in Alain Delattre, Marie Legendre and Petra M. Sijpsteijn, eds, *Authority and Control in the Countryside. From Antiquity to Islam in the Mediterranean and Near East (Sixth–Tenth Century)*, Leiden: E. J. Brill, 2019, pp. 44–93.

Yücesoy, Hayrettin, *Messianic Beliefs and Imperial Politics in Medieval Islam: The ʿAbbāsid Caliphate in the Early Ninth Century*, Columbia: The University of South Carolina Press, 2009.

Zahnisser, A. H. Mathias, "The Forms of *tawaffā* in the Qurʾān: A Contribution to Christian-Muslim dialogue", *The Muslim World* 79 (1989), pp. 14–24.

Zahrāʾ, al-Ḥusayn b. Ibrāhīm, *Hādhihi al-risāla al-musammāt bi-'l-āyāt al-bayyināt fī ẓuhūr mahdī ākhir al-zamān wa ghāyat al-ghāyāt*, Omdurman: 1887.

Ẓahūr al-Dīn, Muḥammad, *Ẓuhūr al-masīḥ*, n.p., 1908

Zakī, ʿĀdil, *al-Mahdī: dawlat al-islām al-qādima wa al-khilāfa al-akhīra ʿalā minhāj al-nubuwwa fī ḍawʾ al-aḥādīth al-ṣaḥīḥa wa al-ḥasana wa rudūd ʿalā mā ushīra ḥawla al-aḥādīth min shubuhāt*. Beirut: Dār Ibn Ḥazm, 2005.

Zamakhsharī, Abū al-Qāsim b. ʿUmar, *al-Kashshāf ʿan ḥaqāʾiq al-tanzīl wa ʿuyūn al-aqāwīl fī wujūh al-taʾwīl*, Riyāḍ: Maktabat al-ʿUbaykān, 1998.

Zarhūnī, ʿAbd al-Raḥmān, *Rihlat al-wāfid fī akhbār hijrat al-wālid*. French translation by Colonel Justinard. *La riḥla du Marabout de Tasaft*, Paris: Librairie Orientaliste Paul Geuthner, 1940.

Zarkashī, Abū ʿAbd Allah Muḥammad b. Ibrāhīm, *Iʿlām al-sājid bi-aḥkām al-masājid*, ed., Abū al-Wafā Muṣṭafā al-Marāghī, Cairo: 1385 AH.

______, *Taʾrīkh al-dawlatayn al-muwaḥḥidiyya wa al-ḥafṣiyya*, Tūnus: al-Maktaba al-ʿAtīqa, 1966.

Zebiri, Kate, *Maḥmūd Shaltūt and Islamic modernism*, Oxford: Oxford University Press, 1993.

Zniber, Mohamed, "L'itineraire psycho-intellectuel d'Ibn Toumert", in Abdelmajid Kaddouri, ed., *Mahdisme: Crise et Changement dans l'histoire du Maroc*, Casablanca: Najah el Jadida, 1994, pp. 15–29.

Index

"breaking the cross and killing the swine" 32
depriving Muslims of landed property 26
disconnected from the eschaton 35, 100, 268, 271–272
his ʿAbbāsī genealogy 25
his conquests 38, 211–213
his denial amounts to infidelity 32 n. 133
his expectation causes lethargy among Muslims 41
his flags 38, 211
his generosity 26, 213
identical with Jesus 6
in Ghulām Aḥmad's thought 276
in the Iranian constitution of 1979 xiii
in Mawdūdī's thought 262–264
in Muslim creeds 27–34
in Shīʿī thought 28–29, 246, 263, 285–286
in Ṣiddīq Ḥasan Khān's thought 211
in Zaydī thought 25
Qurʾānic hints at his appearance 28–29
ruling over the whole world 213, 262, 264, 268–269
sends a military expedition to India 213–214
the idea supporting Sunnī–Shīʿī rapprochement 29
the title related to *mahd* (cradle) 9, 61–63
their achievements 283–285
al-Mahdī (ʿAbbāsī caliph, r. 775–785) 247
mahdī al-dam ("*mahdī* of blood") 35
mahdī al-dīn ("*mahdī* of religion") 35
"Mahdī encyclopaedia" 29
Un mahdī incompris (by Marc Gaborieau) 237
mahdī al-khayr ("*mahdī* of goodness") 35
mahdī al-khurāfa ("*mahdī* of superstition") 41
al-Mahdī wa fiqh ashrāṭ al-sāʿa (by al-Muqaddam) 41
al-Mahdiyya (city) 51
Maḥmūd Bēgaṙhā (d. 1511) 94, 96
Maḥmūd al-Ḥasan (d. 1920) 232
Maḥmūd Shaltūt (d. 1963) 42, 43
Majālis (by Muḥammad Aḥmad) 155, 156, 157, 188
al-Majlisī (d. 1698) 29
al-Makkī, Abū Ṭālib (d. 998) 124. 126
Makkī, Maḥmūd ʿAlī 84
māl al-ẓulm (wrongfully acquired property) 157–158
Malaga 210
malāḥim (apocalyptic wars) 31
Mālik b. Anas (d. 796)
as *mujaddid* 255
his revivalist activities in Mawdūdī's thought 254
Mālikī school of law 47, 86
al-Maʾmūn (ʿAbbāsī caliph) 83
Manḍū 94
manqala (a game) 180
Manṣab-i imāmat ("*Office of the imām*" by Ismāʿīl Shahīd) 238
al-Manṣūr, Abū Yūsuf Yaʿqūb (r. 1184–1199) 59
al-Maqdisī, Ibn Qudāma (d. 1223) 30
Marrākush (Marrakech) 53, 54, 55, 56, 60, 63, 76, 202
al-Marrākushī, ʿAbd al-Wāḥid (d. 1228) 59, 79, 277
Marw 11
Mary 61, 63
Māsa (a town in the Maghrib) 37
masīḥ 1
in Ghulām Aḥmad's thought 276
Maṣmūda, Maṣāmida (Berber clan) 48, 65
Masrūr Aḥmad 272
Masūfa (Berber clan) 80

Index of Qur'ānic Verses

Translations are taken from Arberry, *The Koran Interpreted*, with some emendations.

speak to men in the cradle and of age ..." 9, 62
5:121 "... but when You took me to Yourself ..." 223
7:10 "We have established you in the earth and there appointed for you livelihood ..." 124 n. 153
7:32 "To every nation a term ..." 79 n. 151
7:85 "Do not corruption in the land after it has been set right" 102
7:204 "Remember God in your soul, humbly and fearfully ..." 136 n. 202
8:19 "... and your host will avail you nothing though it be numerous ..." 171
8:41 "Whatever spoils you take, the fifth of it is God's ..." 167
8:46 "When you encounter a fighting force, stand firm and remember God frequently ..." 129
8:69 "Eat of what you have taken as booty, such as is lawful and good ..." 126 n. 164, 167
8:72 "Those who believe and have emigrated and struggled ..." 114
9:14 "Fight them and God will chastise them at your hands ..." 169
9:23 "O believers, take not your fathers and brothers as friends if they prefer unbelief to belief ..." 162
9:24 "Say: 'If your fathers, your sons, ... if these are dearer to you than God ...'" 161
9:26 "Then God sent down upon His messenger His Shechina ..." 154
9:29 "Fight those who believe not in God ..." 14, 80, 82
9:34 "Those who treasure up gold and silver ..." 122
9:5 "Then, when the sacred months are drawn away, slay the idolaters ..." 80, 82, 169, 191
9:60 "The freewill offerings are for the pure and the needy ... the ransoming of slaves ..." 181–182, 190–191
9:111 "God has bought from the believers their selves ..." 81 n. 156
9:123 "O believers, fight the unbelievers who are near to you, and let them find in you a harshness ..." 89
10:99 "And if your Lord had willed, whoever is in the earth would have believed, all of them, all together" 103
11:15–16 "Those who desire the life of the present world and its adornment ..." 122
11:17 "And what of him who stands upon a clear sign from his Lord ..." 109, 112, 131
11:40 "... And there believed not with him except a few." 113
14:11 "Is there any doubt regarding God ...?" 68 n. 99
16:67 "And of the fruits of the palms and the vines, you take from there an intoxicant and a provision fair ..." 189
16:111 "... and every soul shall be paid in full for what it wrought ..." 234
17:23 "... be good to parents, whether one or both of them attain old age with you ..." 70

Index of Prophetic Traditions (aḥādīth)